The DRIVING INSTRUCTOR'S HANDBOOK

Pupil introduction fee now only £30

Reduced pupil introduction fees means higher earnings potential

Some driving schools may charge the same all-inclusive fee each week regardless of whether or not you actually receive any new pupils. Not so with the AA Franchise. We believe in a fair pricing policy tailored fee means your pupils are profitable for you within 2 hours of tuition.

With the AA Franchise you retain complete control over how many pupils you would like to receive and when you need them. Update your requirements at any time.

Driving Schools Supplies Ltd

Supplying Driving Instructors Nationwide

ROOF SIGNS ➤➤ Hard brilliant white gloss finish that stays white. Tri-pac Version - Roof sign plus two matching door panels on soft, all over magnetic flat white material.

DUAL CONTROLS ➤➤ Supply only or have them professionally fitted at our Birmingham fitting bays.

LETTERING SERVICE ➤➤ Computer designed layout for a really good message impact.

BOOKS & MANUALS ➤➤ Full range of training and reference manuals for ADI trainees. Also audio/visual aids. ADI training aids, road layouts, lesson plans etc. Discounts available.

THEORY MOCK DRIVING TEST PAPERS ➤➤ Latest questions from the DSA theory bank. 35 questions per sheet in full colour.

PART 3 ON VIDEO ➤➤ The potential 17 lessons of the Part 3 exam shown on Video or CD Rom.

FULL MAIL ORDER SERVICE DIRECT TO YOU
Order our latest catalogue,
for all your Driving School requirements
ALL MAJOR CREDIT CARDS ACCEPTED

TOP CLASS
SCHOOL OF MOTORING
0121 328 6226

DON'T BUY YOUR NEXT SIGN UNTIL YOU HAVE CHECKED OUT OUR PRICES!

DRIVING SCHOOLS SUPPLIES LIMITED
2-4 Tame Road, Witton, Birmingham B6 7DS
Tel: 0121- 328 6226   Fax: 0121-327 1864
Email: sales@d-ss.co.uk
Web: www.d-ss.co.uk

Driving Standards Agency Approved Driving Instructor (Car)

PASS PLUS

The DRIVING INSTRUCTOR'S HANDBOOK

14th edition

John Miller & Margaret Stacey

KOGAN PAGE

London and Philadelphia

This edition of *The Driving Instructor's Handbook* is dedicated to the memory of Margaret Stacey

Publisher's note

Every possible effort has been made to ensure that the information contained in this book is accurate at the time of going to press, and the publisher and authors cannot accept responsibility for any errors or omissions, however caused. No responsibility for loss or damage occasioned to any person acting, or refraining from action, as a result of the material in this publication can be accepted by the publisher or the authors.

First published in Great Britain in 1982 by Kogan Page Limited
Fourteenth edition 2006

Kogan Page Limited
120 Pentonville Road
London N1 9JN
United Kingdom
www.kogan-page.co.uk

Kogan Page US
525 South 4th Street, #241
Philadelphia PA 19147
USA

ISBN 0 7494 4746 X

British Library Cataloguing in Publication Data

A CIP record for this book is available from the British Library.

Library of Congress Cataloging-in-Publication Data

Miller, John, 1938 Dec. 29–
    The driving instructor's handbook / John Miler and Margaret Stacey.
— 14th ed.
    p. cm.
    ISBN 0-7494-4746-X
1. Automobile driver education—Handbooks, manuals, etc. 2. Automobile driver education teachers—Training of—Handbooks, manuals, etc. I. Stacey, Margaret, 1946–   . II. Title.
TL152.6.M55 2006
629.28'3071—dc22

2006012247

Typeset by Saxon Graphics Ltd, Derby
Printed and bound in Great Britain by Thanet Press Ltd, Margate

BSM
part of RAC

Become a BSM Instructor and help others achieve their dreams

- UK leader since 1910 with over 3,000 instructors
- Drive a fully maintained air-conditioned Vauxhall Corsa
- Excellent earnings potential plus benefits
- Professional training packages
- Flexible hours

Call us today on **08705 276 276**
Quoting HBK06 or visit bsm.co.uk

Need a new direction?

Make BSM your choice.

Established in 1910 and part of RAC, BSM is the UK's most experienced national driver-training organisation. With over 3,000 franchised instructors and a wide network of Centres, BSM currently teaches more than 150,000 learners each year.

What's more, BSM trains instructors for a new career by helping them pass the Approved Driving Instructor (ADI) qualifications. Qualifying as an ADI opens up new opportunities in your life, especially if you become a BSM Franchised Instructor.

Experience job satisfaction, helping learners pass their driving test. Enjoy flexible hours to suit your life. Every working day is different, meeting a wide range of people, with different personalities and differing needs.

Running your own business brings freedom and independence. To help you make the most of this, we provide the most comprehensive support package in the industry, and the brand strength that partnership with RAC brings.

As one of our instructors you'll receive Continuing Professional Development (CPD) training to help you turn your business vision into a reality at no extra cost.*

Whether you're becoming self-employed for the first time, returning to work after a break or want a new career to fit around family commitments, with BSM you can enjoy professional assistance from one of the UK's biggest motoring brands. And with a range of different options available, you're sure to find the franchise that's right for you.

BSM's franchises are about personal choice. You can opt for the full BSM support package or, if you prefer, recruit your own learners. There's also a part-time franchise if you'd rather give fewer lessons each week. And if your circumstances change, you can always switch to a different franchise option, with the agreement of your Regional Manager. It's entirely up to you.

BSM's franchise benefits:

- Flexible choice of franchises
- A new car regularly
- Sickness and non-occupational
  accident benefit (after six months)*
- Learner recruitment and
  marketing support
- A spare car available, just in case
- High-tech, low-hassle administration
- Franchise payment breaks
- Continuing professional development
- Friendly support network
- Financial rewards for
  personal performance.

For more information on becoming a franchised BSM Instructor, call

08705 276 276

bsm.co.uk

BSM
part of RaC

We'll steer regular business your way

We'll also help manage your diary

BSM provides the most comprehensive support package in the industry, backed up by the commercial power of the UK's leading brand.

Our fully-trained centres will help find your new learners for you, plan their course of lessons and help manage your diary. That means you can spend more time doing what you do best – teaching people to drive.

No one looks after their instructors better.

Call us today on 08705 276 276
Quoting HBK06 or visit bsm.co.uk

Contents

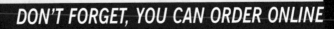

ROD OPERATED DUAL CONTROLS

- Precision made, tailored to suit and fit each individual car
- Pedals can be easily detached for 'out of hours' use
- Pedals can be tailor made for angular pedal pad adjustment
- Rattle free
- Controls can be used to react with the drivers pedal or remain stationary to prevent the trapping of feet under controls
- Fast, efficient fitting service available, with mobile fitters in specified areas
- Controls despatched from stock. Popular makes of vehicles will be despatched on the same day of order
- Each kit comes with comprehensive easy to follow fitting instructions, and free advice during fitting if required

Phone us on:

020 8581 6677

ISO 9001
REGISTERED FIRM

Fax us on: 020 8797 7797
E-mail us: info@dualcontrols.com
or visit our website

www.dualcontrols.com

DESIGN, MANUFACTURE, SUPPLY & INSTALLATION

Unit 14 Abenglen Industrial Estate • Betam Road • Hayes • Middx UB3 1SS

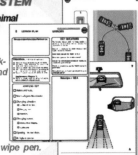

Welcome to
'The Driving Instructor Centre'
At Robinsons Contracts

Robinsons was originally established in 1921 and is still a privately owned small business. We have eight sales advisors Karen, Kevin, Candice, Debbie, Clara, Martin, Dee and Ady who between them have over 50 years experience in the motor industry.

We are the UK's leading suppliers of cars to driving instructors (ADI and PDI's) and driving schools on highly favourable leasing terms. Robinsons Contracts takes all the risk and worry out of obtaining, running and maintaining a driving school car. You can choose from the very latest range of VW, Renault, Ford, Vauxhall, Peugeot, Nissan, Citroen, Toyota and Mazda vehicles.

At Robinsons we take great pride in our ongoing customer service. From helping you to choose the vehicle which best suits your needs to keeping you on the road earning money. We want your business to succeed and we will do all we can to assist you. Our principal aim is to ensure that you are happy with your vehicle and our staff are always at your disposal to help with any problems you may have. Should you have an urgent problem we can even be contacted out of hours, seven days a week. We provide a professional, reliable and unbeatable service backed by knowledgeable and caring staff who look forward to being of service to you.

Leasing a car from Robinsons Contracts frees you from worries, reduces expenses and gives you the chance to concentrate on building a successful business.

Benefits of leasing from Robinsons
1. A brand new car every 7 or 12 months
2. All mechanical repairs and servicing are included in the monthly rental
3. Free replacement vehicle if your car is off the road for more than 48 hours due to mechanical failure
4. All vehicle excise duty is included
5. All vehicles are fitted with he man dual controls
6. Breakdown, homestart and recovery is included
7. You can budget accurately knowing what your expenses will be
8. Your only other expenses will be petrol and topping up of oil, brake fluid
9. Your total monthly rental is upto 100% chargeable against your profits for taxation purposes and if you are VAT registered you can reclaim the VAT portion

What deposit do we require?
We require a small refundable deposit, which is currently £150 for any car. This is lodged against the vehicle to ensure the vehicle is returned to us at the end of

the contract in a good condition for its year and mileage. Thereafter you pay a fixed monthly rental according to the type of vehicle you have chosen. The rentals are fixed for the term of the contract and cannot be increased other than by the rate of VAT imposed by the government or if you have taken our insurance, the yearly premium is increased.

Where do I go if the vehicle needs servicing or warranty work?
When your vehicle needs service or any warranty work take it to your neariest franchaised dealer. We will issue an authorization number and the work will be invoiced to Robinsons.

Insurance
We can now offer fully comprehensive driving school insurance this can be added to your monthly rental.

Sign Writing
We can now organise for your vehicle to be sign writing prior to delivery or collection at a very competitive price.

The 'One Stop Shop'
We have now opened our one stop shop for Instructors supplying products to help you with the day to day running of your business. The shop stocks top boxes, magnetics, safety mirrors, reversing aids, video drive system, books, CD ROMs and videos, we also offer a mail order service. As a He-man dual control agent we stock all dual controls for supply, or supply and fit at very competitive prices and with a team of sign writers on our premises we can now offer a design and sign writing facility giving you a complete service. For a full list of all our products and services please call Jo, Alison or Yvonne for a brochure.

Used Car Contracts
Finally if you are unsure of whether you can afford a brand new car, are a PDI on a trainee licence or just qualified and starting your own driving school, or just want to keep expenses as low as possible, we hire our used vehicles at very favourable rates for shorter periods.

Purchase
If contract hire is not for you we can also quote you on purchasing a car. We specialize in new Ford, Vauxhalls, VW, Renault, Peugeot, Citroen, Mazda, Nissan and Toyota and tailor a finance package to suit your needs or alternatively you can purchase our end of term driving school vehicles. These vehicles come complete with he-man dual controls, service, valet, road tax and remainder of manufacturers warranty.

For further information please visit our web site
www.drivingschoolcontracthire.co.uk
or call us today on **01162 888288**,
our sales advisers are awaiting your call.

TEN TOP TIPS TO AVOID GETTING RICHER

BURN YOUR MONEY AT REGULAR INTERVALS
GET DIVORCED AT LEAST ONCE
BUY EXPENSIVE CARS AND YACHTS
GIVE DRIVING LESSONS ON THE CHEAP
PRODUCE LOTS OF CHILDREN
BUY AN OLD HOUSE AND DO IT UP
GAMBLE PROFUSELY
TREAT THE ENTIRE PUB TO A ROUND OF DRINKS
DON'T PAY OFF YOUR CREDIT CARD BALANCE EACH MONTH

AND LAST BUT NOT LEAST

MAKE SURE YOU DON'T BUY DISCOUNTED DRIVING PRODUCTS
FROM DESKTOP DRIVING TO SELL TO YOUR PUPILS
BECAUSE THAT'S A SURE FIRED WAY OF MAKING EXTRA MONEY

DeskTop Driving Ltd

www.desktopdriving.com
ORDER LINE: 01903 88 22 99
(Just in case you decide you want to be richer)

Give Your Self the Advantages of MSA Membership

Are you aware of the advantages that can be gained by joining the MSA? Here we answer some frequently asked questions, and outline the advantages of membership which is open to qualified ADIs and those becoming ADIs, at any stage of their qualifying process.

The Motor Schools Association of Great Britain is the senior national association for ADIs, first established in 1935. Full membership is reserved for Approved Driving Instructors, however, trainees, potential driving instructors, driving school proprietors and other interested parties may also join but are not allowed to vote at AGMs. Potential Driving Instructors (PDIs) are welcomed into MSA membership and on qualification are converted to full members at no extra charge.

Who owns the MSA?
The MSA is a non-profit making association, without shareholders, owned by and run for the benefit of its membership. With regional centres of activity throughout the country, it is perfectly placed to give you real support and superb value for a modest annual subscription. All these benefits are available to members.

How much does it cost?
For less than 95p per week you will be kept fully informed on all the very latest developments within your industry, belong to the senior association for ADIs and make your opinion count.

What does the MSA do for me?
Most of what the Motor Schools Association does can be divided up into the three headings listed below:

Information
Information is provided to all MSA members every month through the association's own news magazine, Newslink. This contains up-to-the-minute news, views and gossip about the training industry. Each year, every member is sent the association's Annual Report and Handbook, which lists local contacts for both the MSA and the DSA. The MSA also provides inexpensive guides exclusively to members the Driving Test Guide, the ADI Check Test Guide and the PDI Guide.

Representation
Numerous government departments, national and international bodies, consult the MSA including the Driving Standards Agency, Department for Transport, the Driver and Vehicle Licensing Agency, the Parliamentary Advisory Council on Transport Safety, and the European Secure Vehicle Alliance.

In Europe, the MSA represents members through the European Driving Schools Association (EFA).

Services
Free legal advice. Free technical advice. MSA Insurance Services. Personal taxation service. Free public liability insurance for £5million. Free professional indemnity cover for £3million. MSA Visa card with no annual fee and competitive rates. MSA Supplies by RCM Marketing Ltd, everything from roof signs to dual controls and appointment cards to theory test books. Local seminars and meetings with DSA supervising examiners and other officials in attendance and many more...

For tomorrow's motorist today

The Toyota Yaris and Corolla ranges are ideal for instruction, and many schools already reap the benefits of using these vehicles to teach tomorrow's motorists.

You can always rely on Toyota's legendary reputation for reliability and build quality, which makes our cars ideal for tolerating the daily rigours of daily use by all standards of driver.

The recently launched new Yaris offers a comfortable, airy environment, which is particularly important when you spend a considerable proportion of your day in the vehicle. Yet, with its compact form, new drivers can feel confident about controlling the car easily and without being distracted.

Power options include a new 1.4 D-4D 90 diesel engine which benefits from excellent fuel economy achieving 62.8 mpg on the combined cycle. Also available are 1.0 litre and 1.3 litre VVT-I petrol engine versions, both designed to maximise fuel economy whilst providing excellent managed performance. All powerplants meet Euro IV emissions standards and with an eye on costs full services are required only at 20,000 miles. There are currently three grades available, starting with the T2 which offers excellent specification including electric power steering, engine immobiliser and central locking. The T3 grade adds manual air conditioning and height adjustable drivers' seat, the T Spirit trim adds automatic air conditioning.

Meanwhile, the versatile Corolla range is ideal for those who prefer a family sized vehicle to teach in. The latest version of the world's best selling car maintains the traditional features of build quality and reliability which have helped to maintain its global appeal. And to those are added standard features across the range such air conditioning, power steering and trip computer.

As well as offering the ultra efficient 1.4 D-4D 90 diesel engine which returns up to 58.9 m.p.g. on the combined cycle, Corolla engine availability comprises a 1.4, 1.6 and 1.8 litre VVT-i petrol engines as well as a 2.0 D-4D 110 diesel, all of which are Euro IV compliant.

There are currently three specification of the range, available in a combination of hatchback, estate and saloon forms. T Spirit trim is particularly popular. It features climate control air conditioning, plus the automatic dipping rear view mirror and rain sensing wipers. The T3 comes with steering wheel mounted controls, 15 inch five-spoke alloy wheels and manual air conditioning. The entry level T2 comes with an impressive level of specification including air conditioning, Optitron dials, electric front windows and steering wheel which is adjustable for both reach and rake.

Safety is a major feature and the range comes with standard ABS braking with EBD (Electronic Brake force Distribution), front seat occupants have the protection of front, side and curtain airbags, while the body structure has been specifically designed to absorb energy to reduce the effects of front, side and rear impacts.

The Yaris model features highly advanced active and passive safety features including ABS and EBD with brake assist and nine airbags that have contributed to the Euro NCAP five star rating. That's quite an achievement and as you can see the standard specification of both models leaves the main competitors trailing.

For more details on the Yaris and Corolla ranges and offers available to Driving instructors, contact your local Toyota Centre or visit
www.toyota.co.uk

Acknowledgements

My thanks go to Trevor Wedge and John Sheridan at the Driving Standards Agency and also to the many ADIs and trainers who have given valuable feedback and made positive comments about the contents of the *Handbook*.

My special thanks to Sue Vernon of the Queen Elizabeth's Foundation Mobility Centre at Carshalton for her help in updating and revising the chapter on 'Disabilities and Impairments'.

On a personal note, I am grateful to all those people in the industry who have offered help, support and guidance in the preparation of this, the 14th, edition since Margaret's death in September 2005.

John Miller
February 2006

About the Authors

John Miller has been involved with the driver training industry for more than 35 years. He is an experienced instructor trainer and a qualified LGV instructor. For many years he ran his own driving school for car and lorry drivers in Chichester and is now a training consultant. His qualifications include the City & Guilds Further Education Teacher's Certificate and the ADINJC Tutor's Certificate, as well as the ADI and RTITB instructor qualifications. His driving qualifications include the Cardington Special Test and the IAM Advanced Driving Test. He is co-author of *Practical Teaching Skills for Driving Instructors* and author of *The LGV Learner Driver's Guide*. John now updates and edits the *Autodriva Instructor Home Study Programme* that was originally written by Margaret Stacey.

Margaret Stacey operated a driving instructor training facility in Derbyshire and published the *Autodriva Instructor Home Study Programme* for trainees who are preparing for the ADI exams. This programme is widely used throughout the UK by many instructor-training organizations and has now been taken over and published by Kogan Page.

An ADI since 1972, Margaret held the City & Guilds Further Education Teacher's Certificate, the ADINJC Tutor's Certificate and the Pitman NVQ Assessor Award, and had passed the Cardington Special, IAM and RoSPA Advanced Driving tests. She served as secretary on several national committees, including ORDIT (The Official Register of Driving Instructor Training) and the steering group that developed the NVQ in driving instruction.

Margaret's books include *The Driving Instructor's Handbook*, *Practical Teaching Skills for Driving Instructors* (both as co-author), *Learn to Drive in 10 Easy Stages* and *The Advanced Driver's Handbook*.

John and Margaret's books also include *Practical Teaching Skills for Driving Instructors* (with co-author Tony Scriven). This book is recommended by the DSA for candidates for the ADI exams, for qualified instructors preparing for the Check Test and for the Voluntary Register of LGV Instructors. It is a useful resource material for all instructors in their everyday work of teaching driving at all levels and is particularly helpful to anyone wanting to improve their 'continuing professional development'.

John Miller
E-mail: johnmmiller@btinternet.com

Introduction

The Driving Instructor's Handbook was first published by Kogan Page in 1982. At that time it was written by John Miller and Nigel Stacey. Since 1989 it has been recommended by the Driving Standards Agency as a textbook for the ADI exams and the Check Test and is now recommended material for the LGV Instructor's Exam. This, the 14th, edition contains all the latest information on driving licences, driving tests, teaching and coaching skills and the three parts of the ADI Register Exams.

Over the years the *Handbook* has been regularly updated by John Miller and Margaret Stacey and continues to be recommended by the DSA both for new entrants and for qualified instructors. To quote a previous DSA ADI Registrar: 'With the many changes taking place over the whole range of activities in the driver training industry, those involved at all levels of training are strongly recommended to use *The Driving Instructor's Handbook* as resource material.' In this updated and rewritten edition, several new sections have been added, including continuing professional development, eco-friendly driving, and business and customer care skills.

The Check Test for qualified instructors is becoming much more demanding in its assessment of the ADI's skills in identifying, analysing and remedying the pupil's faults. In many ways it can be more like the ADI Part 3 exam. Many instructors with years of experience struggle to retain their ADI grading, with an increasing number now being graded as substandard. Those ADIs who have not kept themselves up to date with modern teaching and coaching skills should appreciate that new entrants to the Register are much better placed to compete for customers who are nowadays much more discerning in their expectations. Rather than finding themselves in a situation where they are downgraded, they might find it well worth their while to consider taking some form of refresher training prior to their Check Test. Coaching and teaching skills are dealt with in more detail in *Practical Teaching for Driving Instructors*.

Drivers of most vehicles now have to pass a theory and hazard perception test for each group of licence acquisition. Additionally, anyone passing the test for car drivers is restricted to driving vehicles of up to 3,500 kilograms or with a maximum of eight seats. Anyone wanting to drive larger vehicles has to take an additional test, as does someone wanting to tow a large trailer behind a car or commercial vehicle.

Under the New Driver Act, newly qualified drivers who accumulate more than six penalty points on their licence within two years of passing the test lose their licence. They then have to reapply for a provisional licence and retake both the theory and the practical test. Recent figures show that about 14,000 drivers each year have their licences revoked, but that only about 8,000 retake and pass the practical test.

All of these requirements mean that, as well as preparing drivers for the ordinary 'L' test, ADIs need to be able to deal with drivers at all levels of ability and experience. To do this they need to be effective teachers who will be able to develop safe attitudes in their pupils.

Teaching people to understand is far more complex than simply telling them where to go and what to do. This is why there is now a move to encourage instructors to use more up-to-date methods of coaching, rather than just 'instructing'. These skills are outlined in more detail in *Practical Teaching Skills for Driving Instructors*.

Training to become a driving instructor is neither cheap nor easy; in fact, it can be relatively costly and certainly time-consuming. However, the time, effort and expense involved in preparing for all three parts of the ADI exam should be considered as an investment in your future.

A wide variety of training courses is available to the prospective instructor. Before you make your choice or pay out any large sums of money in advance, study carefully Chapter 2 of this book. It explains the structure of the examination and how long it may take you to qualify. Chapters 3, 4 and 5 go on to explain, in more detail, the training you will require and the different types of course available.

It's important that you select a tutor who is completely up to date with the examination syllabus and who is a qualified and experienced trainer of ADIs. The ORDIT Register of trainers is a useful guide to available trainers in your area. For details of ORDIT, see page 17. Bear in mind that, although your local driving instructor may be extremely good at teaching new drivers, there is a vast difference between 'teaching to drive' and 'teaching to teach'.

As there is a limit of three attempts on the Part 2 Test of Driving Ability and the Part 3 Test of Ability to Instruct, you should make sure you are well prepared before you attempt these elements of the examination. Listen carefully to the advice given by your tutor. There are no short cuts! Remember, if you fail, there will be more pressure on you at the next attempt.

When you have qualified, you should bear in mind that you are now a professional. You are your best advertisement! Make sure you set a good example by driving correctly at all times. Dress smartly and keep your car in a clean and roadworthy condition. Treat all of your clients with respect and put your best effort in with all of them. If you follow these basic rules, and so long as your instruction is to a high standard, you will get a lot of personal recommendations and your business will flourish.

The number of instructors on the ADI Register remains relatively constant. Therefore, with a changing market and the sustained level of competition in the industry, you cannot afford to sit back and wait for the telephone to ring. You must be proactive and prepared to seek out new markets and prospective customers for yourself. Chapter 1 gives a few ideas and suggestions for maintaining an adequate level of business and keeping ahead of the competition.

As a practising ADI, are you happy with the grading you achieved in your last 'Check Test'? Even though you may have a reasonable pass rate, your teaching style may be a little out of date – especially if you qualified some years ago.

You may find it helpful to update your knowledge and teaching style so that your methods are comparable to those of your newly qualified competitors, who may well have had more rigorous and thorough training. In this respect, listen to any advice given to you by the Supervising Examiner/Approved Driving Instructor (SEADI) at the time of your regular Check Test. Make sure that you are completely up to date with modern driving and teaching techniques and that you are working with the latest editions of *The Highway Code*, *The Official DSA Guide to Driving – the essential skills* and *The Official Guide to Learning to Drive*. These publications should also form the basis of preparing your pupils for the theory test.

With the many changes that have been introduced over the past few years, we have included as much information as is relevant on subjects such as the theory test, the licensing and testing of LGV drivers and the licensing requirements for new drivers. However, because of the changing nature of legislation, some amendments may have been made since this edition was printed. It is recommended, therefore, that you keep fully up to date by joining one of the main trade associations, by subscribing to the various trade magazines and by reading the DSA publication *Despatch*, which is issued to instructors at regular intervals to ensure that your information is up to date.

ALSO AVAILABLE FROM KOGAN PAGE

"All the information you need on how to improve your teaching skills in line with current practices and established criteria."
Approved Driving Instructor Register

"Ideal support material to The Driving Instructor's Handbook *and gives helpful advice to trainee or new instructors."*
Driving

"Not just useful for new entrants to the driver training fraternity, but a source of knowledge on modern, up-to-date skills that could be usefully absorbed by those who have been around a while but need some updating."
John Lepine, MBE, General Manager, The Motor Schools Association

0 7494 4499 1   Paperback   2005

1

The Driving Instructor

This chapter gives an outline of the driving instruction industry and includes information on:

- the instructor's role;
- the qualities of an instructor;
- the ADI qualification;
- how to select your trainer;
- ORDIT – the Official Register of Driving Instructor Training;
- further qualifications;
- driving instruction opportunities;
- ADI associations and organizations.

THE INSTRUCTOR'S ROLE

In today's fast-moving and complex road and traffic systems, the driving instructor's role is now much more challenging than when the driving test was first introduced in 1935. The scope of work within the driving instruction industry has also become much more diverse. Although most qualified ADIs focus their businesses on teaching new drivers, there are now far more opportunities to add interest and variety to the job. These include:

- theory and pre-driver training;
- teaching people with disabilities;
- training under the 'Pass Plus' scheme;
- defensive and advanced driver training;
- company and fleet training;
- minibus driving;
- training in the towing of trailers and caravans;
- corrective training for traffic offenders;
- assessments for older drivers;
- driver training schemes run by police forces and local county councils.

The qualities of the good instructor

To become an effective driving instructor you need to be much more than a good driver who enjoys motoring. The speed and density of today's traffic, together with increasingly complex driving situations, make the ADI's job an extremely demanding one. The aim of the truly professional instructor should be to improve the standards of new and experienced drivers in order to reduce the numbers of accidents, deaths and casualties suffered on our roads.

To become a good driving instructor you need to:

- have a thorough understanding of the rules and principles involved in safe driving;
- be able to put these principles into practice by driving thoughtfully and efficiently;
- be able to patiently teach your pupils how to apply those principles, while other drivers around you are trying to get from A to B as quickly as possible;
- instil safe attitudes into clients at all levels of driving.

One of your main aims should be to produce drivers who will help make our roads safer, but at the same time to ensure that they will enjoy their lessons and future motoring.

The number of drivers killed in road accidents is far too high, particularly among newly qualified, young drivers. You will need to work hard to encourage pupils to develop safe attitudes towards themselves, their vehicle and, last but by no means least, all other road users. Drivers who are taught to accept and compensate for the mistakes of others are far less likely to become involved in 'road rage'.

If you think you have a future in improving driver standards, and that you will be able to carry out all these objectives, to qualify as a Driving Standards Agency (DSA) ADI, you must be prepared to:

- study hard for the theory and hazard perception test, the ADI Part 1;
- work at enhancing your personal driving skills for the driving test, the ADI Part 2;
- be prepared to invest in sufficient, good-quality training to stand a reasonable chance of passing the instructional test, the ADI Part 3.

QUALITIES OF A GOOD DRIVER AND INSTRUCTOR

To be able to enhance your personal driving skills and ensure that you are driving in line with modern techniques, you need to be aware of the qualities required by the good driver as described by the Driving Standards Agency in its book – *The Official DSA Guide to Driving: The essential skills*. Additionally, you will need similar attributes to become an effective instructor.

Responsibility

As a driver: you should always show proper concern for the safety of yourself, your passengers and all other road users. You should also be aware of the need to drive economically and in an environmentally friendly manner.

As an instructor: always have the safety and well-being of your pupils at heart, particularly those in the early stages of their driving careers. Avoid taking them into situations they are unable to cope with. Remember: you are responsible for their safety.

Concentration

As a driver: you must concentrate at all times. Just a moment's distraction from the driving task can have disastrous effects in today's heavily congested and fast-moving traffic.

As an instructor: sitting next to inexperienced drivers, your concentration is even more vital. You have to read the road much further ahead than they will, taking into account any developing situations so that you can keep your pupils safe, relaxed and eager to learn.

Anticipation

As a driver: the ability to predict what might happen is an important part of the skills needed to avoid danger. You need to be aware of any possible hazards in time to safely deal with them.

As an instructor: anticipation is even more important. You will be sitting in the passenger seat beside someone much less able at the controls of your car. You will have to learn to recognize the needs of each individual and anticipate how different pupils may or may not respond to changing situations.

You have to plan as far ahead as possible and anticipate any potential hazards. This will allow time for you to give either positive instructions or prompts, so that your pupil will be able to take any action necessary to avoid problems.

Patience

As a driver: always show patience and restraint with other drivers when they make mistakes. Not everyone is as thoughtful as you!

As an instructor: this display of a positive attitude will not only set a good example to your pupils but, if you have your name on your car, it will also be good advertising.

Remember, we all had to learn to drive, and some find it more difficult than others! If you lose patience with a pupil it will only make matters worse. Most people are aware when they have made a mistake anyway, so be patient and always willing to give more help – even when you have explained things several times before.

Demonstrating tolerance will also go a long way in building up your pupils' confidence and also their belief in you. Hopefully your tolerant attitude will rub off on them!

Confidence

As a driver: the conscientious and efficient driver displays confidence at all times. This confidence results from being totally 'at one' with the vehicle. You should always be travelling at a speed to suit the road, weather and traffic conditions; with an appropriate gear engaged and in the correct position on the road. Planning well ahead and anticipating hazards, the confident driver can avoid the need to make any last minute, rushed, and usually unsafe, decisions.

As an instructor: not only do you need to be confident yourself, but you will also need the skills required to help develop your pupils' confidence. To do this, you will need to ensure that the routes you select for teaching each aspect of the syllabus are matched to each individual's ability. Avoiding those situations a pupil is not ready for will help you gradually build up his or her skills and confidence.

Knowledge

As a driver: if you are to survive on the road, not only do you need a sound knowledge of the rules and regulations contained in *The Highway Code* and *The Official DSA Guide to Driving: The essential skills*, but you also need to be able to apply them in all situations.

As an instructor: you will need to pass on this knowledge so that the drivers you teach will also be able to apply the same principles for driving safely. Remember – they will eventually be sharing the roads with us!

Be prepared to make the effort to keep yourself up to date with the changes taking place so that you are able to:

- handle your vehicle sympathetically and economically;
- apply modern teaching techniques;
- maintain a safe teaching environment;
- recognize the need for keeping your vehicle roadworthy;
- offer advice to pupils on driver licensing requirements, basic mechanical principles, and the rules and regulations for safe driving on all types of road;
- answer their queries confidently.

As well as enhancing your driving skills, having a sound knowledge and understanding will help in your preparations to become an effective instructor. Remember:

- your knowledge will be tested in the theory element of the ADI examination;
- how you apply this knowledge will be assessed in the driving ability test;
- how you pass the information on to pupils will be assessed in the instructional ability test.

Communication

As a driver: you have to continually communicate your intentions to other road users. Methods of signalling these intentions include:

- using the indicators and arm signals;
- brake lights;
- early positioning on the road;
- reversing lights;
- horn and flashing headlights;
- hazard warning flashers;
- eye contact.

As an instructor: you will need to develop ways of communicating effectively with the wide variety of pupils you will be dealing with. You may sometimes have to adapt the terminology you use so that all of your pupils understand exactly what you mean.

Not only will you need to be able to teach them how to apply the relevant procedures and driving techniques, you also need to be able to explain why these procedures need to be followed. This 'why' reasoning should lead to a better understanding that will result in safer drivers sharing the road with us.

There are numerous ways in which you can communicate with your pupils. These include:

- establishing the level of understanding of individual pupils and how best to communicate with them;
- explaining new principles in a clear and simple way;
- using visual aids so that your pupils can 'see' what you mean;
- giving practical demonstrations of complicated procedures;
- developing confidence and success by talking pupils through new procedures;
- giving your directions and instructions clearly and in good time for them to respond safely;
- giving encouragement through positive feedback and praise;
- finding out whether pupils understand your instructions by asking them questions;
- encouraging pupils to ask questions if you can see that they don't understand.

Modern driving techniques are becoming relatively easier through advances in technology and design, making cars much more efficient and safe. However, road and traffic conditions are becoming more and more complex and congested, and in order to keep your clients safe, you need to be aware of the major causes of road accidents. These include:

- other drivers' ignorance of, or total disregard for, the rules of the road;
- lack of concentration and response to developing situations;
- carelessness;
- driving while under the influence of drink or drugs;
- driving when feeling unwell;
- driving with deficient eyesight;
- some drivers' willingness to take risks;
- using vehicles that are un-roadworthy;
- driving while under the stress of modern needs to rush everywhere;
- using mobile phones or other in-car equipment.

All of these elements mean that new drivers have to be taught to a far higher standard than ever, with hazard awareness playing a major role in their development. It will be up to you to ensure that you teach drivers at all levels to:

- handle their vehicle sympathetically and economically;
- drive with courtesy and consideration;
- look and plan well ahead, anticipating what may happen;
- take early action to avoid problems;
- compensate for the mistakes of others;
- understand what they are doing and why they are doing it.

To be able to do all of these things, you, as an ADI, must be prepared to keep yourself up to date with the changes taking place relevant to driving and the teaching of it. We all need to update and adapt our driving procedures and habits from time to time and adjust them to meet current rules and regulations, as well as to deal with ever-changing road and traffic conditions.

The DSA sends a copy of its magazine *Despatch* to all ADIs. This contains some of the latest information. However, most instructors tend to work in isolation and it is very easy to become complacent and just 'plod along' without giving any thought to either updating themselves or improving their skills.

In order to keep up with the times, it is sensible to join some sort of ADI organization. There are a number of national associations that provide information to their members on a regular basis. The main ones are the:

- ADINJC – Approved Driving Instructors National Joint Council.
- DIA – Driving Instructors Association.
- MSA – Motor Schools Association of Great Britain.

More information is given about these organizations on pages 19 to 22.

THE ADI QUALIFICATION

If you wish to teach driving for reward, to either complete beginners or experienced drivers, the only official qualification is that of DSA Approved Driving Instructor (ADI) (car) (or in Northern Ireland, DoEADI). You must have had a minimum of four years' experience as a driver and meet all of the other requirements laid down in the Road Traffic Act. A full explanation of the qualifications for registration is given in Chapter 2.

For an application form and full details of what is involved in the qualification, you should apply for the DSA's information pack *Your Road to Becoming an Approved Driving Instructor* (ADI 14). You can obtain a copy from the DSA for a fee of £5 (at March 2006). For contact details, see page 390. Applicants in Northern Ireland should apply for an ADI 1 (free of charge) to the Driver & Vehicle Testing Agency, Balmoral Road, Belfast BT12 6QL (tel: 0289 068 1831). The pack includes the application forms you will need to get started on the process of taking the exams and qualifying to become an ADI.

To qualify as an ADI, you have to pass an examination that is conducted in three separate tests:

- Part 1: Theory and Hazard Perception Test;
- Part 2: Eyesight and Driving Ability Test;
- Part 3: Test of Ability to Instruct.

You must take and pass all three tests within a two-year period. The format of the exam and how to apply is explained in Chapter 2.

SELECTING A COURSE

One of the most important decisions to be made is on the method of training that can best be fitted in around your other commitments, particularly if you are currently in full-time employment. You also need to bear in mind that, although appointments for theory and hazard perception tests are available virtually 'on demand', the waiting time for practical test appointments is sometimes as long as three months.

Learning to become a driving instructor needs a huge commitment in terms of the time needed to:

- **Study in depth all of the recommended books and other materials.** Not only do you need to prepare yourself for the theory and hazard perception tests, but if you are to become an effective instructor you will need a thorough understanding of all of the principles covered in the full syllabus. This means that learning the question bank by rote will not be sufficient!
- **Enhance your personal driving skills.** This is not only so that you are properly prepared for the ADI Part 2 exam, but also so that your driving will be to a consistently high standard.
- **Invest in sufficient good quality training.** This is not only so that you are prepared for the instructional test, but also so that your teaching techniques will assist you in the future to produce better drivers to share the roads with us.

The Advanced Driving Test

Thinking about becoming a driving instructor? A good first step is to take the DIAmond Advanced Motorists test as we use the DSA standard marking system (six minor faults). It is an excellent preparation for the ADI Part II test. Our test fee is only £45 which includes your first year's membership to the MasterDriver Club. This will entitle you to additional benefits and use of the MasterDriver name for publicity purposes. Once ADI qualified you can increase your income by teaching your clients to advanced standards.

Membership benefits include:–

- Discounted insurance (up to 30%).
- Free legal helpline service.
- Membership and personalised certificate.
- DIAmond Visa card (subject to status).

Contact your nearest professional instructor for more information. Alternatively, write, e-mail or telephone direct for further details and an application form.

Your tutor

The tutor's role includes:

- preparing candidates for all elements of the ADI test;
- retraining/updating experienced instructors;
- preparing qualified ADIs for the Check Test.

Statistics show that less than a third of those beginning the process of training will eventually qualify as ADIs. Before you commit yourself to paying out large sums of money on training, it is sensible to arrange for an assessment with an experienced tutor. Obtaining an honest opinion of your potential can avoid lots of heartache and bitterness later on.

Teaching someone to teach driving is totally different from teaching someone to drive. It doesn't follow that good drivers will always make good instructors. Similarly, it is also very true that not all ADIs, though very good at teaching people to drive, will have the complex skills required to train new instructors. The local ADI may have an extremely good reputation for getting learners through the 'L' test, but because of the higher level of skills and knowledge involved, you may have to look further afield for a tutor who:

- is fully up to date with the requirements of the exams;
- trains instructors on a regular basis;
- has undergone a DSA inspection and is listed in the Official Register for Driving Instructor Training (ORDIT).

With the current pass rate for the instructional test being below 30 per cent, most failures occur at this stage. It's vital therefore that your training is effective and is conducted by someone experienced in the coaching of new instructors.

It is a well-known fact that everyone has a different rate of learning. The good tutor will be able to structure the training programme to suit your particular needs.

The types of course available

The structure of the examination means that you will have to apply for, and pass, each test in sequence and there is often a long waiting list for the practical tests – sometimes as long as three months. You should also bear in mind that, should you fail Part 2 three times, you will not be eligible to take the third part of the exam. Make sure that you will not be paying for what you can't have.

Courses vary a great deal in content, duration and cost. Before deciding on the one that most suits your needs, you should make every effort to find out what you will be getting for your money. Ask for a full description of the syllabus and the format of the training in relation to each element of the exam.

Remember, everyone has a different rate of learning. The training you receive to develop your driving and teaching skills should, therefore, be adapted to suit your particular needs. Examples of the types of training available are:

- distance learning programmes for studying at home for the theory test, with practical training for the driving and instructional tests;
- intensive courses to prepare candidates for all three tests;
- courses preparing candidates for obtaining a trainee licence and working for a driving school while preparing for the instructional test.

Before committing yourself, you should ask for information on the following points:

- What proportion of the training for the practical elements will be conducted in the car?
- How much individual training will you be getting and how much will be on a shared basis?
- If the practical training is shared, how many trainees will be in the car at the same time?
- Does the course allow for training to be structured to suit your particular learning abilities?
- If you opt for working under the Trainee Licence Scheme, will you be receiving proper training and support – particularly prior to being sent out with learners?
- What are your tutor's special qualifications and experience?

Course syllabus

As well as considering these six main points, you should compare the syllabus of the courses on offer with that of the examination. A good training establishment should prepare you properly for each of the three tests. The course should include:

- up-to-date books and materials with questions and answers for the theory test;
- computer-based practice at the hazard perception element;
- sufficient training for Part 2, Eyesight and Driving Ability Test;
- plenty of training, preferably on an individual basis (certainly no more than a ratio of two trainees to one tutor) for the instructional ability test.

(If you opt to take up a trainee licence certain criteria must be met. These are dealt with in Chapter 2.)

Course material

To prepare yourself properly for the examination, you will need the following materials, all of which are recommended by the DSA:

- *The Official DSA Guide to Driving – the essential skills*.
- The *Highway Code*.
- *The Official Guide to Learning to Drive*.
- DL25 Driving Test Report form – see page 336.
- *Practical Teaching Skills for Driving Instructors* by John Miller, Tony Scriven and Margaret Stacey.

- *Instructional Techniques and Practice for Driving Instructors* by L Walklin.
- *Know Your Traffic Signs*.

Other useful material includes:

- *Autodriva Instructor Home Study Programme* by Margaret Stacey.
- *Learn to Drive in 10 Easy Stages* by Margaret Stacey.

How long it will take you to qualify

To be realistic, the qualifying procedure is likely to take around 10 months – that is, if you pass each element at the first attempt and there is no waiting for test appointments. It can take considerably longer than this if:

- there is a long waiting time for appointments;
- tests are postponed;
- you fail any of the tests.

This exam structure and time span should be taken into consideration if you are thinking of taking an intensive course. It is highly likely that you will have to return for 'top-up' training nearer the date of your Part 3 test appointment – and this will probably involve additional fees.

Making the decision

Make sure that you are fully aware of the degree of difficulty of the ADI exams.

Out of 25,000 candidates applying for a theory test in any one year, just over 4,000 actually qualify as an ADI.

Part 3 has the lowest pass rate at below 30 per cent, so this is the test for which you will need plenty of expert training and preparation.

This change of career will involve a great deal of input in terms of time, commitment and cost. Before committing yourself and enrolling on a course, you should seriously consider the following aspects:

- Do I have the potential to become an effective ADI?
- Can I really afford the expense, given that there are no guarantees of qualifying?
- Does the course allow for training to be tailored to the structure of the exam?
- Will I be getting sufficient individual training in preparation for Parts 2 and 3?
- Will the course be structured to suit my own needs?
- Does my tutor have plenty of experience in the training of new instructors?

ORDIT – THE OFFICIAL REGISTER OF DRIVING INSTRUCTOR TRAINING

ORDIT is a voluntary registration scheme administered by the DSA, using criteria that were set originally by representatives of the driver training industry. In Northern Ireland the register is operated by the DVTA (NI).

The Register consists of a list of training establishments that, following inspection by the DSA, have satisfied the criteria of minimum standards.

What is ORDIT?

Members of ORDIT offer professional training to a minimum and consistent standard. They are subject to biannual inspections to ensure minimum standards are maintained.

ORDIT members offer professional facilities and training courses that are designed to:

● develop the skills of those wishing to become driving instructors;
● further develop the skills of existing driving instructors.

All training courses are structured to ensure clients are fully prepared to teach driving as a life skill.

Training programmes

Any type of training programme relating to driver training is acceptable, bearing in mind that quality, and not quantity, is important in all training programmes.

Individual trainers are registered for inclusion on to the ORDIT Register when they have demonstrated to the inspector that they can deliver a satisfactory standard of training in one or all parts of the ADI qualifying examinations, ie Part 1 (Theory); Part 2 (Driving Ability); and Part 3 (Instructional Ability). For example, a trainer can be registered to give only ADI Part 2 training. A trainer who is assessed as giving satisfactory ADI Part 3 training will also be registered to give ADI Part 2 training.

The time allocated for inspections enables training establishments adequate opportunity to plan a structured programme, which should allow the tutor to demonstrate the quality of the training being given.

The inspector's report relates only to the training being seen – training offered by the establishment but not seen by the inspector cannot be assessed.

It is important that inspection programmes are properly planned to show the inspector the range and quality of the training being offered.

What the inspector looks for

The DSA inspector observes and assesses:

- any course material;
- the application and validity of training aids;
- the practical application of the training programme.

The final assessment is based on: 'Did the training programme meet the needs of the student(s) in relation to DSA criteria?'

The inspector also observes and assesses:

- training and interpersonal skills;
- ability to 'teach how to teach';
- subject knowledge;
- role-play and fault simulation;
- fault identification, analysis and remedial action;
- use of routes, timing directions, etc.

It is at the discretion of the DSA to decide whether or not they wish to call for written materials to be presented to assist in the evaluation before placing the establishment on the Register. At the end of an inspection the inspector will offer a debrief and report. The assessment is made on the quality of the training seen in each session and whether it has been matched with the student's needs and his or her level of ability.

Inspection criteria

The criteria used for the assessment of teaching skills are based on:

- the level of teaching;
- the trainer's level, type and style of instruction;
- whether the training meets the needs of the pupil in all situations;
- whether the training is of a consistent standard.

The core competencies must be sound and consistent. The training course should follow a planned structure. Training records must be kept and must be available for inspection.

Lesson plans suitable to the needs of the student should be used. The trainer should be flexible and able to change the original plan in relation to the student's needs. Trainers should show confidence and demonstrate good interpersonal skills. Sound subject knowledge must be evident.

Training aids should be used where appropriate, whether in the classroom or in the car. They should be suitable and capable of showing the key points being covered.

Weaknesses in student skills should be recognized and dealt with constructively at the appropriate time.

During Part 3 training, role-play should be correct and consistent in relation to the character being portrayed. Simulated faults should be realistic in all aspects of training. They should be pitched at the correct level. The student should be clear in his or her own mind when the tutor is in or out of role. 'Question and answer' should be used when appropriate and should be effective.

Future development

The DSA is taking a positive role and is working with the industry to develop and improve the quality of training offered to members of the public. The ORDIT Register is currently under review, and the DSA is committed to keeping the industry fully informed about future developments that might affect training establishments and tutors.

For full details of ORDIT terms and conditions of membership, see page 393.

DRIVING INSTRUCTOR ASSOCIATIONS

When you have qualified you should make an effort to keep yourself up to date, as this will benefit both you and your pupils. Although you will receive the DSA's *Despatch* magazine, it only contains a limited amount of information. To be kept more informed with all of the trends, and also to be able to take advantage of some of the professional and commercial services you will require, you should join at least one of the major national associations.

Three main organizations are open to individual membership:

- Approved Driving Instructors National Joint Council (ADINJC);
- Driving Instructors Association (DIA);
- Motor Schools Association of Great Britain (MSA).

ADINJC

This is a national association that has consultative status with the DSA. Founded in 1973, it was originally set up to bring unity to the driving instructor industry by amalgamating all the major organizations in one body. Membership is made up of associations with varying numbers of members, and an individual ADI Group. It convened the first meetings that led to the setting up of ORDIT and has played an important role in the development of an NVQ in Driving Instruction.

A national conference is normally held in October and as well as providing a forum for both its individual and association members, it is also open to non-member ADIs. Voting is open to all delegates.

For further information on the ADINJC (www.adinjc.com) contact: the Liaison Officer, Clive Snook, on 01747 855091 or e-mail: liaisonofficer@adinjc.com.

The Driving Instructors Association (DIA)

The DIA was founded in 1978 and is now the largest trade association in the UK for professional driving instructors and road safety specialists. Membership is open to Approved Driving Instructors, those training for the ADI qualification and anyone with a professional interest in road safety. The DIA has founded the Driving Instructors' Accident and Disability Fund, a registered charity set up to provide benefits for driving instructors and their families in need. In 1995, the Driving Instructors Association also became a registered charity.

Structure

The DIA remains a proprietary association, the proprietors being DIA (Int) Limited, a trading company and publishers of *The Driving Instructors' Manual*. Individual members are therefore fully protected from any financial liability to the DIA. The DIA is guided by a General Purposes Committee that is elected from the membership at its annual general meeting. It is committed to improving standards of driver education and promoting road safety, while working to promote the welfare and business interests of professional driving instructors.

Consultation

The DIA has consultative status with the Department for Transport (DfT), the Driver and Vehicle Licensing Agency (DVLA), the Driver and Vehicle Testing Agency (DVTA), the Driving Standards Agency and its theory testing organization, and is represented on the Pass Plus Board. It is also represented on the Parliamentary Advisory Council for Transport Safety (PACTS) and other government advisory committees. The DIA maintains extensive links with similar trade associations internationally and has consultative status with the European Parliament and United Nations through its chief executive, who is president of the International Association for Driver Education (IVV).

Membership

The work of the DIA is comprehensive on behalf of its membership and is carried out by a small team of dedicated staff. Each member receives regular copies of *Driving* magazine and *Driving Instructor*, leading high-quality publications for advanced drivers, road safety specialists and driving instructors. Members also receive free professional indemnity and public liability insurance. Services provided for members vary from DIA mail order at preferential rates, training courses, conferences, exhibitions, DIA recovery service, DIA Motor Warranty Direct, medical and hospital plans, discounted car rental and branded advertising schemes to professional accounting services and legal advice. The DIA promotes the DIA Motor Insurance Scheme (formerly DIA Direct Insurance), a service set up to provide the very best training car insurance service to the industry.

Diplomas

The DIA has instituted a higher education programme including the Diploma in Driving Instruction and DIAmond Advanced Instructor qualifications and degree courses at Middlesex University. It promotes the DIAmond Advanced Motorist Test scheme to improve driving skills, and also consults with the DSA on large goods vehicle (LGV), passenger carrying vehicle (PCV), motorcycle, advanced and fleet driver training issues.

Information

A free membership information pack and complimentary copy of *Driving* magazine and *Driving Instructor* can be obtained by telephoning, faxing or writing to: The DIA, Safety House, Beddington Farm Road, Croydon CR0 4XZ (tel: 020 8665 5151; local rate: 0845 345 5151; fax: 020 8665 5565; e-mail: dia@driving.org; website: www.driving.org).

The Motor Schools Association (MSA)

History

The MSA was formed on 31 March 1935, just before the driving test was introduced. The association's principal aims, then as now, are to keep members informed of any matters of interest to them; to represent the views of members to government, its departments and agencies; to provide services which will be of benefit to members; and to set standards of professional and ethical behaviour for teachers of driving.

Membership

Full MSA membership is only available to DSA ADIs. However, those training to become DSA ADIs may join as temporary members and when qualified will be converted at no extra charge to full membership of the association.

How it is run

The MSA is a company limited by the guarantee of its members and is run on behalf of members by the Board of Management. Board members, who are all working driving instructors, are democratically elected at local elections held in each of the association's 10 regions. They are paid no salary for their work on behalf of the association.

Information

The MSA prides itself on the information available to its members. Most of the information passed on to members is contained in the MSA's national publication, *MSA Newslink*. Published monthly, it is sent to all members, who also receive a copy of the regional *MSA Instructor* newspaper every month and a copy of the association's annual report and handbook.

Representation

The MSA represents driver training interests to all relevant government departments and agencies. The association is also a member of the PACTS, the European Secure Vehicle Alliance (ESVA) and the Royal Society for the Prevention of Accidents (RoSPA). European involvement is as the UK representative to the European Driving Schools Association (EFA).

Services

The MSA is always seeking to expand the services available to members. Recently, improvements have been made to both the professional indemnity and the public liability insurance included at no extra charge in the MSA membership fee.

The future

The MSA is a forward-looking organization always open to new ideas and improved methods. It plans to offer further services and benefits to members over the coming year.

For further information, please contact the association by letter, phone, fax or e-mail: The MSA, 101 Wellington Road North, Stockport SK4 2LP (tel: 0161 429 9669; fax: 0161 429 9779; e-mail: mail@msagb.co.uk; website: www.msagb.co.uk).

THE DRIVER TRAINING INDUSTRY

The 'L' driver market

Nearly two million 'L' tests are conducted every year by the DSA, and over 90 per cent of candidates have tuition with an ADI. This is therefore the main source of business for most ADIs. The biggest market for 'L' driver training is in the 17–20 age range and, in order to establish the viability of starting up a driving school in your area, there are various ways of finding out about population trends. These include consulting the local electoral register and contacting local sixth form schools and colleges.

The number of lessons learners need

Teaching driving as a 'skill for life' is much more difficult now than when the driving test was first introduced. However, too many learners seem to think that a driving licence is a right and not a privilege. They want to pass the test as quickly and as cheaply as possible and, even though road systems and the volume of traffic are changing all the time, some parents still compare learning today with 20 years ago. All too common is the statement 'Well, I only had 10 lessons!'

Although you will want your pupils to achieve good test results, your decisions will sometimes need a delicate balance between conscience and reality. You obviously want to keep your clients, and therefore will sometimes have to come to a compromise between your ideal standard and what they will accept. Your main consideration when reaching this compromise is whether the pupil will be at the very least safe on the road.

Putting theory into practice

Driving instruction involves a combination of theory and practice. By encouraging your pupils to study for the Theory Test, you can teach them how to put the principles into practice during their practical lessons. This, in turn, should result in a better understanding of why the rules and regulations are in place.

To teach 'safe driving for life', in addition to the books that are needed to study for the ADI theory test, you will need to have a thorough understanding of the DSA's recommended syllabus for learners. You will find this in the DSA book *The Official Guide to Learning to Drive*.

Theory and hazard perception test training

It will be your responsibility to ensure that new drivers are made aware of the importance of understanding the principles and rules for driving safely. Candidates have to study a number of books for the Theory Test. You can increase your profitability by buying these in bulk (usually at discounted rates) and selling them on at the full price.

Try to encourage pupils to study by emphasizing that the more time they spend studying for the Theory Test, the better they will understand the rules and be able to apply them. This in turn should result in their needing fewer practical lessons.

There are various CD ROMs and DVDs available for the hazard perception test. Have some of these available for your pupils to practise with.

Preparing pupils for the Theory Test does not necessarily mean investing in classroom facilities. There are different ways of organizing training while at the same time increasing your earning potential. These include:

- taking some time out of on-road lessons to cover elements of the theory syllabus;
- teaching small groups of clients in your office;

- hiring a room once a week to run a modular course so that clients can attend at their own convenience and still cover the entire syllabus;
- giving talks at youth clubs and schools;
- setting up a classroom and offering theory training for pupils of other ADIs who do not wish to become involved with theory training.

The personal contact you will build up as a result of running theory courses, particularly for those who are not yet your clients, could result in an expansion of the practical training element of your business.

Information technology

Theory tests are all computer-based and most pupils have access to computers – whether this is at home, or in school or college. It's therefore important for you to be able to offer your pupils the appropriate CD ROMs for effective learning. Interactive programmes can be particularly helpful for pupils who have learning difficulties such as dyslexia. The appropriate computer programs will also enable you to prepare personalized business stationery, handouts and other training aids; and you should be able to reduce the cost of professional fees by 'balancing your books' with an appropriate accounting package.

The 'Pass Plus' scheme

The 'Pass Plus' scheme was set up by the DSA in an effort to encourage newly qualified drivers to undergo further training with an ADI in a wider variety of road and traffic conditions than is required for the 'L' test. You can encourage your pupils to take the extra training by emphasizing that many insurance companies offer substantial discounts to successful participants, usually equivalent to a one year's no-claims bonus.

Pass Plus is designed to 'make newly qualified drivers better drivers'. For details of the Pass Plus syllabus, see page 291. Training can be taken up to a year after passing the Practical 'L' Test. The insurance discount can be deferred for a further two years if the participant is driving on someone else's insurance.

Although the number of drivers taking Pass Plus is slowly increasing, this is still a vastly untapped market with very few instructors taking advantage of its potential. When ADIs were asked by the DSA for the secret behind successful promotion of Pass Plus, some of the tips given were to:

- mention the scheme when pupils first contact you for information;
- try to involve parents, getting them to recognize the added reassurance Pass Plus gives;
- give a reminder about the scheme before and after pupils take the Practical Test;
- inform pupils and parents of the statistics of newly qualified drivers being involved in accidents.

Since the major part of an ADI's work is teaching new drivers, the Pass Plus scheme adds a little more variety to the job.

To register, contact the DSA for your instructor's starter pack. These packs include all the necessary course material and are available from the DSA in Nottingham for £32. For contact details see page 390.

Pre-driver training

Driving is now accepted as a life skill. With this in mind, you might consider getting yourself known to those in the pre-driver age group. Setting up courses will not only give young adults some background knowledge before they take to the roads, but it will also ensure that your name will come to mind when they reach driving age. To highlight the benefits of these courses, you should contact:

- the local education authority;
- schools or colleges with sixth forms;
- youth organizations/groups;
- the local road safety officer.

Defensive driver training

There are now more than 30 million full licence holders in the UK, and a significant number of these would benefit from some form of 'defensive' driver education.

Company drivers

Many companies and organizations now take more seriously the health and safety aspects of operating motor vehicles. More and more of them are beginning to look for professional expertise to conduct assessments and provide remedial training for their employees. These may include current staff members with records of accidents, or potential new employees.

In order to demonstrate a professional approach, you will need to have a properly structured system for making your assessments and presenting reports. Your possible customers might include:

- local companies;
- voluntary groups;
- education departments;
- health authorities.

All of the above are employers of groups of full- and part-time, as well as voluntary drivers.

Traffic offenders

Some traffic offences now attract a compulsory or discretionary order for disqualification and/or a requirement to take a further driving test. Your local solicitors would be interested in a professional assessment and reporting service that could benefit their clients in preparation for court hearings.

Drivers who require their skills to be updated

There are large numbers of drivers who have held a licence for many years but have either not driven for a while, or simply lost their confidence. You could advertise retraining or refresher courses to bring drivers up to date with the latest rules and regulations, to modernize their skills and rebuild their confidence. You could also give short talks about defensive driving to groups such as:

- Young Wives and Women's Institutes;
- Round Table and Ladies' Circle;
- Rotary and Inner Wheel Clubs;
- Lions and Probus clubs.

All you have to do to increase your business and add variety to your work is to carry out a little research and gather information on the above types of company or organization in your area.

Vocational training

With the many changes taking place to driving licence categories and testing procedures for drivers and riders, there is a vast market which is still largely untapped by the ADI. If you have the appropriate licences, you should consider training in the following areas, particularly with the introduction of compulsory training and refresher training for all LGV drivers within the next few years.

Motorcycling

This is an increasing market involving motorcyclists and moped riders at various levels:

- compulsory basic training (CBT);
- pre-test instruction;
- 'Direct Access'.

Special instructional qualifications are needed for the different elements of training. Courses for CBT and Direct Access instructors are conducted at the DSA Training Centre at Cardington. For contact details see page 390.

Minibuses

Drivers with a full licence issued after January 1997 are only allowed to drive vehicles with up to eight seats. A separate test is required to drive vehicles with more than eight seats. Many colleges, schools and other organizations have staff and volunteer drivers who would probably require training or assessments for driving this type of vehicle.

Lorries

With staged testing starting at vehicles of 3.5 tonnes, and the voluntary register of LGV instructors, there is a growing market for training in medium-sized goods vehicles. Although there is, under the voluntary register scheme, a test for LGV instructors, there is no specific instructional qualification as long as you hold the appropriate driving entitlement.

More information on LGV training is included in Chapter 12.

CONTINUING PROFESSIONAL DEVELOPMENT

Teaching learners is very rewarding, but when you have been working as an ADI for a while, you should consider taking more training and other qualifications. The DSA recommend that we should all be seeking to remain updated through continuing professional development (CPD).

The level of competence you attain to pass the ADI examination is the minimum standard required to enable you to teach driving professionally. However, road and traffic conditions, the driver training industry and also the law are in a continual state of change. You should strive to keep your knowledge up to date and also improve your personal driving skills and teaching techniques. This will help to equip you for driver training at all levels.

The most obvious first step is to consider the various advanced driving tests. The Institute of Advanced Motorists (IAM) and RoSPA are probably the most well known. Their tests are outlined in Chapter 6. The Cardington Special Driving Test and the DIAmond Advanced Motorist Test are industry-based.

The Cardington Special Driving Test

This test is available to all ADIs, and the standard required is much higher than that needed to pass the ADI Part 2, Eyesight and Driving Ability Test. Tests are conducted by permanent staff instructors at the DSA's Training and Development Centre at Cardington, near Bedford. You have to demonstrate that you can handle your car efficiently and accurately on all types of road including a motorway and while carrying out a variety of manoeuvre exercises.

For the test, the car you use must have:

- manual transmission;
- an interior instructor mirror;
- integral head restraints for both driver and assessor.

To achieve the grade A assessment you need to show that you have the ability to control the speed and position of the car safely, systematically and smoothly. Your driving will need to be at a consistently high standard, based on concentration, effective observations, anticipation and planning.

During the test, several manoeuvres are included. These will include:

- moving away smoothly from rest to include, where possible, moving off on reasonably steep uphill and downhill gradients;
- moving away at an angle from behind a stationary vehicle;
- overtaking, meeting and crossing the path of other vehicles;
- turning right and left corners;
- stopping as in an emergency;
- driving the vehicle backwards and entering limited openings to the left and right;
- reverse parking (in a car park and on the road);
- turning the car round in the road by using forward and reverse gears.

At the end of the test your assessor will give you the result and a briefing on any faults that were recorded. At a later date you will receive written confirmation of the report. If you attain a grade A, you will be eligible to receive the Special Test Certificate.

The fee for this test at May 2006 was £110 plus VAT but this is under review. For further information write to: Special Test Booking Section, The DSA Training Centre, Cardington, Bedford MK42 0TJ (or tel: 01234 744011).

The DIAmond Advanced Motorist Test

This test is administered by the DIA, whose examiners use the standard DSA marking system. The DIAmond Test is available at two levels: the Advanced Test, incorporating a wide variety of road and traffic situations, during which you are allowed no more than six driver faults in a one-hour drive; and the Special Test, where the standard is two faults or less in a drive of one and a half hours.

Tests are conducted by DIAmond Advanced Examiners. These are normally ADIs who have been awarded the Diploma in Driving Instruction, have passed the Cardington Driving Test (with two faults or less) or the DIA Special Test and have also passed the DIA DIAmond Advanced Examiners' Course.

Once you are an ADI, passing the DIAmond Advanced or Special Test could help you in marketing advanced and defensive driving courses.

The Diploma in Driving Instruction

This qualification is awarded by the DIA. The qualification is not restricted to ADIs, and anyone involved in driving instruction, road safety or other occupations related to driving may apply. The overall aims of the diploma are to improve standards of driver training and to provide wider public recognition of the services offered by those who hold it.

The examination consists of five modules, each tested in a two-hour examination. These are:

1. legal obligations and regulations;
2. management practices and procedures;
3. vehicle maintenance and mechanical principles;
4. driving theory – skills and procedures;
5. instructing – practices and procedures.

A certificate is issued for each module, and the Diploma is awarded when all five have been passed. Examinations are conducted in April/May of each year at any DIA-approved examination centre. Further information about this qualification is available by phoning the DIA on 0845 345515.

City & Guilds Further Education Teacher's Certificate

The qualification is relevant for anyone teaching in adult education – no matter what their specialist subject may be. You may find it particularly helpful for getting into the theory training market. The course will help to build up the confidence needed to adapt your teaching from the normal one-to-one in-car situation, to standing in front of a class. It will also give you a greater understanding of different teaching techniques, and you will discover how and why people learn at different rates.

One of the main advantages of achieving this certificate is that it is a recognized teaching qualification that is accepted by most educational establishments. You will therefore have an advantage over your competitors when you apply to run courses through schools and colleges.

Courses are held at colleges of further education throughout the country and are normally run on a part-time basis. For full details, contact your local college or education authority.

Certificate in Education (CertEd)

This is aimed at those who would like to develop more as professional teachers. It is normally a continuation of initial teacher training (such as the FE Teacher's Certificate) and is designed to build on current teaching experience. The scheme is modular, being broken down into four parts. Continuous assessments are made throughout and there is no examination involved. Depending on current qualifications, this part-time course can be taken over a one- or two-year period.

The CertEd fits into the Credit Accumulation and Transfer Scheme (CATS) that, by accumulation of credit points, can open up a wide range of further training and development opportunities. For information on the availability of courses contact your local education authority.

NVQ in driving instruction

The driving instructor's biggest potential market is the new driver. Most young people now leaving schools and colleges are aware of the NVQ system. They recognize the qualification as a guarantee of a minimum standard of achievement. To gain an NVQ, all you have to do is collect evidence of your everyday work. The evidence has to show that your work is conducted in line with the DSA syllabus. Your portfolio of evidence then has to be verified by assessors who have been qualified by the awarding body.

Although the DSA's ADI qualification is the only official requirement before you can give driving instruction for payment, there is no obvious way for would-be learners to differentiate between the quality of instruction different ADIs give. Sometimes selecting a name from Yellow Pages can be a hit-and-miss affair, but if you have an NVQ, this will immediately be recognized.

THE FUTURE

For some time now, the DSA has been considering the responses received to some of its consultation documents. Those papers sought views on:

- introduction of mandatory record books for provisional licence holders;
- introduction of a compulsory minimum learning period;
- lowering of the age for learning to drive;
- introduction of new pre-test requirements and compulsory basic training;
- theory training;
- training for accompanying drivers;
- professional tuition;
- motorway training;
- skid training;
- the introduction of a four-week period before the Practical driving test can be retaken;
- a probationary licence code for the first two years after passing the Practical driving test;
- a requirement to use 'P' plates for 6 or 12 months after passing the driving test;
- the introduction of a second Practical driving test;
- a lower blood alcohol level for new drivers;
- a restriction to low-powered vehicles for new drivers;
- a lower speed limit for new drivers;
- a restriction on night driving for new drivers;
- a restriction on carrying passengers for new drivers.

All of these are currently still under review. Styles of driving need to be adapted to suit improved vehicle design and changing road and traffic conditions, and this extensive list of topics now under review indicates the necessity for all instructors to keep themselves informed.

No matter what the level of your experience, make a habit of keeping yourself up to date, whether this is through the magazine *Despatch*, or through membership of one of the national organizations. The future safety of your pupils could be in your hands, and remember: we will all be sharing the road with them!

The Road Safety Bill

This bill, which is due to be discussed in parliament during 2006, aims to amend the regulations for driving instructors' qualifications and to change some of the driver licensing and testing regulations. The new legislation makes provision for a whole range of possible changes to the driver training industry. Among many other measures, the bill will probably change the present ADI qualification arrangements to include separate training, testing and registration for all sections of driver training, including lorries, buses, and off-road and fleet driving. It will improve and extend the regulation of instructors to ensure quality standards and value for money, while giving better information to the consumer.

The bill will enable the public to have access to more detailed information about individual instructors, their qualifications and the services they offer. Furthermore, there is provision for regulation about instructor training courses and the persons offering training; a requirement for trainee instructors to complete successfully a period of prescribed training before taking any of the qualifying examinations; and provision for the setting of maximum charges for providing the statutory training.

There will be more extensive use of driver retraining to improve standards generally and to reduce the amount of repeated offences by regular offenders – all of which should be beneficial to the training industry and should be welcomed by all instructors and trainers.

These measures are not likely to be implemented for several years, but at that time it is expected that radical changes to the driver training industry will be required.

2

The ADI Register

This chapter contains information on the regulations relating to the Driving Standards Agency (DSA) Approved Driving Instructor (ADI) Register. It includes information on:

- the Register;
- registered and licensed instructors;
- qualifications for registration;
- applications for registration;
- the structure of the examination:
  - the theory and hazard perception tests;
  - the eyesight and driving ability test;
  - the instructional test;
- the Trainee Licence system;
- registration and the ADI Certificate;
- the Code of Practice for ADIs;
- the Check Test.

To comply with the requirements of the Road Traffic Act 1988, anyone giving driving instruction for money or money's worth must either be registered with the DSA or must hold a current licence to give instruction (the 'trainee licence'). Full details of the requirements are in the Motor Cars (Driving Instruction Amendment) Regulations and are available from The Stationery Office Ltd or at www.opsi.gov.uk.

The official title of a registered driving instructor is 'Driving Standards Agency Approved Driving Instructor (Car)'. (In Northern Ireland it is 'Department of the Environment Approved Driving Instructor'.)

In their efforts to continually improve road safety standards, the DSA has introduced many changes since the Register was first established in 1964. This means that candidates now have to demonstrate a much higher standard of personal driving and instructional skills in order to qualify and to remain in the Register.

QUALIFICATIONS

To become an ADI you must:

- hold a full British or Northern Ireland unrestricted car driving licence;
- have held it for a total of four out of the past six years prior to entering the Register after qualifying (a foreign driving licence, an automatic car driving licence or a provisional licence held after passing the driving test all count towards the four years);
- not have been disqualified from driving at any time in the four years prior to being entered in the Register;
- be a fit and proper person to have your name entered in the Register;
- pass the Register qualifying exam;
- apply for registration within 12 months of passing Part 3.

To accompany a learner driver you must be 21 or over and have held a full UK driving licence for three years. A foreign full licence counts towards this three-year period as long as it is accepted under the 'exchange' scheme.

Candidates with disabilities

The Road Traffic (Driving Instruction by Disabled Persons) Act 1993 came into effect in 1996. This created a new category of ADI who can teach in cars with automatic transmission only. This qualification is only available to candidates whose licence limits them to drive automatic vehicles because of a disability.

The qualifying exam is exactly the same as that for any other candidate except that both practical tests are taken in a car with automatic transmission. (For more information refer to the ADI 14 booklet *Your Road to Becoming an Approved Driving Instructor.*)

Application for registration

The initial application to have your name entered into the ADI Register is made at the same time as applying for the Part 1 Theory and Hazard Perception Test. Application forms are included with the ADI 14 booklet, the cost of which at March 2006 is £5 (or £11 if you also wish to receive the official question bank). It can be obtained by calling 0870 121 4202. Your name will only be entered into the Register when you have passed the final part of the exam and have sent off your pass certificate with the current registration fee, which is £200 at March 2006. (Examination and registration fees are reviewed from time to time. For details of the current fees you should ask your tutor, enquire with the DSA when you apply for the ADI 14 or check the DSA website www.dsa.gov.uk.)

To provide driving tuition for money or the equivalent, you must:

- have passed all three parts of the qualifying examination and be a DSA ADI (Car). The examination consists of:

- Part 1, Theory and Hazard Perception Test;
- Part 2, Test of Driving Ability;
- Part 3, Test of Ability to Instruct;
- have paid the current registration fee;
- agree to take a test of 'continued ability and fitness to give instruction' (Check Test) when required to do so by the Registrar.

Alternatively you must have passed Parts 1 and 2 and hold a Trainee Licence. This allows you to gain experience before taking the Part 3 instructional ability test.

Practising with friends or relatives before your test

To supplement your training, you may wish to practise without giving up your current job to work for a driving school. It is permissible to teach friends or relatives during your period of training, as long as you do not make any charge or receive payment of any kind, for example in petrol or goods. Alternatively, you may opt to work for a driving school under the Trainee Licence Scheme.

TRAINEE LICENCE

Under this scheme, candidates may work for payment for a driving school while preparing for the instructional test. Under the provisions of the Road Traffic Act, a six-month licence to give instruction can be issued to suitable applicants (the fee at March 2006 is £125). If you wish to take up this option, you can apply for a licence after you have passed the ADI driving test and you have a sponsoring ADI. Only one licence will normally be granted and it will be at the Registrar's discretion as to whether a second may be issued. In Northern Ireland, a trainee licence can be applied for at the same time as making an application for a written test. A maximum of two will be issued; each is valid for six months.

To qualify for this six-month licence you must:

- have passed Parts 1 and 2 of the qualifying examination;
- have undergone 40 hours of training with a qualified ADI;
- be sponsored by an ADI.

(In Northern Ireland a Trainee Licence may be applied for at the same time as applying for the written test.)

Trainee licences are granted under the following conditions:

- The trainee instructor is only authorized to give instruction for the school whose address is shown on the licence.
- For every trainee licence holder there must be at least one ADI working from the sponsor's address.
- Trainees must receive 40 hours' practical training from an ADI. This period of training must start no earlier than six months before, and be completed

by, the date of issue of the licence. Training in all of the following subjects must be received:

- explaining the controls of the vehicle, including use of the dual controls;
- moving off and making normal stops;
- reversing into openings to the left and the right;
- turning the car around using forward and reverse gears;
- parking close to the kerb, using forward and reverse gears;
- using the mirrors and making emergency stops;
- approaching and turning corners;
- judging speed and making normal progress;
- road positioning;
- dealing with junctions and crossroads;
- dealing with pedestrian crossings;
- meeting, crossing the path of, overtaking and allowing adequate clearance for other vehicles and anticipating other road users;
- giving correct signals;
- understanding traffic signs, including road markings and traffic lights;
- method, clarity, adequacy and correctness of instruction;
- the general manner of the driving instructor;
- manner, patience and tact in dealing with pupils;
- ability to inspire confidence in pupils.

- You must not advertise yourself as a fully qualified instructor.
- You must abide by one of the following conditions:
  - Your sponsoring ADI must supervise 20 per cent of all the lessons you give. A record of all lessons given, along with the supervision received, must be kept on form ADI 21S. Both you and your sponsor must sign this form which must then be returned to the DSA as soon as the licence expires.
  - Alternatively a minimum additional 20 hours' training covering all of the above topics must be undertaken. This extra training must take place within the first three months of the issue of the licence or before taking a first attempt at Part 3, whichever is the sooner. (A record of this training must be kept on form ADI 21AT and must be sent to the DSA before the end of the three-month period, or presented to the examiner who conducts the Part 3 test, whichever is the earlier.)
  - At least 25 per cent of the period of training has to be practically based and in a car at a maximum instructor-to-trainee ratio of no more than two trainees to one ADI.
  - If the training option is selected and you subsequently fail either the first or second Part 3 test, a further five hours' training must be taken before you are allowed to take another test. A declaration signed by you and your sponsor has to be provided to the examiner on the day of the test. Failure to do this will result in the test being cancelled.

Displaying the Trainee Licence

Whenever a trainee is giving driving lessons under this scheme, the red licence must be displayed in the left-hand side of the car's windscreen. If requested by a police officer or any person authorized by the Secretary of State, the licence must be produced. Failure to do this is an offence.

If you hold a Trainee Licence

If you are working under the Trainee Licence Scheme, have signed for the training option, and are attending for your first attempt at Part 3 within the first three months of the licence, you will have to produce your ADI 21T form. Both you and your trainer should sign this form to confirm you have had a minimum of 20 hours' extra training. This is in addition to the 40 hours' training required to obtain the licence.

If you have to take the test for a second or third time, you will need to provide a declaration, signed by you and your trainer, to confirm that a minimum additional five hours' training has been received. If you fail to produce any of the training declarations your test will be cancelled and you will lose the fee.

Exemptions to the Regulations

Section 123 of the Road Traffic Act only applies to instruction in the driving of cars. It does not apply to instruction in:

- riding motorcycles;
- driving large goods vehicles (although there is a voluntary register for LGV instructors);
- driving large passenger-carrying vehicles.

Under Section 124, police officers are exempted from Section 123 when giving driving instruction as part of their official duties, providing this is with the authority of the Chief Constable.

Under Section 39 and in relation to the responsibilities of local authorities to provide 'traffic education', road safety officers are exempt from the ADI regulations while carrying out their official duties.

These exemptions do not apply where police or road safety officers are giving instruction in cars outside their official duties.

EXAMINATION STRUCTURE

You must take and pass all three parts of the examination in the following sequence:

- Part 1: theory and hazard perception test.
- Part 2: eyesight test and a practical test of your driving.
- Part 3: a test of your ability to give driving instruction.

From the date of passing the theory and hazard perception test, you have two years in which to pass the two practical tests. You may take the theory and hazard perception tests as many times as it takes you to pass both on the same occasion. However, there is a limit of three attempts on the driving and instructional tests.

PART 1: THEORY AND HAZARD PERCEPTION

The application for this part of the exam is included with the ADI 14 starter pack, *Your Road to Becoming an Approved Driving Instructor*. The test covers a wide range of subject knowledge, including:

- the rules and regulations for driving on our roads;
- mechanical principles;
- teaching techniques;
- dealing with disabilities.

Tests are conducted, in English only, at 'L' test theory centres throughout the UK. If you are dyslexic it may be possible for special arrangements to be made. However, you must state this condition on your application form and you will need to supply some proof of it.

Applications can be made online, by phone or by post. For details see page 56.

The test is 'touch screen' based, but don't worry if you are not familiar with interactive computer programmes. You will be allowed to work through a practice session before starting. There will also be staff on hand to help if you experience any difficulty.

You have to answer 100 multiple-choice questions by selecting one answer from a choice of four and you have 90 minutes to complete the test. The screens are easy to read with only one question at a time being shown. The programme allows you to move backwards and forwards through the questions to check on any you may not be sure about, or to change an answer should you wish. The system will also alert you if there are questions you have not answered.

The banding system

The questions are banded into four subject groups. These are:

- road procedure;
- traffic signs and signals; car control; pedestrians; mechanical knowledge;
- driving test; disabilities; law;
- publications; instructional techniques.

There are 12 different set tests, and the questions are set randomly for each candidate. This allows for an equal degree of difficulty for all candidates. For details of the subjects in each band, see page 56.

The pass mark

To pass you need to score an overall mark of 85 per cent. However, the DSA need to ensure that prospective ADIs have an adequate knowledge in all of the subject areas. You must therefore score a mark of 80 per cent in each of the four bands. So, for example, if you get a maximum score of 100 per cent in three of the bands but only 79 per cent in the fourth, you will fail.

Following completion of the theory test, you will be given a short break before taking the hazard perception test.

The hazard perception test

This test consists of watching 14 video clips on the computer. Like the theory element, you will be allowed a short practice session before starting the test. Each hazard is allotted a maximum score of five points, and the earlier you spot it the more points you will achieve. However, you have to be careful not to click too many times as this will result in a negative score.

The pass mark

To pass you must score 57 out of a possible 75 marks. If you fail this part of the test you will have to take both parts again.

Results

You will receive the results for both parts within a few minutes of completing the hazard perception test. If you pass, you will be given information about applying for the Part 2, Eyesight and Driving Ability Test.

Should you fail, you may apply for a retest as soon as you wish. You are allowed to take this test as many times as it takes to pass both elements within the same session. (For more information on the syllabus, sample theory questions and how best to prepare for these two tests, see Chapter 3 of this book and Chapter 5 of *Practical Teaching Skills for Driving Instructors*.)

PART 2: DRIVING ABILITY

You may apply as soon as you have passed the theory and hazard perception tests. You are allowed to take it at any centre of your choice – you will find a list of these on the application form. Send your application with the current fee (£82 at April 2006) to the DSA in Nottingham. You will be sent a letter confirming your appointment. When you attend for the test, take this and your driving licence and some photographic identification (such as your passport) with you.

The format of the test

The test lasts for about an hour and, if you wish, your trainer may accompany you. Sometimes senior DSA staff may accompany examiners on tests. This is to ensure uniformity so don't worry – they're not there to test you.

Eyesight

You will first of all be asked to read a number plate from a distance of 27.5 metres, with glasses or contact lenses if you normally wear them. If you cannot read the plate the rest of the test will not be conducted.

Vehicle safety questions

At the start of the test the examiner will ask several questions about vehicle safety. As with the 'L' test, these questions are on a 'show me'/'tell me' basis. Three questions require you to describe how to check on the condition and operation of various components ('tell me'), and with two questions you need to demonstrate an actual check ('show me').

The syllabus for this part of the test includes:

- tyres and brakes;
- steering;
- lights and reflectors;
- direction indicators;
- audible warning devices;
- fluids used in the engine, braking or steering system;
- coolants and lubrication.

Sample questions are:

- 'Identify where you would check the engine oil level and *tell me* how you would check that the engine has sufficient oil.'
- '*Tell me* how you would check that the brakes are working before starting a journey.'
- '*Show me* how you would check that the power-assisted steering is working before starting a journey.'
- '*Show me* how you would check that the headlights and taillights are working.'

Each incorrect answer is recorded as a *driving fault* up to a maximum of four faults. If all five questions are answered incorrectly a *serious fault* is recorded, meaning that you would fail.

Driving technique

This test is of an advanced nature and a very high standard of competence is expected. You must drive in a brisk and 'business-like' manner, demonstrating that you have a thorough knowledge of the principles of good driving and road safety; and that you put them into practice at all times. Routes used include:

- heavy and fast-moving traffic, for example motorways and dual carriageways;
- rural sections;
- urban areas.

You must satisfy the examiner on your:

- expert handling of the controls;
- application of correct road procedure;
- anticipation of the actions of other road users and taking the appropriate action;
- sound judgement of speed, distance and timing;
- consideration for the convenience and safety of other road users.

The result

During the test the examiner will be making an assessment of your personal driving skills and will mark any relevant faults on the Driving Test Report Form – DL25. You will be given the result as soon as the test is completed.

If you pass

To achieve a pass you need to score six or less *driving faults*. Your examiner will give you an oral debrief and explain any driver faults that have been recorded. You will also be given an application form for the Part 3 instructional test.

If you fail

All faults are recorded throughout the test and *driving faults* (those of a minor nature) will accumulate. You will fail if you commit more than six of these driver faults, or one serious or dangerous fault. Your examiner will give you a brief explanation of the faults recorded. You will also be given an application form for a further test. *If you fail this test three times, you will not be allowed to apply for Part 3.*

After failing a third attempt, should you wish to continue the process of qualifying, you will have to wait until a two-year period has expired from the date you passed the theory test. You will then have to start the whole process again, by taking the theory and hazard perception tests. It therefore makes sense to have sufficient good-quality training to ensure that your personal driving skills are up to the standard required.

For more information on preparing for the ADI driving test see Chapter 4.

PART 3: INSTRUCTIONAL ABILITY

You can apply for this test as soon as you have passed the Part 2 driving test. Tests are conducted at the centres listed on the application form and, as with the driving test, you can take it at the one of your choice. Send your application to the DSA with the current fee (£82 at April 2006). The appointment will be confirmed by letter and, when you attend for the test, take this with you along with your driving licence and some photographic identification such as your passport.

The test

The test lasts for about an hour and is conducted by a Supervising Examiner ADI. It is designed to test whether you can pass on your knowledge to pupils with different levels of ability through your practical teaching skills. The test is conducted in two parts. In Phase 1, you have to teach a beginner or a learner with limited driving skills; and in Phase 2 you have to make an assessment and give remedial instruction to either a learner who is about at test standard or a qualified driver who is undergoing driver development training.

The role play situation

Your examiner will describe each pupil to you, and a different person will be portrayed for each phase. You will need to adapt your instruction to suit the personality and level of ability of each. *It is extremely important, at this stage, that you listen very carefully to the description of each pupil and to the level of experience he or she has.* For example, you may be asked to teach a beginner how to move off and stop. Even this basic subject will require setting the base line at varying levels depending on whether this is the pupil's first attempt to move the car, or the pupil has moved off and stopped before.

As soon as the examiner 'goes into role', you must try to behave as you would with a 'real life' pupil by confirming prior knowledge with a few simple questions. The information given should then allow you to decide on the start point for the lesson. (You will find more information on 'setting the base line' in Chapter 5.) Examiners are trained to play the role of people with a variety of personalities and abilities. Part of this test is to assess whether or not you have the ability to adapt your methods and level of instruction appropriately to suit different pupils so that maximum learning can take place.

The marking sheet

During the test you will be assessed under the following headings:

- Core competencies.
- Instructional techniques.
- Instructor characteristics.

These are sub-divided into the following categories:

1. Core competencies:
   (a) Identification of faults
   (b) Fault analysis
   (c) Remedial action.
2. Instructional techniques:
   (a) Level of instruction
   (b) Planning
   (c) Control of the lesson
   (d) Communication
   (e) Question and answer techniques
   (f) Feedback/encouragement
   (g) Instructor's use of controls.
3. Instructor characteristics:
   (a) Attitude
   (b) Approach to pupil.

The maximum grade attainable in each phase is 6, and to pass you need to attain a minimum grade of 4 in each. By taking into consideration the markings in columns A and B of the ADI 26 marking form, an overall assessment will be made and a corresponding grading awarded. For example, if a candidate fails to identify a serious error, because of this failure, nothing will have been done to correct the problem. The examiner would therefore mark the appropriate box in column A under 'not covered' or 'unsatisfactory'. This would then be transferred to column B under the heading 'identification of faults'. (You will find a breakdown of how these different elements are assessed in Chapter 5.)

At the end of the test

So that your examiner can make a fair assessment of your overall performance, you will be asked to wait for about 30 minutes while all elements of your performance are considered. You will then be given an oral debriefing together with the relevant ADI 26 form. If you do not wish to wait, the form will be posted to you.

As well as studying Chapter 5 of this book, you should find *Practical Teaching Skills for Driving Instructors* particularly helpful for this part of the examination. For details of all reference books see page 392.

When you pass

You will be given a letter confirming the result and you may apply for entry onto the Register of Approved Driving Instructors (Car) as soon as you wish. Complete the application form on the reverse of the letter and send it with the current fee to the DSA in Nottingham. This must be done within 12 months of the date you pass.

Registration declaration

When you apply for registration, you must sign a declaration to the effect that you will:

- notify the Registrar of any change of name, address or place of employment;
- notify the Registrar if convicted of any offence;
- return the certificate if your registration lapses or is revoked;
- agree to undergo, when requested by the Registrar, a Check Test conducted by DSA staff.

The ADI Certificate

You should receive your official green ADI Certificate of Registration within a week. This will remain valid for four years. You will then have to renew your registration. The certificate incorporates:

- your name;
- your photograph;
- your ADI number;
- the date of issue;
- the date of expiry of the certificate.

Displaying your ADI Certificate

As a qualified instructor, whenever you are giving tuition for money or the equivalent, you must display the official green certificate on the left-hand side of the car's windscreen, and produce your certificate if requested by a police officer or any person authorized by the Secretary of State. Failure to do so constitutes an offence. If you can satisfy the Registrar that your certificate has been lost, damaged or destroyed, a duplicate can be issued on payment of the current fee.

If you fail

Using the application form on the reverse of the letter, you may apply for a further test if you are still within the two-year qualifying period, and the failed test was your first or second attempt. Otherwise, if you wish to continue, you will have to wait until a two-year period from passing the theory test has elapsed before you can apply for Part 1 again. It therefore makes sense to have sufficient good-quality training to ensure that your instructional skills are up to the standard required to become an effective driving instructor!

Requesting more information

Whether you pass or fail, if you would like a fuller explanation of your test result, you may ask for an appointment to see your examiner. Examiners are normally available on Friday mornings.

ADI CHECK TEST

Once your name is on the ADI Register, it is a condition of continued registration that you must take a Check Test with your Supervising Examiner (SEADI). The main objective of the test is for the examiner to assess whether your teaching methods, lesson content and fault analysis are up to the minimum standard required to remain in the Register.

Your SEADI will 'sit in' while you conduct a normal lesson. An assessment, similar to that made on the ADI instructional test, will be made of your overall performance. You will then be graded accordingly. Alternatively, it can be the examiner 'role-playing' a pupil.

Test frequency

If you are a newly qualified ADI, you will be invited to attend for a Check Test within a year of passing your instructional test. You will be given a grading of 4, 5 or 6 depending on the examiner's assessment of your lesson. If the examiner feels you are lacking in experience, an 'E' (educational) grading will be given. In this case, you will be invited to attend for a further test within a few months.

Once you have been graded, the frequency of subsequent tests will be dependent on the grade you achieve. It is normally:

- grade 5 and 6 instructors – within four years;
- grade 4 instructors – within two years.

Any test resulting in a grade 3, 2 or 1 will require a retest to be taken fairly quickly. For grade 3 this will normally be within three months, grade 2 within two months, and a grade 1 indicates that the instruction seen was dangerous and this will result in the scheduling of an urgent retest. If you are not able to show an acceptable standard of instruction on three consecutive Check Tests you could be removed from the Register.

The invitation

Tests are conducted during the SEADI's normal working hours and the invitation to attend will specify the date and time, and the place – normally local to the area you work in, and often the local driving test centre. You must acknowledge receipt of this invitation as soon as possible, particularly if the appointment is not convenient and another has to be arranged.

Your pupil

If your pupil is a full rather than provisional licence holder, it must not be another ADI. The most important thing to remember is that the examiner is assessing your ability to teach and not the pupil's ability to drive. You must therefore ensure that your instruction is pitched at the correct level, whatever standard the driver has attained.

If you do not have any pupils available, you may opt for a 'role play' Check Test. This is very similar to the way in which Part 3 is conducted, and the examiner will select the subjects to be covered and the level at which they are to be taught.

The car

A driving school car should always be kept in a roadworthy condition and display 'L' plates if the driver is a provisional licence holder. It should go without saying that a clean and tidy car will create a professional image. If the lesson is to be conducted in a pupil's car, it is sensible for you to check on its condition beforehand. Your ADI Certificate must be displayed if you are charging for the lesson.

You must make sure that all seatbelts (both front and rear) are in good working order.

Presenting the lesson

The format of any driving lesson should follow a similar pattern. The fact that it is a Check Test should make very little difference. Following the initial introductions of pupil to examiner and explaining to the pupil the purpose of the Check Test, follow the basic routine set out below.

- Recap on the previous session.
- Use questions and answers (Q&A) to establish what has been remembered (or forgotten).
- Set the objectives by stating what subjects are going to be covered.
- Give as much help through guided instruction as is necessary.
- Identify, analyse and correct errors, giving valid reasons.
- End with a recap on what has been learnt and what will be covered next time.

You will be assessed on:

- Your flexibility to deviate from objectives if necessary. For example, if the objective was given as a manoeuvre exercise, and the pupil made some serious mistakes at junctions, it may be sensible to attend to these and defer the manoeuvring. You should remember to state why you have deviated from the original plan.
- The level of your instruction. This must be suitable for the ability of your pupil.
- The teaching methods used and the clarity, adequacy and correctness of your instruction.
- The effectiveness of your Q&A technique.

- Your manner, patience, tact and, very importantly, your ability to inspire confidence.
- Your recapping at the end of the lesson and whether feedback on progress is adequate.

Instructor grading

The examiner will be marking your instruction on the working sheet ADI 26 (see pages 47–48). The lowest grade attained in any of the foregoing aspects of your work will normally be the final grade given. The following is an outline of the DSA's description of the six grades:

Grade 6

The instructor's overall performance is to a very high standard with no significant instructional weaknesses.

A concise and accurate recap on the previous lesson was given with realistic, attainable objectives set for the current lesson. There was dialogue, with pupil involvement.

The ADI consistently demonstrated the ability to vary/select the most appropriate instructional techniques to suit the needs, aptitude and ability of the pupil.

He or she was quick to recognize and address all relevant driving faults and provided thoroughly sound analysis. Prompt and appropriate remedial action took place.

An appropriate route was chosen for the pupil's ability and experience and the instructor took every opportunity to develop the pupil's driving skills and awareness using the problems presented en route.

An appropriate learning environment was created to positively encourage the further development of the pupil's skills and good driving practice.

The lesson concluded with a concise recap, which was an accurate overview of the lesson.

The strengths and weaknesses in the pupil's performance were identified and discussed constructively.

Realistic and appropriate objectives were set for the next lesson.

A professional attitude and approach to the pupil was shown throughout the lesson.

Grade 5

A good overall standard of instruction was demonstrated with some minor weakness in instructional technique.

A recap on the previous lesson was given and the pupil was involved. Objectives were set.

DRIVING STANDARDS AGENCY

WORKING SHEET

Cert. Expiry Date ☐ **SOM** ☐ **Vehicle** ☐

Dual Controls: Yes ☐ No ☐ **Pupil:** Male ☐ Female ☐ **Practising Privately:** Yes ☐ No ☐

Hours tuition with this ADI ☐ **Hours tuition with another ADI** ☐

Please circle main content of lesson: 1 2 3 4 5 6 7 8 9 10 11 12 13 14 15 16 17 18 19

DRIVING STANDARDS AGENCY

Test of continued ability and fitness to give instruction (Check Test)

The examiner has marked each aspect of your performance in columns A and B below. See overleaf for explanatory notes.

COLUMN A

	1	2	3
1. Controls			
2. Move away/stopping			
3. Emergency stop			
4. Reverse Left/Right			
5. Turn in the road			
6. Reverse park			
7. Mirrors			
8. Signals			
9. Planning			
10. Use of speed			
11. Junctions			
12. Roundabouts			
13. Meet/Cross/Overtake			
14. Positioning			
15. Adequate clearance			
16. Pedestrian crossings			
17. Anticipation/Awareness			
18. Dual C'way/Motorway			
19. Pass Plus Module			

COLUMN B

Fault Assessment	1	2	3	4	5	6
Identification						
Analysis						
Remedy						
Instructional Techniques						
Recap at start						
Aims/Objectives						
Level of instruction						
Planning						
Control of lesson						
Communication						
Q & A Technique						
Feedback/Encouragement						
Instructor's use of controls						
Recap at end						
Instructor Characteristics						
Attitude & approach to pupil						

Instructor ☐ PRN ☐

Supervising Examiner's Name ☐ Date ☐

S E Signature ☐ Grade ☐

ADI 26CT (A) (Rev 9/97)

Figure 2.1 DSA Working Sheet for the ADI Check Test

ASSESSMENT NOTES

This form is designed to identify the strengths in your instruction and to highlight the areas which need to be improved upon. It is given in conjunction with the de-briefing at the end of your check test with the aims of improving your teaching skills.

COLUMN A

BOX 1 Subject not covered/incorrect or dangerous instruction
BOX 2 Subject covered unsatisfactorily
BOX 3 Subject covered satisfactorily in all aspects

COLUMN B

The marking in this column reflects your performance in relation to the core competencies, the instructional techniques that you employed and your attitude and approach to the pupil and the lesson. Each heading is broken down into a six point rating scale. The closer to the right the mark is, the better you have performed.

A majority of the marks placed to the right does not necessarily reflect a high grade as some of the aspects marked to the left may have played a more significant part in the lesson and therefore have an effect on the overall grading.

The criteria for grading are as follows:

6. Overall performance to a very high standard with no significant instructional weaknesses.

5. A good overall standard of instruction with some minor weakness in instructional technique.

4. A competent overall performance with some minor deficiencies in instructional technique.

3. An inadequate overall performance with some deficiencies in instructional technique.

2. A poor overall performance with numerous deficiencies in instructional technique.

1. Overall standard of instruction extremely poor or dangerous with incorrect or even dangerous instruction.

The ADI demonstrated, with only minor weaknesses, the ability to vary/select the most appropriate instructional techniques as necessary to suit the needs, aptitude and ability of the pupil.

All important driving faults were recognized and addressed with a sound analysis and appropriate remedial action being explained and practised.

An appropriate route was chosen for the pupil's ability and experience, and most opportunities were taken to develop the pupil's driving skills and awareness.

The ADI structured an appropriate learning environment in which the pupil could readily further develop his or her skills and good driving practice.

The lesson concluded with a concise recap, which was an accurate overview of the lesson.

The strengths and weaknesses in the pupil's performance were identified and discussed and the objectives for the next lesson were stated.

The instructor's attitude and approach to the pupil was good throughout the lesson.

Grade 4

The ADI demonstrated a competent overall performance with some minor deficiencies in instructional technique.

The recap was acceptable but with limited pupil involvement and objectives for the current lesson being outlined.

An ability was demonstrated to select/vary the most appropriate instructional techniques as necessary to suit most of the needs, aptitude and ability of the pupil.

The ADI recognized and addressed the important driving faults, providing generally sound analysis and remedial action.

An acceptable route was chosen for the pupil's ability and experience, and advantage was taken of most of the opportunities to develop the pupil's driving skills and awareness using the problems presented en route.

The ADI structured a generally appropriate learning environment that provided opportunities for the pupil to develop their skills and good driving practice.

The lesson concluded with a general summary, giving an accurate overview of the lesson and the main strengths and weaknesses in the pupil's performance identified.

The ADI's attitude and approach to the pupil was acceptable throughout the lesson.

Grade 3

The ADI demonstrated an inadequate overall performance with some deficiencies in instructional technique.

The recap of the previous lesson was inadequate or sketchy.

There was failure to properly set out or explain the objectives for the current lesson – nor was the pupil involved.

The instructor demonstrated only a limited ability to vary/select instructional techniques as necessary to suit the needs, aptitude and ability of the pupil.

There was inconsistent identification, analysis and remedy of driving faults.

Some unnecessary retrospective instruction took place.

The route chosen was unsuitable for the pupil's ability and experience.

Opportunities were missed to develop the pupil's driving skills and awareness using the problems that presented themselves en route.

The ADI failed to structure a learning environment to enable the pupil to develop skills and good driving practice.

The summary at the end of the lesson was inaccurate or incomplete.

Many of the strengths and weaknesses in the pupil's performance were not identified, or were treated superficially.

There were shortcomings in the ADI's attitude and approach to the pupil.

Grade 2

The ADI demonstrated an overall poor performance with numerous deficiencies in instructional technique.

There was little or no recap given on the previous lesson and a failure to set objectives for the current lesson.

The instructor was unable to vary/select instructional techniques as necessary to suit the needs, aptitude and ability of the pupil.

Many problems occurred with the correct identification of driving faults, their analysis, and remedial action was very late.

The route chosen was unsuitable for the pupil's ability and experience and numerous opportunities were missed to develop the pupil's driving skills and awareness.

It was a poor learning environment in which the pupil would be unable to develop skills and good driving practice.

A superficial summary was given at the end of the lesson, with the main strengths and weaknesses in the pupil's performance not being mentioned.

The ADI demonstrated serious shortcomings in attitude and approach to the pupil.

Grade 1

The ADI's overall standard of instruction was extremely poor or dangerous with incorrect or even unsafe instruction.

No recap was given on the previous lesson and no objectives set for the current one.

The instructor was unable even to recognize the need to vary/select the most appropriate instructional techniques as necessary to suit the needs, aptitude and ability of the pupil.

Driving faults were not identified, analysed nor corrected. Many of these were of a serious or dangerous nature.

A totally unsuitable route was chosen for the pupil's ability and experience.

The ADI failed to use the opportunities that presented themselves en route to develop the pupil's driving skills and awareness.

There was no attempt to structure any kind of learning environment.

No summary was given at the end of the lesson.

The ADI demonstrated very serious shortcomings in attitude and approach to the pupil.

At the end of the test

You will be given a verbal debriefing and handed an ADI 26 form showing the markings under the various headings. A copy of the 'working sheet' marked by the examiner during the test is available from the DSA.

Instructor's test results

Your driving school/instructor code is recorded at the beginning of all of your pupils' tests. The DSA collate the information from all tests and you will be provided with a breakdown of your pupils' results. By highlighting those items where there are consistent failures, the analysis should show where there may be shortcomings in your instructional techniques that need to be attended to.

All instructors, whether newly qualified or with years of experience, should use the Check Test as an opportunity to discuss with their SEADI any queries they may have relating to these statistics, or any other matters relating to driving tuition. This applies particularly if:

- a lower grading is achieved than was expected;
- you would like to attain a higher grade;
- pupils are consistently failing for similar errors.

If it's a while since your last Check Test, and there are some areas of instructional techniques you think you may not be up to date with, it may be sensible to have an assessment with a tutor prior to taking your next one!

DSA SERVICE STANDARDS

Information on the DSA's service standards for all matters relating to driving instructors and the Register is available in leaflet form from the DSA. The leaflet is available by contacting the DSA by phone on 0115 901 2500 or at www.dsa.gov.uk. A summary of the content is listed below for your information:

- The DSA's role.
- Its customers.
- Its aims.
- Service standards, for:
    - its customers;
    - those taking theory tests;
    - those taking practical tests;
    - ADIs.
- More information on:
    - keeping customers informed;
    - listening to customers;
    - how customers can help the DSA;
    - equal opportunities;
    - if things go wrong;
    - compensation code;
    - complaints procedure.

The leaflet also lists the various phone numbers for enquiries relating to all subjects listed.

Keeping up to date

Many instructors who have been on the Register for a number of years are now finding it a struggle to retain their grading. In recent years, a higher proportion than ever before are being graded as 'substandard' and subsequently removed from the Register. Even if you have only been on the Register for a short time it may be beneficial to seek some refresher training.

You will find more information on preparing for your Check Test in *Practical Teaching Skills for Driving Instructors*. Detailed advice on preparing for all parts of the qualifying examination and the Check Test is given in Chapters 3 to 5 of this book, and Chapters 5 to 8 of *Practical Teaching Skills for Driving Instructors*. Further information can be found in the ADI 14 starter pack, and on the DSA website: www.driving-tests.co.uk. Details of all books and publications are on page 392.

3

ADI Part 1: Theory and Hazard Perception

This chapter contains information on:

Theory Test

- Syllabus.
- Resource materials.
- Studying and organizing your time effectively.
- The test format.
- The 'banding' system.
- Sample questions.
- Taking the test.
- The pass mark.

Hazard Perception Test

- The test format.
- How to respond to the hazards.
- The pass mark.
- Resource materials.

THEORY TEST

To be a safe driver and an effective instructor, you need a thorough understanding of the principles, rules and regulations that are covered in all of the reading materials recommended by the Driving Standards Agency (DSA). As a good instructor you should be able to:

- apply these principles, rules and regulations whenever you are driving;
- pass on all of this information to your pupils to help them acquire the skills needed to effectively put them into practice;
- answer sensibly any questions your pupils may ask.

Syllabus

To be able to carry out your duties as a responsible ADI, you need a wide range of subject knowledge and skills. The following are all included in the theory test syllabus:

- The principles of road safety in general and their application in specified circumstances.
- Correct and courteous driving techniques:
  - car control;
  - road procedure;
  - hazard recognition and proper response;
  - dealing safely with other road users and pedestrians;
  - the use of safety equipment.
- The theory and practice of learning, teaching and assessment.
- The tuition required to instruct a pupil in driving a car, and:
  - the identification, analysis and correction of errors;
  - your manner and the relationship between instructor and pupil.
- Simple vehicle adaptations for drivers with disabilities.
- A knowledge of the *Highway Code*.
- A knowledge of the DSA book for 'L' test candidates, *The Official Guide to Learning to Drive*.
- How to interpret the 'Driving Test Report', Form DL25.
- A knowledge of basic mechanics and the design of cars adequate for the needs of driving instruction.

Resource materials

To ensure that you cover all the elements included in this syllabus, as well as the book you are now reading, the DSA recommends that you study the following materials:

- *The Official DSA Guide to Driving: The essential skills*.
- The *Highway Code*.
- *The Official Guide to Learning to Drive*.
- The DL25 – the Driving Test Report form (see page 336).
- *Know Your Traffic Signs*, published by The Stationery Office.
- The Motor Vehicles (Driving Licences) Regulations, available from The Stationery Office.
- *Practical Teaching Skills for Driving Instructors*.
- D100 leaflet *What You Need to Know about Driving Licences*.
- *The Official DSA Theory Test Guide for Car Drivers and Motorcycles*.

Other useful materials include:

- *Driving Test Theory* CD ROM.
- *Learn to Drive in 10 Easy Stages*.
- *Autodriva Home Study Programme*.

For details of all books and resource materials, see page 392.

Studying the syllabus

Don't be misled into thinking that it will be enough to just learn the DSA's question bank by rote! Learning by rote means *memorizing through repetition*. This way of learning, although useful for learning such things as multiplication tables and stopping distances, will not give you the understanding you need to be properly prepared to:

- be able to discriminate between the correct and incorrect answers given in the theory test;
- have the proper understanding required if you are to gain the maximum benefit from your practical training;
- pass the practical tests within the limited number of attempts allowed;
- effectively carry out your role as an ADI.

You should consider that, if you are not properly prepared, there is also the cost of failing two or three tests at £50 a time!

Not only do you need to prepare yourself properly for all of the foregoing reasons, but it is highly unlikely that you will be able to effectively memorize the entire official bank of over 900 questions. One hundred questions are set randomly in 12 different papers to allow an equal degree of difficulty for all candidates; and the questions will not appear in 'banded' order. To make things more difficult, some questions are negatively worded and others require you to know exact quotes from the official publications.

Even if you enrol on an intensive classroom course, you will still have lots of studying to do in your own time. There are no short cuts to gaining all of this knowledge and understanding.

Be prepared to exercise a good deal of self-discipline and set enough time aside for your studies.

Organizing your studies

Because of the wide range of topics involved, picking up a book and reading it from cover to cover will be of very little benefit – unless, of course, you have a photographic memory! You need to develop your study skills by:

- making time available;
- finding the best place to carry out your studies;
- formulating a study plan.

You need to make the best use of your time by:

- organizing study periods to fit in with your existing commitments;
- setting yourself achievable objectives;
- not overloading yourself by trying to learn too much at once;
- following a properly structured study programme;
- dividing the materials into related topics;
- monitoring your progress throughout your course;
- seeking the advice of your tutor if there are any points you don't understand.

You will find more information on how to develop your study skills in Chapter 5 of *Practical Teaching Skills for Driving Instructors* and in the *Autodriva Home Study Programme*.

Booking the ADI theory test

You can book the theory test if:

- your application for registration has been processed by the DSA;
- the 'fit and proper' tests on you have been completed; and
- you have received written confirmation from the DSA.

The most convenient way to book is online at www.dsa.gov.uk. To do this you will need:

- a valid UK or EU driving licence;
- your ADI reference number;
- debit or credit card details.

To book by phone, contact the booking office on 0870 0101 372. The office is open from Monday to Friday between 8 am and 6 pm. For bookings by post, send your completed application form to: Driving Standards Agency, Booking Department, PO Box 381, Manchester M50 3UW.

The cost of the ADI theory test (at April 2006) is £50.

The theory test banding system

The questions are banded into four subject groups:

- road procedure;
- traffic signs and signals; car control; pedestrians; mechanical knowledge;
- driving test; disabilities; law;
- publications; instructional techniques.

Sample questions include:

Band 1 – road procedure

Q How should you overtake horse riders?

a Drive up close and overtake as soon as possible
b Speed is not important, but allow plenty of room
c Use your horn just once to warn them
d Drive slowly and leave plenty of room

Q You wish to overtake a long, slow-moving vehicle on a busy road. You should:

a follow it closely and keep moving out to see the road ahead
b flash your headlights for the oncoming traffic to give way
c stay behind until the driver waves you past
d keep well back until you can see that it is clear

Q When taking a left turn a driver should position the vehicle:

a well to the left of the road
b with the offside wheels close to the centre line
c midway between the centre line and the nearside edge of the road
d by steering slightly to the right before turning

Band 2 – traffic signs and signals; car control; pedestrians; mechanical knowledge

Q An anti-lock braking system assists directional control when steering during emergency braking. This is achieved by:

a allowing the driver to apply cadence braking
b preventing the wheels from locking up
c making the brakes more efficient
d taking over the responsibility of the driver

Q You are approaching a zebra crossing where a pedestrian is standing on the footpath with one foot on the crossing. You should assume the pedestrian is:

a intending to cross the road when there is a safe gap
b about to cross the road
c thinking about using the crossing
d unsure whether to cross

Q There are double white lines in the middle of the road. The line nearest to you is broken. You may:

a park on the left
b overtake, but you must not cross the line
c overtake if it is safe to do so
d park on the right

Band 3 – the driving test; disabilities; the law

Q   **A category 'B' driving test candidate with sight in only one eye passes the test. The examiner will issue a:**

a   pass certificate showing the disability
b   normal pass certificate
c   pass certificate with a restriction listing the vehicles the person can drive
d   pass certificate restricting the person to certain speed limits

Q   **When driving, the maximum proportion of alcohol per each 100ml of breath must not exceed:**

a   35 microgrammes
b   50 microgrammes
c   80 microgrammes
d   100 microgrammes

Q   **A candidate who fails the driving test for coasting would be marked on the driving test report under:**

a   clutch
b   gears
c   brakes
d   accelerator

Band 4 – publications; instructional techniques

Q   **The 'learning plateau' sometimes occurs during instruction. This refers to:**

a   a slowing down of the pace of instruction
b   a common difficulty experienced by some persons in hand–foot coordination
c   a temporary halt in the learning process
d   persons who have learning difficulties

Q   **A pupil can be encouraged to develop a good driving attitude by:**

a   persuasion and example
b   an instructor imposing their will
c   letting them learn from experience
d   asking them to study the instruction materials

Q   **In choosing a method of instruction, an instructor should:**

a   maintain a consistent approach to be fair to all pupils
b   vary the method to suit the individual pupil
c   use one of two distinct approaches
d   stick to the lesson plan

Taking the theory test

You are allowed plenty of time for this test – don't rush yourself. As you can see, the questions are very wide-ranging and some will need careful consideration. Don't worry if you see people leaving their computer after only half an hour. Learners use the same centres and their test only takes about 35 minutes compared with the 90 minutes allowed for the ADI test.

Follow these simple rules and, if you have been thorough with your studies, you should have no problems:

- Take your time.
- Read each question carefully and at least twice.
- Carefully consider the choice of answers.
- Sometimes you can eliminate the obviously wrong answers quite quickly, but take time to consider the options when faced with negatively worded questions.
- Leave questions you're not sure about and go back to them when you've answered those you find easier.
- Check that you've answered all of the questions.

Pass mark

The overall pass mark is 85 per cent. However, the DSA need to ensure that you have an adequate knowledge in all of the subject areas and you need a score of 80 per cent in each band to pass. This means that, even if you score 99 per cent in three of the bands and only 79 per cent in the fourth, you will fail. This should emphasize to you the need for a thorough understanding of the principles covered in all of the recommended materials.

Following completion of the theory test, you will be given a short break before taking the hazard perception test.

HAZARD PERCEPTION TEST

Before you start this, as with the theory element, you will be allowed a short practice session.

The test consists of 14 video clips. You must watch carefully and respond to the hazards by clicking on the mouse. As each hazard develops, you need to keep registering a response to the changing situation – just as you would be assessing and reassessing developing situations if you were driving.

Each hazard is allotted a maximum score of five points, and the earlier you spot the hazard, the more points you will achieve. Provided your responses are made to correspond with the potential hazards or changing situations, you should be able to achieve a maximum score.

A skilled driver could be expected to click, on average, 10 or 12 times in one clip. However, you have to be careful not to click too early, or at random, as this will result in a negative score.

Resource materials

It's sensible to practise your skills at responding to 'on-screen' hazards. Your trainer should be able to supply you with one or more of the wide variety of CD ROMs and DVDs that are now available.

The DSA has produced a DVD entitled *Roadsense* in which hazards are highlighted with different colours – similar to the test clips. Yellow indicates potential hazards that you need to keep watching for changes, and red indicates developing situations (those that would need some form of action). For information, visit its website: www.dsa.gov.uk.

Pass mark

To pass you must score 57 out of a possible 75 marks. If you fail this part of the test you will have to take both parts again.

Although this chapter is mainly concerned with the theory and hazard perception tests, try to remember that you are preparing for a job that has serious responsibilities attached to it.

As an ADI you will be preparing new drivers to share the roads with all of us, or assisting more experienced motorists to improve their personal driving skills. You should always be prepared to consistently apply the rules and regulations whenever you are driving, and keep up to date by maintaining a library of the latest publications.

4

ADI Part 2: Driving Ability

This chapter contains information on:

- application;
- format and syllabus;
- resource materials;
- preparing for the test;
- the car;
- taking the test;
- the marking system;
- common faults;
- when you pass;
- profile of the perfect driver;
- on the road;
- the system of car control.

The test lasts about one hour and is made up of three elements:

- an eyesight test;
- vehicle safety questions;
- a practical driving test.

You must pass all three parts on the same occasion.

APPLICATION

You will be given an application form when you pass the theory and hazard perception tests. You may then apply as soon as you wish and can take the Part 2 test at a centre of your choice.

Send the form, together with the appropriate fee (£82 at April 2006), to the DSA at Nottingham. You will be sent a letter confirming your appointment. When you attend for the test, take the letter with you. You will also need to take both parts of your photo card licence. If you still have an old-style paper licence you should take your passport with you as photographic proof of your identity. Without the necessary documents, the test cannot be conducted.

THE CAR

You must provide a suitable vehicle that:

- is properly taxed and insured;
- is a saloon or estate car in proper working condition with front and rear seat-belts in working order;
- is capable of the normal performance of vehicles of its type, with manual transmission;
- has right-hand steering;
- has a readily adjustable seat, with head restraint, for a forward-facing front-seat passenger;
- is not displaying 'L' plates;
- has an additional, adjustable interior mirror for use by the examiner.

From time to time a member of the DSA staff may accompany examiners to ensure uniformity of tests. All seatbelts front and rear must therefore be in working order. If they are not, the test will be cancelled. Anyone accompanying you on test will be expected to wear a seatbelt.

EYESIGHT

You will be asked to read a vehicle number plate from a distance of 26.5 metres, or 27.5 metres if it is an old-style number plate). If you need to wear spectacles or contact lenses to do this, you must wear them for driving.

If you are unable to complete the eyesight test satisfactorily, you will not be allowed to continue with the driving test.

VEHICLE SAFETY QUESTIONS

As outlined in Chapter 2, the examiner will choose three of your car's components and ask you to explain ('tell me') how to carry out checks on their condition and safety. You will be asked to demonstrate ('show me') how to make checks on the condition and operation of two other items. Incorrect answers are marked as 'driving faults', but if all five questions are answered incorrectly this will be marked as a 'serious fault'.

For details of the syllabus for this part of the test and for sample questions, see page 39.

THE DRIVING TEST

During the test you will be assessed driving in a variety of situations, including:

- urban areas;
- rural roads;
- motorway or dual carriageways;
- roads that carry heavy and/or fast-moving traffic.

The syllabus

Your driving skills will be assessed in the following areas:

- handling of the controls;
- application of correct road procedure;
- anticipation of the actions of other road users and taking appropriate action;
- judgement of distance, speed and timing;
- consideration for the convenience and safety of other road users.

Specific exercises include:

- moving away – straight ahead and at an angle;
- dealing with other vehicles, when:
  - overtaking;
  - meeting;
  - crossing their path;
- turning left- and right-hand corners correctly and without undue hesitancy;
- controlled stop;
- reversing into openings to the left and right;
- reverse parking into a space behind another parked vehicle;
- turning the car around in the road using forward and reverse gears;
- reversing into a parking bay.

Resource material

The following is a quote by the DSA on this part of the ADI Test:

> This test is not just a slightly more difficult 'L' test. It is of an advanced nature and a very high standard of competence is required. You must show that you have a thorough knowledge of the principles of good driving and road safety and that you can apply them in practice.

To be able to drive skilfully and safely, you need a thorough understanding and working knowledge of the rules and regulations. You should have done most of your studying when preparing for the theory test, now you must demonstrate that you can apply the rules sensibly and correctly. To help with your application of the correct routines and procedures you should continually refer to:

- *The Official DSA Guide to Driving: The essential skills.*
- The *Highway Code.*
- *Know Your Traffic Signs.*

For details of reference books, and resource materials, see page 392.

PREPARATION

Even if you have already passed an advanced driving test, the syllabus and style of driving of the other motoring organizations may differ from that of the DSA. It is therefore advisable to have an assessment with an experienced ADI tutor. While instructors at the local driving school may be extremely good at preparing candidates for the 'L' test, they may not be fully conversant with the higher level of assessment required for this test.

Tutors registered under the ORDIT scheme know what the DSA's requirements are and are skilled at assessments at this level. They will be able to advise you on any adjustments needed to enhance your driving style and efficiency.

Even if you have been driving for many years, modifications may be needed to streamline your performance in line with modern driving techniques. However, it is often said that 'unlearning' something you've been doing for years is far more difficult than learning something from scratch, and some experienced drivers find it difficult to adapt to a new style of driving.

Effective training

Training with a qualified, experienced tutor is essential for several reasons:

- If you are still driving to the style you were taught many years ago, you may be applying inefficient methods.
- When you have passed the theory test, there may still be some deficiencies in areas of your knowledge that could result in failure. A trained tutor will be able to identify these and teach you how to apply the rules and procedures correctly.
- The standard of driving required by the DSA is higher than that of other advanced driving organizations.
- You may be under false assumptions about the test and its content – a good tutor will be able to advise you correctly.
- An assessment given under test conditions will be invaluable experience.
- The training you receive from your tutor will provide you with a demonstration of the teaching techniques you will need to acquire to become an effective instructor.

Failure is expensive, and it increases the pressure when attending for retests. In addition, if you do not take training with a specialist, you may well be at a disadvantage when it comes to taking your instructional ability test, as you will not have seen demonstrated the teaching skills you need to acquire.

A good tutor will make an objective assessment of the current level of your personal driving skills and be able to guide you along the route to improvement and explain why any changes need to be made to your style.

Be prepared to invest in sufficient training as you are only allowed three attempts at this test. If you are not up to the required standard, not only will failure be expensive, but there will be more pressure on you next time.

It is sensible to have a couple of 'mock test' sessions with your tutor prior to taking the test just in case you have any last-minute doubts or queries, and need any advice or reassurance.

Remember – your examiner will be expecting to see you drive with skill and confidence. You are an experienced driver – it will therefore be obvious to the trained eye if you are trying to put on a show of being 'extra careful'. Doing this will only be a distraction and may cause you to make incorrect decisions and to fail to make proper progress.

To prepare for the test, you should:

- take advice from your tutor on the aspects of your driving that need improvement;
- continue to refer to the recommended books;
- get as much practice as possible on different types of road and in differing conditions;
- apply the correct procedures whenever you are driving so that they become natural;
- try to maintain progress in relation to the conditions, the law and your car;
- practise giving yourself commentaries as you are driving along.

As well as making progress, you should also take into consideration vehicle sympathy, economy and the comfort of your passengers. To maximize progress, you should:

- make sure you can reach all of the controls properly;
- use the controls smoothly and progressively;
- hold, turn and straighten the steering wheel properly;
- demonstrate vehicle sympathy by selecting gears at the correct time and in accordance with speed and power requirements;
- plan well ahead so that you can use 'accelerator sense' to avoid unnecessary stops, excessive use of the brakes and engine braking;
- maximize fuel economy by keeping the engine revs at the correct level.

To maintain progress and demonstrate your personal driving skills, you should:

- look and plan well ahead, anticipating and preparing for hazards before you reach them;
- adjust your speed to avoid any unnecessary stops;
- start looking early at junctions so that you can take opportunities to proceed as soon as you are sure it's safe;

- always be aware of the speed limit and make progress by driving up to it in relation to the road, weather and traffic conditions.

To protect yourself, your passengers and road users all around, you should:

- be aware of what is happening all around your car at all times by using all of the mirrors on a regular basis;
- respond properly to what you see in the mirrors;
- anticipate and make allowances for the mistakes of other road users;
- exercise self-discipline when threatened by others;
- show courtesy and consideration to anyone else using the road;
- always be prepared to give way, even if it's your priority.

Show that you can handle your car efficiently in all of the manoeuvre exercises by:

- maintaining absolute control on all gradients, using the handbrake when necessary;
- making effective observations throughout, and responding correctly to the presence of any other road users – which means giving them priority when appropriate;
- demonstrating accurate steering skills to complete each exercise effectively;
- stopping the car in a controlled manner, avoiding skidding; but if you do skid, you must demonstrate that you can correct it properly.

If you put all of these principles into practice, passing the Test of Driving Ability at your first attempt should not be a problem.

THE SYLLABUS

Try not to be influenced by the examiner sitting beside you. If you are putting into practice the principles of safe driving contained in the recommended books and as taught by your tutor, your decisions should only be influenced by what is happening all around you.

Remember, your decisions to act should be based only on what you know is safe for the circumstances. Examiners are specially trained and should recognize from the all-round situation what you are basing these on.

Your examiner will assess your driving skills under some of the headings listed on the DL25, Driving Test Report form (reproduced on page 336). Any numbers not listed relate to tests on other categories of vehicle. You will be assessed on:

1. (a) *Eyesight* – you must be able to read a number plate from the prescribed distance.
   (b) *Vehicle safety* – you must be able to describe and demonstrate how to check the condition and safety of a number of the car's components.
   (c) *Highway Code* – you must demonstrate that you can apply the rules.

2. *Controlled stop* – you must be able to stop your vehicle safely, promptly and under full control. Firm, progressive braking should result in a prompt and safe stop. Avoid braking so harshly that your car skids, or if your car has an anti-lock braking system, that this is activated. Remember you are supposed to be stopping under control.

3. 4. and 5. *Reverse exercises*

Reverse left into a limited opening:

- *Under control:* taking account of any gradients, full control should be maintained throughout.
- *With proper observation:* all-round checks should be made throughout and you should respond to the presence of other road users. This means giving them priority when appropriate or proceeding if you are sure they are waiting.
- *Reasonably accurately:* you are an experienced driver, you should be able to maintain a reasonable degree of accuracy throughout and end in a safe position.

Reverse right into a limited opening:

- *Under control:* as for the left reverse you should take account of any gradients, and maintain full control throughout.
- *With proper observation:* as you will be manoeuvring on the wrong side of the road you will need to pay particular attention to the front, responding to the presence of other road users. This means giving them priority when appropriate.
- *Reasonably accurately:* as an experienced driver, you may switch the focus of your observations from offside to rear to nearside in order to maintain a reasonable degree of accuracy. This will also help keep up to date with the presence of others.

Reverse parking – either on the road or into a parking bay:

- *Under control:* take account of any gradients, and maintain full control throughout.
- *With proper observation:* as you may be manoeuvring into a more confined space from the middle of the road, you will need to pay particular attention to the presence of other road users. This means giving them priority when appropriate.
- *Reasonably accurately:* whether reversing on the road or into a parking bay, you need to steer into the space accurately and finish up with your vehicle straight.

6. *Turn in the road*

- *Under control:* take account of any gradients, and maintain full control throughout, using the handbrake where necessary.
- *With proper observation:* keep checking in all directions and give other road users priority when appropriate.

      – *Reasonably accurately:* you should be able to complete this manoeuvre in three movements. However, if you're on a particularly narrow road it may take five – don't worry.

11. *Take proper precautions before starting the engine.* Make a habit of checking that the parking brake is secure and the gear lever is in neutral before starting the engine. However, if you happen to stall in an awkward situation and wish to get moving quickly, it is more efficient to keep your footbrake on, clutch down and switch on. You must however, retain full control of your vehicle at all times.

12. *Control – you should make proper use of:*
    – *Accelerator:* progressive, gentle use and good accelerator sense should result in full control, a smooth ride and economical use of fuel.
    – *Clutch:* good clutch control should be demonstrated without excessive wear and tear, as for example happens when it is used for very short stops. Coasting over prolonged distances should be avoided.
    – *Gears:* selective changing up and down the box should be employed to suit the circumstances and to result in maximum fuel economy.
    – *Footbrake:* progressive use of the brakes should result in smooth stopping.
    – *Parking brake:* used for those stops likely to last for more than a few seconds, particularly in situations where other traffic and pedestrians are present and, of course, to avoid any rollback on gradients.
    – *Steering:* an efficient pull–push method should be used to give maximum efficiency, leverage and control.

13. *Move off:*
    – *Safely:* full observations should be made to ensure that no other road users are affected when moving away.
    – *Under control:* full control should be maintained when moving away in all situations – level, uphill, downhill and at an angle.

14. *Use of the mirrors well before:*
    – *Signalling:* mirrors should be checked well before making any decision to signal so that discrimination is effective and signals are timed correctly.
    – *Changing direction:* no action to change direction should be taken unless you are absolutely sure you will not be affecting another road user.
    – *Changing speed:* always be sure of the all-round situation before changing your speed, whether you are speeding up or slowing down.
    – Use the mirror–signal–manoeuvre (M–S–M) routine effectively.

15. *Give signals by direction indicators/arm:*
    – *Where necessary:* if any other road user (including pedestrians) would benefit from a signal, use one. If appropriate, that is, if you have time and your window is open, consider giving an arm signal for stopping at a zebra

crossing if you think an oncoming driver or pedestrian might benefit. The horn should be used as a warning of your presence and can be helpful when you're approaching a blind bend or summit.

- *Correctly:* use only signals that clearly show your intentions to move off, stop or change direction.
- *Properly timed:* signals should be timed so as not to confuse. For example, if you're waiting to move away from the kerb and there are a couple of vehicles approaching from the rear, too early a signal may alarm the drivers into thinking you're going to pull out in front of them; or if you're taking a second road on the left make sure you time your signal so as not to encourage a driver waiting in the first one to emerge in front of you. You should also remember that early positioning helps confirm your intentions, for example when passing parked vehicles where you may not think a signal is needed.

16. *Clearance/obstructions:* where there are parked vehicles, work out whose priority it should be, but also anticipate what the oncoming driver is likely to do. Priorities don't really matter if the other driver is determined to take the road space. Sometimes it is courteous to make a positive decision to give way, for example if you are travelling downhill and there is a larger vehicle coming up the hill towards you.

17. *Response to signs and signals – take appropriate action on all:*
- *Traffic signs:* road signs are there for your information and guidance. Respond to them early by checking your mirrors and taking the appropriate action. Check for signs whenever you are approaching a different type of road, and make sure you are always aware of the speed limit for the road you are travelling on.
- *Road markings:* are also for your guidance. Look and plan well ahead, and respond to hazard warning lines by checking your mirrors and looking for any possible dangers. Plan early for any lane changes so that you don't have to take any late action that might affect others. Be aware of any stop lines and make sure you bring your vehicle to a complete stop.
- *Traffic lights:* plan your approach according to the colour already showing – remember they could change at any moment. If the lights are on green, check your mirrors, adjust your speed and be prepared to stop until you reach that point of no return when it would be unsafe to stop. Demonstrate that you know the meaning of amber. If, when it shows, you are so close to the line that you would need to brake sharply to stop, you should continue – particularly if someone is close behind you. If red is showing, check your mirrors, adjust your speed and be prepared to stop if it remains on red, or to change to an appropriate gear and proceed if it changes to green.
- *Signals given by traffic controllers:* obey any signals given by authorized persons such as police officers or school patrol wardens.

- *Other road users:* although most drivers use signals correctly, some do not! Make sure, if another driver is signalling to turn into your road, that he or she actually is going to turn. Similarly, if another driver flashes his or her headlights at you to proceed, don't just go without checking all-round safety for yourself.

18. *Use of speed.* Speed limits are not targets and although you should make proper progress, your speed should be dictated not only by the limit for the road you are on, but also by the weather, the condition of the road surface, the traffic volume and any pedestrian activity.

19. *Following distance:* always keep a safe distance between yourself and other vehicles. If the vehicle in front of you stops, you should have time to take action without getting too close to it. Leave a gap of at least a metre for every mph of your speed – or use the two-second rule. In very wet conditions you should at least double this distance. If someone is following you too closely, drop back even further. This will allow you to give the following driver more time to stop.

20. *Maintain progress:* drive at a realistic speed appropriate to the road and traffic conditions. Approach all hazards at a safe and controlled speed, without being over-cautious or interfering with the progress of other traffic. Be ready to move away promptly from junctions. When you have to stop, keep looking in all directions for a suitable gap in the traffic and have your car ready to move smoothly into it, building up your speed and changing up efficiently so as not to affect any other road user.

21. *Junctions (including roundabouts)*
    - *Speed on approach:* try to time your arrival at junctions in accordance with the sightlines. That is, if the junction is opening up, without slowing down excessively, give yourself time to start making early observations. If the sightlines are totally restricted, don't waste too much time on the approach if you won't be able to see until you get there!
    - *Observations:* you cannot make any safe decision to proceed until you have looked properly in all directions. On the approach to T-junctions, as soon as sightlines begin to open up (no matter in which direction), start looking and keep looking in both directions until you are absolutely sure you will not affect another road user. At crossroads, keep looking in all directions – even when you have priority. Remember, even a green light does not give you 100 per cent safety – check there's no one proceeding through on the wrong colour.
    - *Approaching traffic:* your actions should never make another driver slow down or change direction. Before you make any decision to cross another driver's path, make sure you have enough time and, just as importantly, make sure you know what's happening in the new road.
    - *Turning right:* when turning from main roads, if there is sufficient width for two vehicles on either side, make sure you position your car so as not to

hold up the following traffic. Make sure you know what's happening in the new road before you commit yourself to turning in. When emerging from wide roads, position yourself just to the left of the centre line so as not to impede the flow of left-turning traffic. However, if the road is narrow, keep farther to the left to allow more room for vehicles turning in.

- *Turning left:* whether turning in or emerging, maintain your normal driving position, about a metre from the kerb, to allow plenty of room for the rear wheels to clear the kerb.

- *Cutting corners:* make sure you position correctly, according to the width of the road, and if you have to wait for oncoming traffic, that you wait just short of the point of turn. This should ensure that you turn in on your own side of the road, avoiding cutting corners. However, if there are parked vehicles near the end of the road making an ideal turn impossible, proceed a little farther forward prior to turning, to give you a better view.

22. *Judgement:*

- *Allow adequate clearance to stationary vehicles and obstructions.* Allow sufficient room for doors opening, drivers moving off without signalling or people walking between vehicles. This means you should, in ideal circumstances, be allowing about a metre's clearance.

- *Meeting other traffic:* when the width of the road is restricted, be prepared to give way, no matter whose priority it may be. Remember, the oncoming driver may not be as courteous as you are! If there are vehicles parked on both sides, but there is room to proceed through, then allow an equal amount of clearance to both sides – in other words, drive down the centre of the road. On roads where there is a need to maintain the traffic flow but you cannot give the ideal clearance, then slow down and drive through cautiously, allowing time to respond if the situation changes.

- *Overtaking:* this is *the* most dangerous manoeuvre! Before you decide to overtake you should ask yourself, *is it safe, legal and necessary?* Make sure you know what's happening behind you and that you can see far enough ahead so you know you'll have sufficient time to execute the manoeuvre quickly and efficiently without affecting any other road user. Allow plenty of room when overtaking cyclists and motorcyclists.

- *Crossing the path of other traffic:* never rush to beat an oncoming vehicle when turning right. If you have to rush, there is a risk involved, and you should never put your car (or your body) into a situation your eyes haven't visited first.

23. *Positioning*: normally position your vehicle well to the left. On a road of reasonable width, your normal driving position should be about a metre from the kerb – or even a little farther out if there are large puddles and pedestrians around. Give cycle lanes the same distance. On narrower roads, in rural areas for example, you may have to drive a little nearer the edge of the road, in which case you will need to adjust your speed according to the

situation and the presence of any other road users. On left bends, keep to the centre of your lane to maintain safety from oncoming vehicles. On right bends, keep to the left to improve your view.

– *Driving in lanes:* exercise lane discipline and drive in the centre of your lane, avoiding straddling the lines. Look and plan ahead and select your lane early. When a lane change is necessary, apply the M–S–M routine early, carrying out the manoeuvre safely and gradually.

24. *Pedestrian crossings:* dealing with the light-controlled crossings is fairly straightforward as you have to obey the light sequences. Anticipate when they are likely to change and apply the M–S–M routine in good time. Stop at the stop line and secure your car with the parking brake.

At zebra crossings, it's a bit more complicated. You need to be on the lookout for pedestrians likely to step out at any moment. Look and plan well ahead, apply the M–S–M routine and always be travelling at a speed at which you can stop within the distance you can see is clear. Be patient and only proceed when you know it's safe. Pedestrians have priority anywhere in the road – be ready to anticipate their actions and, if possible, give them time to get onto the pavement.

At toucan crossings, be prepared to give way to cyclists as well as pedestrians.

25. *Position/normal stops.* Sometimes when drivers are under test conditions they feel they must stop as soon as they are asked to do so! However, you must make sure that you only stop where it's safe, legal and convenient. Remember, you should be demonstrating that you know and understand the rules by applying them correctly.

26. *Awareness and planning:*
    – *Pedestrians:* people don't always do as they should, and pedestrians don't normally read the *Highway Code*. Always expect the unexpected, and, in any area where there is pedestrian activity, try to anticipate what might happen. Check your mirrors and be ready to slow down or stop.
    – *Cyclists:* give as much clearance as you can to cyclists. They are unpredictable and could wobble into your path at any time, particularly in windy conditions. Expect them to ride off pavements without warning and to cycle in between lanes. Always check to your sides before moving off in queues of traffic.
    – *Drivers:* these are pedestrians on wheels – they don't always act as they should. That they know the rules does not mean they will always apply them. Look and plan all around, watching out and allowing for drivers: moving off, changing lanes or stopping suddenly; cutting corners; turning across your path; taking priority when it should be yours; not using signals correctly; following you too closely; not obeying traffic signs and signals.

27. *Ancillary controls.* You should maintain constant all-round visibility in your car. Without needing to look down at the controls, use the washer/wipers,

demisters and fan as necessary. If you use the air conditioning, make sure you switch it off if you open your window – this includes during any of the manoeuvre exercises. For normal driving, having the windows open in hot weather causes drag and will use more fuel than the air-conditioning unit does.

ECO-SAFE DRIVING

As an experienced driver, in the Part 2 ADI exam you will need to show that you are aware of the need for fuel efficiency and an environmentally friendly approach in all aspects of your driving. As an ADI you will need to be able to encourage your new drivers in the use of all these various techniques.

Eco-friendly driving can make a significant impact on the global use of conventional fuels and make a positive contribution to the reduction of carbon emissions. This process starts with an awareness of the availability of vehicles with alternative fuels such as electric and 'dual fuel' power.

Fuel-efficient driving is now part of the ADI Part 2 exam and could be included in the 'L' driver test within the next few years.

To make an improvement in your own fuel-efficient driving, there are many areas that can be considered, including:

- *Acceleration.* Your use of acceleration should be steady, smooth and progressive whenever possible, avoiding unnecessary speed peaks. A smooth driving style can save up to 10 per cent of fuel used. Where appropriate, cruise control should be used, as this can be more efficient on fuel usage.
- *Braking.* Any use of the footbrake should be smooth and positive, with a certain amount of tapering on and off. Avoid any harsh use of the brakes by easing off the accelerator earlier where possible.
- *Gear changes.* Gear changes need to be made effectively, with block changes up and down where appropriate. Move into the higher gears reasonably quickly. Cars with manual gear change are more fuel-efficient than automatics.
- *Hazard awareness* and forward planning techniques should be used effectively to minimize any unnecessary or harsh changes of speed or direction.
- *Vehicle sympathy.* Engine speeds should be kept relatively low whenever possible. Generally, keeping the engine speed to about 3,000 rpm can save a considerable amount of fuel. All controls should be used smoothly to avoid any unnecessary sharp fluctuations in speed.
- *Manoeuvring.* Reversing into a parking space and then driving out forwards is regarded as more fuel-efficient than reversing out when the engine is cold.
- *Speed.* Keep to all legal speed limits and plan well ahead for any changes. Some experts reckon that by reducing top from 80 mph to 70 can save a considerable amount of fuel.

- *Air conditioning.* Avoid using air con or climate control unless it is necessary, as this can be detrimental to fuel consumption. Avoid driving with the car windows or sunroof open, as this can create 'drag' and an increase in fuel consumed.

Individually, these savings may not seem much, but collectively they can make substantial reductions, not only on your own costs but also on the global use of carbon fuels.

Marking

Eco-safe driving faults are marked on the DL25 as a 'driving fault' by the examiner, using one of the spare boxes on the form. The DL25 form is illustrated on page 336.

The main areas that the examiner will be looking for include:

- *Hazard awareness and planning:* Hazards identified at an early stage, giving adequate time to respond and to decelerate as appropriate.
- *Speed limits:* Complied with all speed limits. Speed is appropriate to all road, traffic and weather conditions.
- *Starting up and moving off:* Avoids excessive use of the accelerator. Moves off promptly and smoothly.
- *Accelerator:* Used smoothly. Accelerator was properly coordinated with the other controls.
- *Gears:* Used efficiently and effectively, with the appropriate gear engaged at all times.
- *Engine braking:* Used effectively to take advantage of engine braking power where appropriate.
- *Engine power and torque:* Utilized higher gears at lower engine speed where appropriate without causing the engine to labour.
- *Cruise control:* Used in appropriate situations, but without compromising road safety.

Remember – this is not just about saving fuel in your vehicle; it's more to do with releasing less polluting chemicals into the atmosphere and conserving fuels globally.

MARKING SYSTEM

This test demands a high level of driving skill and the marking system is fairly critical. Faults are assessed under three categories:

- *Driving faults* – these are errors that detract from the *'perfect'* drive.
- *Serious or potentially dangerous faults* – faults that cause potential danger or damage, and in different circumstances could lead to a serious situation arising.
- *Dangerous faults* – faults that cause actual danger.

To pass this part of the exam you must have no serious or dangerous faults and a maximum of six driving faults.

The following are some examples of faults.

- *Driving faults:* ineffective use of the mirrors and lack of response; making too many unnecessary gear changes; signalling incorrectly; lack of observations during manoeuvre exercises.
- *Serious or potentially dangerous faults:* failure to respond to the presence of other road users during a manoeuvre exercise; cutting a right corner with no other road user present.
- *Dangerous faults:* turning right across the path of an oncoming vehicle; emerging from a junction and slowing down another driver; driving too slowly for the conditions and missing opportunities to proceed in busy situations.

Your examiner will give you the top copy of the DL25 form and will explain any faults that have been marked. If you have passed you will also be given an application form for the test of instructional ability. If you fail, you will be given an application form for a further attempt at the driving test.

Remember, you may only have three attempts at this test. If you fail on the third, and still wish to continue with the qualifying process, you will have to wait until a two-year period elapses from passing the theory/hazard perception test. You will then have to start the whole process again by taking Part 1.

YOUR DRIVING SKILLS

In preparation not only for your ADI driving test, but also for a future of effective, economical and safe driving, you need to know something about the theory behind good driving principles. Driving is mainly a practical skill that can only be fully developed through effective practice and experience. It involves a complex mix of:

- knowledge;
- understanding;
- awareness;
- attitude.

As well as being able to identify all of these elements in order to effectively practise 'safe driving for life', in order to coach the inexperienced there are other aspects of driver behaviour that you need to understand.

It is extremely unlikely that 'the perfect driver' exists. However, perfection is something that we should all try to achieve. As instructors, we should take a pride in our driving and be able not only to analyse and improve our own performance, but also to offer constructive criticism to our pupils. In striving for perfection we need to recognize some of the main ingredients and characteristics of 'the perfect driver', which include skill, knowledge and attitude elements.

PROFILE OF 'THE PERFECT DRIVER'

Skill

To the perfect driver, 'vehicle sympathy' means being 'at one' with, and in total control of, the car at all times. All actions should be smooth, positive and precise. The vehicle should always be:

- in the correct position;
- travelling at a safe speed for the road and traffic conditions;
- with an appropriate gear engaged to suit the speed and power requirements.

Observation, anticipation and forward planning – all of which require total concentration – are essential at all times. Too often, a driver's ability is judged purely on the basis of manipulative and control skills. Perfection in these practical skills alone, however, will not compensate for a lack of knowledge or a defective attitude. Optimum performance requires not only the ability to think for oneself, but also the skill to read effectively the road and traffic conditions and to take account of what other road users may do.

Knowledge

The good driver will know and understand the laws, rules and regulations relating to road procedure. Without this knowledge, even the most skilfully adept person cannot become a complete driver. Knowledge is thought to generate positive attitudes. In driving instruction, as in general education, the more the knowledge and understanding is developed, the better and safer the outcomes will be.

Attitude

Knowledge of the subject and skill in handling the car are not sufficient qualities in themselves. They need to be applied in a safe, sensible manner. This means taking into account mistakes other drivers make and being prepared to make allowances for them.

Attitudes have a profound effect on the quality of driving, and although relatively easy to define in general terms, they are more difficult to assess in the individual driver. The perfect driver is:

- considerate;
- courteous;
- tolerant; and
- never drives in a spirit of competition or takes revenge on another road user.

For the instructor, these qualities are even more important. The attitude you display during lessons or on demonstration drives will be transmitted to your pupils.

Attitude is assumed to influence the behaviour of drivers, with reckless or unsafe actions being attributed to a negative one. Opinions are not always objective when judgements are made about a traffic situation or another driver. Judgement in any situation may be influenced by attitudes assumed previously in a similar event. An incorrect attitude can sometimes make drivers see things not as they actually are, but as they imagine them to be. One of your most important jobs as an instructor will be to develop favourable attitudes in your pupils and change any negative ones they may have.

Motivation describes the personal needs and drives of the individual. It ranges from the need to survive to a feeling of well-being and achievement of desires. It can be used in a positive way to improve driver behaviour. However, motivation may sometimes cause illogical and potentially unsafe driving. For example, drivers may take risks that are uncharacteristic if they:

- are late for work or an important appointment;
- want to get the better of another driver;
- wish to demonstrate a superiority of skill;
- would like to gain the admiration of friends.

Emotion is the general term used to describe feelings such as love, hate or fear. Intense emotions like anger, frustration and grief tend to turn the focus of the mind in on itself. This in turn lowers the attention on the driving task and limits perceptive abilities.

Anger may result from an argument. Frustration may result from being held up behind a slow-moving vehicle. Anxiety may be the result of worries about work or other personal problems.

Inexperienced drivers who lack self-confidence may suffer from ill-founded fears that they cannot cope. Driving is in itself a stressful activity, and deficient knowledge or skill can result in frustration and may generate destructive emotions.

Personality is described as 'distinctive personal qualities'. However, what we may think of ourselves may be completely different from the way in which others see us. Personality tends to be inconsistent, and faced with varying circumstances, drivers may display different sides of their personality.

There is some evidence to suggest that extrovert drivers are more likely to be involved in accidents than the introvert. This may be partly explained by the extrovert driver's inability to concentrate on the driving task for longer periods of time.

Perception is the brain's interpretation of information it receives from the eyes, ears and other senses. The perception of a particular traffic hazard involves the primary information-processing functions of the brain. This involves a need to compare the current situation with existing knowledge and previous experience.

Hazard recognition requires an active and rapid assessment of the potential risks involved in a particular situation, and the driver must then anticipate events before they occur. This anticipation relies heavily on stored memories of similar experiences.

Perception is the driver's visual and mental awareness, and it provides information on:

- speed;
- position;
- timing.

Drivers have limited perceptual capacity and are frequently faced with an overload of information from the environment. In order to maintain safety when this happens, it becomes necessary to prioritize. This means that the important pieces of information will need to be attended to while other aspects will have to be ignored.

A more detailed explanation and analysis of driver behaviour is given in Chapter 8, Driver Training.

ON THE ROAD

Road sense

Driving is a continuous process of observing, responding and attending to constantly changing needs involving the vehicle, the road layout and traffic conditions. You need to continually recognize, assess and reassess hazards and respond correctly in good time. These responses involve the M–S–M and P–S–L (position–speed–look) routines.

Within the individual elements of these routines you should:

- look, assess and decide what action can safely be taken in relation to the information received from the all-round situation;
- look, assess and decide whether a signal is required;
- assess whether the signal is having the required effect on others;
- look, assess and decide what effect any changes in position and speed are likely to have on others;
- decide what further looks may be required.

The good driver needs to assess the part he or she is taking in the changing road and traffic environment. For example, you should not only respond to developing situations, but you should also see yourself as an active part of those situations – often contributing to them. Assessing risks, and deciding on the appropriate response to a hazard, involves a continuous process of assessing and reassessing the constantly changing traffic situation. This involves:

- assessing the degree of risk;
- deciding on the priorities;

- focusing attention on the most important aspect;
- deciding on a specific course of action;
- responding in good time;
- reassessing.

Anticipation is having the ability to predict the actions of other road users. It should be interlinked with the visual search skills. As a good driver you need to know:

- why, where and when you must look;
- the kind of things to look for;
- what to expect;
- how to see effectively as opposed to just 'looking'.

Risk assessment is influenced by knowledge and previous experience. It may be learnt on a trial-and-error basis or through controlled exercises. Most drivers will recognize that there is a bend in the road; however, they might not all think of the possibility of there being an obstruction hidden from view.

Most collision accidents result from deficiencies in a driver's information-processing skills and not from deficient car control. A large proportion of accidents could be avoided if drivers were more aware of the risks involved, knew what to look for and what to expect, and were prepared to drive defensively by take avoiding action.

Visual awareness

The good driver is constantly gathering information from the all-round traffic scene. An active visual scan not only provides more information at an earlier stage, but also gives more time to respond. The eye movements of experienced drivers need to be very rapid, moving quickly from one point of interest to another, checking and rechecking areas of risk. Drivers should practise an effective visual search system that involves:

- looking well ahead – allowing you to steer a safe and smooth line;
- keeping the eyes moving – to help you build up a more complete picture and improve awareness;
- getting the big picture – looking all around assists with the judgement of speed and position;
- allowing others to see you – positioning your car so that you can see and be seen;
- looking for alternatives – working out an action plan that may be required if events change.

Hazard recognition

The natural inclination of many drivers is to keep going, unless it is obviously unsafe; for example, by steering away from a moving hazard rather than slowing down to avoid it. You need to:

- actively search the road ahead;
- assess the safety of proceeding;
- recognize the consequences of your actions.

When reading the road ahead, rather than waiting for something to happen, you need to anticipate it and respond in good time so that problems can be avoided. To do this you need to obtain as much relevant information about the road and traffic situation as you can. For example:

- *To steer accurately and adjust to safe speeds before reaching a hazard*, look well ahead for bends, gradients, road signs, junctions and obstructions such as parked cars, roadworks and traffic hold-ups.
- *To maintain tyre and road surface adhesion*, drive smoothly and approach hazards at a suitable speed, taking into account weather conditions, road surface and any camber on bends.
- *To anticipate and act on the actions of other road users*, scan the road for anything with a potential for moving into or across your path.
- *To be able to stop well within the distance you can see to be clear*, you need to identify any blind areas and adjust your speed accordingly.
- *To avoid problems with road users to your sides and rear*, make full use of all of the mirrors and use your peripheral vision. You also need a good understanding of the principles of communicating with other road users. You also need to exercise good lane discipline.

Making decisions

Some drivers' decisions often polarize between 'stop' and 'go' where neither is necessarily correct. Inadequate information and hurried assessments are often major causes of incorrect decisions. Try to make decisions early enough to create extra time and leave you with alternative choices. For example, when you are approaching a parked vehicle where there is a line of slow-moving traffic approaching from the opposite direction, there could be three choices. These are:

- It's safe to proceed.
- It's unsafe to go at the present time.
- More information is needed to reassess the situation before a decision can be made.

Any decision – whether it's to proceed, hold back, give way, or stop – must be continually reassessed. Make your assessments in advance and keep all options open. For example, when approaching a green traffic light you should be anticipating the possibility of it changing and be ready with the decision to stop. At some point on the approach, however, you will be too close to pull up safely, and the only safe decision is to continue. When approaching any traffic lights, no matter what colour is showing, you need to continually reassess what to do if they change.

Response and control skills

Communication

Methods of communication between road users are complex, and involve much more than merely using the commonly recognized means of:

- indicators;
- brake lights;
- arm signals;
- horn;
- flashing headlights;
- hazard warning flashers.

An effective communication system involves:

- the position of the vehicle on the road;
- the speed of the vehicle;
- implied signals of intent;
- eye contact;
- courtesy signals and acknowledgements.

Signalling by position

In general terms, the driver who maintains a correct course and position on the road should not need to signal. Although this is not completely valid for all circumstances, there is an element of truth, and anticipating an intended act from another vehicle's position should not be ignored.

Taking up the correct position will help to confirm your signals. Where the position does not appear to confirm a signal, other drivers may become confused. For example, a vehicle may be signalling left, but if the car is positioned towards the centre of the road, other drivers may understandably become confused as they are receiving conflicting information.

Signalling by speed

Changes in speed can also be used as an indication of an intended action. For example, in a situation where a vehicle is signalling to turn left, is positioned correctly and is obviously slowing down, there is a combination of evidence to suggest a left turn will be made, and other road users do not have to rely on one single factor.

Other examples of where speed clearly signals another driver's intentions are when a car is approaching a junction far too quickly for it to give way, and when a driver is accelerating rather than slowing down near a zebra crossing. By slowing down well before crossings, you can clearly signal your intentions to the pedestrians waiting to cross as well as letting any other drivers know what you are doing.

Defensive signals

These are the signals you might use to warn other road users of your presence. They include the use of flashing headlights, the horn and hazard warning lights. The use of the horn would normally be considered in relatively slow-moving traffic conditions. Use it when you think another road user might not be aware of your presence, for example when approaching blind summits, sharp bends on narrow roads, or when you see vehicles reversing from driveways. On higher speed roads, such as motorways, because the noise of traffic would drown the sound of the horn, flashing the headlights would be more effective.

Hazard warning lights should only be used when stationary and in an emergency, unless you are coming to a stop for a traffic hold-up on a motorway.

Implied signals, eye contact and courtesy

Not only do you need to recognize and interpret the speed and movement of other traffic, but you must also be alert to implied or potential movement, for example the pedestrians standing at the edge of the pavement near a zebra crossing.

A vehicle waiting at a give-way line always has the potential to move into your path. Treat the implications with respect and be ready to slow down.

Eye contact is another valid form of communication. For example, when you are slowing down on the approach, or waiting at a pedestrian crossing, it helps to reassure pedestrians they have been seen; or when you are waiting to pull into a line of slow-moving traffic it may persuade others to hang back and allow you to move out into the traffic stream.

Speed adjustment

The senses used in the judgement of speed are:

- sight;
- hearing;
- balance;
- touch.

The interpretation of speed can be very difficult at times, particularly in a modern car with a sound-insulated interior. In the absence of vibration and noise on a smooth road that has no nearby side features such as buildings, speed can seem deceptively slow.

Speed is assessed through a combination of factors that appear to involve an established speed 'norm' learnt from previous experiences. It can be judged from:

- the rate at which visual images disappear to the sides;
- road, wind and engine noise;
- the sense of balance when changing speeds and direction;

- the general 'feel' of the vehicle on the road;
- comparisons with established 'speed norms'.

These speed norms can sometimes be misleading, for example when approaching the intersection at the end of the slip road after leaving a motorway.

Speed adjustments are required to maintain sufficient safety margins so that you can stop well within the distance you can see to be clear and in accordance with the traffic conditions, visibility and regulations. These adjustments must take into account the critical perceptual and attention overload limitations of any driver.

As your speed increases your focus point needs to be farther ahead, while there will be a corresponding reduction in your peripheral vision. Where you need to attend to foreground detail, you must reduce your speed. Peripheral vision will assist in the judgement of your speed and position. If you don't reduce your speed you may well miss important risk factors, and your awareness of lateral position and safety margin will be limited.

To attain maximum awareness you need to apply an active visual scanning process for observing the road and traffic environment in its entirety, including signs, markings and traffic flow. By using this scanning process, and by maintaining proper control of your speed, you should be able to maintain a safe course, whilst at the same time watching for the potential movement of other road users and compensating for them in good time.

You should always be travelling at a speed at which you can stop safely within the distance you can see to be clear. This means also taking into consideration how closely you are being followed. If a driver is far too close for comfort, you will need to take responsibility for his or her safety as well as your own. To do this you should:

- ease off the gas gradually;
- drop back from the vehicle ahead;
- look and plan as far ahead as possible;
- slow down early, braking gently when you see a hazard.

By allowing more space between you and the vehicle ahead, and braking early and gently, you will be creating more time for the following driver to respond.

Position

As well as being in the correct position on the road in relation to its type and any change in direction you may be considering, you also need to consider your distance from the vehicle ahead. Positioning properly, safely and with consideration involves:

- your driving position in the road;
- driving in the centre of your lane;
- changing lanes early and gradually;
- allowing sufficient safety cushion between you and the vehicle ahead;

- allowing sufficient safety margins when passing parked vehicles or other obstructions;
- maintaining safety margins that will allow for the unexpected movement of others;
- selecting safe parking positions;
- taking up suitable positions on the approach to junctions so that you can take effective observations;
- positioning correctly when turning so that minimum disruption is caused to the traffic flow.

To position yourself correctly in order to maintain good sightlines and visibility of the road ahead, you need to:

- position out towards the centre of the road when approaching parked vehicles;
- be prepared, when giving way to oncoming traffic, to wait well back from the obstruction.

Other considerations when waiting in traffic are:

- not blocking crossings or access to side roads and entrances;
- not stopping so close to the vehicle ahead as to be unable to pull out around it should the need arise.

Gathering information

Failing to take precautionary measures in doubtful situations can often result in the situation becoming critical and extreme measures becoming necessary. Before making any commitment to act, you need to gather relevant information so that you can deal with any situation safely and effectively.

Driving is not just a series of decisions to stop or go. In many situations, you will need to put into effect an information-gathering exercise. For this, you will need to slow down to create time for the situation to develop, and keep your options open before making a definite commitment to keep moving or stop. Precautionary measures should also be taken when vision is restricted or where there may be an unseen hazard, for example over the brow of a hill or around a bend.

Hold-back procedure

There are varying ways of holding back from problems. These range from just a momentary easing off the accelerator, to taking more active measures to maintain safety. Maintaining safety where there are hazards normally means:

- looking and planning well ahead;
- anticipating any changing circumstances and potential hazards;
- maintaining good vehicle control at all times;
- slowing down early enough to hold back from the hazard.

Hold-back procedure involves actively reducing the speed with a view to looking, deciding or waiting, and maintaining safe options in moments of uncertainty to create a safety cushion.

Progress

Whereas the hold-back procedure involves slowing down with a view to looking, waiting and deciding on what action is required, *powered progress* involves proceeding after considering all the available information and deciding it's safe to go. This often includes *creeping and peeping*. Using first gear clutch control, slowly edge forwards so that you can look round any obstruction, or in all directions at blind junctions, before making any commitment to proceed.

For making powered progress away from hazards, the point at which the decision to go is taken will dictate which gear to select. Remember, *gears are for going – not for slowing!* Select a gear that will be appropriate for the speed and power requirements.

Speed control and steering

The control skills required will depend on the need to either make powered progress or to hold back. *Powered progress* involves holding the car still or moving off under full control on all gradients, then making efficient progress through the gears, taking into account changing conditions and gradients. *Holding back* involves slowing down using either deceleration or controlled rates of braking, depending on gradients; and stopping if the need arises and securing the vehicle. Which procedure is necessary depends on the road and traffic environment.

You need to demonstrate that you have a thorough knowledge of all the different skills involved in proper speed control. You also need to demonstrate that you understand about the safe use of speed in relation to the acceleration, braking and cornering limitations of your vehicle, and the qualities of adhesion between the tyres and road surface. You should be aware of the overall stopping distances in both good and poor driving conditions, and have the ability to apply them.

You need to pay attention to signs and markings so that you are aware of the speed limit for the road you are travelling on. You should be aware of the need to make proper progress according to the road and traffic conditions. Demonstrate that you are a confident driver – inconvenience and danger can be caused to others if you are putting on a show of being over-cautious. Maintain all-round awareness by keeping a check on what is happening all around your vehicle before you make any changes to your speed or direction.

SYSTEM OF CAR CONTROL

An efficient system of car control should take into account the natural and mechanical forces that affect the stability of a vehicle in motion. Your system of driving must take into consideration other road users' actions, by having built-in safety margins that should help to compensate for:

- human error;
- deficient skills;
- minor lapses in concentration;
- mistakes by other road users.

Applying an efficient system should ensure that you will always have time to maintain control of your vehicle in a sympathetic manner. Points to remember are:

- The speed of your vehicle should always be such that you can stop in a controlled manner well within the distance you can see to be clear. To do this you need to look for, and respond to:
  - obstructions on your intended course;
  - the potential for other road users to move into your intended course from blind areas;
  - restrictions to your sightlines caused by road features such as bends, hill crests or dips in the road;
  - obstructions that may be hidden by restricted sightlines.
- Control and speed should take into account the natural and mechanical forces that affect the stability of vehicles in motion. You should demonstrate an awareness of the:
  - physical roadholding and handling limitations of your car;
  - tyre and road surface adhesion;
  - increased stopping distances in wet and icy conditions;
  - effects of camber and gravity;
  - aerodynamic forces acting on the vehicle.
- To minimize the effects of the forces that affect the stability of vehicles in motion, you should:
  - use the accelerator, brakes and steering smoothly and progressively;
  - avoid excessive acceleration or braking when negotiating bends and corners;
  - avoid changing gear when your hands would be better engaged on the steering wheel, for example when negotiating sharp bends and turns;
  - avoid unnecessary gear changes when selective changing is more appropriate;
  - keep both hands on the wheel when braking, accelerating and cornering;
  - accelerate progressively when negotiating a curved path.

If you are sympathetic to the needs of your vehicle, not only will you prolong its working life, but you will also make more efficient use of fuel. Try to:

- avoid unnecessary or fidgety movements on the accelerator;
- use the accelerator and footbrake early and progressively;

- avoid excessive clutch slip, drag and unnecessary coasting;
- avoid excessive tyre wear by cornering at lower speeds;
- avoid using the gears to reduce speed;
- use cruise control if it's available.

The handbrake

The handbrake should normally be used:

- when the vehicle is stationary on up- and downhill slopes;
- if you're going to be stationary for more than a few seconds, that is, for longer than the time it would take to apply and then release it again; and of course,
- when parked.

However if you're planning ahead properly and anticipating changing circumstances, you should be able to minimize the number of times when you need to come to a complete stop. By planning and creeping slowly forwards you are creating time for the hazard to clear, making the stop either unnecessary or very minimal. For such short waits the use of the handbrake is obviously unnecessary.

Using the brakes and gears

When slowing down, keep both hands on the wheel and (unless you're on an uphill gradient) use the footbrake to reduce speed. After slowing down, change to a gear that's appropriate for negotiating the hazard. For example, when approaching a left turn in, say, fourth or fifth gear, brake to reduce the speed sufficiently and then change into the gear required to negotiate this particular corner. When approaching a T junction where your view of the main road is restricted, brake to slow down until the car has almost stopped, push down the clutch and release the pressure from the brake to allow the vehicle to roll slowly. Just before stopping, change into first gear, ready to go again. As well as being a waste of fuel, changing down to reduce the speed is unsympathetic and causes unnecessary wear and tear to the clutch, gearbox and transmission.

However, it is sometimes useful to use a lower gear on downhill gradients to offset the effects of gravity. In these circumstances, the brakes should be used initially to bring the speed under control before the appropriate gear is selected. This provides increased engine braking and reduces the risk of brake failure from overheating due to continuous use on long downhill stretches of road.

Double declutch

This technique is not generally necessary. Although still recommended in some advanced driving manuals, it can be inappropriate in a modern vehicle with gears protected by synchromesh and increases unnecessary wear on the transmission system. However, when it is required, this is how it should be carried out.

To change up:

- Hand to gear lever and cover the clutch.
- Clutch down, off the accelerator.
- Move the gear lever to neutral.
- Clutch up quickly and then down again.
- Engage the higher gear.
- Raise the clutch and accelerate.

To change down:

- Hand on gear lever and cover the clutch.
- Clutch down, off the accelerator.
- Move the gear lever to neutral.
- Clutch up and depress the accelerator quickly, releasing it immediately.
- Clutch down quickly and engage the lower gear.
- Raise the clutch; continue braking/accelerating.

Factors influencing stopping distances

The overall stopping distance consists of two separate components, the thinking distance and the braking distance. Thinking distances are based on the average person's reaction time in normal driving conditions, which is about two-thirds of a second. This reaction time is that between reacting to an emergency and the act of beginning to apply the footbrake. In an artificial 'emergency stop' situation this reaction may be reduced – but only slightly.

The conversion of speed from miles per hour to metres per second shows that, at a speed of 60 mph with a reaction time of two-thirds of a second, the 'thinking distance' will be about 18 metres (or 60 feet). This distance is proportional to the speed. The exact distance may vary slightly from one driver to another and from one situation to another, depending on the driver's:

- fitness;
- health;
- reactions;
- state of mind.

Braking distances are affected by a combination of factors, including the:

- size and weight of the vehicle;
- effectiveness of the vehicle's braking system;
- type of tyres, their pressure and depth of tread;
- condition of the road surface.

Whereas thinking distances increase proportionally with speed, braking distances increase much more rapidly at higher speeds. For example, if you increase your speed from 20 mph to 40 mph it is going to take four times the distance to stop (24 metres instead of 6 metres). At 60 mph, the braking distance is nine times the distance compared with 20 mph.

With good brakes and tyres on a dry road, the car should normally stop in the distances shown in Table 4.1. On wet or slippery roads, these distances will be much greater, and can be up to 10 times the braking distance in extreme conditions.

The cause and correction of skidding

Although the vehicle and road surface condition may contribute to a skid, the main cause of most skids is without any doubt the driver. There are three different types of skid and these are caused by:

- excessive speed for the road conditions and/or traffic situation;
- excessive acceleration, braking and/or cornering forces being applied to the tyres;
- a combination of both.

The rear-wheel skid occurs when the rear wheels lose their grip. It's usually the result of excessive speed and cornering forces. Sometimes it also occurs in combination with harsh acceleration or, more usually, excessive braking. This type of skid is easily recognized because the rear of the car slides away from the centre of the corner. If uncorrected it could cause the vehicle to turn completely round.

It's essential to eliminate the cause, for example to release the accelerator and/or footbrake and compensate with the steering.

Because, in this type of skid, the driver will see that the vehicle is pointing in the wrong direction, the natural reaction will be to steer back on course. There is a danger however, particularly with the quick response of radial tyres, for drivers to over-steer, causing the vehicle to spin the other way.

Table 4.1 Stopping distances

Speed			Thinking distance		Braking distance		Overall stopping distance	
mph	Metres per sec	Feet per sec	Metres	Feet	Metres	Feet	Metres	Feet
20	9	30	6	20	6	20	12	40
30	14	45	9	30	14	45	23	75
40	18	60	12	40	24	80	36	120
50	23	75	15	50	38	125	53	175
60	27	90	18	60	55	180	73	240
70	32	105	21	70	75	245	96	315

The front-wheel skid occurs when the front wheels lose their grip, leaving the driver with no directional control. It usually occurs as a result of turning sharply into a corner or bend at excessive speed and/or under hard acceleration or braking. It can be recognized when the vehicle fails to go in the direction in which it is being steered.

To correct the skid, the cause must be eliminated and steering control regained by momentarily straightening the wheels and/or reducing pressure on the accelerator or brake.

The four-wheel skid occurs when all four wheels lose their grip. It's usually caused by excessive speed for the road conditions or traffic situation, resulting in uncontrolled overbraking. On a wet or slippery surface drivers may even feel that their speed is increasing. Steering control is lost and the vehicle may turn broadside. The control can be partially restored by momentarily releasing the brake to allow the wheels to start turning again and then quickly reapplying the brake in a rapid on–off action. Many new cars are now fitted with an anti-lock braking system which will work in the same way, allowing the driver to regain control much more easily.

More information on skids is contained in the DSA publication *The Official DSA Guide to Driving*. The prevention of skids is better than the cure! It's important to recognize danger signs early and act on them. For example, slowing down early when you see a group of children playing near the road will mean less braking pressure is needed if one of them dashes out. Concentration, planning and the early anticipation of the possible actions of others is essential.

In snow and ice, slow down early with light braking pressure. Gentle braking is less likely to cause skidding than changing into a lower gear. Use gradual acceleration and keep in the highest gear possible without distressing the engine. When going uphill in snow, try to maintain a steady momentum by staying well back from the vehicle ahead.

Drive at safe speeds for the road surface conditions. Accelerate, brake and corner gently. Drive more slowly on wet, icy and slippery surfaces. Watch out for loose gravel, fallen leaves and damp patches under trees. Make sure your tyres are correctly inflated and that they have a minimum of 2 mm of tread all around. Never mix cross-ply and radial tyres on the same axle. If you must use a mix of tyres, fit the cross-ply to the front and the radials to the rear axle.

Keep off soft verges! Read the surface conditions and slow down well before reaching any bumpy parts and speed humps. Avoid heavy braking on loose gravel and muddy surfaces and when driving through damp patches under trees.

The combination of oil, rubber dust and water can make the surface very slippery after a light summer shower following a long dry spell. In freezing temperatures, remember that black ice forms on exposed bridges first.

Emergency braking

You need to be realistic about the distance it can take to stop, particularly in wet conditions. When you have to brake quickly:

- Pivot promptly from accelerator to brake.
- Apply the brake progressively and firmly.
- Keep both hands on the wheel to keep the vehicle on a straight course.
- Apply maximum braking force just before the wheels lock up.
- Avoid braking so hard that the wheels lock up, as this will considerably lengthen the stopping distance.

If the wheels lock up, particularly in wet, slippery conditions, the brake should be momentarily released and then quickly reapplied – this is called cadence braking and it will allow the tyres to regain their grip. This method of rapid on–off braking is how an anti-lock braking system works. It gives the driver greater braking efficiency and increased directional control should the wheels lock.

Please bear in mind that although your car may have an anti-lock braking system, it's normally a sign of lack of anticipation and/or bad planning if it's needed.

Whenever you drive, you need to:

- exercise self-discipline;
- concentrate all the time and read the road well ahead;
- drive at speeds at which you can stop safely within the distance you can see is clear;
- anticipate actual and potential hazards;
- be courteous, patient and considerate;
- apply the controls gradually and smoothly;
- drive in a safe, sympathetic, effective and economic manner.

As an instructor, your driving should be an example to your pupils and to the public in general. Your aim should be to teach them to drive confidently and to a similar style.

Remember: PRACTISE WHAT YOU PREACH! Try to maintain a good, professional standard with your driving at all times.

5

ADI Part 3:
Instructional Ability

This chapter contains information on the topics that make up the syllabus for learning *safe driving for life*. Your future job will entail teaching all of these topics to pupils with varying degrees of skill and ability.

In Part 3 of the ADI test, your ability to teach pupils at different stages of learning will be assessed. This chapter explains the different aspects of your instructional techniques that are tested, including:

- application for a test;
- the car you use;
- the format of the test;
- structuring lessons at the correct level;
- subjects tested and their key elements;
- the marking system;
- training and practice.

APPLICATION

When you pass the Part 2 Eyesight and Driving Ability Test, the examiner will give you an application form for Part 3. Tests are conducted at the centres listed on this form and can be taken at whichever one you choose. Send your application to the DSA with the current fee and you will receive written confirmation of your appointment. Take this confirmation letter with you when you attend for the test, along with both parts of your photo card licence. If you still have the old-style paper licence you will need to take your passport as photographic proof of your identity. A trainee licence is also acceptable.

THE CAR

You must provide a suitable vehicle for the test. It must:

- Be properly taxed and insured, including any liability of the examiner as a driver. The insurance should cover any DSA examiner, as the DSA cannot guarantee that the test will be conducted by a specific person.
- Be a saloon or estate car in proper condition with front and rear seat belts in working order.
- Have manual transmission and right-hand drive.
- Have a readily adjustable driving seat and a seat for a forward-facing front passenger, both with head restraints.
- Display the statutory 'L' plates (or 'D' plates in Wales, if you prefer).

As a working instructor, you must be continually aware of the all-round situation. You also need to know how your pupil is responding to the situation behind and to the sides of your car. It is therefore essential that you have at least one extra rear view mirror. Many instructors also fit a supplementary mirror in order to discreetly monitor pupils' mirror work and their response to the situation to the rear.

From time to time members of the DSA staff accompany examiners on tests to ensure uniformity. All seat belts must therefore be in working order. If they are not, the test will be cancelled. Similarly, anyone accompanying you on your test must wear a seat belt. If you want your tutor to accompany you, you will need to inform the examiner before leaving the waiting area.

TEST FORMAT

The test lasts for about an hour and is conducted by a Senior Examiner ADI (SEADI). You will have to demonstrate, through your practical teaching ability, that you are able to pass on your knowledge to pupils with different levels of ability.

The test is conducted in two parts. In the first (Phase 1), the examiner will play the role of a beginner or a learner with limited driving skills. In the second part (Phase 2), the examiner will play the role of either a learner who is about at driving test standard or a qualified driver undertaking driver development training.

If the examiner is to portray the qualified driver there are several situations that might be described:

- a driver who is preparing for a job interview that will require a driving assessment;
- someone who has not driven in the UK for a few years;
- someone who has not driven regularly for some time, but who now needs to commute between different urban locations;
- the driver who has difficulty with reverse parking because he or she was not taught this manoeuvre.

The 'qualified driver' role is selected randomly, with the examiner making an amendment to the marking sheet as appropriate.

Structuring the lesson at the correct level

At the beginning of each phase, the examiner will give you a brief description of the pupil with an outline of the current standard of his or her driving. You must:

- listen very carefully to this information;
- ask the examiner to repeat anything you have not understood;
- structure your tuition at an appropriate level to suit the pupil described.

You must make every effort to add realism to the lesson. You can do this by:

- trying to treat the examiner as a real pupil;
- getting into your 'instructor role' by asking questions to establish the pupil's knowledge;
- listening very carefully and giving extra useful information.

If the examiner is to portray a full licence holder (rather than a 'partly trained' learner) in the second part of the test, you should use a slightly different approach. Your technique should take into account the previous experience of the 'pupil', and would apply particularly to:

- the person who is a regular driver, but who is now preparing for a job interview that will involve a driving assessment;
- the driver who has a lot of driving experience abroad, but who is now returning to the UK;
- someone who has not driven for some time, but who will now need to drive for work or business purposes.

In these circumstances, avoid being over-fussy about driving habits that might have built up over a period of years, but at the same time do not expect too much from the person who might not have driven since passing the test.

You will need to be reasonably diplomatic but firm if there are any major problems to rectify but, for example, do not be too pedantic about methods of steering. If the pupil has been using a rotational method for a number of years rather than pull/push, your task will be to make sure that his or her steering is safe and under complete control, rather than introducing a new method.

Similarly, you may well find that the person who has been driving for some time will be in the habit of changing up and down through the gears consecutively and using intermediate gears unnecessarily. You might need to be diplomatic but firm in dealing with this problem and changing a long-standing habit; use your coaching skills by emphasizing modern techniques and the changes in vehicle technology.

With this type of pupil there will be a tendency to overdo the use of signals – frequently signalling when unnecessary and often with a late or inadequate mirror check. Try to guide the pupil (particularly with the use of questions) into being selective by encouraging him or her to make early and appropriate use of mirrors and all-round observations. By doing this, the pupil should begin to develop a feel for when signals should be given, as well as the importance of correct timing.

Examination topics

The list of topics tested in this part of the exam covers some of the subjects included in the DSA's officially recommended syllabus for learners. You will find full details in *The Official Guide to Learning to Drive*. Your tutor should show you how to teach all of the subjects in the syllabus, as well as teaching you how to:

- structure lessons;
- check pupils' knowledge;
- assess the needs of pupils with differing abilities;
- plan routes suitable for the level of the learner and the subject under instruction;
- teach hazard perception and anticipation.

You will find information on all of these topics in Chapter 8 of this book, and guidance on how to put them into practice in *Practical Teaching Skills for Driving Instructors*.

The examiner will select one topic from each of the following lists:

Subjects specified in Phase 1

- Safety precautions on entering the car and explanation of the controls.
- Moving off and stopping.
- Turn-in-the-road exercise.
- Reversing (to the right or left).
- Emergency stop and use of mirrors.
- Dealing with pedestrian crossings and giving signals by indicators/arm as appropriate.
- Approaching junctions to turn either right or left.
- Dealing with emerging at road junctions.
- Dealing with crossroads.
- Meeting, overtaking and crossing other traffic, allowing adequate clearance for other road users and anticipation.

Subjects specified in Phase 2

- Dealing with crossroads.
- Meeting, overtaking and crossing other traffic, allowing adequate clearance for other road users and anticipation.
- Approaching junctions to turn either right or left.
- Dealing with emerging at road junctions.
- Dealing with pedestrian crossings and giving signals by indicators/arm as appropriate.

- Making progress and general road positioning.
- Reverse parking.

Where a particular exercise includes two or more subjects the examiner will, in the initial briefing, nominate which topics you are to cover. Listen carefully, taking brief notes if you wish, to make sure that you cover the important items and avoid wasting time on irrelevant ones.

Dealing with the key elements

Each subject is made up of a number of key elements. You may only have time to cover some of these briefly during your explanation. However, once on the move, you must ensure that all of the correct procedures and routines are put into practice.

Lesson format

Please note that, throughout this chapter, the word 'pupil' is used to describe either your 'real life' pupil *or* the examiner playing that role for the test. On the test, once the pupil has been described to you and that role is assumed, you must try to treat the examiner as a 'real life' pupil. Remember that a different pupil will be portrayed for each phase, and you will have to adapt your instruction to suit each one.

Each 'lesson' should be tailored to suit the time available and the standard of the pupil described. How much instruction you give while stationary should be dictated by the pupil's prior knowledge and you must also remember that this is a test of your practical teaching ability. Do not 'waffle' – try to focus on the key elements of the subject and ensure that learning then takes place through practice.

During your introduction to the lesson, you may refer to brief notes or subject headings if you need to. However, you need to look professional. This will not be achieved if you quote lengthy paragraphs from books. Training aids should be used where appropriate, particularly if the subject is a new one for the pupil, or where an illustration would be helpful to explain something a little more complex.

Keep the pupil involved by asking the occasional question. This could be to confirm a *Highway Code* rule or a principle outlined for example in *The Official DSA Guide to Driving: The essential skills*. Do not, however, completely bombard the pupil with complicated questions that are not appropriate to the skill level being portrayed. Remember, you're supposed to be building up your pupil's confidence, not destroying it!

STRUCTURE OF THE TEST

Phase 1 – key elements

- Establish the base line for the lesson by asking a couple of questions and correcting any misunderstandings.

- Explain the routines and procedures to be learnt.
- Offer a demonstration if it's appropriate.
- Give talk-through instruction until the pupil's skills begin to develop.
- Gradually reduce the amount of instruction and use questions to prompt and to develop independence.
- Do not restrict yourself to the nominated topic, but also react to what is happening around you. When opportunities arise to teach awareness and anticipation, take advantage of them.
- Identify and analyse faults when they arise and give advice on how to improve.
- Give the pupil plenty of encouragement and feedback, quoting the *Highway Code* or other driving principles outlined in *The Official DSA Guide to Driving: The essential skills*.

The examiner will assess your ability to teach a new subject to the pupil, or to reinforce and practise a subject where the pupil has some prior knowledge.

Establishing the base line for the lesson

Setting the base line will often include confirmation of why the topic is necessary in order to build up the skills required to become a 'safe driver for life' and not just to prepare for the 'L' test. Each lesson has to have a start point. To set this 'base line' you will need to listen carefully to the SE's description of the pupil and what previous experience he/she has. You can do this by asking a few questions relevant to the subject. As learners have to prepare for the Theory Test, asking questions at this point will help you establish whether the pupil is studying or not. Depending on the responses, you may have to either go through all the key elements, or reinforce anything the pupil omitted or appeared to misunderstand.

Visual aids

If the pupil appears to be having difficulty in understanding, you should use training aids. Not only do these help pupils because they can see what you mean, but they can also serve as memory joggers for you.

Demonstrations

These may be offered where appropriate: for example if, when you're explaining a difficult principle or manoeuvre to your pupil, there appears to be some confusion or misunderstanding. In the test situation, time is limited and demonstrations are normally declined. If, however, your offer of one is accepted it must be accurate. You might even consider combining a 'talk-through' explanation with the demonstration.

There are times when you may need to carry out part of a manoeuvre or procedure, and other times when the exercise has to be executed in slow motion.

You may also need to replicate the way the pupil is carrying out the procedure and compare this with the correct routine.

Learning through practice

If the subject is relatively new, you should be prepared to give full 'talk-through' instruction to build up the pupils' confidence. In the early stages of learning the pupil will need plenty of help. You have to be prepared, therefore, to repeat procedures and to give as much assistance as is necessary.

Remember that your instruction should not be restricted to the lesson topic. Any unusual situations that arise during the drive should be mentioned. For example, if you are dealing with junctions, you should not ignore the possibility of meeting oncoming traffic where there are vehicles parked on the road.

Question and answer (Q&A) on the move

Avoid over-instruction and be ready to decrease the instruction when you can see skills beginning to develop. Asking a few simple questions early enough can encourage pupils to take a little responsibility for carrying out routine procedures. For example, to encourage the pupil to make effective safety checks before moving off, you could ask, 'Is there anyone to your right?' or 'Is there anyone in your blind area?' When using Q&A on the move, try to ensure that the pupil does not have to respond with a lengthy answer.

Positive correction

When correcting pupils, it is far more effective to make a positive comment. For example if your pupil applies the handbrake without releasing the ratchet, the positive correction would be something like, 'When you apply the handbrake, remember to press in the button first.' If the car is being driven too far from the kerb, you could advise, 'Try to drive about a metre from the kerb.' If while waiting to emerge from a junction, the pupil only looks in one direction, you could encourage better observations by asking, 'Can you see clearly both ways?'; or giving a direct instruction to 'Keep looking both ways until you know it's safe to go.'

Maintaining control and safety

As an instructor, you are responsible for the all-round safety of your pupil, other road users and, of course, yourself. Do not allow potentially dangerous situations to arise. You must maintain control of the lesson. Sometimes this will mean preventing an unsafe situation from arising. For example, if you feel your pupil is going to emerge from a junction and you know that he or she has not looked effectively, or can't see far enough because of restricted sightlines, a positive instruction to 'wait' may be all that is required.

Retrospective correction

If you allow a pupil to emerge unsafely, giving a reprimand afterwards, it could be too late! It will be no consolation after a 'near miss' situation to confirm that 'You shouldn't have pulled out without looking properly!' Learning is more likely to take place if the pupil deals with the situation correctly in the first place. In this example, it would be more effective to ask your pupil, 'Can you see if there's anyone approaching?' However, sometimes things happen quickly before you have time to act. In these cases, you may have to give corrective advice after the event. Make sure you do!

Developing the pupil's understanding

Whenever an error is committed and you are giving corrective advice, you must give a valid reason by finishing with the 'because' element. This does not mean saying, 'Because I say so!' or 'If you don't, you'll fail your test!' Your reasoning should be based on the correct application of the rules, regulations and procedures for driving safely and considerately – in other words, in order to survive. You could also quote the official publications to add authority.

Giving feedback and encouragement

This is an important aspect of your job as an instructor! No matter what the standard and ability of your pupils, at the end of each practice element, you should let all of them know what progress has been made and where improvement and practice are needed. Encourage pupils to ask for more information if they don't understand something you've been working on. Confirm that you will record any items necessary for pupils to revise before the next lesson. Encourage them to study for the Theory Test or to revise rules and procedures for topics that are going to be covered on the next training session.

Remember to finish on a 'high'. Give praise for those areas where improvement took place.

Phase 2 – key elements

During this part of the exam, you will be assessed on your ability to:

- assess what the pupil already knows and can do;
- identify and analyse errors or weaknesses;
- give remedial instruction to achieve improvement.

Establish any underlying problems

Listen very carefully to the examiner's description of the pupil and of previous driving experience. Ask a couple of questions to confirm that the key elements of the topic are understood and in order to pitch the lesson at the correct level. Again, listen carefully, as the answers given may hint at an underlying problem or misunderstanding. If so, confirm the correct routines and procedures.

Assessing ability through practice

You should aim at getting the car moving as soon as possible. Your first priority, with pupils at this level, is to make an assessment of their strengths and weaknesses, and then to give the necessary advice to improve understanding and skills.

Over-instruction

Unlike the Phase 1 'lesson', which is all about your teaching ability, your skills at assessment are now being tested. Treat your pupil as a driver and avoid the temptation to carry on where you left off with the first pupil by giving too much instruction and assistance. Allow your pupil to demonstrate the ability to make decisions and to put the correct procedures into practice. If any patterns of error occur, you can then intervene and start working on correcting the faults.

Identifying faults

Never assume that your pupil will carry out all the correct routines and procedures.
    Part of your job is to identify, analyse and correct faults. You need to be able to identify those faults that could lead to problems, whether or not they relate directly to the topic under instruction. You then need to give some corrective advice and create opportunities to practise the correct routines.

Dealing with faults on the move

Although you have been given a specific subject to deal with, you may find that unrelated driving faults are introduced. These must be dealt with, but without 'nit-picking'. Where minor mistakes occur on a one-off basis, they may not even be worth a mention. But if similar errors keep recurring, or if you are unsure, then query them. You may be able to deal with these minor errors on the move by asking a simple question or making a positive comment. For example, if your pupil forgets a couple of checks of the nearside door mirror prior to turning, you could ask, 'Where should you be checking before you turn left?'

Dealing with more serious faults

Errors of a more serious nature – for example, if your pupil turns right across closely approaching traffic before you have time to prevent it – will need to be dealt with in more detail. This is a dangerous error and needs some corrective advice. To discuss the problem safely, and to avoid distracting the pupil's attention from the driving task, you should confirm that you'll discuss the point as soon as you can find somewhere safe to stop. Whatever the error, remember to finish with the WHY!

Recognizing faults

You must watch what the pupil is doing all of the time. Mistakes can be made at any time. The following are a few of the basic mistakes that might be made.

- Doors – not properly closed.
- Seat – not adjusted properly.
- Seat belt – forgotten or twisted.
- Mirrors – not adjusted properly; not checked regularly; incorrect response to what is happening.
- Safety checks – handbrake and neutral checks omitted before switching on.
- Observations – no shoulder checks prior to moving away.
- Control – jerky use of clutch – could be caused by lapse between lessons, practice in a different car or incorrect seat adjustment.
- Signals – unnecessary; badly timed; not cancelled or reapplied; or incorrect.
- Observations – ineffective looks in all directions at junctions.
- Positioning – normal driving; driving in lanes.

Try to make learning a positive experience by watching for these errors and correcting them by asking:

- Are all the doors closed properly?
- Can you reach and operate the controls comfortably?
- What do you need to put on before you drive?
- Can you see to the rear and sides?
- Do you need to check anything before you turn the key?
- What should you be looking for before moving away?
- The clutch may feel strange at first; take your time until you get used to it.
- Who were you signalling to? What does the *Highway Code* say about flashing headlights?
- Where should you be looking before you emerge?
- What is the normal driving position?

ASSESSMENT OF INSTRUCTIONAL ABILITY

During the test you will be assessed on each of the following:

1. Core competencies:
    (a) Identification of faults;
    (b) Fault analysis;
    (c) Remedial action.

2. Instructional techniques:
    (a) Level of instruction;
    (b) Planning;
    (c) Control of the lesson;
    (d) Communication;
    (e) Question and answer techniques;
    (f) Feedback/encouragement;
    (g) Instructor's use of controls.
3. Instructor characteristics:
    (a) Attitude;
    (b) Approach to pupil.

1. Core competencies

(a) Identification of faults

Having passed Part 2 you have shown that your driving is of a very good standard. Your job as an instructor is to prepare your pupils to share the road with you. You should therefore be teaching them to drive to a similar style, and although they won't achieve the same standard until they have had more experience, they will be learning to apply a sound system of car control that will result in *safe driving for life*.

When accompanying new drivers you should therefore base your judgement on what you would be doing in similar circumstances. Where anything deviates from your driving norm you need to ask yourself, 'What would I be doing here?'

Based on this concept you need to:

- recognize all faults that you consider need correcting;
- identify, and bring to the pupil's attention, any faults that are serious, or that are repeated;
- categorize the errors as minor, repeated, serious or dangerous.

You have to clearly identify faults that require correction as part of an effective teaching/learning process. When you have identified a fault, you have to ask yourself whether it is a 'one-off' minor error and not really worth mentioning, or whether it could lead to future problems and needs to be addressed.

When you have ascertained that a fault is worthy of a mention, you now have to decide when to deal with it. With minor errors, it may be appropriate to draw the pupil's attention to it at the time. If the error is of a more serious nature, you may have to delay your explanation until a more appropriate and safe time arises.

(b) Fault analysis

When you have identified an error, you have to accurately analyse the cause of it. Key elements in the fault analysis process are as follows:

- You must accurately analyse faults you have identified.
- The analysis must be complete.
- You need to follow it with a remedy.

For example, if your pupil swings out to the right after turning left, you need to confirm what caused the problem. Was it because of:

- too high a speed on the approach?
- incorrect positioning on the approach?
- late gear selection affecting the steering?
- an inefficient steering technique?
- the pupil's failure to look well down into the new road?
- a combination of some of these errors?

(c) Remedial action

- You need to be able to offer solutions for all of the identified problems.
- Your corrective advice must be effective; remember to explain the 'why'.
- You must create opportunities to practise the correct procedures to help eradicate the problems and improve the pupil's knowledge, skill and understanding.

When you have identified and analysed an error, you should give some constructive advice on how to remedy it. Using a visual aid if appropriate, explain to the pupil what should have been done. Finish your explanation with an appropriate reason for the action, by explaining what might have happened if the error had not been corrected. In the example it would be the problems caused to any oncoming traffic or the following driver who might have decided to overtake.

With some more complex faults, a demonstration might be appropriate if you have time. Finally, you should create opportunities for the correct procedure to be practised.

(More information on fault identification, analysis and remedy can be found in Chapter 4 of *Practical Teaching Skills for Driving Instructors*.)

2. Instructional techniques

(a) Level of instruction

To be an effective instructor, you need to be able to match your instruction to suit the level of ability of each individual pupil, and then adapt it to suit the driving skills demonstrated. You therefore have to follow these rules during each phase of the test, ensuring that you are neither under- nor over-instructing. You should then be prepared to further adapt the level of your instruction to suit the pupil's strengths and weaknesses as each 'lesson' develops.

There should be a complete match of your instruction to the stated level of experience, knowledge and needs of the pupil. This should ensure that the tasks you set for the inexperienced driver are not too difficult, and those set for the more experienced are not too easy. Having matched the level of your teaching to the stated experience and ability of the pupil, you must ensure that your instruction remains consistent. This is necessary to avoid confusing the pupil. If the pupil does appear to become confused, then you will need to make further adjustments to the level of your instruction to ensure that some learning or improvement takes place.

As each lesson progresses, make any adjustments necessary so that your instruction matches the pupil's apparent strengths, weaknesses and perceived improvement.

(More information on levels of instruction can be found in Chapter 4 of *Practical Teaching Skills for Driving Instructors.*)

(b) Planning

This section covers how you plan the lesson according to the pupil's needs and in relation to what actually happens. It relates to the sequence of your instruction, the amount of practical activity, and the aptness and effectiveness of your teaching methods. While assessing your teaching ability, the examiner will also take into consideration the complexity of the lesson topic.

Your instruction should be planned methodically and delivered in a clear and logical manner. To do this, you first of all have to base the work on what the pupil already knows, then lead into the new elements. In other words you are moving from the 'known' to the 'unknown'.

Key elements involved with lesson planning are:

- Each 'lesson' must be well planned and properly structured.
- Each subject should be dealt with in a logical and methodical way.
- The time between theory and practice should be allocated sensibly.
- Your presentation of the subject should be well organized.
- You must demonstrate that you understand the level of complexity of the subject.
- Take all opportunities that arise during each lesson to develop your pupils' skills through practical experience.
- Opportunities should be created to revisit situations to confirm skill and understanding.

(More information on lesson planning can be found in Chapter 4 of *Practical Teaching Skills for Driving Instructors.*)

(c) Control of the lesson

Maintaining safety, while at the same time building up pupils' confidence, requires good interaction with pupils and the ability to remain in full control in all situations. The assessment under this heading will be made on:

- how you allocate the available time between theory and practice;
- whether you are capable of changing the plan according to how the pupil responds;
- your reaction to critical situations;
- your response to the needs of other road users.

You will need to demonstrate an ability to anticipate what the pupil may do, taking appropriate action on any potential errors or danger in order to maintain a firm degree of control over the pupil.

To maintain safety, and to ensure that positive learning takes place, you need to constantly check on your pupil's reactions to each set of circumstances. To do this, you must:

- allocate a proper balance between theory and practice, to ensure that learning is reinforced;
- be alert and show awareness and perception to changes in the all-round situation;
- judge the pupil's ability to identify and react to the different situations and changing circumstances;
- watch the pupil's actions, observations and reactions at critical times, such as at junctions and other hazards;
- be ready to take control when necessary.

(More information on maintaining control can be found in Chapter 4 of *Practical Teaching Skills for Driving Instructors*.)

(d) Communication

It's important that your instructions are easily understood. Your ability to adapt and to use language and terminology that suits each pupil will be assessed under this heading.

Don't restrict yourself to 'technical' or 'authoritative' jargon simply because you've read it in books. You should adopt an easy, descriptive and concise style of instruction and communication that suits your personality, and will be easily understood by each individual pupil. For example, if you wanted to encourage a younger learner to make sure it was safe before emerging from a T-junction, which of the following statements do you think would be most appropriate?

Take effective observations, looking for a suitable opportunity to emerge.

Or:

Keep looking both ways until you can see that it's safe to go.

When you are giving any verbal information, make sure it is given fluently and avoid repeating yourself. You should be able to adapt and make adjustments to your vocabulary so that the less able can clearly understand you, and the more able are not patronized.

Give your directions clearly and in good time. Use simple and straightforward instructions so that there is no chance of any misunderstanding. Be ready to give more information if a junction does not conform to normal rules.

Key elements involved in the communication process include:

- the presentation of new information in an easy-to-understand manner;
- explaining routines and procedures in a logical sequence;
- explaining the meaning of any jargon you use;
- using simple terminology;
- the avoidance of repetition;
- adjusting your method of communication to suit the level of understanding of each pupil.

(More information on communication skills can be found in Chapter 4 of *Practical Teaching Skills for Driving Instructors*.)

(e) Question and answer (Q&A) technique

Your pupils will eventually be sharing the roads with all of us! Your job will be to teach all your pupils to cope safely and effectively with today's road and traffic conditions. To do this you will have to help each pupil to develop a proper understanding of the need to drive defensively and to maintain a safe attitude towards themselves, their vehicle and all other road users.

To assist in the development of this level of understanding, you will need to incorporate an effective Q&A technique into your driving instruction.

According to the pupil you are teaching, and the circumstances you are in, you will need to decide on when Q&A is appropriate. Your early-stage pupils should be made to feel comfortable about the Q&A process, so don't bombard them with complicated questions to which they are not likely to know the answers. Ask a simple one when you feel it will help to improve their skills or promote a better understanding of a routine or driving rule. As pupils' skills progress, use questions that are more searching. This should help you establish whether there is an understanding of the correct procedures and a safe attitude.

There are times when you don't need to ask any questions at all: for example, when your pupil is driving well and dealing safely with everything that is happening. There are also circumstances when you should not distract a pupil's attention from the driving task: for example, when you are in a complicated situation that requires full concentration.

Questions that require a simple 'Yes' or 'No' response will not tell you what the pupil thinks or understands. For example, if you ask a pupil, 'Should you look round before moving off?' the answer 'Yes' does not confirm that the pupil understands what he or she is looking for. To be effective you should use more searching questions based on:

- what;
- when;

- where;
- why;
- how.

The '*why*' is the most important element. As in the example given above, this will give you feedback on whether or not the pupil understands the reason for a particular action or shows a safe attitude for the particular circumstances. It would therefore give you better feedback if you ask, 'Where should you look before moving off, and what are you looking for?'

After asking a question, you can usually tell from a pupil's body language whether or not the point has been understood. Respond if you think the pupil is unsure by asking what hasn't been understood.

Questions can be asked to:

- recap on a previous lesson or topic;
- prompt;
- establish knowledge and understanding;
- encourage pupil participation.

Questions used should:

- be relevant to the pupil's ability and the circumstances;
- be asked at the correct time;
- be worded in such a way as to be thought-provoking;
- not distract the pupil at a crucial moment.

Q&A works both ways.

From the beginning of a course of training and at the start of a lesson, encourage your pupils to ask questions, and allow time for this to take place. Irrelevant questions, however, should not be allowed to distract from the topic under instruction. If questions are asked that don't relate to the lesson, you can tactfully delay any discussion by confirming that you will deal with it later.

Key elements involved in the successful application of Q&A include:

- Use it only when it will be of obvious benefit to the pupil.
- Use questions that are set at a suitable level for the needs of each pupil.
- Word questions simply so as not to cause confusion.
- Use Q&A only when it's the most appropriate method for dealing with a problem.
- Only use it when there is sufficient time for the pupil to respond.
- Make sure it is not too late for a question to be relevant.
- Do not ask questions when the pupil needs to concentrate on driving.
- Encourage the pupil to ask you questions.
- Do not ignore pupils' questions.
- Answer questions correctly.
- If your pupil appears to have become demoralized by your over-use of Q&A, or cannot respond correctly, then drop it for a while.

- Ask questions that will encourage pupils to think about their skills and progress and, depending on the responses, adjust the level of your instruction accordingly.

In order to be able to correctly answer questions asked by your pupils, you need to keep yourself continually up to date with the official publications.

(f) Feedback/encouragement

We all respond to positive feedback and praise! When your pupils achieve success, you need to let them know by giving lots of encouragement and positive feedback. You should be able to:

- give feedback to clearly indicate each pupil's level of achievement at any given point during a lesson;
- respond with the appropriate advice and guidance when you recognize from your pupil's body language that he or she is unsure or uncertain;
- confirm when a pupil has done well by using verbal confirmation, positive eye contact or body language;
- make use of all opportunities to give praise and encouragement where appropriate to develop the pupil's confidence;
- encourage pupils to ask questions so that you can give accurate feedback.

Key elements in giving and gaining feedback include:

- Ensure that your feedback is not ambiguous or confusing.
- Act positively on the feedback you get from the pupil.
- Acknowledge and give praise for good performance.
- Demonstrate your skills as a teacher by promoting questions from your pupil.
- Answer all questions, giving correct and complete information.
- Respond to your pupil's uncertainties by providing positive confirmation on his or her achievements, confirming which aims and objectives have been achieved.
- Confirm how progress will lead into the next subject to be covered.

(g) Your use of controls

As an instructor, maintaining safety in all situations is an important part of your job. This does not just mean being able to use dual controls. You will be assessed on how you use any control necessary to maintain safety for you and your pupil and to avoid inconvenience to other road users. You will be assessed on how you:

- use the dual clutch and brake;
- protect the gear lever at appropriate times;
- assist with the handbrake;
- correct steering problems;

- help with, or explain about, the use of other controls such as indicators, lights, horn, demister, visor.

If you have to use the dual controls or any ancillary controls in the car, make sure your pupil knows the reason you did so. For example, giving a left signal when leaving a roundabout, tell the pupil, 'I put the signal on for you there so that the drivers wanting to enter the roundabout won't be waiting unnecessarily for you.'

If condensation develops, show your pupil how the demisters work and explain about the importance of maintaining good all-round vision. Similarly, respond if you can see that your pupil is becoming too warm by explaining about the fan or air conditioning. If pupils are squinting because of bright sunlight, help by lowering the visor – before they remove both hands from the wheel to do it themselves!

It can sometimes be helpful to use the dual controls as a positive supplement to your instruction, for example when giving a demonstration of clutch control during a manoeuvre. Remember however, dual controls are primarily installed in driving school cars to prevent damage or danger. If your pupil isn't responding to a developing hazard, give a verbal prompt. If this doesn't work, then give a definite instruction, avoiding the use of the dual controls until it becomes a necessity – that is, no action being taken by the pupil.

The usual sequence of actions following this pattern would be:

Do you think you can get through that space safely? (The prompting question)

Check your mirror, slow down and give way to that oncoming car! (The instruction to take some action)

Wait! (The firm request)

Take some action by either using the dual controls to stop the car or by helping the pupil steer through the space. (The final action necessary to maintain safety)

Following your use of the dual footbrake, you must confirm why you took action. You could explain, 'I had to stop you there because it was the other driver's priority and there wasn't room for us both to get through.'

There may be times when you need to use the dual controls to prevent a stall in heavy traffic, or to stop the car from moving off at an inappropriate time. These should be kept to a minimum, as you should always try to prompt the correct action from your pupil. When any form of control has been used, you must explain when and why it was used. Key elements involved in using the controls include:

- Use them only in a positive manner to:
  - prevent danger or damage;
  - encourage understanding through demonstration;
  - assist with in-car vision and comfort;
  - help other road users.

- Use them only when other methods of prompting a pupil's response to potential hazards have failed.
- Explain why it was necessary for you to take action.
- Avoid using the dual controls as a punitive measure.

3. Instructor characteristics

(a) Attitude

The skills needed by instructors to create a relaxed, but supportive and learning, environment are extremely important. It is vital that you show a positive attitude towards your job, your pupil, and other road users as well as towards road safety in general. The more positive you are in demonstrating a safe and considerate attitude, the more likely your pupils will be to develop these attributes.

(b) Approach to pupil

You will need to be able to establish a good rapport with all of your pupils, striking a balance between being friendly, fair and firm so that you create the right learning atmosphere for each individual. At the same time, you will need to show a professionalism that will gain respect and that will encourage the pupil to work with you. You should endeavour to:

- put pupils at ease;
- instil confidence;
- establish an atmosphere that is conducive to a good instructor/pupil relationship and positive learning.

Key elements in the characteristics of a good instructor are:

- Try to be natural, using an approach that suits your personal characteristics.
- Combine friendliness with professionalism.
- Be approachable without being patronizing, so that the pupil remains at ease.
- Show that you are:
  - responsible and considerate;
  - keen for your pupils to learn;
  - interested in your work and also road safety.

More information on instructor characteristics can be found in *Practical Teaching Skills for Driving Instructors*.

PREPARATION

While studying for the ADI theory test you should also be gathering a good deal of the background knowledge you will need for teaching new drivers. Similarly, while training you for the ADI driving test, your tutor will be demonstrating the teaching skills that you will have to learn to put into practice as an instructor. A good tutor should teach you how to:

- establish prior knowledge by using Q&A techniques;
- break down subjects into their key elements;
- adopt the teaching principle of explanation–demonstration–practice;
- use Q&A techniques to maximize understanding and obtain feedback during practical sessions;
- give full talk-through instruction;
- give more responsibility to learners by decreasing the level of instruction at the appropriate time;
- improve learners' awareness and understanding by encouraging commentary driving;
- supervise and assess more experienced learners;
- use visual aids to assist learners' understanding;
- identify, analyse and correct errors made by drivers of differing abilities;
- avoid problems on the road by early verbal intervention;
- explain about the use of the dual and ancillary controls.

Training and practice

Although practice with real learners can be beneficial in the later stages of your training, it's not sensible to try it too soon. So whether you're practising with friends or relatives, or are gaining experience under the Trainee Licence Scheme, it's absolutely essential that you get plenty of properly structured training from your tutor before you practise with learners.

To teach you the main elements outlined previously and to give you a feel of the job under controlled conditions, a good trainer will realistically portray drivers with differing abilities and learning aptitudes. Your tutor should be covering:

- setting the baseline for lessons by establishing prior knowledge;
- planning the instruction to suit the level of ability of each pupil;
- organizing routes so that pupils can cope;
- how to avoid inconveniencing other road users;
- maintaining safety for your pupils, yourself and others;
- how to transfer responsibility as skill levels increase;
- the avoidance of danger and damage;
- how to give positive feedback and advice;
- how to link forward to the next lesson.

THE TEST

Part 3 is not a test of your knowledge – that is assessed in the theory test. Neither is it a test of your driving skills – those are assessed in Part 2. It is purely a test of your ability to give practical driving instruction.

You need to be able to demonstrate that you can pass on your knowledge and skills in a way that results in understanding and good driving practices being acquired by your pupils.

The two 'phases' of the test are conducted as follows, with the examiner playing the role of a beginner or partly trained learner in Phase 1, and a learner at about driving test standard or a full licence holder seeking development training in Phase 2.

Your examiner will describe the pupil to be portrayed and nominate the subject to be covered. You will be asked if you wish anything to be clarified, and once this has been done, the role of the pupil will be taken on. During the remainder of this chapter, the word 'pupil' refers to your examiner in that role.

During the test you should demonstrate your ability to do the following:

- Explain clearly the key elements of the topic.
- Give the necessary help and talk-through instruction to develop and improve the pupil's skill.
- Use Q&A to help the pupil understand why certain rules and procedures must be followed. For example, to encourage effective observations at junctions, you could ask the following questions:
  - 'Keep looking each way – can you see in each direction?'
  - 'How far can you see?'
  - 'Is it clear all around?'
- Develop the pupil's confidence by transferring responsibility when skills improve.
- Identify, analyse and correct errors by explaining how you would have dealt with situations.
- Create opportunities to practise the correct procedures.
- Give feedback and encouragement when improvement takes place.

Because of the time constraints of this test, you may not be able to cover every essential detail of the topics to be taught. However, you must ensure that all the key elements are included, whether this is during the explanation at the beginning of each 'lesson' or while the pupil is driving.

Fault assessment

An important part of your job is fault identification and assessment. Although you should not nit-pick at every minor error, you should deal with any mistakes which could develop into bad habits and, of course, any that are potentially serious or which could result in danger. The easiest way to recognize and deal with faults is to ask yourself, 'Would I be doing this if I were driving?' You can then transfer your thoughts by asking pupils for a reason and explanation as to why they did it. Their response will then dictate how you need to deal with the problem.

During this test, any major faults will normally be associated with the lesson topic. However, other faults will be introduced and you should deal with them effectively. When you recognize that something has deviated from a normal driving pattern, you should:

- query the fault;
- ask the pupil if he or she understands the correct procedure for dealing with such a situation;
- explain how you would have dealt with it;
- give the reason;
- practise the correct procedure to reinforce the point.

Subjects tested

Your tutor should give you guidance on how to teach the officially recommended syllabus as outlined in the DSA book *The Official Guide to Learning to Drive*. The instructional test does not encompass all these subjects, but you will need to be able to teach them to your pupils. For this reason the next section includes guidance on how to deal with the more complex subjects of dual carriageways and roundabouts.

Key learning points

The topics for instruction are itemized along with a list of their key learning points. It is important that these key elements are covered, in either the explanation or the practical part of the lesson. There are 10 preset tests, and the DSA's marking sheets for these are shown on pages 158 to 167. You will also find more information on them in Chapter 7 of *Practical Teaching Skills for Driving Instructors*.

We deal here with the subjects in a logical (staged) sequence, rather than list them in the preset test numerical sequence. The test topics are mixed so that your teaching skills can be tested during Phase 1 and your assessment and correction skills can be tested during Phase 2.

Learning to teach

Teaching driving can be a complex set of tasks. It is not always possible to work through each topic individually in a set sequence – there will often be an overlap. To help with your training, the subjects are covered in the next section in a logical sequence, as if you were working through the syllabus with a genuine learner. You will need to adapt your instruction and terminology for each pupil to suit the varying road and traffic situations. You cannot hope to teach different subjects to people of varying abilities by learning set scripts.

You should refer to the books *The Official DSA Guide to Driving: The essential skills* and *The Official Guide to Learning to Drive* for more information on the subjects covered in the official syllabus for learners. Use this syllabus to help formulate some lesson plans. If you do this, it will help to reinforce the key elements in your memory.

The DSA officially recommend the following books to help you in your preparations for the Part 3 exam: *Practical Teaching Skills for Driving Instructors*, by John Miller, Margaret Stacey and Tony Scriven; and *Instructional Techniques and Practice for Driving Instructors*, by Les Walklin. For details of all books and resource materials, see page 392.

THE PRESET TESTS

The controls lesson

Preset Test 01 – Phase 1

The main objectives of a first driving lesson are to:

- allow you and your pupil to get to know each other;
- reassure the pupil and gain his or her confidence;
- explain the use and functions of the main driving controls;
- give the pupil experience in moving off and stopping if time allows.

Lesson structure

The first lesson is normally booked either on the phone or in the office. When you meet the pupil for the first time, therefore, you need to establish how you will address each other. This usually depends on the pupil's age, gender and background. For example, if your pupil is a teenager you will probably be on first-name terms. However, if you are teaching a more mature person, it may be appropriate to take a more formal approach. In the test your examiner will describe the 'pupil' and give you an outline of his or her background, and you will then need to establish how you will be addressing each other.

You now have to *set the base line for the lesson*. This means establishing whether or not the pupil knows anything about the controls of the car, and if he or she has any previous driving experience. For example, if the pupil is an 18-year-old garage mechanic, you should not have to go into quite as much detail as you would need to with a middle-aged learner who has absolutely no knowledge of cars. Ask a couple of questions to find out what is known, then decide on the level of instruction needed to cover the key elements.

For the purposes of your training, we are covering this subject in detail so that you will be able to deal with someone with no knowledge. Your tutor should explain how to adapt your instruction so that you can also deal with the same subject with someone who has more experience. However, do not be patronizing. Most people have been passengers in cars and consequently will have picked up some knowledge.

Confirm that your pupil has a valid driving licence and can read a number plate from the prescribed distance. On your test, you may be asked to conduct the lesson at the test centre. However, it's normal, with pupils who have no experience, to drive them to a quiet training area with a stretch of reasonably straight road and very few hazards. During this drive, find out a little about the pupil and their reasons for learning to drive. You can ask if another pupil recommended you.

Ask whether the pupil has taken, or applied for, the Theory Test. While driving, you can explain some of the routines you are putting into practice.

Lesson content

Remember that this is not a test of your knowledge! Consider how much information the pupil is likely to absorb. Avoid overloading your explanations with irrelevancies. For example, at 9 am on a sunny morning, do you really need to include information about all the lights, gauges, dials and other equipment? You can confirm that this information will be covered in a future lesson when the need arises; for example, how to use the wipers, lights and other ancillary equipment.

Timing your explanation

The time you spend on each of the key points should depend on whether the pupil has any prior knowledge or understanding. Most people have been passengers and will probably know about seat belts; and a trained mechanic will probably be able to tell you a thing or two about how the clutch works and the relationship between power requirements and gears. Many new pupils will also have ridden a bicycle or motorbike. This means that they will have an understanding of the use of gears and some road sense. Remember to ask questions at intervals to confirm what the pupil may already know. Learning a script for the lesson is a total waste of time – you must adapt your instruction to take prior knowledge into consideration and in line with how your pupil responds.

Driver checks

Doors

If you have driven the pupil to the training area, explain the need for safety checks before opening any door, looking either for pedestrians on the pavement side or traffic in the road. It's sensible to wait by the driver's door while the pupil gets seated. You can then ensure it's closed properly. Using your own door, explain about the safety catch by opening it and demonstrating the light click when the door isn't closed properly. Do this by getting the pupil to check in the door mirror for body alignment. Get him or her to listen to the firmer sound when you close the door properly. Confirm the dangers of driving along with doors not properly closed. Also explain how to open the doors safely in windy conditions.

Handbrake and neutral

Explain how the extra weight of people getting into a car can affect it; and of the need to check the handbrake and neutral for security.

Seat adjustment

Explain how to adjust the seat and back rake to ensure that all the controls can be reached comfortably and controlled properly. The left knee should be slightly bent when the clutch is fully depressed, and there should be a slight bend at the elbows when the hands are placed on the steering wheel in the 'ten to two' or 'quarter to three' positions.

Remember that everyone is different. You have to be flexible with what you want your pupils to do. For example, for most people, keeping the left heel down on the floor when using the clutch will result in good control as well as taking the pressure off the calf muscle. However, if you have a very tall or short pupil this position may not be possible or comfortable.

If your car has steering height adjustment, explain how it works if appropriate.

Head restraints

Tell the pupil how to adjust the head restraints and explain their purpose: that is, to prevent neck and spinal injuries. You could demonstrate what happens to the body if the car has to be stopped suddenly.

Mirrors

Teach the pupil to adjust the interior and two door-mounted mirrors to give maximum vision to the rear and sides. Explain why they are made of different types of glass, confirming that all decisions must be made from the true image seen in the interior mirror. You could get the pupil to compare the size of objects in the three mirrors to confirm what you are saying.

Even with three mirrors, explain that there are still areas around the car that can hide things. These are known as 'blind areas'. You can confirm that they will be covered in more detail prior to moving off.

Seat belts

Explain how to put on and release the seat belt safely by keeping hold of the buckle. Watch for any twists across the lap or chest. Remember, your pupil will have been a passenger and will therefore have some experience in using these; do not be patronizing. It may be more appropriate to ask one or two relevant questions on *Highway Code* rules to confirm his or her knowledge about drivers' responsibilities. If this is lacking, then ask the pupil to study the relevant rules, as you will be asking more questions in the next lesson.

Switching on the engine

At this point you may wish to complete the 'cockpit drill' by getting the pupil to check the handbrake is on and neutral selected prior to switching on the engine. You may, however, prefer to leave this until later, when you have explained about the main controls.

The steering

Hand position

Explain how to position the hands between 'ten to two' and 'a quarter to three' and the importance of not holding the steering wheel too tightly. Describe how the hands will naturally follow the eyes, and emphasize the importance of looking well ahead up the road to help maintain a straight course. Emphasize the importance of maintaining full control by using the pull–push method described in *The Official DSA Guide to Driving: The essential skills,* and by trying to keep each hand on its own side of the wheel.

Indicators

Remember not to be patronizing – most people know something about cars. Ask the pupil to work out which stalk is the indicator, and also which way it's operated for signalling left and right. Relate this to the direction in which the wheel will be turned. You could ask, 'Which way will you turn the wheel for going to the right? So, which way do you think the indicator will need to go?'

Let the pupil practise a couple of times by keeping the hand on the wheel and extending the fingers to switch the indicators on and off for left and right.

Horn

Show the pupil where the horn is, confirming that it should not normally be used while stationary. Refer to the *Highway Code* and ask a couple of questions about when not to use it. Confirm that you will be asking more questions on the next lesson.

The need for explaining other ancillary controls will be dependent on the light and weather conditions. Remember not to overload the pupil with too much information not directly relevant to the lesson.

Handbrake

Explain how this operates on the rear wheels. Explain its purpose:

- It holds the car securely when stationary.
- It acts as a back-up system for securing the car.
- It allows the driver to hold the car on a slope when both feet are occupied with accelerator and clutch.

Give one or two examples of where to use it, such as pedestrian crossings and traffic lights, and when stationary for more than a few seconds. Let the pupil practise releasing and applying the handbrake. Before doing this, it's a good idea to tell the pupil where the footbrake is and ask him or her to apply it. This should help the pupil develop an understanding of the relationship between these two controls. (Explain that you will be giving more information about the footbrake later in the lesson.)

Gear lever

While stationary, give a simple explanation on gears and their use. Remember, a visual aid might help the pupil as well as serve as a memory jogger for you. Explain about the power and speed requirements – for example, first gear is normally used for moving off because it is the most powerful and has to get the weight of the car moving – and the spring-loaded mechanism on most new cars that allows the lever to come back to its natural position between third and fourth gear.

In order for the pupil to develop a feel for smooth and accurate gear selection, allow for plenty of practice. You might demonstrate with your right hand, showing how to 'cup' the lever in the direction it has to go. Explain the 'palming' method, relating the position of the first four forward gears to that of the road wheels on the car. (This may help those will less natural aptitude for driving.) Allow practice at changing up and down in sequence, and then show the pupil how to use the 'block-changing' method. Finally, ensure the pupil looks ahead through the windscreen while moving the gear lever.

Encourage the pupil to ask questions, so that anything that has not been understood can be repeated.

Accelerator, footbrake and clutch

Explaining that it's more important to be able to stop the car than to make it go faster, ask the pupil to position the right foot squarely over the brake pedal, with the heel acting as a pivot between it and the accelerator. Remember – be flexible. Although it's preferable to keep the heel on the floor, if it's not comfortable or possible (because of the pupil's height, for example) don't insist on it. Discomfort can be a distraction from the driving task.

Explain what each of these controls does in simple terms. The *accelerator* works like a tap; the more the pedal is pushed down, the more fuel will flow into the engine to make it go faster. Releasing the pressure will slow down the flow of fuel, therefore slowing the car. It should be used gently and progressively. The *brake* works on all four wheels to slow the car down and eventually to stop it. Initial pressure should be light, gradually becoming firmer and then eased just prior to stopping in order to bring the car to a smooth stop. The mirrors should be used prior to use; the initial pressure on the brake will activate the brake lights to warn following drivers.

Outline some of the terminology you will be using, for example:

- 'gas' relating to the accelerator;
- set the gas;
- cover the brake;
- more gas/less gas;
- brake gently/brake firmly.

How the clutch works

Keep your explanation simple – use an illustration if you think it will help. The main purpose of the clutch is to connect and disconnect the power from the engine to the road wheels so that gear changes can be made smoothly.

When you have explained about the main controls, encourage questions by asking if there is anything that has not been understood. Stationary practice will build confidence and also some vehicle sympathy.

Before turning on the engine, allow the pupil to cover and feel for the pedals without looking down. Explain how to use the ignition key and, to encourage good habits from the outset, remind the pupil to check the handbrake is on and the gear lever is in neutral before switching on. Allow some practice of:

- pivoting the right foot between the brake and gas pedals;
- setting the gas;
- checking the mirror before braking, explaining about the brake lights;
- listening and feeling for the range of the clutch.

On a normal driving lesson, you would go on to explain how to move off and stop. However, in the test situation, time is limited and you may not get this far. We are therefore covering the subject briefly. A full explanation is given in Preset Test 2.

Moving off and stopping

- Explain how to put the mirror–signal–manoeuvre (M–S–M) routine into practice for moving off and stopping.
- Confirm the need to make safety checks of the blind areas before moving. It's important at this stage to confirm what the driver is looking for.
- Ensure that your instructions for moving off are properly timed to ensure initial success.
- Give full talk-through for moving off, changing gear, steering and stopping, including the selection of safe places, referring the pupil to rules in the *Highway Code.*

Building up confidence

Try to ensure early success by giving your instructions in the correct sequence and properly timed. By doing this you can assure the pupil that driving is not as hard as he or she might previously have thought. These first attempts at moving and stopping the car will show the pupil what effect the main controls have on it. Plenty of practice at this, and in gear changing, will also help build that all-important self-confidence of the more anxious pupil, or help to satisfy the expectations of the more able.

Summary of the key points

- Entering and leaving the car safely (safety in opening and closing doors).
- Carrying out the driver checks (doors, handbrake, neutral, seat, head restraint, mirrors, seat belt and switching on engine).
- Assuming a correct seating position for reaching the foot controls and steering wheel.
- Use, adjustment and purpose of seat belts and head restraints.
- Checking the handbrake and neutral and starting the engine.
- Identifying the function of the main driving controls: steering/indicators/ handbrake/gear lever/accelerator/footbrake/clutch.
- Stationary practice with gears and foot controls to build up pupil confidence.
- Explaining the M–S–M routine and giving 'talk-through' instruction for moving off, changing gear, steering, and stopping in a safe position.

Moving off and stopping
Preset Test 02 – Phase 1

The main purposes of this lesson are for you to help the pupil to understand the principles behind the M–S–M routine, and develop basic car control skills in order to:

- move off safely and under control;
- stop smoothly and parallel with the kerb;
- understand why we need to stop in safe places.

Lesson structure

Following the initial introductions, you need to establish the base line for the lesson. Use Q&A to establish what was covered on the previous session. For example:

What did your last instructor teach you?

Did you move off and stop at all?

Was the M–S–M routine explained? Tell me what it means.

The point at which you start the lesson will depend on the answers given. With a real pupil you would normally drive to a reasonably quiet training area and use the time to establish any prior knowledge. However, because of the time constraints of the test, you may have to begin the lesson at the centre.

If the pupil has moved off before

If the pupil has moved off and stopped before, you will need to confirm what he or she understands and can do. To do this, ask a few questions such as:

Are you familiar with this type of car?

Can you reach all the controls comfortably?

Have you made all your driver checks?

What can you see in the mirrors?

What can you tell me about the blind areas?

Do you know what 'set the gas' and 'find the biting point' mean?

Have you moved off and stopped before?

Are you studying for the Theory Test?

Do you understand the M–S–M routine? Can you explain it to me?

You will need to reinforce what has already been learnt and then work on improving car control skills for moving off and stopping in different circumstances.

If the pupil has not yet moved a car

If the pupil has no previous experience, the objective will be, 'By the end of today's lesson, you should be able to move off and stop safely and under control.' You will need to:

- explain about the M–S–M routine;
- allow the pupil to practise using the foot controls and selecting gears as necessary while stationary;
- give a full talk-through of, and practice in:
  - moving off and stopping (level, uphill and downhill, if circumstances allow);
  - moving off, building up speed and changing gear;
  - driving along and checking the mirrors;
  - slowing down and changing down;
  - stopping smoothly in safe places;
- give feedback and encouragement.

Explanation of the M–S–M routine

Mirrors

Decisions should be taken on what is seen in the interior mirror. To confirm why this is so, ask the pupil to compare the images between the three mirrors. Confirm what blind areas are and the importance of checking there is no other road user in them prior to moving off.

Explain that M–S–M routine should be applied when any change in speed or direction is intended. That is, it is used for:

- signalling;
- moving off;
- changing direction (passing parked vehicles, overtaking, turning corners);
- slowing down and stopping.

Confirm that no decisions should be taken before assessing what effect any actions may have on other road users.

Signals

Explain the purpose and use of signals and relate this to the *Highway Code*. Discrimination should be introduced, even at this stage, in order to develop the pupil's 'look, assess and decide' processes. Before moving away you could ask, 'Is there anyone around who would benefit from a signal?'

M–S–M routine

Explain how and why this sequence should be followed for every change of speed or direction, including moving off, overtaking and stopping.

Precautions before moving off

Explain about the blind areas. If parked at the side of the road, pick out an object on the offside pavement that will be in the pupil's blind area. Ask if he or she can see it without turning round to check. Confirm what could happen if he or she moved off when a cyclist was emerging from a driveway into that blind area.

Another way of emphasizing the need to look round is to get the pupil to watch in the mirror for a vehicle approaching from behind. Then get him or her to follow it into the offside mirror and keep watching until it disappears into the blind area. It is important that the pupil develops an understanding of what might happen if blind areas are not checked.

Coordination of the controls

By giving full and properly timed 'talk-through' instruction you should be able to ensure that success is achieved first time. This will do wonders in building up the pupil's own confidence and his or her faith in you as a teacher. Remember that your learner may be feeling a little anxious during the first few attempts. Don't attempt too much too soon. Talk the pupil through moving off and stopping over quite short distances until you can see skill and confidence are improving. You can then lead gently into building up a little more speed and progressing through the gears.

Recognizing and avoiding problems

In the early stages, pupils will often do only what they are told to do – no more and no less. You must ensure that you tell them everything in the correct sequence to enable them to control the car smoothly and build up their confidence.

During initial practice at moving off, and so that problems can be avoided, you must ensure that you respond immediately should things start to go wrong. For example, if the pupil eases pressure from the accelerator, you could say, 'Keep the gas set.' If the clutch is allowed to come up too far, say, 'Clutch down a little.' Try to imagine how your pupil will feel if, when moving off for the first time, the engine stalls – hardly the best way to build up confidence!

Be ready to correct any steering errors. If the pupil is steering towards the kerb or out towards the centre of the road, ask where he or she is looking and explain how 'The hands follow the eyes. Look well ahead at where you want to go.'

Normal stop control

Before moving off, explain how the M–S–M routine will be applied when stopping. After moving off for the first time and driving for a short distance, prepare the pupil for stopping. To encourage early development of mirror use, ask if there is anyone behind. Give the instruction to apply the left signal if needed. Be ready to help with this if necessary.

Give full talk-through instruction to ensure a smooth and safe stop is attained. That is, say, 'Cover the brake and the clutch. Brake gently. Clutch down, brake gently to a stop.' Give the instruction, 'Keep both feet still. Put the handbrake on and the gear lever into neutral. Now, rest your feet.' This will ensure that the engine is kept running and will assist in building the pupil's confidence in his or her ability. (Sometimes a feeling of relief at stopping can cause pupils to release the foot controls before the car has been secured. The resultant stall can lead to a sense of inability and disappointment.)

Carry out the moving off and stopping exercise a couple of times, and if the pupil begins to respond favourably, encourage them to try the procedure without your assistance. You should, however, be ready to give more help if needed.

Normal stop position

Introduce the *Highway Code* rules relating to stopping. Ask the pupil for a couple of examples of where and why it would not be safe or legal to stop. For example:

Give me three examples of where you shouldn't stop or park your car.

Why should you not stop near a bend or the brow of a hill?

What problems could you cause if you stopped too near or opposite a bus stop?

Try to time your initial instructions to coincide with safe stopping places. If, however, the pupil stops somewhere unsafe or inconvenient, ask, 'Why do you think this is not a good place for stopping?'

Making progress by building up speed and using the gears

Practice should now be given at:

- moving off;
- building up speed;
- changing through the gears to make progress;
- stopping.

It is vital that your pupil's confidence is built up through the car's response. Remember to time your instructions so that it sounds and feels smooth. For example, after moving off and building up a little speed you will need to ensure the change to second gear is smooth. Your instructions should allow for the pupil being a little slow and the car losing some momentum. You can compensate for this by allowing a little more speed to be built up than is necessary, particularly if driving uphill; and preparing the pupil for the change by saying, 'Can you hear the engine getting louder? We're going to change to second gear.'

Next get the pupil to put his or her left hand on to the gear lever, palm towards you, before adding the instructions:

Off the gas and clutch down.

Gear lever straight back to second.

Ease up the clutch and back to the gas.

Hand back on the wheel, check the mirrors and gently accelerate.

Encourage the pupil to build up speed and progress through the gears following the above instructions, changing the wording to suit whichever gear is being selected. Encourage use of the mirror while driving along. This will help pupils develop the habit of regularly checking on the situation to the rear. This, in turn, should result in a more natural application of the M–S–M routine for dealing with hazards.

Teach the differences between moving off on the level, uphill and downhill. To develop vehicle sympathy explain about the effects of different gradients on the power requirements (uphill) or the use of the footbrake (downhill).

Summary of the key points

- Setting the base line for the lesson (the briefing): confirm what the pupil knows; explain the objectives of the lesson, that is, to further improve or to learn how to move off, change through the gears and stop the car, applying the M–S–M routine.
- Mirrors: explain the need to use them well before changing speed or direction, and stopping.
- M–S–M: explain the system of car control as defined in the *Highway Code, The Official Guide to Learning to Drive* and *The Official DSA Guide to Driving: The essential skills.*
- Precautions before moving off – confirming problems associated with blind areas.
- Coordination of the controls – explain and practise using the controls smoothly.
- Normal stop: explain and practise how to stop smoothly.
- Normal stop position: explain about the importance of selecting safe places for stopping.

The emergency stop and using the mirrors

Preset Test 05 – Phase 1

Teaching pupils about using the mirrors effectively should be part of an ongoing programme from their first driving lesson. You should also, during the early stages of learning, be introducing an element of hazard perception and anticipation by pointing out possible problems and explaining how to respond.

By definition, the word 'emergency' means 'a situation of a serious and often dangerous nature, developing suddenly and unexpectedly, and demanding immediate action'.

Emergencies cannot therefore be planned for, as you do not know when they will arise, so one could happen at any time during a pupil's career as a learner. You need to know that your pupil will be able to cope. Introducing this exercise during the early stages, as an extension of braking and stopping exercises, will help develop the pupil's control skills and confidence.

The main purposes of the lesson are to:

- confirm what the pupil knows about the adjustment and use of mirrors;
- improve the pupil's general driving skills and all-round awareness;
- teach the pupil how to stop promptly and under control;
- give basic advice on how to correct a skid.

Lesson structure

As there are two topics to be dealt with, this Phase 1 exercise can be split into two sections. The first covers how to adjust and use the mirrors. You can then check, during the drive to the training area, whether all the correct routines and procedures are understood and being put into practice. Give feedback confirming the importance of using the mirrors correctly and being aware of the all-round situation. The second phase involves explaining how to stop in an emergency and what to do in the case of a skid.

Introduce yourself in the usual manner and establish the base line for the lesson by confirming the pupil's previous knowledge. This means that you should:

- check that the pupil is in the correct seating position and has adjusted all the mirrors so that they can be checked without an exaggerated head movement;
- confirm the reason for checking blind areas and make sure that these checks are made properly;
- ask a few questions about when mirrors should be checked in relation to moving off/speeding up and slowing down/changing direction/passing parked cars/overtaking/M–S–M routine.

Fault analysis

During the drive to the training area, watch the pupil closely to ensure that regular checks are being made of the appropriate mirrors. Assess the pupil's understanding through their actions: that is, checking the mirrors regularly before moving off, changing speed or direction, signalling or stopping; and reacting properly to what is seen in the mirrors, putting into practice the M–S–M routine by:

- deciding whether or not a signal is required;
- deciding how actions may affect any following driver;
- delaying signals if necessary;
- signalling earlier and braking more gently if appropriate before turning and when stopping;
- keeping a safe distance from the vehicle ahead if someone is following too closely.

Avoiding conflict

No matter how good an instructor you may be, it is not possible to check every time a driver uses a mirror. In order to avoid arguments, if you are not quite sure whether a mirror check was carried out, simply ask, 'Did you check the mirrors before signalling?' Then follow this up with, 'Why is it important to check the mirrors before you do anything else?' The responses given will confirm whether or not the pupil understands the principles behind the M–S–M routine, and whether you will need to give more information when you reach the training area for carrying out the emergency stop.

You can now link the two subjects by confirming that:

- A good driver uses all of the mirrors regularly and is aware of the all-round traffic situation.
- Emergencies can arise at any time.
- If an emergency arises, there may be no time for another mirror check, but you should be aware of the situation behind.

How to avoid emergencies

Emphasis should be placed on the fact that good drivers plan well ahead, taking into consideration what is happening. They also anticipate what might happen where they can see a possible hazard developing, or where they cannot see at all. For example, no one can see around a bend, so how can a driver know what may be there? What you can't see, you don't know.

Quick reactions

In an emergency, the priority is to react promptly and stop the car quickly and safely. Referring to the stopping distances in the *Highway Code*, relate these to the road and weather conditions, and explain how these will dictate what is a safe amount of pressure to apply to the brakes. Explain that progressive, firm pressure is required as harsh braking may result in a skid and this will only create further risk. Allow the pupil to practise the pivot between the accelerator and footbrake.

Ask your pupil where the driver's hands should be when braking. Confirm that a firmer hold than usual is necessary since more than normal braking pressure is being applied. This should also help to keep the car travelling in a straight line. Remind the pupil that engine braking can help to slow down the car more quickly. Confirm what the clutch is used for when stopping the car, and ask the pupil whether it will be different in an emergency situation.

Stopping the car is a priority, not keeping the engine running. Reassure the pupil that stalling is not a serious error as long as the necessary precautions are taken before restarting the engine. Explain about securing the car after stopping and confirm that this is even more important in an emergency, as the all-round situation needs to be checked before moving off again. Also confirm that, because the car was stopped in an unusual (a driving) position, checks of blind areas all around the car sides will need to be made prior to moving off again.

Skidding

What is required here is to provide information on what can cause the most common types of skid, and to reassure the pupil of what to do if he or she brakes too harshly and the car skids. Ask the pupil about the causes of skidding, and confirm that these normally only occur when a driver is not responding properly to the road and weather conditions. Harsh braking can cause a skid, and the most common type is the rear-wheel skid.

Explain that if a skid occurs the driver needs to remove the cause, in this case by releasing the brake pedal, and apply and release the brakes until they take effect again. Explain that this is how an ABS system works and confirm whether or not your car has one. Then explain how to steer into the skid by straightening up the front of the car. Use a model car, or show an illustration to clarify what you mean by 'steering into the skid'.

Maintaining safety

Explain the signal you will be giving when you want the pupil to stop. Once on the move, sit still and try not to make any movements that may distract the pupil into stopping prematurely. Remember, as an ADI, you will be responsible for the safety of yourself, your passenger, your vehicle and other road users. Make sure that this exercise is carried out in complete safety. Ideally this should be:

- not too near to any parked vehicles;
- where there are no nearby pedestrians;
- clear of junctions.

Check properly to the rear, and only give your stopping signal when there is no one close behind. After stopping, make sure that the car is secured. Get your pupil to check on the position in the road, and ask what blind areas will need to be checked before moving away. Practise the exercise two or three times, giving any remedial advice in relation to the pupil's reactions and use of the controls.

Summary of the key points

- Establish what the pupil knows about mirror adjustment and use.
- Identify and analyse faults, giving remedial advice as necessary.
- Explain how to avoid emergencies by planning ahead.
- Describe how to react quickly and use the controls to stop promptly and under control.
- Explain about skids and how to correct them.
- Practise the emergency stop and give feedback and advice.

Approaching junctions to turn left and right

Preset Test 07 – Phase 1

Preset Test 03 – Phase 2

It's important to gradually build up pupils' skills and confidence by introducing topics in a logical manner. When a reasonable level of skill in moving off and stopping has been attained, introduce basic junction routines. Beginning with simple left turns, it's normal to teach pupils how to turn into a side road and continue to the next left turn, which might be another side road on the left, or involve emerging onto a main road. Practise until a sound routine is established, then transfer this knowledge into dealing with right turns, following a similar pattern and introducing the differing elements.

The objectives of the lesson are to:

- establish what the pupil already knows about the M–S–M routine and how this system is applied at junctions;
- teach the inexperienced how to deal safely with junctions;
- assess how the more experienced learner deals with junctions;
- identify and analyse faults;
- give remedial advice and create opportunities to practise the correct routines.

As a working ADI you will already know your pupil. However, unless the examiner says that previous lessons were with you, you will need to introduce yourself. Establish the base line for the lesson by asking a few questions and assessing what the pupil already knows and can do.

The main element of the lesson is the correct application of the M–S–M routine, breaking this down as follows:

- *Mirrors:*
    - checking early to see what is happening;
    - working out how any other road user may be affected by the manoeuvre;
    - deciding if and when to signal.
- *Signal:*
    - to warn or inform other road users at the correct time, and so as not to confuse.
- *Manoeuvre:*
    - *position:* early to confirm the signal; appropriately for the direction, the width of the road, any obstructions, vision;
    - *speed:* appropriate for vision, the required gear, obstructions, oncoming traffic, pedestrians;
    - *look:* all around prior to turning for obstructions, other road users, pedestrians.

Phase 1 – Dealing with a pupil who has very little or no experience

Where you set the base line will depend on whether the pupil has any previous knowledge or experience at dealing with turning left and right. Remember pupils *should be* studying for the Theory Test and therefore should be able to answer simple questions on the M–S–M routine. However, assume nothing! Their answers will give you feedback of their level of knowledge and understanding – or lack of it.

If the pupil has not yet dealt with any turns, you will need to give a more detailed explanation of the routines. Use a visual aid if you think it will help. Here are a few examples of questions that you can use, either during your explanation or during the practical part of the lesson:

What routine do you use when you are moving off and stopping?

Why is it important to check the mirror and what are you looking for?

When does the Highway Code tell you to use signals?

If a pedestrian is crossing the road you are turning into, who has priority?

Whose priority is it when you're turning right, yours or the oncoming driver's?

How will you be able to work out whether it's safe to turn right when there's an oncoming car?

Why would it be dangerous to cut the corner?

To begin with, you will need to give full talk-through instruction to confirm the correct routines, decreasing the level of help as the pupil's skill and understanding improves. However, be ready to give more help when necessary.

If the pupil has some previous experience

Following your Q&A session, if it is confirmed that the pupil has some previous experience, find out what is known about the routines and then get on the move so that you can make an assessment. You should soon be able to tell how much or how little help is needed, and adapt the level of your instruction to:

- give full talk-through instruction;
- help only when things are forgotten or routines carried out in incorrect sequences;
- assist when more difficult circumstances arise;
- intervene to ensure safety is maintained.

Encouraging hazard awareness

Whenever your car is moving, take advantage of every opportunity that can be used to develop hazard awareness. Do not restrict your teaching to the topic in hand, but be ready to deal with other problems as they arise. For example, if there are parked vehicles or obstructions, encourage the pupil to think about the possibility of oncoming traffic and give a full talk-through to maintain confidence and safety.

Phase 2 – Dealing with the more experienced pupil

Ask a few questions to confirm knowledge and understanding. Listen carefully – something may be quoted out of sequence or omitted altogether. Reaffirm any points you think are necessary, and get on the move so that you can make a practical assessment. If your pupil appears to be experiencing difficulty, or shows a lack of understanding, give as much help as is necessary until there is an improvement in his or her understanding and skills.

Not all errors committed will relate directly to the subject in hand. Any potentially serious problem must be dealt with. The degree of the error will dictate whether it can be dealt with on the move, or whether you will need to find somewhere safe to stop for a more detailed discussion.

Fault assessment

Whatever the standard of the pupil, *positive* correction is better than *negative* or *retrospective* correction. If you can see a problem developing ahead and the pupil isn't responding, it's sensible, in the first instance, to give some positive prompt to encourage some action. This is far safer, and more effective, than allowing a potentially dangerous situation to arise, particularly where other road users are involved.

During any drive you should assess whether your pupil is putting all of the established routines into practice. Identify and analyse any problems. Give advice on how to improve, and *give your reasons.*

Common faults

- A lack of understanding of the M–S–M routine.
- Not checking the mirrors effectively.
- Signalling at the same time as checking the mirror.
- Signalling too early or too late.
- Not positioning correctly according to the circumstances.
- Not using the brakes effectively to slow down in good time.
- Making unnecessary gear changes or changing down too early or late.
- Coasting around corners.
- Approaching too fast and swinging out on left turns.
- Lack of awareness of pedestrians and the need to give priority.
- Crossing approaching traffic.
- Not looking effectively into the new road.
- Cutting corners.

Summary of the key points

- Confirm the correct application of the M–S–M/position–speed–look (P–S–L) routine for turning left and right.
- Assess the pupil's ability and adapt the level of your instruction to suit.
- Identify, analyse and give remedial advice on weaknesses, and allow practice to improve.
- Give more help/tuition when required.

- Give feedback on where improvement has taken place and where more work is needed.

T-junctions – emerging
Preset Test 8 – Phase 1
Preset Test 4 – Phase 2

It is clear that you cannot keep turning into roads without eventually coming to the end of one. Most instructors therefore initially deal with 'emerging' in conjunction with turning into side roads. The main objectives are to:

- establish what the pupil already knows about the M–S–M routine and its application at T-junctions;
- teach inexperienced pupils how to approach and emerge safely;
- assess how the more experienced learner deals with T-junctions;
- identify and analyse faults;
- give remedial advice and create opportunities to practise the correct routines.

Introduce yourself and establish the base line for the lesson by finding out what the pupil already knows and understands about junctions. The main elements of the lesson are to:

- confirm the application of the M–S–M routine;
- explain about 'Give Way' and 'Stop' junctions;
- emphasize the importance of taking effective observations;
- encourage safe decisions to proceed or hold back according to sightlines;
- outline correct position according to circumstances:
    - turning left or right;
    - wide or narrow roads;
    - obstructions;
    - one-way streets;
    - pedestrian activity.

Phase 1 – Dealing with a pupil with very little or no experience

Set the base line for the lesson. Confirm previous experience by asking a few questions on the M–S–M routine and its application when turning left and right into side roads. Ask what the pupil knows about 'emerging' from junctions.

Although 'emerging' may be a new topic, the pupil should already have turned left and right into side roads. You now need to build on this knowledge and transfer it to the new circumstances. You should explain about:

- the different types of junction, 'Give Way' or 'Stop' – ask the pupil to describe the signs and markings and to tell you their different meanings;
- positioning on the approach, depending on:

- the direction to be taken;
- the width of the road;
- vision:
  - restricted sightlines in one or both directions;
  - good vision in one direction only;
  - good vision all around;
  - emerging safely without affecting others, including pedestrians.

Practice

You will need to give full talk-through instruction until the pupil's understanding and control skills begin to develop. Gradually reduce the amount of instruction as the pupil's skills develop. However, be ready to give more help when necessary, and to intervene to prevent a pupil from emerging unsafely.

Phase 2 – Dealing with the more experienced pupil

The more experienced pupil will have had plenty of practice at emerging but may have weaknesses. Try to establish what these are as quickly as you can so that you can create maximum time for practising the correct routines. If the weaknesses do not become obvious in your short Q&A discovery session, you will need to get on the move and watch carefully to see what problems develop. You must ensure that the correct routines and procedures are being put into practice.

Pay attention to the all-round traffic situation and assess how your pupil is responding to it. Do not allow a potentially unsafe situation to arise. For example, if you feel the pupil is about to emerge unsafely before being able to see properly in all directions, you should give some positive command, such as 'Wait!' Follow this up with 'Have you checked both ways?', 'How far can you see?' or 'What if something is approaching out of the blind area at 40 mph?'

It may be appropriate, when convenient, to pull in and give more information on sightlines and the importance of being able to see properly before emerging.

Fault assessment

As previously stated, positive correction is better than negative or retrospective correction. Preventing a potentially dangerous situation, such as emerging unsafely, should result in a greater degree of safety for everyone, and more positive learning and understanding taking place.

Common faults

- A lack of understanding of the M–S–M routine.
- Ineffective application of the M–S–M routine.
- A failure to identify or respond to the type of junction, 'Give Way' or 'Stop'.

- Not taking into consideration restrictions to sightlines.
- Not looking early enough at 'open' junctions.
- Stopping unnecessarily when safe to proceed.
- Not looking effectively in all directions.
- Not responding to pedestrians.
- Emerging unsafely.

Summary of the key points

- Establish prior knowledge and understanding of the M–S–M/P–S–L routines.
- Confirm the correct application of the routines.
- Ensure that the pupil has a good understanding of sightlines and vision.
- Identify and analyse faults.
- Give remedial advice with reasons.
- Create opportunities to practise the correct routines.
- Give feedback where improvement has been made.

The reverse and turn in the road manoeuvres

Preset Tests 3 and 4 – both Phase 1

Because of their similarity, and to avoid a great deal of repetition in this book, we are combining the explanation for these two manoeuvres. You will find detailed information on each exercise in the DSA publications, *The Official DSA Guide to Driving: The essential skills* and *The Official Guide to Learning to Drive*. Use the information in these books to build up your lesson plans.

The main purposes of the manoeuvre exercises are to:

- develop the pupil's car control skills;
- improve car control skills and confidence;
- develop an awareness of the importance of observations;
- teach the pupil how to respond to other road users.

Lesson structure

Introduce yourself and establish the base line by asking a few questions about what the pupil has learnt previously and understands about clutch control. All of the manoeuvre exercises are based on coordination between:

- clutch;
- accelerator;
- footbrake;
- steering;
- observations.

Safe and smooth control can be affected by something as basic as sitting too close or too far from the pedals. You should therefore confirm, at the beginning of the lesson, that the correct 'cockpit drill' is carried out and the controls can be reached comfortably.

Confirm prior understanding by asking how to control the car at low speed. For example:

How do you hold the car steady when moving off up a hill?

How do you creep slowly forwards to get a better view at junctions?

Which pedals would you use to control the car on a downhill slope?

Confirm that you will be assessing these control skills during the drive to the practice area. This may be some distance away, so giving an explanation of the exercise at this point will be of little use. The pupil will have other things to concentrate on and also may have forgotten all you said, resulting in you wasting valuable practice time having to repeat what you said before.

Use this opportunity to check on the pupil's application of the M–S–M routine and particularly watch out for any problems with car control skills. As you drive along, use simple questions for confirming understanding of any relevant points.

When you arrive at the training area, give positive feedback on progress, adding any necessary remedial advice where improvement is needed.

Lesson content

Put into practice the general teaching principle of 'explanation/demonstration/practice'. Confirm that it is a safe, legal and convenient place to carry out the exercise. Relate this to the rules in the *Highway Code* and ask a few questions, for example:

Are there any signs or road markings that would make the manoeuvre illegal?

Do you think we will be inconveniencing other road users?

Are there any parked vehicles or obstructions nearby that could affect us?

Transferring previously learnt skills

If the pupil has previous experience, ask for the procedures to be explained to you. Listen carefully, and add any information or clarification you feel is necessary. Allow the pupil to practise the exercise so that you can make your assessment. Be ready to give help if the pupil experiences difficulty.

Dealing with the subject for the first time

If the pupil has not carried out the manoeuvre previously, give some reassurance by confirming that it only involves coordinating all of the skills previously learnt:

that is, combining the use of the foot controls to keep the speed low, which in turn will give more time to work on the steering and make the observations.

Explanation

Use a visual aid if you think it will help the pupil understand the main principles. Your explanation should include:

- The importance of good all-round vision. For reversing to the left this will involve turning round in the seat, removing the seat belt where necessary.
- Confirming the position of reverse gear and letting the pupil practise selecting it while stationary.
- Describing each element of the exercise, including:
  - the control of speed with either the clutch and gas, or the footbrake if downhill;
  - steering;
  - observations: that is, where to look and how to respond;
  - checking into the new road for safety and convenience prior to the exercise.
- Confirm that control is of major importance and accuracy will come with practise.

Demonstration

Offer a demonstration if you think the pupil will benefit. Remember, however, you will have more time to do this on a real lesson than during the Part 3 test. You might consider combining a demonstration with your explanation. Do this by changing seats and talking yourself through the exercise. This could benefit you in two ways: the more anxious pupil will see the exercise is easier than it sounds, and it will take less time than giving the explanation and demonstration separately.

Practice

One of your main aims when teaching a new topic should be for the pupil to achieve a reasonable degree of success. To build up the pupil's confidence, therefore, you should ensure that your talk-through is effective and that you respond promptly if the pupil is having difficulty.

Try to imagine how your pupil might be feeling. All of the control skills learnt in previous situations now need to be combined; and the pupil has the extra task of checking around for other road users. Expect a little loss of memory, and give as much help as possible to encourage success and confidence. If after a couple of attempts you can see the pupil's skill developing, ease off on the level of instruction. Be ready, however, to give more help if necessary.

Making sure all-round safety is maintained

You are responsible for the safety of yourself, your pupil and other road users! Because at this stage pupils' observations are likely to be very superficial, you must remain fully aware of what is happening all around you, all of the time. If you see anyone approaching, draw the pupil's attention to their presence by telling them to pause, then ask: 'Have you seen that other car? Let's wait and let it pass.'

At this early stage, the pupil does not need the extra pressure of knowing he or she is holding someone up. As long as it is safe – and you have checked all around – avoid this pressure by encouraging the other driver to proceed. Confirm that other road users should be given priority. As their confidence increases you will be able to encourage your pupils to respond to others according to the circumstances – for example, if it's obvious that another driver is being considerate and has decided to wait. On these occasions, you must emphasize that observations should also be made in the other directions to check that it's safe before proceeding.

Giving feedback

Praise goes a long way in building confidence. Confirm where progress and improvement has taken place. Explain any weaknesses; confirm that more practice will be given. Encourage revision of the main points before the next lesson.

Summary of the key points

- Set the base line by confirming previous knowledge.
- Assess the pupil's control skills and general driving, giving remedial advice as necessary.
- Explain the manoeuvre, including observations and how to respond to others.
- Give full talk-through and decrease the help as skill improves.
- Ensure the pupil is given feedback of progress.

Meeting, crossing the path of, and overtaking other traffic. Allowing adequate clearance to other road users and anticipation

Preset Test 2 – Phase 2

Preset Test 8 – Phase 2

Preset Test 10 – Phase 1

If you are to develop safe attitudes in your pupils, anticipation is something that you should introduce during the early stages of learning. There are so many vehicles parked on our roads that it's almost impossible for a new driver not to encounter some of them. It is important, therefore, that you take advantage of situations that arise to teach your pupils how to:

- read the road ahead and to the sides;
- consider the all-round situation;
- think about priorities;
- anticipate what others might do;
- work out the safest way to respond.

The main objectives are to:

- establish how much experience the pupil has in dealing with other traffic;
- teach the partly trained driver about priorities when:
    - dealing with parked vehicles;
    - turning right;
    - dealing with pedestrians and cyclists;
- assess the trained pupil on all of the above aspects of driving;
- explain how to overtake safely;
- identify and analyse faults;
- give remedial advice and create opportunities to practise the correct routines.

As there are a number of different elements involved in the preset tests covering them, your examiner will identify those topics on which you must concentrate. Listen very carefully so that you can plan the lesson around the selected topics, and do not fall into the trap of trying to cover everything.

Introduce yourself and establish the base line for the lesson by finding out what the pupil already knows about the topics. Confirm the M–S–M routine for approaching all hazards, then focus on those subjects that need either teaching or reinforcing.

Meeting other traffic, allowing adequate clearances

The key elements are:

- *looking* and planning ahead for parked vehicles;
- *deciding* on priorities by acting on available information:
    - obstruction on the left side of the road;
    - obstruction on the right side of the road;
    - speed, position and size of oncoming traffic;
    - uphill or downhill situation;
- *applying* the M–S–M routine and waiting in the *hold back* position, to:
    - maintain a view of the road ahead;
    - be able to steer through in a straight line when safe;
- *allowing* clearances for parked vehicles relative to:
    - the volume of traffic;
    - pedestrian activity;
- adjusting the speed to suit the available space: the narrower the gap, the lower the speed to give more time to respond;
- clearances for cyclists.

Crossing other traffic

The key elements are:

- Priorities when turning right:
  - Speed and distance of oncoming traffic;
  - If there's time to walk across, there should be time to turn safely.
  - Is it safe to turn? What is happening in the new road?
  - Is there time to turn without cutting the corner?
- Selecting lanes in good time to avoid cutting across the path of others.

Overtaking

The key elements are:

Safe

Is there an adequate view of the road ahead? Consider vision:

- bends/brows of hills/dead ground;
- any junctions ahead.

Legal

Refer to the *Highway Code*:

- Are there any pedestrian crossings ahead?
- What road markings are there?
- Are there any signs that would make overtaking illegal or dangerous?
- What is the speed limit and will it have to be exceeded to complete the manoeuvre?

Necessary

- At what speed is the vehicle ahead travelling in relation to the speed limit?
- Will we be turning off soon?
- Do we need to get by to make progress?

Following at a safe distance

Explain that this is to give a better view of the road ahead.

Mirror–position–speed–look (MPSL), M–S–M

- Mirror.
- Position – to get a view to the nearside.
- Mirror – position to get a view of the road ahead.
- Speed – select a lower gear to give sustained power.
- Look – check all around again.

- Mirror – check to ensure that the manoeuvre will be safe.
- Signal to let other drivers know of the intended manoeuvre.
- Manoeuvre – quickly and efficiently.
- Mirrors – check before returning to the left without cutting in and accelerating away.

Anticipation

Teaching anticipation is an ongoing process that should start from day one of a pupil's driving career. The key elements are:

- looking for other vehicles whose drivers may:
  - emerge from junctions;
  - open doors or move off without warning;
  - take priority when they should be giving way.
- looking and planning ahead for any pedestrian activity:
  - expecting them to walk into the road;
  - at junctions between parked cars/behind buses/at crossings – in fact, anywhere.
- looking and planning ahead for cyclists, expecting them to:
  - ride into the road without warning;
  - change position or turn at junctions without signals;
  - cycle around obstructions without checking;
  - ride alongside near crossings, at junctions and in traffic lanes.

Dealing with pupils who have very little experience

Establish prior knowledge and driving experience. Using a visual aid if appropriate, explain how to approach and deal with the different types of hazard. If the pupil has very little experience of driving in busier areas, you must give sufficient talk-through to ensure both safety and confidence. Look and plan well ahead and describe what you can see happening, and encourage the pupil to respond early enough to avoid problems.

Even where the pupil has previously driven in busier areas, you must be ready to assist when necessary to avoid uncomfortable or unsafe situations developing. Remember – you are responsible for the safety of your pupil and all other road users around you! Identify any weaknesses in the pupil's general driving and explain how improvements can be made. Remember, when you suggest alternative action, you need to give a valid reason for it. Give encouragement where routines are carried out correctly and safely.

Dealing with more experienced pupils

At this stage, the pupil will be experienced at driving in traffic. You may only need to confirm prior knowledge by asking a few questions on how to approach and deal with the different types of hazard. If overtaking is to be covered, you will need to know whether or not the pupil is familiar with the difference from the normal M–S–M routine. You may need to give an explanation, and should an opportunity to overtake arise during the drive, talk the pupil through the procedure.

At this stage, you should be constantly monitoring the pupil's performance in relation to correct driving procedures and hazard recognition. Anything that deviates from the driving 'norm' needs to be addressed, either briefly if the error is minor, or by stopping somewhere safe if it is of a more serious nature.

Common faults

- Failing to anticipate hazards or potential risk situations.
- Taking priority when it should have been given.
- Not applying the M–S–M routine when approaching hazards.
- Shaving parked vehicles on the left.
- Shaving parked vehicles on the right on narrow roads.
- Moving out too far and meeting oncoming traffic dangerously.
- Not allowing for the actions of pedestrians, cyclists or other drivers.
- Turning right across the path of approaching traffic.
- Showing an unsafe attitude and general lack of consideration.

Summary of the key points

- Establish prior knowledge and experience.
- Give adequate information on any new subject, particularly when meeting other traffic/passing parked vehicles/driving in busy areas/overtaking.
- Ensure that all the correct routines are put into practice.
- Identify and analyse weaknesses.
- Give remedial advice and create opportunities to practise the correct routines.
- Give feedback where improvement has taken place and confirm where more practice is needed.

Crossroads and roundabouts

Preset Test 1 – Phase 2

Preset Test 9 – Phase 1

Having taught your pupils how to turn into and out of T-junctions, you will then need to transfer this knowledge and develop their skills at dealing with the differences that apply at crossroads. The main objectives are to:

- establish what the pupil knows about the M–S–M routine and the different types of junction;
- teach partly trained pupils how to adapt the procedures to deal safely with crossroads;

- assess how the trained pupil deals with crossroads;
- identify and analyse faults;
- give remedial advice and create opportunities to practise the correct routines.

Establish the base line for the lesson by finding out what the pupil already knows and understands about different types of junction. Confirm that the M–S–M routine also applies at crossroads, emphasizing that more observations are needed in all directions.

The main elements of the lesson are to explain or confirm:

- the application of the M–S–M routine at crossroads;
- priorities at junctions with different markings;
- the requirement for extra all-round observations, regardless of the direction being taken;
- positioning for turning right, offside and nearside;
- observations and priorities when turning right.

Dealing with the less experienced pupil

Confirm the pupil's knowledge of the M–S–M routine by asking a few questions on it. Check whether crossroads have been dealt with in previous lessons, and if so, what the pupil knows about them. If the pupil has no experience and there are quiet crossroads nearby, this will give you the opportunity of establishing the different aspects to be introduced without the hassle of too much traffic.

Use a visual aid if you think it will help to explain the need for the extra all-round observations at crossroads, no matter whose priority it may be. Explain how to respond to other road users and be willing to give way if unsure, particularly when turning right.

While allowing the pupil to drive and put into practice what is known about junctions, you should be ready to help with talk-through instruction at the crossroads. This applies particularly to the observations. Make sure that the correct routines are applied as opportunities arise when:

- driving through crossroads with the priority;
- approaching uncontrolled crossroads;
- emerging from 'Give Way' or 'Stop' lines;
- dealing with traffic lights.

Watch carefully to ensure that observations are being made in all directions at crossroads, no matter who has priority. Confirm that the pupil should be looking for anyone who may be emerging across his or her path.

If the local road layout dictates that you have to deal with traffic-light controlled or busier junctions, you may need to explain how to turn nearside and offside. Remember the level of ability of your pupil – you will probably have to give lots of help until confidence is built up.

Dealing with more experienced pupils

By this stage, the pupil should have experienced driving on most types of urban road. The procedures for dealing with crossroads should therefore merely need confirming with a few relevant questions. Listen carefully for any weaknesses in knowledge or understanding. Confirm what the main dangers are when turning right at crossroads, and what the pupil should be looking for.

Once on the move, you should assess how the pupil is responding in all situations. Look and plan well ahead. Should you feel that the pupil is not reacting early enough to any situation, try to instigate the correct action by prompting with a question or suggestion, particularly where lane changes are necessary. Be careful, however, not to over-instruct. Avoid giving definite instructions unless you can see a potentially serious situation developing.

Minor or one-off errors can usually be dealt with on the move, as long as this will not distract the pupil. However, if more serious faults occur it may be necessary to stop to discuss them.

Fault assessment and feedback

Whatever the level of the pupil, you must be constantly looking for:

- weaknesses in his or her knowledge;
- correct application of the rules;
- effective, all-round observations – including at traffic lights;
- response to the all-round traffic situation.

Let the pupil know when improvement has taken place and confirm where more work has to be done.

Common faults at crossroads

When driving along main roads:

- proceeding through without adjusting speed or checking the side roads;
- turning left and/or right without checking in all directions;
- turning left and/or right without applying the correct M–S–M routine;
- cutting corners.

Approaching 'Give Way' or 'Stop'-controlled crossroads:

- failure to apply the correct routine on the approach;
- lack of awareness of the type of junction being approached;
- lack of effective all-round observations before emerging;
- incorrect response to other road users;
- failing to stop at 'Stop' signs.

Traffic-light controlled junctions:

- lack of forward planning and anticipation;
- incorrect application of the M–S–M routine on the approach;
- incorrect positioning for:
  - the type of junction;
  - road markings;
  - presence of other drivers;
- proceeding before it's safe;
- crossing closely approaching traffic;
- failing to look in all directions before turning.

Roundabouts

Roundabouts are junctions designed to improve traffic flow. Although they are not dealt with as a separate entity in Part 3, you will find them in most urban areas, including the test routes! You will need to teach your pupils how to deal effectively with the different types of roundabout.

In order to avoid too much repetition here, refer to the section dealing with approaching junctions and, structuring the lesson as described to suit each individual pupil, ensure that you include information and practice on:

Forward planning and anticipation

- Reading signs and markings.

Application of the M–S–M routine

- Emphasizing the use of all mirrors on multi-lane roads.
- Lane selection and discipline.
- The 'give way' rule.
- Looking in all directions in order to anticipate gaps in the traffic and maintain road position.
- Making progress by taking opportunities to proceed.
- Mirrors and signal before leaving.
- Position in the new road.

Encourage your pupils to learn the relevant *Highway Code* rules and also the procedures described in *The Official DSA Guide to Driving: The essential skills* and *The Official Guide to Learning to Drive.*

Dealing with a pupil with no experience

Introduce this subject by including 'basic rule' roundabouts, progressing to more complex ones as skills increase. If possible, and of course depending on local geography, begin with left turns, progressing to following the road ahead, then introduce taking roads to the right.

In order to build up skills and confidence, as with any new subject, you will need to give full talk-through instruction until the pupil can cope. Give as much help as you can to assist with this building of confidence.

Try to imagine how a pupil feels when entering a large roundabout for the first time. It can be very confusing and all of the exits may look similar. You will need to clearly identify the exit road. For example, if you want your pupil to take the road to the right, which is the third exit, you can identify this by similar wording to this:

At the roundabout, I'd like you to take the road to the right, that's the third exit.

It's the one where (for example) there's a pelican crossing.

You can then give further assistance as you proceed through the roundabout by adding as you pass the first two exits:

This is the first exit.

This is the second.

We're taking the next exit so check your mirror and signal left for leaving.

Dealing with more experienced pupils

As with all of the foregoing subjects, you will need to find out what your pupil knows and what sort of roundabouts have been dealt with previously. You will then need to make an assessment of skills and continue the pupil's development.

During the later stages of training, you should try to create opportunities for practice on as many different types of roundabouts as your area will allow. If necessary, plan for longer lessons to drive to different areas for this purpose. If this isn't possible, then encourage pupils to sign up for further training under the Pass Plus scheme.

Common faults at roundabouts

- Lack of planning and anticipation.
- Failure to read signs and markings.
- Incorrect application of the M–S–M routine.
- Late mirror use resulting in unsafe lane changes.
- Failure to look in all directions resulting in:
  - missing gaps in the traffic;
  - an incorrect course being followed through the junction.
- Lack of anticipation of other vehicles taking an incorrect course.
- Driving in the blind areas of larger vehicles.
- Lack of mirror use before changing lanes, resulting in:
  - a lack of awareness of drivers to the rear and sides;
  - leaving in the wrong lane for the circumstances.

Summary of the key points of these topics

- Establish prior knowledge and understanding for dealing with crossroads and roundabouts.
- Confirm extra observations required.
- Ensure that all the correct routines are being put into practice.
- Identify, analyse and give remedial advice on any weaknesses.
- Give feedback where improvement has been made and where more practice is needed.

Pedestrian crossings and the use of signals

Preset Test 06 – Phase 1

Preset Test 07 – Phase 2

Preset Test 09 – Phase 2

The main objectives involved with teaching these subjects are:

- establishing what pupils know about the use of different methods of signalling;
- assessing whether they understand and can correctly apply the M–S–M routine;
- teaching them how to approach and deal safely with pedestrian crossings;
- identifying and analysing faults;
- giving remedial advice;
- creating opportunities to practise the correct routines.

Lesson structure

Establish the base line for the lesson by finding out what your pupil already knows. Bear in mind that, when you start to use busier areas, he or she should have a reasonable level of car control skills and an understanding of the basic driving routines. This should include knowledge of the M–S–M routine, and the use of signals. Also remember that, as pedestrians, your pupils should already know quite a bit about crossings and their use.

Using signals

Whether you're dealing with a partly trained or a more experienced pupil, he or she should have previously learnt how to:

- check the mirrors regularly;
- be aware of the all-round situation;
- decide whether or not a signal is required;
- use the signals:

- correctly;
- when necessary;
- at the appropriate time;
- respond safely to signals given by others.

Confirm the M–S–M routine by asking a few relevant questions. Also ask for examples of the different methods of signalling. These should include:

- using the brake lights;
- indicators;
- reversing lights;
- early road positioning;
- the appropriate use of arm signals.

Arm signals

Although seldom used, in the appropriate conditions arm signals can be helpful when approaching zebra crossings. Ask your pupil if he or she has ever been waiting at a crossing when a driver from one direction has stopped but the one approaching from the opposite way has not. An arm signal would have alerted that driver to the fact that the other was stopping.

Allow some stationary practice in the use of this signal; and advise study of the others contained in the *Highway Code*. Draw pupils' attention to the fact that, should the indicators fail on their car, they need to be able to let others know of their intentions.

Dealing with pedestrian crossings

Your pupils will all have used pedestrian crossings – do not be patronizing. Most of them will also be studying for the Theory Test. By asking a few relevant questions, you should be able to confirm whether or not they understand the basic rules relating to the different types of crossing. Ask how many types of crossing they can think of. The list should include:

- zebra;
- pelican;
- puffin;
- toucan;
- pegasus (equestrian);
- school crossings.

Sample questions include:

What sort of sign might you see on the approach to a pedestrian crossing?

What markings would you see on the road?

What do the zigzag lines mean?

How would a pedestrian claim priority at a zebra crossing?

What is the sequence of the lights at a pelican crossing?

What is the difference at a puffin crossing?

Who is a toucan crossing for?

How is the pegasus (equestrian) crossing different?

Because of the number of different types of crossing, and the limited time available, you will probably only be able to deal with the main types, zebra and pelican. However, if the lesson is taking place at the relevant time and there are children making their way to or from school, it may be appropriate to mention school crossings and the patrol staff. If you are asked questions relating to a specific crossing, or there are any other types peculiar to the local area (for example toucan, pelican, puffin or equestrian), then obviously you will need to include these.

The key elements to be emphasized are:

- looking ahead for signs and markings;
- anticipating and planning for pedestrian activity;
- the effective application of the M–S–M routine;
- approaching at the correct speed to allow a safe stop if necessary;
- planning for the lights to change at controlled crossings;
- using all signals safely and correctly.

Dealing with the less experienced driver

If the pupil has never dealt with crossings, you will need to give some talk-through instruction to encourage forward planning, the correct application of the M–S–M routine, and also to build up confidence. As skill improves, gradually reduce the level of tuition and transfer the responsibility by asking the pupil to tell you how far ahead they are looking and what they plan to do. Remember – always be ready to give further assistance if required, particularly if safety is at risk.

Dealing with the more experienced driver

Allow the pupil to drive for a few minutes so that you can make an assessment of their level of skill and understanding. If any problems arise, identify and analyse them. Whether you can do this on the move, or whether you will need to stop will depend on:

- the degree of the error;
- how much detail you need to go into;
- the situation you are in;
- whether there is anywhere convenient to stop.

Fault assessment

Where fault assessment is concerned, no matter what the standard of the pupil is, *positive* correction is better than *negative* or *retrospective* correction. If your pupil is not responding to a developing hazard, it is sensible to give a positive prompt to encourage some action to be taken. This is far safer and more effective than allowing a potentially dangerous situation to arise, particularly where pedestrians are involved.

For example, say you are approaching a pelican crossing and have noticed the 'Wait' sign lit up and pedestrians waiting to cross. Your pupil appears not to be anticipating any change in the situation. Which of the following options do you think will result in more positive learning taking place: trying to get the pupil to react by asking, 'What do you think is going to happen at that crossing?', or waiting to see if action is going to be taken and then, when nothing happens, using the dual controls to stop the car at the latest possible moment?

Practice

Plan the lesson to include as many crossings as possible. During the drive, assess whether the pupil is putting all the established routines into practice. Identify and analyse problems. Give advice on how to improve, and when you make a correction, remember to give a good reason for it. On the Part 3 test, of course, route planning is done for you by the examiner.

Common faults

- Lack of planning and anticipation.
- Incorrect application of the M–S–M routine.
- Signals:
  - given incorrectly;
  - unnecessarily;
  - badly timed.
- Not reinstating signals that have cancelled themselves.
- Not cancelling signals after use.
- Misuse of the horn and/or flashing headlights.
- Inviting pedestrians or other road users to move forward.
- Approaching crossings too fast.
- Failure to respond to traffic lights.
- Failure to stop when necessary.
- Blocking crossings in traffic queues.
- Not securing the car when necessary.
- Moving off from crossings prematurely.
- Not responding safely to others' signals.

Summary of the key points

- Establish what the pupil knows about the different methods of signalling.
- Confirm use of the M–S–M routine in all situations.
- Outline the rules relating to the different types of crossing.
- Emphasize the importance of approaching at the correct speed and stopping when necessary.
- Identify and analyse weaknesses.
- Give remedial advice with valid reasons.
- Create opportunities to practise the correct routines.
- Give feedback on where learning or improvement has taken place and link forward to the next lesson.

Reverse parking
Preset Test 6 – Phase 2

This exercise is important in further developing the pupil's control skills, and teaching the pupil to park in smaller spaces. By the time you introduce this manoeuvre, the pupil's control skills should be well developed. The skills learnt previously will be transferred into dealing with parking in more challenging conditions.

The main elements of the lesson are to:

- assess the pupil's general driving;
- confirm the site for parking: safe – legal – convenient;
- teach the manoeuvre if it has not been done before, with coordination of controls, accuracy and observations;
- reinforce each element of the exercise as above if it has been practised before;
- confirm how gradients and cambers will affect control;
- identify and analyse any problems.

Lesson content

Confirm what the pupil already knows about manoeuvring and the control skills involved. Confirming that you will be driving to a suitable site, ask the pupil to drive on, putting all previously learnt routines and procedures into practice.

During this drive make an assessment, identifying strengths and weaknesses. Analyse these and give remedial advice if necessary. You should be able to deal with most of the minor errors on the move, but if any serious ones occur, comment on them and, if necessary, deal with them in more detail when you stop.

Confirm that the site is safe, legal and convenient. Explain that the exercise sometimes has to be carried out where there are other road users and that traffic flow must be maintained. Consideration needs to be exercised if too much delay will be caused to others.

Pupils who have previous experience

If the pupil has practised the exercise before, ask a few questions on the different elements and then assess the level of knowledge, understanding and skill. Should problems arise, you must be ready to help in order to encourage improvement.

The pupil with no previous experience

Prior to starting the exercise, get the pupil to work out what effect any up- or downhill gradient may have on control of the car. Encourage an initial look around for pedestrians and other road users. A full talk-through for the first attempt should encourage success and build confidence. Depending on progress, you can then either give more help or encourage the pupil to try the exercise unaided.

The most common problems are caused by:

- the pupil not taking the gradient into consideration;
- the amount of movement of the wheel required for cars with and without power-assisted steering;
- lack of observations, or response to the presence of others.

With a pupil who has been driving regularly but who has never been taught this manoeuvre, try to build on what he or she already knows and can do. For example, the pupil will probably have a lot of experience in reversing generally and may have tried reverse parking on his or her own, but without much success. You can use your question and answer skills to determine where and how to start the lesson and should employ your coaching skills, rather than simply 'instructing', as the lesson progresses.

The manoeuvre

Confirm the application of the M–S–M routine to get into position alongside the other vehicle. The signal element will depend on the presence of other road users – indicator, confirming arm signal, brake lights and/or reversing lights. Assess the gradient and confirm how the speed will need to be controlled.

Building on the pupil's current knowledge of reversing round a corner to the left, confirm the point at which the wheel will need to be turned, and explain that it will need to be straightened earlier than when driving around a corner, and then turned to the right and straightened again. Explain that less effort is required if the car has power-assisted steering.

Emphasize the need for regular observations and of responding to other road users' actions. Ensure the pupil checks the front of the car is clearing the other vehicle. Confirm that, once the other car is cleared, looking through the rear window well down the road will give a better perspective for keeping the car straight. Complete the manoeuvre with the wheels straight.

Practising the reverse park

Plenty of practice may be required to ensure consistency. However, from the point of view of good public relations you should not reverse around the same vehicle more than twice. It will be of greater benefit to drive somewhere else so that the exercise can be carried out under different circumstances – for example, on a different gradient or a narrower road.

Use simple terms for reference. For example, a 90-degree angle would be used for reversing around a right-angled corner before straightening, while a 45-degree angle would be needed for reverse parking.

It can also be useful for you to work out reference points appropriate to your car for commencing the turning and straightening-up elements. This will enable you to get the pupil to respond to something he or she can actually see.

Common faults

- Not putting into practice the M–S–M routine prior to the exercise.
- Lack of consideration of the gradient or camber, resulting in incorrect use of the controls.
- Lack of coordination of the controls.
- Not looking in the direction of travel.
- Under- or over-steering.
- Not keeping a check on the all-round traffic situation.
- Not responding to other road users.
- Finishing in an unsafe position.

Summary of the key points

- Confirm the pupil's previous experience.
- Assess driving and give remedial advice where necessary.
- Confirm the elements involved – control/accuracy/observations and response.
- Practise the exercise and encourage confidence.
- Give feedback of improvement and confirm where more practice is needed.

Making progress; hesitancy and road positioning
Preset Test 05 – Phase 2
Preset Test 10 – Phase 2

To deal with today's congested conditions and complex road systems, drivers need to be skilful, confident and considerate. As an ADI, it will be your job to teach your pupils to become safe and effective, and to develop in them positive attitudes towards themselves, their vehicle and other road users. Therefore, even though they probably won't achieve the same standard, you should be teaching your pupils to drive to a similar style to the one you use in your own driving.

Your main objectives will be to teach new drivers to be aware of the need to make progress when it's safe, according to the type of road and the road, weather and traffic conditions; and to have the confidence to take all safe opportunities to proceed at junctions, and to drive positively on roads with higher speed limits.

Make sure they are aware of the need to:

- be travelling at a safe speed for the conditions;
- have the correct gear engaged for the speed and power and economy requirements;
- be in the correct position in relation to:
  - the type of road;
  - width of the road;
  - vision and safety margin;
  - other road users.

By the time your pupils are approaching test standard, their personal driving skills should be well developed. They should be applying all of the correct routines and procedures for driving in different road and traffic situations. Your main objectives are to confirm knowledge of:

- the speed limits for different types of road;
- braking, following and stopping distances and the 'two-second rule';
- the factors which should influence the speed – for example the type of road/surface/weather conditions/volume of traffic/pedestrian activity;
- the need to make progress when safe;
- what effect driving too slowly for the conditions may have on other drivers.

At junctions, ensure that your pupils look early for gaps in the traffic, and that they have the car ready for moving off efficiently. When they have moved into a gap, ensure they build up speed positively. Ensure that they position correctly for the type of road, direction to be taken, speed and position of other vehicles, and volume of pedestrian activity.

Lessons for the more advanced

Explain what the objectives are and establish the pupil's knowledge and understanding by asking a few questions. For example:

What's the speed limit in a built up area?

What's the speed limit on a two-way road with a national speed limit sign?

What's the stopping distance at 30 mph?

Explain the 'two-second' rule to me.

Would you drive at 30 mph past a school at 3.30 in the afternoon?

What happens to your stopping distance on wet roads?

Driving on dual carriageways

An important part of your job is to prepare your pupils for driving on all types of road. Dual carriageways are normally safer than single-carriageway roads, as the traffic on each carriageway is all travelling in the same direction. There are also fewer problems caused by traffic having to cross the path of other drivers. Teach your pupils to:

- look and plan well ahead for obstructions or junctions;
- use all of the mirrors even more frequently;
- maintain lane discipline;
- read the signs and markings;
- anticipate early changes in direction;
- apply the M–S–M routine in good time to allow for safe lane changes;
- keep up to date with traffic to the rear and sides;
- avoid driving in other drivers' blind areas for prolonged distances;
- drive positively to suit the conditions.

Fault assessment

You will need to assess how your pupils are driving in relation to the conditions. Remember to query anything that deviates from normal standards.

Failure to make progress

If pupils are missing too many gaps at junctions, you must encourage them to:

- start making their observations earlier;
- work out when their gap is going to arrive;
- have the car ready to move promptly into the space;
- build up the speed and change up through the gears efficiently.

When pupils drive too slowly for the conditions, or miss opportunities to proceed, you must encourage them to make progress by talking them through a few situations to demonstrate what you mean. This should not be classed as over-instruction because, after all, if they can't drive appropriately to suit the conditions, then you have to teach them how to do so.

Driving too fast for the conditions

When pupils drive too fast, without considering the possible dangers, you must be firm and get their speed under control. When this becomes necessary, you must give valid reasons. For example, if you are on a road where there's a lot of pedestrian activity, you will need to confirm what speed you would be driving at and explain what you would be looking for.

Positioning

Encourage correct positioning at all times. Ensure that your pupils:

- maintain the normal road position when driving along;
- position correctly at junctions, according to the type and width of the road;
- plan well ahead and select the correct lane in good time;
- maintain lane discipline.

Common faults

- Moving off slowly and not changing up through the gears efficiently.
- Driving too slowly on roads with higher speed limits.
- Breaking the speed limit.
- Driving too fast in unsafe conditions.
- Missing opportunities to proceed at junctions.
- Not looking in all directions at junctions.
- Looking only to the right at roundabouts and getting out of position.
- Not using the mirrors regularly.
- Being unaware of drivers to the rear and sides.
- Lack of planning on dual carriageways resulting in becoming 'boxed in'.
- Positioning incorrectly on narrow roads or one-way streets.
- Driving too close to the kerb, or too far out.
- Incorrect positioning on bends.
- Not maintaining lane discipline.

Summary of the key points

- Establish prior experience.
- Confirm the importance of planning ahead and making progress where safe.
- Ensure that safety margins are maintained according to the conditions.
- Confirm the importance of being in the correct place on the road at all times.
- Identify and analyse faults and give remedial advice with reasons.
- Give feedback on improvement and emphasize where more practice is needed.

The preset tests

To ensure that all candidates have a test of equal difficulty, and that there is a balance between the two phases, the exercises are arranged as 'preset tests' (PST). Some subjects – for example, pedestrian crossings and signals – are used more often than others. Where a test exercise involves several subjects, for example 'meet, cross and overtake other traffic', your examiner will give a clear indication of those subjects you are to include. Make sure that you listen carefully and structure your lesson accordingly.

Interpreting the marking sheet

The marking sheets for the PST are reproduced on pages 158 to 167.

Using the markings in columns A and B on the marking sheets, your overall performance on both phases is assessed. In particular, the examiner will make an assessment of your ability under the three main headings of core competencies, instructional techniques and instructor characteristics. The maximum grade attainable in each phase is 6. The minimum level for a pass is grade 4 in each phase. However, the examiner makes an overall assessment by taking into consideration the markings of both columns A and B.

For example, if a candidate fails to identify a serious error and does nothing to correct the problem, the examiner would mark the appropriate box in column A under 'not covered' or 'unsatisfactory'. This would then be transferred to column B under the heading 'identification of faults'.

Criteria for grading

6   Overall performance to a very high standard with no significant instructional weaknesses.
5   A good overall standard of instruction with some minor weakness in instructional technique.
4   A competent overall performance with some minor deficiencies in instructional technique.
3   An inadequate overall performance with some deficiencies in instructional techniques.
2   A poor overall performance with numerous deficiencies in instructional techniques.
1   Overall standard of instruction extremely poor or dangerous with incorrect or even dangerous instruction.

You must remember that because of this overall assessment of what actually happens on the day, no two tests can ever be the same. Even the manoeuvre exercises cannot be rehearsed, and you will need to be able to adapt to what is happening in different circumstances. This is all part of the test of your potential to become an effective teacher of driving.

WHEN YOU PASS

You will be given a letter confirming the result, and you may apply for entry on to the Register of Approved Driving Instructors (Car). Complete the application form on the reverse of the letter and send it with the current fee. This must be done within 12 months of the date you pass. Registration then becomes renewable every four years.

Registration declaration

When you apply for registration, you must sign a declaration to the effect that you will:

- notify the Registrar of any change of name, address or place of employment;
- notify the Registrar if convicted of any offence;
- return the certificate if your registration lapses or is revoked;
- agree to undergo, when requested by the Registrar, a Check Test conducted by DSA staff.

IF YOU FAIL

Using the application form on the reverse of the letter, you may apply for a further test if you are still within the two-year qualifying period, and the test was your first or second attempt. Otherwise, if you wish to continue, you will have to wait until the two-year period has elapsed before you can apply for Part 1 again. It is therefore sensible to be prepared to invest in sufficient training with an experienced tutor before taking your Part 3.

Whether you pass or fail, if you would like a more detailed explanation of your test result ring your SE on a Friday morning. The examiner will normally be happy to give further advice to help with your instructional techniques.

THE ADI CERTIFICATE

After passing the instructional test, you should receive your official green ADI Certificate of Registration within a week. This will incorporate your name, photograph, ADI number and the date of issue and expiry of the certificate, which will be four years from the date of its issue. As a qualified instructor, whenever you are giving tuition, you must display the official green certificate on the left-hand side of the car's windscreen, and produce your certificate if requested by a police officer or any person authorized by the Secretary of State. (Failure to do so constitutes an offence.) If you can satisfy the Registrar that your certificate has been lost, damaged or destroyed, a duplicate can be issued on payment of the current fee.

PUPILS' PASS RATES

Records will be kept of the test results of all the pupils you present for test, and a printout of these will be sent to you on a regular basis. Use this information to monitor your tuition. If you notice that pupils are failing for similar faults, it could be that your teaching methods need to be adjusted. If you wish to discuss any subjects relating to driving tuition, your SEADI will normally be happy to oblige.

Instructional Test - Part III

The Examiner has marked each aspect of your performance in columns A and B below. Please see overleaf for explanatory notes.

Candidate's Declaration

I certify that
- the vehicle I have provided for the test is properly insured under the Road Traffic Act 1988 and
- I do/do not have to wear seat belts under the Motor Vehicles (Wearing of Seat Belts) Regulations 1982

Signed

Date

Centre

Date

Make & model

Reg Mark

Dual Controls   Fitted   Not Fitted

Candidate's Name

Ref. No

Column A

PST No.1 Exercises 1B and 10T

Phase 1-1B Beginner-Controls

	Not Covered	Unsatisfactory	Satisfactory
Doors			
Seat/Head Restraint			
Seat Belt			
Mirrors			
Accelerator			
Footbrake			
Clutch			
Handbrake			
Gears			
Steering			
Indicators			
Starting			
Precautions before moving off			
Normal stop position			
Normal stop use of MSM			
Normal stop control			

Phase 2-10T Trained-Crossroads

Mirror-Signal-Manoeuvre			
Speed			
Gears			
Coasting			
Observation			
Emerging			
Position right			
Position left			
Pedestrians			
Cross approaching traffic			
Right corner cut			

The results of your test are:

Phase I Grade		Phase II Grade	

Supervising Examiner's name

Location   Section No.

S E Signature

Column B

In this column the top line of boxes to Phase I and the bottom line of boxes refer to Phase II

1/2/3 = Unsatisfactory   **4/5/6 = Satisfactory**

Core Competencies

	1 2 3	4 5 6
Identification of faults		
Fault analysis		
Remedial action		

Instructional Techniques

	1 2 3	4 5 6
Level of instruction		
Planning		
Control of lesson		
Communication		
Q/A Techniques		
Feedback/Encouragement		
Instructor use of controls		

Instructor Characteristics

	1 2 3	4 5 6
Attitude and Approach to Pupil		

ADI 26/PT/01 Rev 7/98

FORMS UK plc FCN17651400

Figure 5.1   Marking sheets for the ADI Preset Tests

 **DRIVING STANDARDS AGENCY**

Instructional Test - Part III

The Examiner has marked each aspect of your performance in columns A and B below. Please see overleaf for explanatory notes.

Candidate's Declaration

I certify that
- the vehicle I have provided for the test is properly insured under the Road Traffic Act 1988 and
- I do/do not have to wear seat belts under the Motor Vehicles (Wearing of Seat Belts) Regulations 1982.

Signed

Date

Centre	
Date	
Make & model	
Reg Mark	
Dual Controls	Fitted ☐ Not Fitted ☐
Candidate's Name	
Ref. No	

Column A

PST No.2 Exercises 2B and 11T

Phase 1-2B Beginner-Moving off / stopping

	Not Covered	Unsatisfactory	Satisfactory
Briefing on moving off/stopping	☐	☐	☐
Mirrors vision and use	☐	☐	☐
Mirrors, direction, overtaking and stopping	☐	☐	☐
Mirror signal manoeuvre	☐	☐	☐
Precautions before moving off	☐	☐	☐
Co-ordination of controls	☐	☐	☐
Normal stop position	☐	☐	☐
Normal stop control	☐	☐	☐

Phase 2-11T Trained-Meet, cross and overtake other traffic allowing adequate clearance for other road users and anticipation

Mirror-Signal-Manoeuvre	☐	☐	☐
Meet approaching traffic	☐	☐	☐
Cross approaching traffic	☐	☐	☐
Overtake other traffic	☐	☐	☐
Keep a safe distance	☐	☐	☐
Shaving other vehicles	☐	☐	☐
Anticipation of pedestrians	☐	☐	☐
Anticipation of cyclists	☐	☐	☐
Anticipation of drivers	☐	☐	☐

The results of your test are:

Phase I Grade		Phase II Grade	

Supervising Examiner's name

Location		Section No.	

S E Signature

Column B

In this column the top line of boxes to Phase I and the bottom line of boxes refer to Phase II

1/2/3 = Unsatisfactory   4/5/6 = Satisfactory

Core Competencies

	1	2	3	4	5	6
Identification of faults	☐	☐	☐	☐	☐	☐
Fault analysis	☐	☐	☐	☐	☐	☐
Remedial action	☐	☐	☐	☐	☐	☐

Instructional Techniques

	1	2	3	4	5	6
Level of instruction	☐	☐	☐	☐	☐	☐
Planning	☐	☐	☐	☐	☐	☐
Control of lesson	☐	☐	☐	☐	☐	☐
Communication	☐	☐	☐	☐	☐	☐
Q/A Techniques	☐	☐	☐	☐	☐	☐
Feedback/Encouragement	☐	☐	☐	☐	☐	☐
Instructor use of controls	☐	☐	☐	☐	☐	☐

Instructor Characteristics

	1	2	3	4	5	6
Attitude and Approach to Pupil	☐	☐	☐	☐	☐	☐

ADI 26/PT/02 Rev 7/98

FORMS UK plc FCN17651500

Instructional Test - Part III

The Examiner has marked each aspect of your performance in columns A and B below. Please see overleaf for explanatory notes.

Candidate's Declaration

I certify that
- the vehicle I have provided for the test is properly insured under the Road Traffic Act 1988 and
- I do/do not have to wear seat belts under the Motor Vehicles (Wearing of Seat Belts) Regulations 1982.

Signed

Date

Centre

Date

Make & model

Reg Mark

Dual Controls   Fitted   Not Fitted

Candidate's Name

Ref. No

Column A

PST No.3 Exercises 4P and 7T

Phase 1-4P Partly trained-Turn in the road

	Not Covered	Unsatisfactory	Satisfactory
Briefing on turn in the road			
Co-ordination of controls			
Observation			
Accuracy			

Phase 2-7T Trained-Approaching junctions to turn either right or left

	Not Covered	Unsatisfactory	Satisfactory
Mirrors			
Signal			
Brakes			
Gears			
Coasting			
Too fast on approach			
Too slow on approach			
Position			
Pedestrians			
Cross approaching traffic			
Right corner cut			

The results of your test are:

Phase I Grade

Phase II Grade

Supervising Examiner's name

Location

Section No.

S E Signature

Column B

In this column the top line of boxes to Phase I and the bottom line of boxes refer to Phase II

1/2/3 = Unsatisfactory   4/5/6 = Satisfactory

Core Competencies

	1	2	3	4	5	6
Identification of faults						
Fault analysis						
Remedial action						

Instructional Techniques

	1	2	3	4	5	6
Level of instruction						
Planning						
Control of lesson						
Communication						
Q/A Techniques						
Feedback/Encouragement						
Instructor use of controls						

Instructor Characteristics

	1	2	3	4	5	6
Attitude and Approach to Pupil						

ADI 26/PT/03 Rev 7/98

FORMS UK plc FCN17653300

Instructional Test - Part III

The Examiner has marked each aspect of your performance in columns A and B below. Please see overleaf for explanatory notes.

Candidate's Declaration

I certify that

- the vehicle I have provided for the test is properly insured under the Road Traffic Act 1988 and
- I do/do not have to wear seat belts under the Motor Vehicles (Wearing of Seat Belts) Regulations 1982.

Signed

Date

Centre	
Date	
Make & model	
Reg Mark	
Dual Controls	Fitted Not Fitted
Candidate's Name	
Ref. No	

Column A

PST No.4 Exercises 3P and 9T

Phase 1-3P Partly trained-Reversing

Left Reverse   Right Reverse

	Not Covered	Unsatisfactory	Satisfactory
Briefing on reversing			
Co-ordination of controls			
Observation			
Accuracy			

Phase 2-9T Trained-T Junctions-Emerging

	Not Covered	Unsatisfactory	Satisfactory
Mirror-Signal-Manoeuvre			
Speed			
Gears			
Coasting			
Observation			
Emerging			
Position right			
Position left			
Pedestrians			

Column B

In this column the top line of boxes to Phase I and the bottom line of boxes refer to Phase II

1/2/3 = Unsatisfactory   4/5/6 = Satisfactory

Core Competencies

	1	2	3	4	5	6
Identification of faults						
Fault analysis						
Remedial action						

Instructional Techniques

	1	2	3	4	5	6
Level of instruction						
Planning						
Control of lesson						
Communication						
Q/A Techniques						
Feedback/Encouragement						
Instructor use of controls						

Instructor Characteristics

	1	2	3	4	5	6
Attitude and Approach to Pupil						

The results of your test are:

Phase I Grade   Phase II Grade

Supervising Examiner's name

Location   Section No.

S E Signature

ADI 26/PT/04 Rev 7/98

FORMS UK plc FCN17651700

Instructional Test - Part III

The Examiner has marked each aspect of your performance in columns A and B below. Please see overleaf for explanatory notes.

Candidate's Declaration

I certify that
- the vehicle I have provided for the test is properly insured under the Road Traffic Act 1988 and
- I do/do not have to wear seat belts under the Motor Vehicles (Wearing of Seat Belts) Regulations 1982.

Signed

Date

Centre	
Date	
Make & model	
Reg Mark	
Dual Controls	Fitted / Not Fitted
Candidate's Name	
Ref. No.	

Column A

PST No.5 Exercises 6P and 8T
Phase 1-6P Partly trained-Emergency stop/Mirrors

	Not Covered	Unsatisfactory	Satisfactory
Briefing on emergency stop/mirrors			
Quick reaction			
Use of footbrake/clutch			
Skidding			
Mirrors vision and use			
Mirrors, direction, overtaking and stopping			
Mirror-signal-manoeuvre			

Phase 2-8T Trained-Progress / Hesitancy – Normal position

	Not Covered	Unsatisfactory	Satisfactory
Progress to fast			
Progress too slow			
Hesitancy			
Normal position too wide from the left			
Normal position too close to the left			

The results of your test are:

Phase I Grade ___   Phase II Grade ___

Supervising Examiner's name

Location ___   Section No. ___

S E Signature

Column B

In this column the top line of boxes to Phase I and the bottom line of boxes refer to Phase II

1/2/3 = Unsatisfactory   4/5/6 = Satisfactory

Core Competencies

	1 2 3	4 5 6
Identification of faults		
Fault analysis		
Remedial action		

Instructional Techniques

	1 2 3	4 5 6
Level of instruction		
Planning		
Control of lesson		
Communication		
Q/A Techniques		
Feedback/Encouragement		
Instructor use of controls		

Instructor Characteristics

	1 2 3	4 5 6
Attitude and Approach to Pupil		

ADI 26/PT/05 Rev 7/98

FORMS UK plc FCN17651800

Instructional Test - Part III

The Examiner has marked each aspect of your performance in columns A and B below. Please see overleaf for explanatory notes.

Candidate's Declaration

I certify that
- the vehicle I have provided for the test is properly insured under the Road Traffic Act 1988 and
- I do/do not have to wear seat belts under the Motor Vehicles (Wearing of Seat Belts) Regulations 1982.

Signed

Date

Centre

Date

Make & model

Reg Mark

Dual Controls   Fitted   Not Fitted

Candidate's Name

Ref. No

Column A

PST No.6 Exercises 12P and 5T

Phase 1-12P Partly trained-Pedestrian crossings and the use of signals

	Not Covered	Unsatisfactory	Satisfactory
Briefing on pedestrian crossings/signals			
Mirror-signal-manoeuvre			
Speed on approach			
Stop when necessary			
Overtaking on approach			
Inviting pedestrians to cross			
Signals by indicator			
Signals by arm			
Signals - timing			
Unnecessary signals			

Phase 2-5T Trained-Reverse parking

	Not Covered	Unsatisfactory	Satisfactory
Briefing on reverse parking			
Co-ordination of controls			
Observation			
Accuracy			

The results of your test are:

Phase I Grade   Phase II Grade

Supervising Examiner's name

Location   Section No:

S E Signature

Column B

In this column the top line of boxes to Phase I and the bottom line of boxes refer to Phase II

1/2/3 = Unsatisfactory   4/5/6 = Satisfactory

Core Competencies

	1	2	3	4	5	6
Identification of faults						
Fault analysis						
Remedial action						

Instructional Techniques

	1	2	3	4	5	6
Level of instruction						
Planning						
Control of lesson						
Communication						
Q/A Techniques						
Feedback/Encouragement						
Instructor use of controls						

Instructor Characteristics

	1	2	3	4	5	6
Attitude and Approach to Pupil						

ADI 26/PT/06 Rev 7/98

FORMS UK plc FCN17651900

Instructional Test - Part III

The Examiner has marked each aspect of your performance in columns A and B below. Please see overleaf for explanatory notes.

Candidate's Declaration

I certify that
- the vehicle I have provided for the test is properly insured under the Road Traffic Act 1988 and
- I do/do not have to wear seat belts under the Motor Vehicles (Wearing of Seat Belts) Regulations 1982.

Signed

Date

Centre

Date

Make & model

Reg Mark

Dual Controls   Fitted   Not Fitted

Candidate's Name

Ref. No

Column A

PST No.7 Exercises 7P and 12T

Phase 1-7P Partly trained-Approaching junctions to turn either right or left

	Not Covered	Inadequately Covered	Adequately Covered
Briefing on approaching junctions	☐	☐	☐
Mirrors	☐	☐	☐
Signal	☐	☐	☐
Brakes	☐	☐	☐
Gears	☐	☐	☐
Coasting	☐	☐	☐
Too fast on approach	☐	☐	☐
Too slow on approach	☐	☐	☐
Position	☐	☐	☐
Pedestrians	☐	☐	☐
Cross approaching traffic	☐	☐	☐
Right corner cut	☐	☐	☐

Phase 2-12T Trained-Pedestrians crossings and the use of signals

	Not Covered	Inadequately Covered	Adequately Covered
Mirror-Signal-Manoeuvre	☐	☐	☐
Speed on approach	☐	☐	☐
Stop when necessary	☐	☐	☐
Overtaking on approach	☐	☐	☐
Inviting pedestrians to cross	☐	☐	☐
Signals by indicator	☐	☐	☐
Signals by arm	☐	☐	☐
Signals timing	☐	☐	☐
Unnecessary signals	☐	☐	☐

The results of your test are:

Phase I Grade   Phase II Grade

Supervising Examiner's name

Location   Section No.

S E Signature

Column B

In this column the top line of boxes to Phase I and the bottom line of boxes refer to Phase II

1/2/3 = Unsatisfactory   4/5/6 = Satisfactory

Core Competencies

	1 2 3	4 5 6
Identification of faults	☐☐☐	☐☐☐
Fault analysis	☐☐☐	☐☐☐
Remedial action	☐☐☐	☐☐☐

Instructional Techniques

	1 2 3	4 5 6
Level of instruction	☐☐☐	☐☐☐
Planning	☐☐☐	☐☐☐
Control of lesson	☐☐☐	☐☐☐
Communication	☐☐☐	☐☐☐
Q/A Techniques	☐☐☐	☐☐☐
Feedback/Encouragement	☐☐☐	☐☐☐
Instructor use of controls	☐☐☐	☐☐☐

Instructor Characteristics

	1 2 3	4 5 6
Attitude and Approach to Pupil	☐☐☐	☐☐☐

ADI 26/PT/07 Rev 7/98

FORMS UK plc FCN17652000

Instructional Test - Part III

The Examiner has marked each aspect of your performance in
columns A and B below. Please see overleaf for explanatory notes.

DRIVING STANDARDS AGENCY

Candidate's Declaration

I certify that
- the vehicle I have provided for the test is properly insured under the Road Traffic Act 1988 and
- I do/do not have to wear seat belts under the Motor Vehicles (Wearing of Seat Belts) Regulations 1982.

Signed

Date

Centre

Date

Make & model

Reg Mark

Dual Controls   Fitted [ ]   Not Fitted [ ]

Candidate's Name

Ref. No

Column A
PST No.8 Exercises 9P and 11T

Phase 1-9P Partly trained-T Junctions-Emerging

	Not Covered	Unsatisfactory	Satisfactory
Briefing on T junctions	[ ]	[ ]	[ ]
Mirror-signal-manoeuvre	[ ]	[ ]	[ ]
Speed	[ ]	[ ]	[ ]
Gears	[ ]	[ ]	[ ]
Coasting	[ ]	[ ]	[ ]
Observation	[ ]	[ ]	[ ]
Emerging	[ ]	[ ]	[ ]
Position right	[ ]	[ ]	[ ]
Position left	[ ]	[ ]	[ ]
Pedestrians	[ ]	[ ]	[ ]

Phase 2-11T Trained-Meet, cross and overtake other traffic allowing adequate clearance for other road users and anticipation

	Not Covered	Unsatisfactory	Satisfactory
Mirror-Signal-Manoeuvre	[ ]	[ ]	[ ]
Meet approaching traffic	[ ]	[ ]	[ ]
Cross approaching traffic	[ ]	[ ]	[ ]
Overtake other traffic	[ ]	[ ]	[ ]
Keep a safe distance	[ ]	[ ]	[ ]
Shaving other vehicles	[ ]	[ ]	[ ]
Anticipation of pedestrians	[ ]	[ ]	[ ]
Anticipation of cyclists	[ ]	[ ]	[ ]
Anticipation of drivers	[ ]	[ ]	[ ]

The results of your test are:

Phase I Grade [ ]   **Phase II Grade** [ ]

Supervising Examiner's name

Location   Section No.

S E Signature

Column B

In this column the top line of boxes to Phase I and the bottom line of boxes refer to Phase II

1/2/3 = Unsatisfactory   4/5/6 = Satisfactory

Core Competencies

	1	2	3	4	5	6
Identification of faults						
Fault analysis						
Remedial action						

Instructional Techniques

	1	2	3	4	5	6
Level of instruction						
Planning						
Control of lesson						
Communication						
Q/A Techniques						
Feedback/Encouragement						
Instructor use of controls						

Instructor Characteristics

	1	2	3	4	5	6
Attitude and Approach to Pupil						

ADI 26/PT/08 Rev 7/98

FORMS UK plc FCN17652800

Instructional Test - Part III

The Examiner has marked each aspect of your performance in columns A and B below. Please see overleaf for explanatory notes.

Candidate's Declaration

I certify that
- the vehicle I have provided for the test is properly insured under the Road Traffic Act 1988 and
- I do/do not have to wear seat belts under the Motor Vehicles (Wearing of Seat Belts) Regulations 1982.

Signed

Date

Centre

Date

Make & model

Reg Mark

Dual Controls Fitted ☐ Not Fitted ☐

Candidate's Name

Ref. No

Column A

PST No.9 Exercises 10P and 12T

Phase 1-10P Partly trained-Crossroads

	Not Covered	Unsatisfactory	Satisfactory
Briefing on crossroads	☐	☐	☐
Mirror-signal-manoeuvre	☐	☐	☐
Speed	☐	☐	☐
Gears	☐	☐	☐
Coasting	☐	☐	☐
Observation	☐	☐	☐
Emerging	☐	☐	☐
Position right	☐	☐	☐
Position left	☐	☐	☐
Pedestrians	☐	☐	☐
Cross approaching traffic	☐	☐	☐
Right corner cut	☐	☐	☐

Phase 2-12T Trained-Pedestrian crossings and signals

	Not Covered	Unsatisfactory	Satisfactory
Mirror-Signal-Manoeuvre	☐	☐	☐
Speed on approach	☐	☐	☐
Stop when necessary	☐	☐	☐
Overtaking on approach	☐	☐	☐
Inviting pedestrians to cross	☐	☐	☐
Signals by indicator	☐	☐	☐
Signals by arm	☐	☐	☐
Signals timing	☐	☐	☐
Unnecessary signals	☐	☐	☐

The results of your test are:

Phase I Grade [   ]   Phase II Grade [   ]

Supervising Examiner's name

Location   Section No.

S E Signature

Column B

In this column the top line of boxes refer to Phase I and the bottom line of boxes refer to Phase II

1/2/3 = Unsatisfactory   **4/5/6 = Satisfactory**

Core Competencies

	1 2 3	4 5 6
Identification of faults	☐☐☐	☐☐☐
Fault analysis	☐☐☐	☐☐☐
Remedial action	☐☐☐	☐☐☐

Instructional Techniques

	1 2 3	4 5 6
Level of instruction	☐☐☐	☐☐☐
Planning	☐☐☐	☐☐☐
Control of lesson	☐☐☐	☐☐☐
Communication	☐☐☐	☐☐☐
Q/A Techniques	☐☐☐	☐☐☐
Feedback/Encouragement	☐☐☐	☐☐☐
Instructor use of controls	☐☐☐	☐☐☐

Instructor Characteristics

	1 2 3	4 5 6
Attitude and Approach to Pupil	☐☐☐	☐☐☐

ADI 26/PT/09 Rev 7/98

FORMS UK plc FCN17652200

DRIVING STANDARDS AGENCY

Instructional Test - Part III

The Examiner has marked each aspect of your performance in columns A and B below. Please see overleaf for explanatory notes.

Register of Approved Driving Instructors (Car)

Candidate's Declaration

I certify that
- the vehicle I have provided for the test is properly insured under the Road Traffic Act 1988 and
- I do/do not have to wear seat belts under the Motor Vehicles (Wearing of Seat Belts) Regulations 1982.

Signed

Date

Centre

Date

Make & model

Reg Mark

Dual Controls   Fitted   Not Fitted

Candidate's Name

Ref. No

Column A

PST No.10 Exercises 11P and 8T

Phase 1-11P Partly trained-Meet, cross and overtake other traffic allowing adequate clearance for other road users and anticipation

	Not Covered/ Incorrect	Unsatisfactory	Satisfactory
Briefing			
Mirror-signal-manoeuvre			
Meet approaching traffic			
Cross other traffic			
Overtaking other traffic			
Keep a safe distance			
Shaving other vehicles			
Anticipation of pedestrians			
Anticipation of cyclists			
Anticipation of drivers			

Phase 2-8T Trained-Progress / hesitancy - normal position

Progress too fast			
Progress too slow			
Hesitancy			
Normal position too wide from the left			
Normal position too close to the left			

The results of your test are:

Phase I Grade

Phase II Grade

Supervising Examiner's name

Location

Section No.

S E Signature

Column B

In this column the top line of boxes to Phase I and the bottom line of boxes refer to Phase II

1/2/3 = Unsatisfactory   4/5/6 = Satisfactory

Core Competencies

	1	2	3	4	5	6
Identification of faults						
Fault analysis						
Remedial action						

Instructional Techniques

	1	2	3	4	5	6
Level of instruction						
Planning						
Control of lesson						
Communication						
Q/A Techniques						
Feedback/Encouragement						
Instructor use of controls						

Instructor Characteristics

	1	2	3	4	5	6
Attitude and Approach to Pupil						

ADI 26/PT/10 Rev 7/98

FORMS UK plc FCN17652/00

GENERAL INSURANCE – A BEGINNERS GUIDE

C.A.R. Insurance Centre has been supplying cover for Driving Instructors for over 10 years and are recognised as one of the largest providers in the U.K.

With this experience our specialist team are dedicated to ensuring that our customers, old and new, are fully covered for every eventuality.

Shopping for insurance can be confusing and when trying to run a business the last thing you want to do is spend time shopping around. At C.A.R. we have recognised what is most important in a policy for you, some of which are listed below

- *Our policies offer a replacement car after an accident whether your fault or not*
- *Our policies will provide cover for any driver over the age of 25 for Social, Domestic & Pleasure use*
- *We can provide Breakdown cover which includes home start and European cover*

All of our policies are underwritten by Allianz Cornhill and will provide legal cover as standard. We can also offer various payment facilities.

C.A.R. is very proud to offer other classes of insurance as well such as motor, travel, vans and all types of commercial risks. Not only that but as a policyholder with Allianz Cornhill, you would be entitled to a further 20% off your household policy as well!

Our team are here to answer all your questions. You can call us on **0845 600 1300** or visit us on **www.car-insurance.com**

Our service standards are excellent and we aim to provide our clients peace of mind so that they can carry on their business confident that they are fully covered. Just ask one of our many clients, Mr Toye:

'What I look for in my insurance is the peace of mind that if anything goes wrong, and at times it does being a driving instructor, that I have instant access to a professional team. To a growing business like mine, I can say C.A.R. Insurance provides this in every way.'

Motor Insurance for Driving Instructors

 Legal Cover and Dual Controlled Car
(Following an accident/claim)
  (i) Non-Fault Claims
  (ii) Fault Claims - Maximum period 14 days

 £100 standard excess for all pupils

 Any driver over 25 can use your vehicle for
social, domestic and pleasure
(Driver under 25 for S,D&P must be notified & approved)

 Any qualified Instructor over 25
can instruct in your vehicle

 Public liability as an Instructor whilst
instructing

Automatic cover for teaching previously
banned/convicted drivers & pass plus

C.A.R. INSURANCE CENTRE

0845 600 1300
(Local call rate)

6

The Driver

As a professional driving instructor you need to have a thorough working knowledge of the regulations and procedures relating to driving licences. Just as importantly, you need to know where to obtain up-to-date, detailed official information about the law and current procedures. Your pupils will frequently need your advice and assistance with their licence applications and with the various licence entitlements.

This chapter deals mainly with a summary of the legal responsibilities of the driver and instructor in relation to:

- driving licence regulations;
- licence categories and minimum driving ages;
- health and eyesight requirements;
- vocational driving licences;
- photo card licences;
- driving on a foreign licence.

Also included are a summary of road traffic law; driver improvement and driver rectification schemes; the 'New Driver' Act, and advanced driving tests.

To make sure that you are completely up to date with your information you should regularly check some of the following useful points of contact:

- The Driving Standards Agency (DSA) publication *Despatch*. This magazine is issued at regular intervals to all instructors and various organizations;
- The DSA and Driver and Vehicle Licensing Agency (DVLA) websites at www.dsa.gov.uk and www.dvla.gov.uk;
- The trade magazines that are published by the main ADI organizations such as the Motor Schools Association of Great Britain (MSA) and Driving Instructors Association (DIA).

DRIVER LICENSING

The DVLA at Swansea issues licences for all categories. The licence shows details of all categories for which the driver has entitlement, including lorries and buses. Any provisional entitlement is shown, together with any relevant restrictions such as maximum trailer weight or 'not for hire or reward'. Driving without the appropriate driving licence entitlement usually invalidates the insurance cover.

Only photo card licences are now issued by DVLA, with the old-style paper licences being phased out. To apply for a photo licence you need to send off the form D750 as well as the licence application form D1, together with your original licence and an identifying document (your passport or birth certificate). To voluntarily exchange an old-style 'paper' licence for a photo licence the fee is £19. Details of other licence fees are shown on page 175.

Whereas a paper licence normally has an extended expiry date (usually to age 70), the photo licence has to be renewed after 10 years to keep the photographic likeness up to date. To avoid the necessity of sending off an important document such as your passport or birth certificate, an additional service is available at most main post offices whereby your details and documents can be checked and verified at the time. For this service there is an additional fee as well as the cost of the licence. To take advantage of this service you need to attend in person at a participating post office. Some form of personal identity such as a current UK passport must support your application.

A fact sheet on photo licences (INF61) is available from DVLA by telephoning the automated fact sheet service on 01 792 792 792 or by visiting the DVLA website at www.dvla.gov.uk. Fact sheets are also available from DVLA Customer Services for:

Driving a Minibus	INF28
Minimum Test Vehicles	INF29
Towing Trailers	INF30
Motorcycles	INF31
Driving in GB as a Visitor or a New Resident	INF38
Renewing Your Car Driving Licence	INF40
Drivers of Large Vehicles	INF52

Provisional driving licences

In order to learn to drive and to take the official driving test, a provisional driving licence must be obtained before a vehicle can be taken out on the public roads. The holder of a provisional licence may drive a vehicle only when accompanied by, and under the supervision of, a driver who holds a full licence for that type of vehicle. The supervising driver must be over 21 years of age and have held a full driving licence for the type of vehicle being driven for at least three years. This rule, however, does not apply under certain circumstances and when driving certain vehicles, for example when taking a driving test or when riding a motorcycle. More information on the supervision of learner drivers is provided on page 194.

To validate a provisional motorcycle licence the rider must also hold a valid certificate of basic training (CBT). Note that a provisional motorcycle licence holder must not carry any pillion passenger, even if that passenger is a qualified rider or driver.

In Northern Ireland, a vehicle displaying the prescribed 'L' or 'R' plates is restricted to a maximum speed of 45 mph.

Licence categories

The whole subject of driving licence entitlement is now extremely complex. There are so many variables, including different types of vehicle; when the original licence was first issued; and the age of the driver. The DVLA has a 16-page document on the subject, *What You Need to Know about Driving Licences* (D100). As the title suggests, this publication includes full details of licence entitlements for cars, motorcycles, lorries and buses, as well as the different eyesight and medical requirements for each type of licence.

The main categories of licence and the minimum driving ages are shown in Table 6.1, but for full details you need to refer to the D100, or visit the DVLA website at www.dvla.gov.uk.

Your entitlement to drive a particular type of vehicle (or vehicle/trailer combination) depends on several factors including your age, the date your first full licence was issued and the weight of the vehicle. The minimum age for certain types of vehicle is sometimes governed by other factors, particularly in relation to larger and specialized vehicles. The normal minimum age for driving is varied in the case of:

- drivers who receive Disability Living Allowance;
- members of the armed forces;
- trainees in the Young Driver scheme;
- drivers of minibuses and PCVs in limited circumstances.

Passing a driving test for a particular category may entitle you to drive vehicles of some other categories, and may also entitle you to use the licence as a provisional licence for other vehicles. There are also certain restrictions. For example:

- If you pass the test in a car with automatic transmission you are not entitled to drive a car with manual gears.
- Passing the test on a moped does not give you motorcycle entitlement.
- When you pass a test on a category C (rigid) vehicle, this automatically gives to you a provisional licence category CE (articulated or drawbar).

Driving licence application

You may apply for a full licence if you have:

- passed the driving test and you exchange the pass certificate for a full licence within two years of the date of the test;

Table 6.1 Driving licence categories for tests passed on or after 1 January 1997

Category	Type of vehicle	Min. age
A	Motorcycle	17
A1	Light motorcycle	17
B1	3 or 4 wheel light vehicle	17
B	Motor car	17
B+E	Car with trailer	17
C1	Medium goods vehicle	18
C1+E	Medium goods vehicle with trailer	18/21
C	Large goods vehicle (LGV)	21
C+E	LGV with trailer	21
D1	Minibus	21
D1+E	Minibus with trailer	21
D	Bus or coach	21
D+E	Bus or coach with trailer	21
f	Agricultural tractor	17
g	Road roller	21
h	Tracked vehicle	21
k	Mowing machine/pedestrian controlled vehicle	16
l	Electric vehicle	17
p	Moped	16

- held a full licence issued in the Channel Islands or the Isle of Man, valid within the last 10 years; or
- held a full British licence or a full licence issued in Northern Ireland granted on or after 1 January 1976.

You may also apply for a full licence if you have been resident in Great Britain for less than one year and you surrender a valid full licence issued in the EC or some other countries (see page 179). Application may be made at any time up to two months prior to the date from which the licence is required, and should be made at least three weeks before the date of commencement of the licence. The appropriate forms are normally available from post offices and local vehicle licensing offices. The completed form should be sent to the Driver and Vehicle Licensing Authority, Swansea SA99 1AB. If you need to make an enquiry about your licence, you are advised to contact the Driver Enquiry Unit, DVLA, Swansea SA6 7JL (tel: 0870 240 0009) quoting your driver number. It is worth making a note of this number in case your licence is mislaid.

If you are disqualified from driving, you will normally have to pay £50 for a new licence (or £75 for some drink/drive offences). Licences are normally valid until the applicant's 70th birthday, at which time a new licence may be issued for one, two or three years at a time, depending on health and other factors. Renewal in these circumstances is free of charge.

A duplicate or exchange licence is valid for the period of the original licence. A replacement licence that is issued after a period of disqualification is charged at the same rate as a duplicate licence. A driver who is adding an extra category to an existing licence may require an exchange licence, which is also issued where motorcycle entitlement is required, or when a licence contains out-of-date endorsements. A Northern Ireland full licence may be exchanged for a GB licence for the appropriate fee.

A duplicate licence is needed to replace a licence which has been lost, mislaid or defaced. Replacement of a licence following a change of address is made free of charge.

Driving licence information codes

When checking a pupil's licence details you will often find certain information codes adjacent to the entitlement section. These codes specify any particular restrictions that might apply to the individual driver for a variety of reasons (see Table 6.3).

Table 6.2   Driving licence fees (March 2006)

Licence type	Fee
First provisional licence	
– car, motorcycle, moped	£38
– bus or lorry	Free
Changing provisional for first full	
– first provisional issued before 1/3/2004	£9
– first provisional issued after 1/3/2004	Free
Duplicate licence	
– licence lost, stolen, destroyed or defaced	£19
Replacement	
– change of name and/or address	Free
Exchange	
– removing expired endorsements or exchanging an old-style licence for new-style photo licence	£19
Adding a test pass to a full licence	Free
New licence after revocation under the New Drivers Act	£38
Renewing a licence	
– car licence at age 70 or over	Free
– full licence for medium/large goods vehicles, minibus/bus	Free
– provisional for medium/large vehicles, minibus/bus	Free
– for medical reasons	Free
Exchanging a licence from other countries:	
– full Northern Ireland licences	Free
– full EC/EEA or other foreign licence (including Channel Islands and Isle of Man)	£38
New licence after disqualification	
– car, motorcycle, medium/large vehicle, minibus/bus	£50
– if disqualified for some drink/drive offences	£75

Note: All vocational licences for buses and lorries are now free of charge.

Health and eyesight

When applying for a licence the driver has to make various declarations regarding health and eyesight. You must declare, for example, any disability and any illness that might affect your driving. The law also requires the driver to notify the licensing authority if there is likely to be any worsening of any condition, and if there has been a change in any disability since the issue of the licence. Examples of the kind of health conditions in question are listed in the leaflet D100, but if there is any doubt about whether or not the condition should be reported, drivers are advised to consult their doctor. It is not necessary to report any medical conditions that are not likely to last more than three months.

Table 6.3 Driving licence information codes

Code	Description
01	eyesight correction
02	hearing or communication aid
10	modified transmission
15	modified clutch
20	modified braking systems
25	modified accelerator systems
30	combined braking and accelerator systems
35	modified controls layouts
40	modified steering
42	modified rear view mirror(s)
43	modified driving seat
44	modifications to motorcycle
45	motorcycle only with sidecar
70	exchange of licence
71	duplicate of licence
78	restricted to vehicles with automatic transmission
79	restricted vehicles (details in brackets)
101	not for hire or reward
102	drawbar trailers only
103	subject to certificate of competence
105	not more than 5.5 metres long
106	restricted to vehicles with automatic transmission
107	not more than 8250 kg
108	subject to minimum age limit
110	limited to invalid carriages
111	limited to 16 passenger seats
113	limited to 16 passenger seats except for automatics
114	with special controls required for safe driving
115	organ donor
118	start date is for earliest entitlement
119	weight limit does not apply
120	complies with health standards for category D1

Epilepsy: under certain circumstances a licence may be issued to someone who has been free of attacks for one year.

Pacemakers: people who are subject to sudden fainting or giddiness have, in the past, not been issued with a licence. The law, however, has been changed, and a licence may now be granted if this disability is corrected by the fitting of a cardiac pacemaker and if other medical conditions are satisfied.

Disabilities: drivers who are physically and mentally capable of driving but are otherwise disabled may be issued with a licence which restricts them to driving a vehicle of special design or construction. This type of licence does not entitle the driver to use it as a provisional licence for other groups of vehicles. If the driver then wishes to learn to drive a vehicle of a different type, he or she must first apply for the appropriate provisional entitlement to be added to the original licence.

Eyesight: in order to conform to the law there is a minimum standard of eyesight which must be reached (with glasses or contact lenses if necessary). The requirement is to read a motor vehicle number plate in good daylight at a distance of 20 metres (65 ft) or 20.5 metres for the old-style plates with seven digits. In the case of the driver of a mowing machine or pedestrian-controlled vehicle the relevant distances are 45 feet and 40 feet.

If you need glasses or contact lenses in order to attain these standards, you must wear them every time you drive. It is an offence to drive if your eyesight does not meet the required standard.

An applicant who declares a disability to the DVLA may be asked for permission to obtain a report from the applicant's doctor. A licence may be issued for a limited period so that the condition can be reviewed or the licence may be restricted to certain types of vehicles.

Procedure for medical assessment

When information about a disability is received, the applicant may be required to authorize his or her doctor to give information about the disability to the Medical Adviser at the DVLA. If the applicant or licence holder fails to do so, or if the information available from the doctor is not conclusive in relation to fitness to drive, the applicant may be required to have a medical examination by a nominated doctor.

Motorcycle licences

A full car licence usually acts as a provisional licence for motorcycles and as a full licence for mopeds. A new provisional motorcycle licence is issued for a maximum of two years. If a full licence is not obtained in this time it is not possible to renew the licence for a period of one year. The provisional licence entitles the rider to use a solo motorcycle with an engine capacity of up to 125 cc. Pillion passengers are not allowed to accompany a learner rider, even if the passenger has a full licence for that type of machine.

CBT is required for all riders of mopeds and motorcycles. The learner has to undergo a short course of off- and on-road training before riding unaccompanied on public roads. On successful completion of the course, the learner is issued with a certificate that validates the provisional licence. This applies to anyone riding a motorcycle or moped on 'L' plates, irrespective of when their licence was issued, and includes full Category B (car licence) holders who have not passed the motorcycle test.

After taking CBT the learner may ride on the road, but is limited to machines of up to 125 cc with a maximum power output of 11 kw. 'L' plates must be displayed and pillion passengers are not allowed on a solo motorbike. CBT certificates are valid for two years. To obtain a full licence, both the Theory and Practical Tests have to be passed within a two-year period.

Motorcycle licence categories

Category A1: light motorcycle – not exceeding 125 cc and a maximum power output of 11 kw. This type of licence can be obtained by taking the practical test on a bike between 75 and 120 cc.

Category A: standard motorcycle – any motorcycle. The test must be taken on a bike of more than 120 cc that is capable of at least 100 kph. For the first two years the rider is restricted to a bike of 25 kw unless he or she takes the Direct Access route to obtaining the licence.

Direct Access

Direct Access is a means of achieving an unrestricted licence without waiting for two years. It is available only to those over the age of 21, and must be taken on a motorbike that exceeds 35 kw. Training and practice can only be undertaken under the direct supervision of a specially qualified instructor, with radio communication between instructor and pupil.

Licence application

Provisional licence entitlement for motorcycles is normally granted for a maximum of two years. Learners are not permitted to ride on the roads until they have successfully completed CBT. The only exception to this is when they are under the supervision of an authorized instructor during the training.

Mopeds may be ridden at 16 years, subject to the CBT requirements.

A full car licence normally includes provisional entitlement for motorcycles but a CBT certificate is needed to validate the licence. A full car licence issued before 1 February 2001 includes full entitlement for mopeds, and CBT is not needed in those circumstances. Anyone passing their car test on or after 1 February 2001 will need to take CBT before riding a moped.

Vocational licences

The DVLA issues all licences, including those for large goods vehicles (LGVs) and passenger carrying vehicles (PCVs). The entitlement is shown on the photo card licence, with provisional entitlements indicated on the paper counterpart.

A driver who passes the 'L' test is now issued with a licence for driving vehicles up to 3,500 kg or a maximum of eight passenger seats. For driving anything over these limits, a separate test is needed for each type of vehicle. For example, you need to hold a full licence for cars before obtaining a provisional licence for medium-sized goods vehicles, and a full rigid vehicle licence is required before you can drive an articulated vehicle or draw-bar combinations. There are also restrictions on the type of trailer that can be towed. For example a separate test and licence entitlement would be needed to tow a large trailer behind a heavy motor car if the combined weight was more than 4,250 kg or if the gross weight of the trailer was more than the unladen weight of the towing vehicle.

The rules relating to vocational licences, medicals and test procedures are dealt with in more detail in Chapter 12, which also deals with training and qualifications for vocational licences.

DRIVING ABROAD

Visiting another country

To drive in any country belonging to the European Community or the European Economic Area (EC/EEA) you are allowed to use your GB licence. If you want to drive in a non-EC/EEA country you should check with one of the motoring organizations whether you need an International Driving Permit (IDP). IDPs are issued by the AA, the RAC, RSAC and Green Flag. To qualify for an IDP you must be resident in Great Britain, have passed a driving test and be over 18 years of age.

Moving to another country

If you move abroad you should check with the licensing authority of that country for information about the exchange of licences. If you return to Great Britain from a non-EC/EEA country you may drive for up to 12 months on your foreign licence.

VISITORS AND NEW RESIDENTS

You normally have to be resident in this country to qualify for a full driving licence. There are, however, special rules for the exchange of foreign licences and for driving in this country as a visitor or new resident. These rules vary, depending on the country that issued the licence. There are also some variations for vocational licences – for example for lorries and buses.

European Community and European Economic Area countries

A visitor to Great Britain from these countries can drive using his or her Community licence for as long as the licence remains valid. The licence will show the various types of vehicle that can be driven.

A new resident in Great Britain can exchange his or her Community licence for a GB one at any time. Alternatively, he or she may drive on their foreign licence up to the age of 70 or for three years, whichever is the longer. Vocational licence holders who do not exchange their licence for a GB one may drive:

- until age 45 or for five years after becoming resident, whichever is the longer;
- if aged over 45 (but under 65), until reaching 66 or for five years, whichever is the longer;
- if aged 65 or over, for 12 months.

Northern Ireland

A licence from Northern Ireland can be used until it runs out. Alternatively, it can be exchanged for a full car, motorcycle or moped licence if the original licence has been valid since 1 January 1976. A lorry or bus licence can be exchanged if it was issued on or after 1 April 1986. A driving test pass certificate is acceptable for exchange.

Gibraltar and designated countries

The 'designated countries', other than Gibraltar, are Australia, Barbados, British Virgin Islands, Canada, Falkland Islands, Hong Kong, Japan, Malta, Monaco, New Zealand, Republic of Cyprus, Republic of Korea, Singapore, South Africa, Switzerland and Zimbabwe. Anyone visiting Great Britain and holding a licence from one of these countries is allowed to drive vehicles up to 7.5 tonnes and with up to 16 passenger seats for up to 12 months, whether or not the vehicle was brought into the country with them. Holders of licences for larger vehicles may only drive vehicles that have been brought into Great Britain from the designated country.

For new residents the rules are slightly different. Small vehicles may be driven for up to 12 months, during which time the foreign licence must be exchanged for a GB one. New residents must not drive medium or large goods vehicles or PCVs until they have passed the relevant GB test.

Vocational licence holders from Gibraltar may drive for 12 months and can exchange the licence within five years of residency.

Jersey, Guernsey and the Isle of Man

Visitors from these islands with ordinary licences can drive any category of vehicle shown on the licence for up to 12 months. Vocational licence holders from Jersey or the Isle of Man can drive large vehicles for up to 12 months. If the vocational licence was issued in Guernsey, only vehicles that have been imported temporarily can be driven.

New residents from Jersey, Guernsey or the Isle of Man may drive for up to 12 months, but should exchange their licence during that period.

All other countries

Visitors from other countries are allowed to drive vehicles up to 7.5 tonnes and with up to 16 passenger seats, provided that the original licence is still valid. With large vehicles, only those that have been registered outside Great Britain and that have been driven into the country may be used.

For new residents, provided that the full licence remains valid, any small vehicle shown on the licence may be driven for up to 12 months. During that time a GB licence must be obtained.

New residents with vocational licences may not drive larger vehicles without passing the GB driving test for that type of vehicle.

Licences from these countries are not exchangeable.

Please note that these are guidelines only. For precise details, go to the DVLA website at www.dvla.gov.uk, or contact DVLA Customer Services on 0870 240 0009.

ROAD TRAFFIC LAW

Most people are unsure about the law for motorists, although at any time when driving or using a car, they may find themselves faced with some aspect of it. The purpose of this section is to enable you to find out how the law affects you and your pupils.

The motorist is affected by civil as well as criminal law, and an offence in a criminal court may well be followed by another case in a civil court. For example, someone who injures a pedestrian and is found guilty of dangerous driving might later find him or herself being sued for damages in a civil court.

Most of the relevant criminal law is found in the Road Traffic Act (RTA) 1991. Apart from criminal law, the RTA 1991 gives the Secretary of State for Transport the power to make other regulations regarding various motoring matters. The most important of these are the Motor Vehicles (Construction and Use) Regulations.

Much of the civil law that affects motorists is not contained in special rules relating to the roads. It is a part of the general law of the land. For example, the law of negligence applies to anyone, whether driving or not. Motorists are most likely to encounter the civil law after they have been involved in a road accident in which there has been injury to a person or damage to property. In these cases, the law allows the person injured to claim against the other driver, or the insurance company.

However, a motorist may be guilty of an offence under criminal law even if no accident has taken place. An offence may have been committed even if it was not intended; for example, driving without lights at night is an offence even though the driver checked the operation of the lights before starting his or her journey. There is also a certain amount of confusion regarding the *Highway Code*. Although the *Code* is based on the specific rules of the RTA, a breach of it is not necessarily a punishable offence. However, the *Highway Code* can be used as a reference in a court when assessing the actions of a driver. A breach of a particular part of the *Highway Code* may in some cases amount to a breach of a specific part of the RTA. Nevertheless, the offence will be found to be against a section of the RTA.

Questions of liability may arise when drivers are using vehicles to carry out their normal work or when a vehicle is being used for driving instruction. These questions of liability often arise under the Construction and Use Regulations when the driver, supervising driver and the employer may all be equally guilty of an offence.

Driving offences

Offences that are covered by the 1991 RTA include:

- causing death by dangerous driving;
- dangerous driving;
- causing death by careless driving when under the influence of drink or drugs;
- causing danger to other road users.

These offences are based more firmly than previously on the actual standard of driving. 'Dangerous driving' has to have two main features: the standard of driving falls far below that expected of a competent and careful driver, and the driving must involve actual or potential danger of physical injury or serious damage to property.

The standard of driving is judged in absolute terms and takes no account of factors such as inexperience, age or disability of the driver. It is not intended that the driver who merely makes a careless mistake, of a kind that any driver might make from time to time, should be regarded as falling far below the standard expected of a competent and careful driver.

The danger must be one that a competent and careful driver would have appreciated or observed. It means any danger of injury (however minor) to a person or of serious damage to property.

Careless and inconsiderate driving is defined in relation to 'a person driving a mechanically propelled vehicle on a road or other public place'. This means that non-motorized vehicles and offences on private property to which the public have access may be included. The main constituents in this offence are referred to in terms of 'driving without due care and attention, or without reasonable consideration for other road users'.

Offences of driving without a licence, without 'L' plates, without supervision, or under the age when a licence can be obtained, are now dealt with under the offence of 'driving otherwise than in accordance with a licence'. Penalty points for this offence vary from three to six depending on the circumstances and seriousness of the offence.

Offences incurring disqualification

The following offences carry automatic disqualification:

- manslaughter caused by the driver of a motor vehicle;
- causing death by dangerous driving;
- causing death by careless driving when unfit through drink;
- dangerous driving;
- motor racing on the highway;
- driving, or attempting to drive, when under the influence of drink or drugs, or with more than the permitted blood alcohol level;
- failure to provide a blood or urine sample.

Drink/drive offences

The legal alcohol limits are:

- 35 microgrammes of alcohol per 100 millilitres of breath;
- 80 milligrammes of alcohol per 100 millilitres of blood;
- 107 milligrammes of alcohol per 100 millilitres of urine.

The minimum period of disqualification is 12 months, with a minimum of three years for a second offence within 10 years.

Driver rehabilitation scheme

Drivers who are convicted of a drink/drive offence are normally offered the opportunity to take a voluntary 'driver rehabilitation course'. This enables them to have a reduction of up to one quarter off the period of disqualification. Courses are usually organized at weekends and during the evening, with a total of about 20 hours' instruction. The cost of the course (typically about £135) has to be paid by the offender.

The Extended Driving Test

Courts have the power, for some of the more serious offences, to order disqualification until an 'appropriate' driving test is passed. These offences include motor manslaughter, causing death by dangerous driving and dangerous driving. The test is longer and more rigorous than the normal 'L' test. It therefore provides scope for the driver to be tested in a greater variety of road and traffic conditions.

In determining whether to make such an order, the court must have regard to the safety of road users. For offences involving obligatory disqualification, the 'appropriate' test is the Extended Driving Test, and this might therefore apply to the driver who has been disqualified under the 'totting up' procedure, and who has been ordered by the court to retake the test. For offences involving obligatory endorsement (as opposed to obligatory disqualification), the appropriate test is the ordinary Test of Competence to Drive.

Penalty points for some offences are graded according to the seriousness of the offence (see Table 6.4). An accumulation of 12 points within three years means that the driver will automatically be disqualified from driving, although the courts are given powers not to disqualify in exceptional circumstances. The three-year period is measured backwards from the date of the latest offence.

The period of disqualification as a result of an accumulation of penalty points is:

- six months, if there has been no disqualification in the past three years;
- one year, if there has been one disqualification in the past three years;

Table 6.4 Penalty points for driving offences

Offence	Points
Being in charge of a vehicle when unfit to drive	10
Failing to stop after an accident	5–10
Failing to report or to give particulars	5–10
Careless and inconsiderate driving	3–9
Driving while uninsured	6–8
Driving while disqualified by a court	6
Driving other than in accordance with a licence	3–6
Exceeding a speed limit	
– in court proceedings	3–6
– by fixed penalty	3
Contravention of temporary prohibition or restriction	
– in court proceedings	3–6
– by fixed penalty	3
Contravention of motorway regulations	
– in court proceedings	3–6
– by fixed penalty	3
Failure to give identity of driver	3
Unlawful carriage of motorcycle passenger	3
Contravention or failure to comply with C & U Regs.	3
Driving with defective eyesight	3

- two years, if there has been more than one disqualification in the past three years.

Disqualification may be imposed for a single offence if the court feels that the offence is serious enough.

A penalty points endorsement can be removed after four years from the date of the offence.

An endorsement of disqualification may be removed four years after the date of conviction (11 years for drinking and driving offences).

After a disqualification for a period of more than two years the driver can apply for the disqualification to be lifted after a period of:

- 2 years if the disqualification period is less than 4 years;
- half the period of disqualification if the disqualification period is between 4 and 10 years;
- 5 years if the disqualification was for more than 10 years.

The 'New Driver' Act

This Act affects any newly qualified driver who accumulates six or more penalty points within two years of passing his or her driving test. The accumulation of six or more points (whether arising from court convictions or from fixed penalty offences) means that the licence is automatically revoked by the DVLA and the driver has to revert to a provisional licence. Both the Theory and Practical Tests will need to be retaken before a full licence can be issued. After passing the tests a new full licence will generally include all previous licence entitlements, but the points will carry forward, as these could count towards any future 'totting up'. Recent figures from the Driver and Vehicle Licensing Agency show that about 14,000 new drivers have their licences revoked each year.

Disqualification and the ADI

One of the requirements of ADI qualification is, 'will have held a full driving licence for four years'. An important point to be remembered by professional driving instructors is that any period of disqualification from driving will involve a further period of disqualification from the ADI Register. For example, a one-year disqualification for a driving offence is followed by a four-year disqualification from the official Register. The instructor would, therefore, be unable to work as an ADI for a total period of five years.

Fixed penalties

Traffic wardens and police officers are empowered to enforce the law in connection with various offences by use of the fixed penalty system. The relevant offences include waiting, parking, loading and obstruction as well as offences relating to vehicle tax, lights and reflectors. Driving offences such as making an unauthorized 'U' turn and driving the wrong way in a one-way street are also included.

The ticket is given to the driver or is fixed to the vehicle. Payment must be made within 28 days or alternatively the offender may request a court hearing. If the driver who committed the offence cannot be identified or found, the registered owner of the vehicle is ultimately responsible for payment of the fine. However, in the case of hired vehicles, special rules apply and the person who hires the vehicle will become liable for any fines or excess charges.

The extended fixed penalty scheme covers various moving traffic offences including speeding, failure to comply with traffic directions and vehicle defect offences. The following categories are included in the scheme, and for these offences the issuing of the ticket is normally the responsibility of the police:

- Contravening a traffic regulation order.
- Breach of experimental traffic order.
- Breach of experimental traffic scheme regulation in Greater London.
- Using a vehicle in contravention of a temporary prohibition or restriction of traffic on a road, such as where a road is being repaired.
- Contravening motorway traffic regulations.
- Driving a vehicle in contravention of an order prohibiting or restricting driving vehicles on certain classes of roads.
- Breach of pedestrian crossing regulations.
- Contravention of a street playground order.
- Breach of a parking place order on a road.
- Breach of a provision of a parking place designation order and other offences committed in relation to it, except failing to pay an excess charge.
- Contravening a parking place designation order.
- Breach of a provision of a parking place designation order.
- Contravention of minimum speed limits.
- Speeding.
- Driving or keeping a vehicle without displaying a registration mark or hackney carriage sign.
- Driving or keeping a vehicle with the registration mark or hackney carriage sign obscured.
- Failure to comply with traffic directions or signs.
- Leaving vehicle in a dangerous position.
- Failing to wear a seat belt.
- Breach of restrictions on carrying children in the front of vehicles.
- Driving a vehicle elsewhere than on the road.
- Parking a vehicle on the path or verge.
- Breach of Construction and Use Regulations.
- Contravention of lighting restrictions on vehicles.
- Driving without a licence.

- Breach of provisional licence provisions.
- Failure to stop when required by constable in uniform.
- Obstruction of highway with vehicle.

Penalty tickets for endorsable offences are handed to the driver, as the driving licence will have to be surrendered for possible endorsement with the appropriate penalty points. If the licence shows an accumulation of points which, together with the current offence, would bring the total to 12 points or more, the fixed penalty ticket would not be issued. In those circumstances a prosecution for the offence would follow.

If the licence is not immediately available, it must be produced within seven days at a nominated police station. A receipt for the licence is then issued, and this is an accepted document if for any reason the licence has to be produced at a later date.

The fixed penalty fines of £30, £40 or £60 are payable within 28 days (or as specified in the notice). If payment is not received in time, the charge is increased by 50 per cent. A court hearing may be requested if the driver feels that the ticket was issued incorrectly or unfairly.

Driver Improvement Scheme

Several police forces are now offering this scheme as an alternative to prosecution for drivers committing some less serious or careless driving offences.

Offenders are given the opportunity to attend a short (one- or two-day) course at their own expense. The aim is to address driver behaviour and to provide remedial instruction tailored to suit the individual driver's needs. The scheme is not normally used for more serious offences, or where there is an element of dangerousness or deliberate recklessness.

Driver identity

The 1991 Act defines the circumstances in which a person can be required to give information about the identity of a driver who is alleged to be guilty of a road traffic offence. This is particularly important in connection with the identification of drivers involved in speeding or other offences detected by automatic devices, including cameras.

A photograph, showing the registration number, is taken of the offending vehicle. It is not intended that the registered keeper of the vehicle should bear responsibility for the offence detected by the device, if someone else was driving at the time of the offence. It is, therefore, necessary to trace the driver through the registered keeper. The penalty for not providing the information has been increased to three penalty points to provide an incentive to do so.

The existing fixed penalty system requires the vehicle and the person committing the offence to be present at the time the fixed penalty ticket is issued. However, under the provisions of the RTA 1991, a conditional fixed penalty offer is available for all fixed penalty offences, including those detected by automatic cameras and other devices. These provisions allow for the police to issue a notice to the alleged offender by post.

The notice is first issued to the registered keeper of the vehicle, requiring information about the identity of the driver. The conditional offer of a fixed penalty will then be issued to the person identified as the driver of the vehicle when the offence was detected. If the information about the driver is not given, the 'keeper' of the vehicle will have committed an offence, which is now endorsable.

If the driver wishes to take up the offer of the fixed penalty, the driving licence and payment are sent to the Fixed Penalty Office and the payment is accepted, so long as the licence shows that the driver would not be subject to a 'totting up' disqualification. In those circumstances, the payment and licence would be returned and a court summons would then be issued.

Driving licence endorsements

Endorsement offences appear on a driving licence in a coded version which includes details of the court, the offence and of the fine and endorsement (see Table 6.5).

Speed limits

A speed limit of 30 mph normally applies to all vehicles on a road where street lamps are positioned at regular intervals. On occasions a higher speed is allowed on such a road, in which case appropriate signs show the higher limit.

Speed limits apply to roads and vehicles, and where there is a difference the lower limit applies. The maximum speed on motorways and dual carriageways is 70 mph and on single carriageways 60 mph. However, these limits apply to cars, car-derived vans and dual-purpose vehicles adapted to carry not more than eight passengers. A different set of speed limits applies to other types of vehicles (see Table 6.6).

Mobile phones

It is illegal to use a hand-held mobile phone while driving. This includes situations such as waiting at traffic lights or level crossings and in queues of stationary traffic. To make a call or to answer the phone you should find a safe and suitable place to park. However, in a lengthy stoppage on a motorway it would be obvious that you were not 'driving' if the engine was switched off.

The only exemption from the regulations is for calls to 999 (or 112) in a genuine emergency where it would be unsafe or impractical to stop.

Using a hand-held phone while driving can incur a fixed penalty fine of £30. This amount can increase to a maximum of £1,000 if the case goes to court. The regulations also apply to anyone supervising a learner driver. As an instructor

Table 6.5 Driving licence endorsement codes

Code	Offence
	Accidents
AC10	Failing to stop and/or give particulars after an accident
AC20	Failing to report an accident within 24 hours
AC30	Undefined accident offence
	Driver banned from driving (disqualified)
BA10	Driving while disqualified
BA20	Driving while disqualified by virtue of age
	Careless driving
CD10	Driving without due care and attention
CD20	Driving without reasonable consideration for other road users
CD30	Driving without due care and attention or without reasonable consideration for other road users
	Construction and use offences
CU10	Using a vehicle with defective brakes
CU20	Causing or likely to cause danger by reason of use of unsuitable vehicle or using a vehicle with parts or accessories (excluding brakes, steering or tyres) in a dangerous condition
CU30	Using a vehicle with defective tyres
CU40	Using a vehicle with defective steering
CU50	Causing or likely to cause danger by reason of load or passengers
CU60	Undefined failure to comply with Construction and Use Regulations
	Dangerous driving
DD10	Driving in a dangerous manner
DD20	Driving at a dangerous speed
DD30	Reckless driving
DD40	Driving in a dangerous or reckless manner, etc
DD50	Causing death by dangerous driving
DD60	Culpable homicide while driving a vehicle
DD70	Causing death by reckless driving
	Drink or drugs
DR10	Driving or attempting to drive with blood alcohol level above limit
DR20	Driving or attempting to drive while unfit through drink or drugs
DR30	Driving or attempting to drive then refusing to supply a specimen of blood or urine for laboratory testing
DR40	In charge of a vehicle while blood alcohol level above limit
DR50	In charge of a vehicle while unfit through drink or drugs
DR60	In charge of a vehicle then refusing to supply a specimen of blood or urine for laboratory testing
	Insurance offences
IN10	Using a vehicle uninsured against third party risks
	Licence offences
LC10	Driving without a licence
LC20	Driving when under age
	Miscellaneous offences
MS10	Leaving a vehicle in a dangerous position
MS20	Unlawful pillion riding

MS30	Playstreet offences
MS40	Driving with uncorrected or defective eyesight or refusing to submit to eyesight test
MS50	Motor racing on the highway
MS60	Offences not covered by other codes
MS70	Driving with uncorrected defective eyesight
MS80	Refusing to submit to an eyesight test

Motorway offences

MW10	Contravention of Special Roads Regulations (excluding speed limits)

Pedestrian crossing

PC10	Undefined contravention of Pedestrian Crossing Regulations
PC20	Contravention of Pedestrian Crossing Regulations with moving vehicle
PC30	Contravention of Pedestrian Crossing Regulations with stationary vehicle

Provisional licence offences

PL10	Driving without 'L' plates
PL20	Driving while not accompanied by a qualified person
PL30	Carrying a person not qualified
PL40	Drawing an unauthorized trailer
PL50	Undefined failure to comply with conditions of a provisional licence

Speed limits

SP10	Exceeding goods vehicle speed limit
SP20	Exceeding speed limit for type of vehicle (excluding goods or passenger vehicles)
SP30	Exceeding statutory speed limit on a public road
SP40	Exceeding passenger vehicle speed limit
SP50	Exceeding speed limit on a motorway
SP60	Undefined speed limit offence

Traffic directions and signs

TS10	Failing to comply with traffic light signals
TS20	Failing to comply with double white lines
TS30	Failing to comply with a 'Stop' sign
TS40	Failing to comply with directions of a traffic constable
TS50	Failing to comply with a traffic sign (excluding 'Stop' signs, traffic lights or double white lines)
TS60	Failing to comply with a school crossing patrol sign
TS70	Undefined failure to comply with a traffic direction or sign

Theft or the unauthorized taking of vehicle

UT10	Taking and driving away a vehicle without consent (or attempting to)
UT20	Stealing or attempting to steal a vehicle
UT30	Going equipped for stealing or taking a vehicle
UT40	Taking or attempting to take a vehicle without consent; driving or attempting to drive a vehicle knowing it to have been taken without consent; allowing oneself to be carried in or on a vehicle knowing it to have been taken without consent

Special code

XX99	Signifies a disqualification under the 'totting-up' procedure

Notes

Aiding and abetting offences are as listed above, but with the 0 changed to 2 (eg UT20 becomes UT22).
Causing or permitting are as listed, but with the 0 changed to 4 (eg PL20 becomes PL24).
Inciting offences are as listed, but with the 0 changed to 6 (eg DD10 becomes DD16).

Table 6.6 Statutory speed limits

Vehicle	Single carriageway	Dual carriageway	Motorway
Motorcycles	60	70	70
Cars, including car-derived vans	60	70	70
Cars, towing trailer or caravan	50	60	60
Goods vehicles up to 7.5 tonnes	50	60	70
– towing trailer	50	60	60
Large goods vehicles			
– over 7.5 tonnes	40	50	60
Buses and coaches:			
– up to 12 metres length	50	60	70
– over 12 metres length	50	60	60

you should be concentrating on what your pupil is doing and not be using a phone.

Hands-free equipment is not covered by the regulations, provided that the phone can be used without actually holding it.

MOTOR VEHICLE INSURANCE

Compulsory motor vehicle insurance was introduced in 1930. At that time it was decided that insurance was necessary to make sure that people who were injured in a road accident were not left uncompensated. Property damage should be included within the minimum insurance, and this cover is required by the RTA 1988.

Other types of insurance policies have been in operation for many years, as it is recognized that there is a need for more cover than the minimum requirements of the RTA.

Types of insurance

Compulsory insurance

Users of motor vehicles must be insured with an authorized insurer against third party risks. The cover must include compensation in respect of death, injury to another person and also the cost of any emergency medical treatment. All passengers must be covered and no 'own risks' agreements are allowed between passengers and the user of the vehicle. This type of insurance policy (which is very rare) is sometimes known as a 'road traffic only' policy, and leaves the user with a vast amount of risk. As an alternative to insurance, application may be made to the Secretary of State at the Department for Transport for a warrant to enable a deposit of £500,000 in cash or securities to be made with the Accountant-General.

Third party property damage is a compulsory requirement under the RTA 1988.

Third party insurance only

A 'third party' insurance policy usually requires at least the minimum cover as that described above.

This type of policy would normally cover:

- liability for injuries to other people (including passengers in your car);
- liability in respect of accidents caused by them (for example, causing injury to a passer-by, or damaging his or her property by opening a car door);
- liability for damage to other people's property (for example, damage to another vehicle may be paid in full or in part by your insurance company).

For an additional fee the policy may be extended to include the risks of fire and theft. An additional premium may be required if the car is not kept in a locked garage overnight.

A 'third party, fire and theft' policy offers slightly more than the bare minimum but still leaves a lot of risk with the driver/owner/operator.

Comprehensive insurance

In view of the heavy cost of repairs, two out of three owners these days take out a 'comprehensive' insurance policy. However, there is no such thing as fully comprehensive insurance, and care should be taken in reading the small print. The term 'comprehensive' as applied to motor insurance means that a variety and a great deal of protection is provided under one policy document, but does not mean that cover is provided against every conceivable contingency of whatever nature.

This type of insurance cover will normally include the risks for third party, fire and theft, together with cover for accidental damage to your own car, medical expenses, and loss or damage to personal effects in the car.

The policy will specify the uses to which the car may be put. For instance, a policy restricting use to social, domestic and pleasure purposes will not provide cover for any business use (including use by a driving school). There may also be a restriction to cover driving by specified drivers only, or the policy may exclude driving by certain persons.

Other restrictions vary from one insurance company to another, but it is normal practice for the company to specify an 'excess' when a young or inexperienced driver is driving the car. The excess is the amount that you would normally have to pay towards the cost of repairing your vehicle in the event of a blameworthy accident. If the accident was the fault of another driver, you might need to recover this amount from that person. In the case of driving school vehicles, the excess can vary and might be up to £250 depending on who was driving the car (or who was in charge of it) at the time of the accident.

Policies are usually invalidated if the vehicle insured is not maintained in a safe and roadworthy condition. Proof that the vehicle is insured in accordance with the RTA is given by insurers in the form of a Certificate of Insurance. The certificate is quite distinct from the policy of insurance itself. It is the certificate that has to be produced when renewing the car licence; it must also be produced to a police officer on request.

Driver's responsibilities

As a driver you must provide details of your insurance to the person who holds you responsible for an accident which results in damage to his or her property. The law also requires you to give insurance details following an injury accident.

For your own convenience you should be prepared to give your insurance details following an accident, or to a police officer, who can ask to see evidence of your insurance at any time.

Therefore it is in your interest, as well as those of accident victims, to keep your insurance details to hand when driving. You are advised, however, not to leave them in the car in case they are stolen.

Even with the new insurance requirements, drivers and other road users can find themselves without a source of compensation. This can happen where the accident is nobody's fault, or where you yourself are in some measure to blame. It is for you, as a driver, to consider whether you take out additional insurance cover against such risks as injury to yourself or damage to your own car in these circumstances.

EC requirements

All UK motor insurance policies must include cover against any third party liabilities that are compulsorily insurable in any other EC member state. The full cover provided under a comprehensive policy can be extended for travel in Europe, if required. A 'green card' is no longer legally necessary but it may be prudent to obtain the card from the insurance company in order to have much wider cover. Possession of the green card can also help to eliminate some of the problems of procedure and language.

Accident procedures

An 'accident' is generally and legally regarded as one that causes injury to another person or animal, or one that causes damage to another person's vehicle or property. If you are involved in an accident you must stop and give your name, address and vehicle registration details. If there is personal injury, your insurance details must be produced to anyone who has reasonable cause to see them. You must also give information about the ownership of the vehicle. If it is not possible to exchange these details at the time, the accident must be reported to the police as soon as possible, and in any case within 24 hours. A police officer may, in certain circumstances, ask for driver and vehicle details if it is thought that the driver may have been involved in an accident.

These responsibilities apply regardless of who is to blame for the accident. Even if you feel that the accident is relatively trivial or that it was not your fault, you still need to follow the procedure outlined in Figure 6.1. The figure and the notes on page 195 give useful guidance for instructional purposes.

With regard to your responsibility as an instructor, it should be noted that the duty to carry out these procedures applies to a person accompanying the holder of a provisional licence and not only to the driver of the vehicle.

LEGAL OBLIGATIONS OF A SUPERVISING DRIVER

Anyone supervising a learner driver must have held a full GB licence for at least three years and be over 21 years of age. It is the learner's responsibility to check that anyone supervising his or her practice is covered by these regulations. An offence against the regulations carries a penalty of a fine, discretionary disqualification or two penalty points.

The tuition or practice vehicle must display regulation-size 'L' plates (or 'D' plates in Wales, if preferred) that are clearly visible within a reasonable distance from the front and rear of the vehicle. 'L' plates should be removed from the vehicle when a full licence holder is driving it, except in the case of driving school cars.

As well as all the legal obligations, any driver supervising a learner has certain moral obligations relating to the safety of passengers and other road users. If a driving instructor commits or aids and abets a traffic offence, the subsequent punishment resulting from a successful prosecution is likely to have disastrous effects. Even relatively minor offences will attract a disproportionate amount of bad publicity that not only causes disgrace and inconvenience, as well as possible loss of livelihood, but also stains the character of the driving school industry as a whole.

In addition to the responsibilities as driver, already covered in this chapter, the instructor has further responsibilities. Where a supervisor sees that the 'L' driver is about to commit an unlawful act, whether it is through ignorance or lack of skill, and takes no verbal or physical action to prevent it, a prosecution for aiding and abetting could ensue. For example, if a learner was about to ignore a red traffic light and the instructor allowed the car to be stopped after passing the solid line, an offence would have been committed by both persons – even though it was the instructor who finally brought the car to a stop.

Accident Procedure

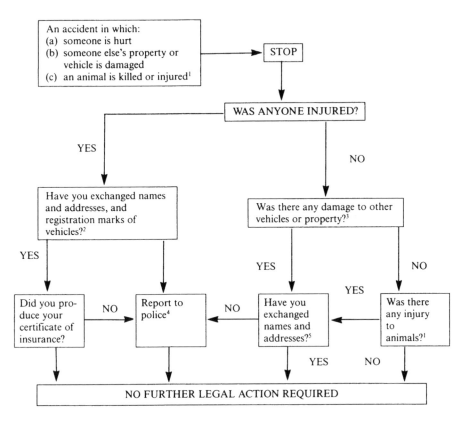

Note:
The chart shows the *minimum* legal requirements.

Accident procedure – notes

1. An 'animal' is regarded as horse, cattle, ass, mule, sheep, goat, pig or dog.
2. You must exchange details not only with the other driver, but also with any person who has reasonable grounds for asking for them.
3. 'Damage' includes roadside furniture, for example lamp posts and other fixtures.
4. You must report an accident as soon as possible, and at least within 24 hours. Your insurance certificate must be produced at the time of reporting or within seven days.
5. Your details must be given to the owner of the vehicle, property or animal.

Figure 6.1   Accident procedure flowchart

Tuition vehicle

You need to pay particular attention to ensure that the tuition vehicle is in a roadworthy condition and that it is taxed and adequately insured for driving instruction and driving test purposes. The vehicle must carry 'L' plates (either 'D' or 'L' plates in Wales) of the prescribed size, showing clearly to the front and rear of the vehicle.

Driving licence and eyesight

Before allowing pupils to drive your vehicle you should make sure that they have a current, valid, signed driving licence and that the eyesight requirements can be met. You must check this even though the pupil may have signed a declaration to this effect on the licence application form. Where glasses are required to meet the minimum standard, they must be worn at all times while driving.

Make sure you are aware of your responsibilities as a driver and an instructor.

Tuition in client's vehicle

On occasions where clients may choose to provide their own car for professional driving lessons, you must give special consideration to all the points previously mentioned, but in particular to the roadworthiness, MOT certificate and insurance cover of the vehicle.

Before agreeing to give tuition in a non-dual-controlled vehicle, you should give serious consideration to the standard, or estimated standard, the client has reached. This is particularly important if you have not had an opportunity to make a valid assessment (for example, a new client booking by telephone).

Due consideration should also be given to the type of vehicle, to see if you can easily reach the handbrake (some cars have the handbrake on the right of the driver or under the dash). Your safety, as well as that of your client and other road users, may be at stake.

ADVANCED DRIVING TESTS

The Cardington Special Test

This high-level driving test is open to all Approved Driving Instructors who want to keep their own driving up to standard as part of their continued professional development. One of the strictest tests available, it is conducted by permanent staff instructors operating out of the Driving Standards Agency's Training Centre at Cardington near Bedford.

You have to provide your own car for the test. It must have:

- manual transmission;
- an interior instructor mirror;

- integral head restraints for both the driver and the assessor.

The test normally lasts approximately 90 minutes, and covers a variety of road and traffic conditions, including motorways. The test syllabus includes:

- driving on all types of road;
- a left- and right-hand reverse;
- turning in the road;
- reverse parking;
- hill and angled starts.

Commentary driving is not expected, and there is no element of theory testing.

You will be assessed on your driving technique, and you are expected to demonstrate a systematic and professional approach to all hazards and plan expertly for safe progress at all times. In particular, the assessor will be checking your:

- expert handling of the vehicle controls;
- use of correct road procedures;
- anticipation of the actions of other road users and taking the appropriate action;
- sound judgement of distance, speed and timing;
- consideration for the convenience and safety of other road users.

During the test you will be asked to carry out some or all of the following manoeuvres:

- moving off uphill and downhill on reasonably steep slopes;
- moving off at an angle from behind a parked vehicle;
- overtaking, meeting and crossing the path of other vehicles;
- turning right- and left-hand corners;
- stopping the car as in an emergency;
- reversing into limited openings to the left and right;
- reverse parking (car park and road);
- turning the vehicle round in the road using forward and reverse gears.

Each individual fault will be fully assessed in the light of the prevailing conditions. The result is normally confirmed by post within 48 hours and, whether you pass or fail, you will receive a report on those faults observed. If you achieve a grade A, you will also receive the Cardington Certificate.

The fee at March 2006 is £129.25 (£110 plus VAT), but this is currently under review. For more details or to make a booking, contact DSA Training Centre, Harrowden Lane, Cardington, Bedford MK44 3ST (tel: 01234 744000; fax: 01234 744010; e-mail: training.dsa@safedriving.org).

The Institute of Advanced Motorists (IAM)

The IAM was founded in 1956 for the purposes of raising driving standards and to establish an Advanced Driving Test. The Institute believes that a higher standard of behaviour by all road users, and drivers in particular, could reduce road accidents and their grim social consequences more effectively than any other method. The Advanced Driving Test offers to drivers of cars, trucks, and motorcycles an opportunity to check their own abilities under today's road conditions; membership of the Institute for those who achieve the Institute's standards then demands the responsibility that goes with proven skill.

The standard of the test is based on the police system of car control as taught in Home Office Approved Police Driving Schools. The examiners, all of whom are either serving or retired police officers, have to hold an Advanced Driving Certificate. This qualification has never been challenged by the public as it is probably the highest available in the world. The 120 test routes are designed to provide all types of driving conditions and are about 35 miles long. The test takes 90 minutes, which does not include the briefing and debriefing.

There are many books available on the subject of advanced driving, including *Roadcraft: The police driver's handbook* and *How to Be an Advanced Motorist*.

The advantage of taking an advanced test is that IAM members have a 50–75 per cent lower accident rate than the general public. Over 400 commercial concerns put their staff through the test in order to cut costs, as does the British Army. Many insurance companies grant a discount off normal motor insurance premiums of up to 20 per cent. The conviction rate among members appears to be five times lower than the general public. Anyone with a full British driving licence can take the test; it is advisable to receive instruction from an ADI, preferably an IAM member, or contact the local IAM group who will give guidance in preparation for the test.

The IAM is a registered charity and receives full moral support from the Department for Transport, all UK police forces and the Ministry of Defence. The IAM motto is 'Skill with Responsibility'.

Application forms for the test can be obtained from the Institute of Advanced Motorists, IAM House, 510 Chiswick High Road, London W4 5RG (tel: 020 8996 9600; fax: 020 8996 9601; website: www.iam.org.uk).

Candidates will be expected to make reasonable use of the vehicle's performance within the speed limits and normal parameters of safety with regard to the road traffic and weather conditions. Candidates are expected to reverse into a side road and execute a hill start, and will be assessed on their powers of observation.

The test is something that any driver with a reasonable amount of experience and skill should be able to pass without too much difficulty. Candidates do not fail for committing minor faults. Even those who do fail should learn some important lessons from the examiner conducting the test. Successful candidates may:

- display the Institute's badge on their car;
- take advantage of special insurance terms;
- receive *Advanced Driving*, the motoring magazine especially written for those with a keen interest in driving;
- join their local IAM group and participate in the road safety, driving and social events which they organize.

During the test

Examiners look for the following points:

- *Acceleration* should be smooth and progressive. It should be used at the right time and right place. Acceleration should not be excessive or insufficient.
- *Braking* should be smooth and progressive. Brakes should be used in conjunction with the mirror and signals. They should not be used late or fiercely. Candidates will be expected to take account of the road conditions.
- *Clutch control.* The engine and road speeds must be properly coordinated when changing gear. Candidates should not slip or ride the clutch, nor should they coast with the clutch disengaged.
- *Gear changing.* Gears should be selected smoothly and fluently. If automatic transmission is fitted, candidates should make full use of it.
- *Use of gears.* Candidates must make correct use of the gears. The correct gear should be selected before reaching a hazard.
- *Steering.* The wheel should be held correctly with the hands at the quarter-to-three or ten-to-two position. The use of the crossed arm technique, except when manoeuvring in a confined space, is not recommended by the Institute.
- *Seating position.* Candidates should be alert and not slumped at the wheel. They should not rest an arm on the door while driving.
- *Observation.* Candidates should read the road well ahead and anticipate the actions of other road users. They must be able to judge correctly the speeds and distances of other vehicles.
- *Concentration.* Candidates should concentrate on the road and traffic situation and not allow themselves to be easily distracted.
- *Maintaining progress.* With regard to the road, traffic and weather conditions, candidates should make use of their vehicle's performance by driving at a reasonable pace, maintaining good progress throughout.
- *Obstruction.* Candidates should not obstruct other road users by driving too slowly, by positioning incorrectly on the road or by failing to anticipate and react correctly to the traffic situation ahead.
- *Positioning.* Candidates should keep in the correct part of the road, especially when approaching and negotiating hazards.
- *Lane discipline.* Candidates should drive in the appropriate lane and be careful not to straddle white lines.

- *Observation of surfaces.* Candidates should continually assess the road surface, especially in poor weather, and look out for slippery conditions.
- *Traffic signals.* Candidates must observe and respond correctly to signals, signs and road markings, and extend proper courtesies at pedestrian crossings.
- *Speed limits and other legal requirements.* Speed limits and other legal requirements must be observed at all times.
- *Overtaking* should be carried out safely while maintaining a correct distance from other vehicles and using the mirrors, signals and gears correctly.
- *Hazard procedure and cornering.* Candidates must have full control over their vehicle on the approach to a hazard. They must negotiate it in the correct position, driving at an appropriate speed with a suitable gear engaged.
- *Mirrors* should be used frequently, especially before signalling and making changes to speed or course.
- *Signals* given by direction indicator, or arm if required, should be given in the right place and in good time. The horn and headlight flasher should only be used in accordance with the *Highway Code.*
- *Restraint.* Candidates should display reasonable restraint, without being indecisive.
- *Consideration.* Candidates should extend consideration and courtesy to other road users.
- *Car sympathy.* Candidates should not over-stress the vehicle, for example by revving the engine needlessly or by fierce braking.
- *Manoeuvring* should be carried out smoothly and competently.

The RoSPA Advanced Driving Test

RoSPA advanced tests are conducted at locations throughout the UK by Police Advanced drivers. The test normally lasts about 1¼ hours. The cost of the test includes the first year's membership of the RoSPA Advanced Drivers Association.

RoSPA has a unique system of grading successful candidates into gold, silver and bronze grades, which seems to be a fairer way of assessing performance over a wider range of driving ability. It provides incentives for the less experienced seeking to improve on their standard continuously, and at the same time, gives a meaningful measure of attainment to the more skilful driver. The highest grade is unlikely to be achieved without a thorough knowledge of *Roadcraft*, the police drivers' manual, and the system of car control it advocates.

Application forms can be obtained from The Administrative Officer, RoSPA Advanced Drivers Association, Edgbaston Park, 353 Bristol Road, Birmingham B5 7ST, tel: 0121 248 2000 or at www.rospa.co.uk.

The test

At the start of the test, examiners try to put candidates at east. Cars used for the test must be in a roadworthy condition and the candidate's visibility must not be obscured in any way. Examiners will take a serious view of candidates who, for example on a rainy day, attempt to drive while visibility is restricted by condensation on windows and mirrors.

Use of the controls

Before starting off, candidates are required to carry out the cockpit drill followed by a brake test shortly after moving.

Candidates are expected to demonstrate their mechanical appreciation by controlling the vehicle smoothly. Examiners will assess the steering method and position of the hands and arms when turning the wheel. The clutch should be used smoothly. Slipping and riding the clutch is frowned upon. Examiners will assess the position of the hand on the gear lever when executing selections, the matching of engine revolutions to road speed and the correct timing of gear changes. The intelligent use of intermediate gears will make a difference to the final grade achieved. The use of the brakes is assessed for smoothness, early braking in correct sequence relating to the 'system', skid avoidance through correct technique and progressive reduction in pedal pressure as the vehicle is brought to a smooth stop. The accelerator should be used firmly when needed, precisely and under control at all times. Acceleration sense in overtaking will be assessed, along with anticipation and the smooth variation of speeds to meet changing road and traffic conditions without braking.

Candidates are expected to use the mirrors in the correct sequence and have an accurate and continuous knowledge of the traffic situation behind. Over-the-shoulder looks are expected at appropriate times. Candidates are also assessed in their use of the horn.

Driving performance

Moving off and stopping should be smooth and carried out safely. Examiners will assess the correct application of the system of car control, whether candidates brake before or after changing gear, and whether they signal too late or too early. Particular emphasis is placed on the way the vehicle is positioned at junctions, on the approach to roundabouts, on the open road and in lanes on the approach to hazards.

Candidates will be assessed on their course when cornering and whether the line taken optimizes visibility and safety, and allows for any tendency of the vehicle to over- or understeer to be compensated for. The use of speed and vehicle controls while cornering will be assessed.

Candidates are assessed on whether necessary signals are omitted or wrongly timed, or unnecessary ones are used. The examiner will look for reinforcement of intention by an arm signal where necessary, and assess reactions to traffic signs.

Candidates are required to perform a reversing exercise safely and accurately, and in normal driving to make reasonable use of their vehicle's performance within legal limits and as safety allows, according to the prevailing road and traffic conditions. Examiners will assess whether candidates are asking themselves the appropriate questions before executing an overtaking manoeuvre.

General ability

Consideration for others and self-control will be assessed. Temperament while driving should be calm, relaxed and decisive.

Candidates are expected not to abuse their vehicles by 'kerbing' and the like.

Examiners will assess candidates' powers of observation, hazard recognition and planning. Candidates may, if they choose, elect to give a commentary drive or are invited to 'think aloud' for a few minutes by the examiner. Candidates will also be assessed on their ability to judge their own speed and the speeds and distances of other vehicles. This will be linked to candidates' use of braking and acceleration.

The test is concluded with questions on the *Highway Code* and other motoring matters such as those contained in most vehicle handbooks.

After the test

The examiner will discuss any points that have arisen during the test and then allocate a grade according to the performance of the candidate. Candidates are allocated a grade and are expected to take a refresher test within three years. Candidates who are ungraded are permitted to take the test again after three months. All retests are free of charge, as the fees are included in the annual membership subscription.

The DIAmond Advanced Motorist Test

The test is administered by the Driving Instructors Association and conducted by specially qualified DIAmond Advanced Examiners. These examiners are ADIs who have qualified for the Diploma in Driving Instruction, have passed the Cardington Special Driving Test and have also passed the DIAmond Advanced Examiners' Course.

The test is based on the DSA method of marking, with no more than six minor faults allowed. During the test a wide variety of road and traffic conditions are covered.

One of the advantages of taking this extra qualification is that you should be able to generate more and different types of business opportunities, such as advanced and defensive driving courses.

More details of the test are available from DIAmond Advanced Motorists Ltd, Safety House, Beddington Farm Road, Croydon CR0 4XZ, tel: 020 8665 5151.

ECO-DRIVING

All advanced driving tests these days – including the ADI Part 2 and the Cardington Special Test – include an element of eco-friendly driving.

Some of the main points that you should bear in mind include:

- Don't leave the car engine to warm up – drive off as soon as practicable after starting the engine.
- Harsh acceleration, sharp braking and generally aggressive driving can all cause an increase in fuel usage.
- Improved engine technology makes it possible to move up through the gears more rapidly – for petrol cars about 2,500 rpm, and for diesel about 2,000 rpm.
- Missing out intermediate gears by 'block changing' up and down through the gears can save fuel.
- Remember that very short journeys of less than 2 miles produce 60 per cent more pollution than journeys with a warm engine. Catalytic converters can take up to 6 miles to become really effective.
- Switching off the engine when waiting in queues of traffic uses less energy.
- The optimum speed range for minimum emissions is regarded as being 40–60 mph.
- Make sure that the engine is regularly maintained and properly tuned to keep emissions to a minimum.
- Make sure that tyre pressures are set at the recommended level. If the pressures are low, fuel consumption can be increased by about 2–3 per cent.
- Don't carry unnecessary loads such as roof racks or heavy items in the boot. In these circumstances, fuel consumption can increase by up to 10 per cent. With a heavy trailer – a boat or a caravan, for example – this figure can rise to 30 per cent.

More detail on eco-friendly driving techniques is given in Chapter 4. The latest edition of *The Official DSA Guide to Driving* has a complete chapter on eco-safe driving.

7

The Car

It is not necessary for driving instructors to know every last detail of the construction of a motor car. However, it is extremely helpful to have a thorough understanding of the basic principles involved, because it will help you to:

- have a better appreciation of your tuition car's workings, resulting in more cost-effective use of it;
- recognize when there is a need to undertake minor repairs and the early diagnosis of potential major faults;
- easily explain to your pupils in simple terms how the controls work;
- assist your pupils in developing more vehicle sympathy and a keener interest in driving generally.

For these reasons it is important to understand what happens when the driver uses the controls. This chapter includes a general view of mechanical principles, vehicle control and operation, vehicle safety checks, factors affecting vehicle stability and a summary of the legal requirements of using a motor car. It also gives an outline syllabus for teaching learners the basics of car mechanics and an understanding of how the car works.

MECHANICAL PRINCIPLES

The motor car is a complex assembly that includes the following main units and systems:

- *Power unit*, including the engine and the systems essential to its operation – for example, cooling, fuel, ignition and lubrication systems.
- *Transmission system* (power train) – this includes a gearbox to match the engine speed to the power required for the road conditions, and a final drive unit that transmits the power to the front and/or rear wheels.
- *Braking system* – to slow or stop the motion of the vehicle in either direction.
- *Steering system* – to move the vehicle in the desired direction.

- *Suspension system* – to reduce as far as practicable the shock and vibration from the road wheels to the vehicle body/chassis.
- *Body/chassis* – to act as a mounting for all the other units and assemblies.

The engine

The function of the engine is to convert the heat energy contained in the fuel into mechanical energy for powering the vehicle. Most cars are powered by four- or six-cylinder engines; each cylinder is a hole bored in a cylinder block. Pistons move up and down in sequence inside these cylinders in a sequence called the Otto cycle. The four strokes of this cycle are induction, compression, power (combustion) and exhaust.

The flow of fuel and air mixture into the cylinders and the flow of the burnt exhaust gases out is controlled by a system of valves incorporated into the cylinder head. The cylinder head bolted to the top of the cylinder block seals off each of the bores, and a gasket is fitted between them to make the joint pressure tight. Combustion of the fuel and air mixture takes place in combustion chambers, formed in the cylinder head above each of the cylinders.

Inlet stroke (a in Figure 7.2). During the inlet stroke, the inlet valve is open and the exhaust valve remains closed. The piston moves downward and the suction or vacuum created by this movement causes air and fuel to be drawn into the combustion chamber.

Compression stroke (b). During the compression stroke, both inlet and exhaust valves are closed. The piston moves upwards to compress the air–fuel mixture into a small volume.

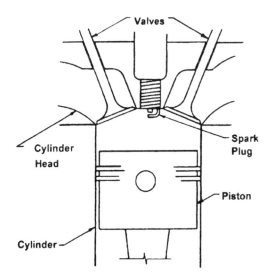

Figure 7.1 The engine

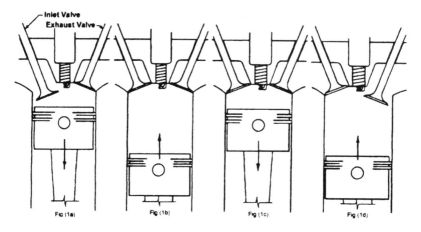

Figure 7.2 The four-stroke cycle (Otto)

Power stroke (c). During the power stroke, both valves remain closed. A spark from the spark plug ignites the air–fuel mixture and the piston is driven downward. This stroke delivers the power to propel the vehicle.

Exhaust stroke (d). During the exhaust stroke, the exhaust valve is open and the piston moves upward to push out the burnt gases. On completion of the exhaust stroke, the process begins immediately with another inlet stroke.

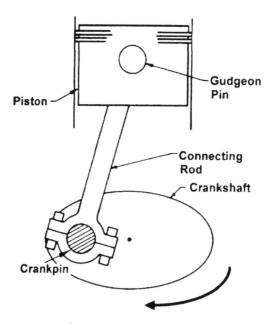

Figure 7.3 Power conversion

Power conversion. The pistons connected by connecting rods to the crankshaft convert the power produced on the power stroke into a rotary motion. A heavy disc called a flywheel is bolted to the crankshaft to make it revolve more evenly and thus ensure a continuous flow of power to the gearbox and driving wheels. One complete Otto cycle rotates the crankshaft twice.

Valve and ignition timing. The arrangement of the valve and ignition timing gears ensures perfect coordination with the motion of the pistons; a camshaft controls the opening and closing of the valves. It rotates at precisely half engine speed and in perfect coordination with the distributor, which controls the exact timing of the spark to initiate the ignition stroke.

The fuel system (petrol engines)

An engine operates on a mixture of petrol and air drawn from the carburettor. The carburettor basically consists of a tube through which the air passes, drawn in by the downward movement of the pistons, and a float chamber that distributes the fuel pumped from the petrol tank. Air passes into the tube of the carburettor through an air filter, the flow being controlled by a flap known as a 'butterfly valve' and operated by the accelerator pedal.

As the accelerator is depressed, more air is drawn in; this in turns sucks more petrol from the float chamber through small jets which spray petrol into the tube. The combined petrol and air mixture is drawn through a series of pipes, known as the inlet manifold, which are connected to each cylinder. When starting a cold engine, a much richer mixture is required and this means a higher proportion of petrol to air than for normal running. This is achieved by restricting the amount of air entering the carburettor by means of a flap in the air intake known as a choke. Some cars have an automatic choke that is controlled by the engine temperature; others are manually operated.

With a fuel-injection system, the amount of petrol injected and the timing of its supply is controlled electronically. The accelerator operates a throttle butterfly valve that regulates the amount of air that flows through to the cylinder. At the same time a pump pressurizes the fuel, which is then directed through the injectors into the cylinders.

Faults

- Dirty air filter: causes rich mixture, increased fuel consumption, loss of power, increased carbon deposits in engine.
- Sediment in petrol tank: causes fuel pipe blockage, dirt in petrol pump and carburettor float chamber that will block the jets, resulting in starvation of fuel at the cylinders.
- Incorrect petrol and air mixture: too rich or too weak. Wrong grade of petrol causing poor engine performance. Driver not returning choke when the engine is warmed up.

The ignition system

The combustible mixture of air and petrol is ignited by a spark that occurs between two electrodes (spark plug) in the combustion chamber, at the end of the compression stroke. It is the function of the ignition system to provide a spark of sufficient heat intensity to ignite the charge mixture at the predetermined position in the engine's cycle under all speed and load conditions.

The ignition system converts the low voltage from the battery into a high-tension voltage by means of an ignition coil. High-tension voltage is transmitted through the HT lead from the coil to the distributor cap. As the engine rotates, the rotor arm inside the distributor acts as an automatic switch that times the spark and distributes it to each cylinder spark plug in turn.

The timing of the spark is advanced or retarded automatically to ensure that it occurs at the correct moment for the load and engine speed. Most modern cars are now equipped with electronic ignition systems that involve less maintenance, longer spark plug life and make starting the car easier.

Faults

- Badly worn, dirty or poorly adjusted contact breaker points and/or spark plugs.
- Cracked, worn or dirty distributor cap.
- Worn rotor arm.
- Poor-fitting, dirty, cracked or perished HT leads, faulty or damaged electronic ignition systems.
- Incorrect ignition timing settings.

Engine lubrication

If two surfaces that rub together are examined under a microscope, it will be seen that each surface has a jagged edge (A in Figure 7.4). If these edges touch one another during operation, friction and heat are generated. If they are left without lubrication, these components will either wear excessively or weld themselves together, ultimately resulting in component seizure.

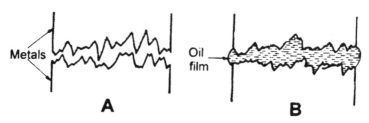

Figure 7.4 Engine lubrication

If this situation occurred in the internal combustion engine, it would first lead to audible knocking noises, then to a reduction in power output, and finally to the failure of the component concerned. To overcome these problems, a film of oil (B in the figure) must separate the two surfaces. It is the function of the 'force-fed' lubrication system to maintain a film of oil between all moving engine components under all operating conditions.

Force-fed lubrication systems are generally of the 'wet sump' type in which the sump acts as both an oil drain return and a storage container. A pump draws oil from the sump and forces it through a filter up into the engine to lubricate all moving parts. Provision of a dipstick enables the level of oil in the sump to be checked. It is vital that the oil level does not drop too near or under the low mark. Should this happen, the moving parts of the engine are starved of the lubrication and protection they need.

An oil level that is too high can result in 'foaming' of the oil, so that air enters the lubrication system, causing inconsistent oil pressure. Excess oil splash on to the cylinder bores can also give rise to an increase in oil consumption.

It is essential that the engine oil and oil filter are replaced at the manufacturer's recommended service intervals. Failure to carry out this fairly basic service will cause unnecessary engine wear and tear.

An oil pressure gauge or oil pressure warning light indicates a condition of low oil pressure. Should this occur, the engine should be switched off immediately.

Faults

- Excessive oil consumption: oil level too high, wrong grade of oil, worn engine components.
- No oil pressure: low oil level, worn/faulty oil pump, blocked oil ways and/or filter.
- Low oil pressure: low oil level, wrong grade of oil, worn/faulty oil pump, very high oil temperature, worn engine components.
- High oil pressure: wrong grade of oil, faulty oil pump.
- Oil leaks: worn and/or faulty seals and gaskets; oil level too high.

The cooling system

The principle of the petrol engine, which derives its power from the combustion of fuel and air, necessitates the use of some type of cooling system in order to keep the engine's components at an acceptable working temperature. A typical water-cooled engine comprises a radiator, a water pump driven by a drive belt from the crankshaft, a series of passages running through the engine, and a thermostat. Water is pumped from the radiator, up through the engine past the thermostat and back into the top of the radiator, where it is cooled by the fan and the natural airflow as the car is being driven. Cooled water from the radiator then flows back into the cylinder block.

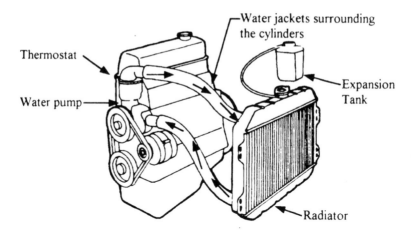

Figure 7.5 The cooling system

Driving school cars in particular do a lot of manoeuvring and slow driving work where there is very little natural movement of air through the radiator to cool the system. Under these circumstances, an electrically operated fan that only functions when a predetermined engine temperature is reached provides additional airflow.

Faults

- Engine overheating: water level low, loose or worn drive belt, faulty thermostat, blocked radiator matrix, collapsed radiator hoses, ignition timing incorrect, vehicle overloaded or brakes binding.
- Overcooling: thermostat faulty (jammed open), electric cooling fan continuously operating (faulty thermostat switch).
- Coolant loss: worn out hoses or loose clips, leaking radiator, water pump or core plugs, failed cylinder head gasket, cracked cylinder head or block.

The transmission system

The transmission of a car (see Figure 7.6) consists of a clutch (B), a gearbox (C) and a final drive unit (F). Their combined purpose is to transmit the drive from the engine (A) through to the road wheels. In the past, cars had an engine and gearbox at the front, with a propeller shaft relaying the drive to the rear wheels via a rear axle unit (D).

Nowadays, a more common layout is a system in which the engine, clutch and gearbox are in one unit driving the front wheels. This design allows more space for passengers and tends to give improved handling and control. However, it requires more complicated engineering, including the use of drive shafts fitted with constant velocity (CV) joints (E). These ensure the smooth transmission of power to the drive/ steered wheels throughout all wheel movements.

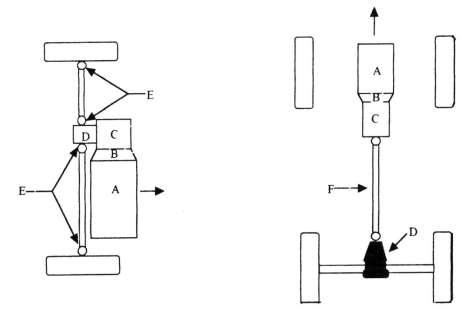

Figure 7.6 The transmission system

The clutch

The clutch enables the engine to be disconnected from the transmission in order to engage or disengage the gears. It provides the means for a smooth engagement of the drive between the engine and the road wheels, and it also allows the car to be controlled at a crawling pace.

The clutch consists of three main parts: a release bearing, a spring-loaded pressure plate and a centre plate. At the back of the engine there is a flat, heavy wheel called the flywheel, which is attached to the crankshaft and revolves at the same speed as the engine. The clutch centre plate comprises a friction material similar to a brake lining. It is connected to the transmission and held firmly against the flywheel by the pressure plate. When the engine is turning, the clutch is also turning.

When the clutch pedal is depressed, the pressure plate is pulled away from the flywheel, thus freeing the centre friction plate and disengaging the drive. When the pedal is released, the centre friction plate is forced against the flywheel by the pressure plate and the drive between the engine and transmission is complete.

Partially engaging (slipping) the clutch allows the car to be controlled at a crawling pace. A release bearing is situated behind the pressure plate and provides the means to allow the pedal linkage to operate the clutch.

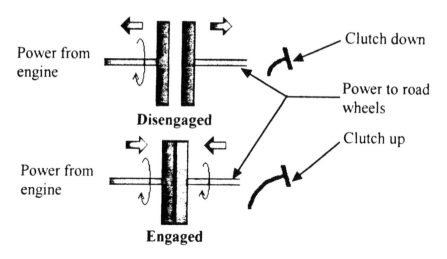

Power from engine

Clutch down

Disengaged

Power to road wheels

Power from engine

Clutch up

Engaged

Figure 7.7 The clutch

Faults

- Clutch slip (no or little power is transmitted when a gear is selected and the clutch pedal is fully released): incorrect clutch linkage adjustment, worn out clutch components, oil contamination of clutch friction faces, riding the clutch (resting foot on clutch in normal driving).
- Clutch judder: worn out rubber engine and gearbox mountings, distorted, damaged or worn clutch components, oil or grease contamination of clutch friction faces.
- Drag or spin (clutch fails to disengage fully when pushed down completely): incorrect clutch linkage adjustment (excess clearance), distorted, damaged or worn clutch components, oil or grease contamination of clutch friction faces.
- Noisy operation: worn or faulty release bearing (noise on disengaging clutch), worn or faulty spigot bearing (noise engaging clutch), worn or damaged clutch components.

Gearbox

The purpose of the gearbox is to enable the car to be driven at varying speeds with the minimum strain on the engine. Lower speeds and harder work will call for lower gears, while for normal cruising a higher gear should be selected.

The modern gearbox usually has four or five forward gears and a reverse gear. It also has a neutral position that disengages the engine from the road wheels. All forward gears have a synchromesh mechanism that allows changing from any one gear to another to be accomplished quietly and smoothly. Very simply, it synchronizes the speeds of the gears to be engaged before actually coupling them together.

Lubrication in the gearbox is as essential as it is in the engine. Most gearboxes have a filler/level plug on the side that allows the oil level to be checked at regular intervals. Failure to maintain the correct level of oil could lead to over-heating and unnecessary wear and tear.

Faults

- Noisy or difficult gear selection: faulty or worn synchromesh units, clutch drag.
- Jumping out of gear: worn or faulty synchromesh units, worn out gear selector mechanism.
- Noisy operation: worn bearings, damaged or worn gear teeth.
- Oil loss: worn gearbox oil seals, damaged or broken gearbox gaskets.

Automatic transmission

Most modern automatic transmission systems use a torque converter, together with an epicyclic gearbox. This enables the system to take up the drive smoothly and for gear changes to be made automatically with the power on. A control system determines when a gear change is needed by a system of sensors, and by comparing the speed of the vehicle with the amount of acceleration. The driver can override the system by, for example, changing to a lower gear by pressing hard on the accelerator (kick down).

Differential units

The differential is comprised of a small unit that is bolted to the crown wheel and pinion assembly, which contains a number of small gears. Together they form part of the final drive unit. The differential gears enable the inside wheel to turn at a slower rate than the outer wheel when on a curve.

Sometimes a 'limited slip' differential is fitted to cars. It is a device that allows normal differential action of the driving wheels when cornering, but prevents loss of traction in the event of either driving wheel losing adhesion. Its action therefore affords the driver better vehicle control under slippery road conditions.

Faults

- Noisy operation: worn out final drive gears, lack of lubrication (check oil level).
- Oil loss: worn oil seals, broken or damaged gaskets, oil level too high.

Exhaust system

An exhaust system is installed for the purpose of collecting burnt gases issued from the engine cylinders and discharging them outside the vehicle. A series of silencers ensure that the gases are exhausted without excessive noise. Exhaust

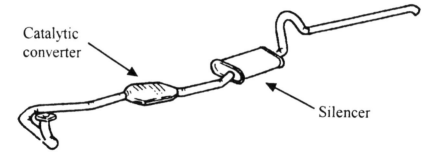

Catalytic converter

Silencer

Figure 7.8 The exhaust system

emission consists of a mixture of carbon monoxide (CO), carbon dioxide (CO_2), hydrocarbons (HC) and oxides of nitrogen (NO_2). Some of these emissions are harmful to the environment so most engine exhaust systems include a catalytic converter to reduce the level of pollutants.

The catalytic converter functions by providing an additional area for continued burning of HC and CO. HC and CO burn completely (or are converted) to water vapour, nitrogen (N) and carbon dioxide (CO_2).

The fuel used in cars equipped with catalytic converters must be lead-free. If lead coats the internal elements of the converter, its effectiveness is greatly reduced.

Precautionary measures

- Use only unleaded petrol.
- Do not use fuel additives.
- If difficult cold starting is experienced, contact dealer as soon as possible.
- If engine misfires, contact dealer as soon as possible.
- Do not use oil additives.
- Allow the engine to return to idle before switching off.
- Keep to the recommended service intervals.
- Never push or tow start the vehicle.
- Avoid running out of fuel.
- Avoid leaving the engine idling for long periods.
- Do not park or drive over inflammable materials.
- Exhaust gas is very hot; keep away from the tailpipe.

Exhaust turbocharging

A turbocharger is a device that uses the exhaust gases to turn an air pump or compressor that forces an increased amount of air into the engine cylinders. If a corresponding amount of fuel is then added, a large increase in engine power will be obtained. Both petrol and diesel engines can use a turbocharger.

Brakes

Most modern cars use a combination of disc brakes on the front wheels and drum brakes on the rear. Disc brakes are more efficient than drum brakes owing to the improved flow of cooling air over the discs. When the footbrake is applied, a hydraulic system multiplies the pedal pressure. Pistons located inside a caliper squeeze the disc between two friction pads, thus providing the braking force required for slowing the car down.

Drum brakes work on the same friction principle, but wheel cylinders expand the brake shoes outward against a rotating drum in order to provide the braking force. Drum brakes, being enclosed, are not so easily cooled by an air stream, and generation of excessive heat may result in a condition known as 'brake fade'.

The hydraulic system consists of a master cylinder and a fluid reservoir, connecting pipes, hoses and wheel cylinders. Footbrake pressure is transmitted directly from the master cylinder and applied to the brake shoes and disc pads. This action ensures that the vehicle will pull up smoothly and in a straight line.

All modern brake systems are of the 'divided line' type, where the addition of a second brake line and a special master cylinder (tandem) ensures that in the event of a failure of either line, at least two wheel brakes remain in service.

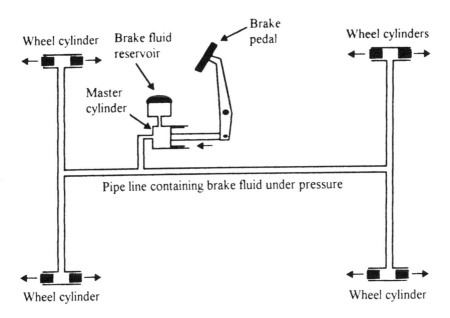

Figure 7.9 Hydraulic braking system

Faults

- Excess pedal-free travel: drum brakes need manual adjustment. Drum brake automatic adjusters not working. Excess disc hub bearing end float. Distorted discs.
- Brake pulling to one side: other side shoes or pads contaminated. Other side wheel cylinder piston seized. Other side caliper piston seized.
- Pedal feels spongy: air trapped in system.
- Pedal sinks slowly: external leakage from hydraulic system. Faulty master cylinder seals.
- Brakes binding: drum brakes over-adjusted. Wheel cylinder piston seized. Caliper piston seized.

Handbrake

The parking brake or handbrake is a separate braking system from the foot-brake. It is usually mounted on the floor of the car and is connected by cable to the two rear wheels. Care should be taken when applying the brake to squeeze the pawl, thus saving unnecessary wear and tear on the ratchet.

Faults

- Excess travel: cable or rear brakes need adjustment. Worn handbrake mechanism.
- Rear brakes binding: seized handbrake mechanism.

Anti-lock braking system (ABS)

Increasingly being fitted as standard equipment, these systems provide near optimum braking under most prevailing road conditions. When braking on wet or icy roads, the system virtually eliminates the tendency for wheels to lock up. This means that braking efficiency is used to the maximum, so that very short braking distances can be achieved (it does not make the brakes more efficient). By preventing the wheels from locking, ABS also assists directional control during braking when cornering.

To prevent the wheel from locking, the system provides pressure modulation in the braking circuits. Sensors fitted to each wheel monitor the rotational speeds of the wheels and are able to detect when there is a risk of wheel locking. Solenoid valves are positioned in the brake circuits to each wheel, and these valves are incorporated in a modulator assembly, which is controlled by an electronic control unit (ECU). The ECU controls modulation of the braking effort applied to each wheel, according to the information supplied by the wheel sensors.

Should a fault develop in the system, a self-diagnostic facility is incorporated in the ECU, which can be used in conjunction with special diagnostic equipment that is available to a dealer, to determine the nature of the fault.

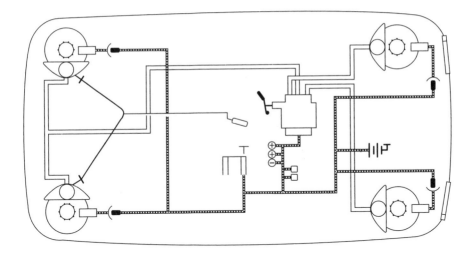

Figure 7.10   Anti-lock braking system

The braking system components used with ABS are similar to those used on models with a conventional braking system. Although ABS provides a major contribution to vehicle safety and driver control, it does not remove the need for responsible driving and for an awareness of road and traffic conditions.

Rack and pinion steering gear

Steering

The steering system is used to control the direction of the vehicle. It is designed to control the front wheels over all types of road conditions, through turns and at different speeds. It comprises a linkage system that is attached to the front wheels, the steering wheel and the steering gear. Manual and power steering units are used.

'Rack and pinion' steering is the most popular system used on front-wheel drive cars. The system is used in conjunction with MacPherson strut suspension, which gives more engine compartment room for transverse-mounted engines. Rack and pinion steering consists of a flat gear (the rack) and a mating gear (the pinion). When the steering wheel and shaft turn, the pinion meshes with the teeth on the rack. This causes the rack to move left or right in the housing. This motion moves the remaining steering linkage to turn the front wheels. The system is very practical for small cars that require lighter steering capacity. It is a direct steering unit that is more positive in motion (less lost motion) than steering box/steering linkage systems.

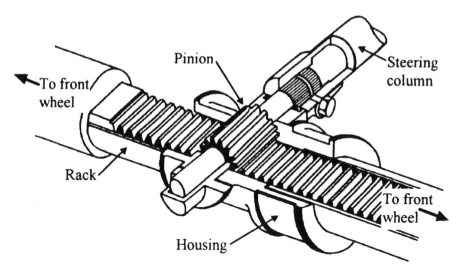

Figure 7.11   Rack and pinion steering gear

Suspension

The suspension system of a car is used to support its weight during varying road conditions. The suspension system is made up of several subsystems. These include the front and rear suspension assemblies and the shock absorbers. All these systems must work together in order to control three different types of body movement – bounce, roll and pitch. *Bounce* occurs when a car hits a bump or dip in the road. *Roll* is produced when cornering, particularly at speed, when centrifugal force causes the car to lean away from the centre of the curve – that is, the car leans to the left when you are trying to steer to the right. In extreme cases, a car will roll over. *Pitch* is the reaction of the rear wheels following the front wheels over a bump. As the front of the car rises, the rear dips; as the rear wheels strike the bump, the front of the car drops, causing a forward and backward movement, similar to a ship pitching in and out of waves.

The suspension assemblies incorporate springs that are interposed between the wheels and the body so that the body is partially isolated from the axles. When a vehicle rides over rough ground, the wheels rise as they roll over the bump and deflect the springs. The energy created as a result of the movement is momentarily stored in the spring and is then released as the spring returns to its original length (rebound). Various types of spring can be utilized – for example, leaf, coil or helical, torsion bar and gas springs.

The suspension design of most modern cars provides for the inclusion of independent front- and rear-wheel suspension systems. These ensure optimum handling and ride comfort.

Several car manufacturers now offer 'active' ride control systems that allow the driver to switch between 'normal' and 'sport' suspension settings. One such system uses a hydro-pneumatic springing medium that is controlled electroni-cally via sensors. The 'normal' setting provides maximum comfort and adapts automatically to driving and road conditions. The 'sport' setting provides a stiffer suspension that is more suited to a sporting driving style.

Shock absorbers

Shock absorbers (dampers) are fitted between the car's body and axle in order to prevent excessive rolling and bouncing of the body during motion. They also minimize unwanted up and down movement of the wheel and axle when the car negotiates uneven road surfaces.

One shock absorber is used on each wheel. Each shock absorber must control one wheel and axle motion. The springs support the body, but the shock absorbers work with the springs to control movements of the car body. The

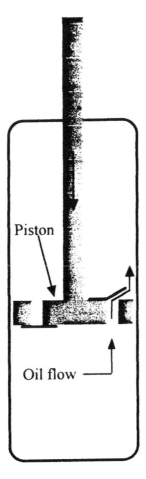

Figure 7.12 Shock absorbers

construction of a basic shock absorber consists of an internal piston contained within an oil-filled cylinder. The piston moves with the axle, and the resistance to movement produced by forcing the oil through small valves in the piston restricts quick action, preventing a continual bouncing movement.

Faults

- Hard ride: tyres over-inflated. Stiff operation of suspension struts. Excess friction in leaf springs.
- Uneven trim: road spring on front, rear or on one side settled (weak). Broken leaf (if the main leaf is broken, the whole axle unit is partially disconnected from the body). The car should not be driven. Hydrogas suspension loss of fluid pressure, causing collapse of the suspension on either side.
- Noisy operation: worn suspension pivots or mountings. Loose mountings. Defective shock absorbers.
- Poor vehicle handling: worn out or defective shock absorbers. Weak road springs. Worn suspension ball joints. Loose clamping (U) bolts (these clamp the springs to the axle).

Tyres

Basically, there are two types of tyre in use on the modern car – cross ply and radial ply. It is important that a driving instructor understands the difference and value of each.

Modern cross-ply tyres have casings made from plies of rayon, polyester or nylon, laid at opposing angles to each other and at approximately 40 degrees to the circumference of the tyre. They are wrapped around two steel wire hoops or beads that prevent the tyre from stretching and parting from the wheel. The tyre

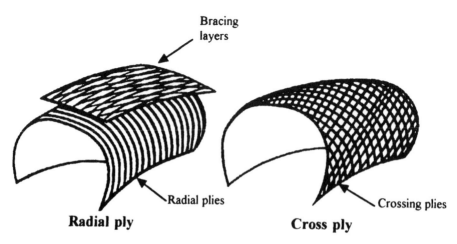

Figure 7.13 Radial and cross-ply tyres

tread, which is moulded to the casing, is manufactured mainly from a blend of synthetic rubbers in order to provide a good road grip, especially in wet weather.

The construction of the radial-ply tyre reduces cornering wear and considerably increases the overall life of the tyre, but this is usually at the expense of a slightly harder ride at lower speeds. It gives greater high-speed cornering grip than a cross-ply of equivalent size. The cords in the plies run from bead to bead across the crown at right angles, not diagonally as in the cross-ply tyre. This gives great pliability and comfort, but little or no directional stability. Stability comes from the tread-bracing layers, a belt of cords running round the circumference of the tyre beneath the tread. These cords are usually spun from rayon textile or fine steel wire, and are flexible but do not lose their tautness. This firmly restricts any lateral stretching of the tread.

Most cars today are fitted with tubeless tyres; these are basically the same as tubed tyres but are made airtight by having a soft rubber lining to the casing, thus dispensing with the need for an inner tube. The main advantage of tubeless tyres is that they are less liable to deflate suddenly when punctured, and can be driven without an appreciable loss of air when penetrated by small flints or nails. Statistics show that the risk of tyre failure with a tubed tyre is about three-and-a-half times greater than with a tubeless tyre.

You should ensure that your tyres meet the legal requirements. They should have a tread depth of 1.6 mm throughout the central three-quarters of the breadth of the tyre and around the entire outer circumference.

You should not have a mixture of cross-ply and radial tyres as they each have completely different road-holding characteristics.

VEHICLE SAFETY CHECKS

To do the job of driving instruction efficiently, the instructor should not be worrying about the condition of the driving school car. Both instructor and pupil must have confidence in the knowledge that the car is in a sound condition, both mechanically and bodily. Regular servicing and preventive maintenance are both of the utmost importance to an instructor. It is false economy to skimp on car maintenance. Unplanned time off the road causes loss of income as well as the cost of the repair. Cancelling and rebooking lessons causes problems that should not arise if the car is serviced regularly.

Driving test examiners can refuse to conduct a test in a car that their pre-test visual check shows to be in an unroadworthy condition.

Listed below are examples of the regular car checks and services that should be carried out.

Daily checks

Windows and mirrors should be kept clean, and dangling mascots, badges or self-adhesive 'L' plates should not impair the driver's vision. When cleaning, use

Faults

- Over-inflation: causes excessive wear along the centre of the tread.

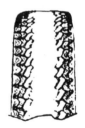

- Under-inflation: causes excessive wear around the outer edges of the tread.

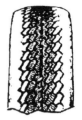

- Serious structural damage: a break or cut in the tyre fabric that is deep enough to reach the body cords. Any exposed portion of ply or cord. Any lump or bulge caused by separation of the tyre structure. These faults usually result from heavy contact with the kerb or a foreign body.

- Incorrect wheel alignment: causes wear (feathering) on either the inner or outer edge of the tread.

- Spot wear: unbalanced tyres will cause a steering wheel shimmy, and rapid and uneven tyre wear. Wear in steering and/or suspension components may also promote excessive tyre wear.

Figure 7.14 Tyre faults

a solvent to remove any windscreen smears, but avoid damaging the rear window heating element with any abrasive cleaner. Operation of the lights should be checked each day, with particular attention to the brake lights.

Carry spare bulbs in the car in case of sudden failure. In order to save time in the event of bulb failure, an instructor should consult the manufacturer's manual for instructions on bulb replacement.

There should also be a daily visual check of the car tyres for any cuts or bulges, stones in the tread and so on. Checking the operation of the horn, indicator, screen washers and wipers should be part of an instructor's daily routine.

Weekly checks

Engine oil level

Make sure that the car is standing on level ground. Remove the dipstick, which is usually situated halfway down one side of the engine, and clean it on a piece of cloth or kitchen paper. Replace it in the dipstick hole, then remove it again and look for the oil mark. The oil level should be between the high (maximum) and the low (minimum) marks. If the oil is near or below the low mark, up to a litre of fresh oil will be needed to top up to the high mark. Care must be taken not to overfill as this could lead to excessive oil pressure in the engine and cause leaks or damage.

Oil leaks

Oil leaks can be detected quite easily by having a quick look round the engine, gearbox, rear axle and the insides of the wheels. Common places for leaks are drain plugs, oil filters, valve cover gasket or any oil or brake pipe. If the car has a regular overnight parking spot, look for drops of oil on the ground. Any leak inside the wheels could mean a faulty brake cylinder, which must receive immediate expert attention.

Cooling system

While the engine is cold, remove the pressure cap from the radiator header/ expansion tank. Check the coolant level and top up as necessary with a mixture of water and antifreeze of the appropriate type and strength. If the water level falls regularly, check for leaks or suspect engine overheating which may require expert attention. Never remove the radiator cap when the engine is hot. High pressure is built up inside the radiator when the engine is running. The steam released when the cap is removed can cause serious scalding.

Brake and clutch fluid levels

Consult the manufacturer's manual for advice on the fluid levels. When topping up brake or clutch reservoirs, always use new fluid. Reusing old brake fluid may damage the brake or clutch systems. Remember that if frequent topping up is required, the fluid must be escaping somewhere. What may be a slight leak one day could be a major loss the next. Never make do with brakes: any suspected fault should receive expert attention without delay.

Windscreen/rear screen washers and fluid levels

It is a legal requirement for screen washers to be in working order and topped up with water. Add a screen washer solvent to the container, as water alone is insufficient to clear the combinations of road grit, exhaust fumes and the like that congeal on the windscreen. In winter add a proprietary winter screen wash to prevent the system freezing up. Do not add antifreeze as this could damage or discolour the paintwork.

Windscreen wipers

Clean the wiper blade rubbers. Dirt and grit stuck on the rubbers could scratch the glass. Renew blades if there is any sign of perishing or brittleness.

Tyre pressures

Check the tyre pressures, including the spare, at least once a week. Don't forget to replace the valve dust-cap. Remove any flints caught in the tread and inspect the sidewalls for any cuts or bulges. Driving school cars are susceptible to damaged tyre walls as a result of kerbing. Any sign of uneven tread wear should be reported and rectified as soon as possible.

Lights

Check the operation of all lights, including indicator flashers and brake lights.

Battery

Check the electrolite level. Top up if necessary, using only distilled water, to about 6 mm above the electrode plates.

Drive belt

Check the tension, looking for cuts and fraying. A loose drive belt can affect the operation of the alternator, which may lead to undercharging of the battery. A fan belt is a fairly simple item to replace if it is unserviceable.

Periodic checks

Driving instructors should be able to carry out their own daily and weekly vehicle checks. Some instructors may have sufficient mechanical knowledge and experience to tackle the larger services that must be made. It is worth considering further study in this field – for example at evening classes or by home study.

Car manufacturers produce handbooks with service recommendations and do-it-yourself advice. There are many good, clear textbooks on this subject, including the *Haynes Glovebox Guide: Your car*. The oil companies, like Mobil, Castrol, Shell and BP, produce very good, sound manuals explaining car facts and car care. Vehicle maintenance record sheets are also available and very valuable. The majority of instructors, however, will go to a garage or a professional mechanic. Nevertheless, it is recommended that you should have some knowledge of the work that must be covered by periodic servicing.

Seasonal checks

At the first sign of winter get the strength of the antifreeze checked with a hydrometer at a garage. Top up as necessary. If the radiator requires topping up during the winter, use an antifreeze mixture. In modern cars it is advisable to leave the antifreeze in all year round as it contains an anti-corrosive additive to prevent rusting in the system. A good-quality antifreeze will keep its strength for about two years, after which the cooling system should be drained, flushed and refilled, using the manufacturer's recommended amount of antifreeze.

In the springtime the car should be thoroughly hosed underneath to remove all the corrosive salt and sand that has accumulated from the gritted roads.

VEHICLE CONTROLS AND OPERATION

There are three major operating systems in a motor car:

- *The main controls:* these enable the driver to start and stop the engine and to control the speed, position and direction of the vehicle.
- *Driving aids:* these assist the driver to see, to be seen by, and to communicate with other road users.
- *Instrumentation:* this provides the driver with information about the vehicle, how it is functioning and the speed at which it is travelling.

The main controls

The *steering* provides a means of controlling and changing the direction of the vehicle. To operate the steering, keep both hands on the wheel as much as possible and in particular at high speeds, when braking and also cornering. Position the hands at about the 'ten to two' or 'a quarter to three' position. Try to use the 'pull–push' method of steering outlined in *The Official DSA Guide to Driving: The essential skills*, but directional control and accuracy of the steering is the most important objective. Avoid sudden, jerky movements on the wheel and hold it firmly, but do not grip too tightly. Remember that when cornering, the rear wheels cut into a turn.

The *handbrake* secures the car when it is parked or stationary for more than a short pause. The handbrake should be used only when the car is stationary, except in an emergency, such as failure of the footbrake system. The ratchet release button should be operated before releasing or applying the handbrake, which is used when parking and also to provide a greater degree of safety and control for some temporary stops. Check that the handbrake is on after entering the vehicle, before starting the engine and particularly before leaving the vehicle.

The *gear lever* provides a permanent means of disconnecting the engine from the driving wheels (neutral). It also provides a selection of different ratios to allow the optimum and most economical engine speeds to be maintained at all road speeds and load requirements. The gears also provide a means of driving the vehicle backwards. Avoid looking at the gear lever when changing. Use a 'cupped' hand on the gear lever and do not use excessive force when moving the gears.

First gear: the most powerful, but slowest. Used for moving off, low-speed clutch control and for manoeuvring.

Second gear: also powerful, but faster than the first gear. Useful for rapid acceleration and for driving at slower speeds through some hazards.

Third gear: a faster gear, used for acceleration from over 15 mph. Used for driving through some hazards.

Fourth gear: the most economical gear, with insufficient power for speeds of much lower than 25 mph. Used to provide progressive acceleration from about 25–30 mph and for cruising at constant speeds.

Fifth gear: used as an aid for cruising at sustained higher speeds.

The *clutch* temporarily disconnects the engine from the gearbox/driving wheels to facilitate changing gear and stopping. It provides the means to engage the power source (engine) smoothly and progressively to the load (the road wheels). It is operated by the left foot and is used for moving off, low-speed control, changing gear and stopping. Clutch control involves finding and holding the clutch plates at the first point of contact, the bottom of which is called the 'holding point' and the top the 'driving point'. The full range is called the 'biting range'. Slipping the clutch is an important part of low-speed control. Excessive clutch slip over prolonged periods, however, causes undue wear and should be avoided. Also, try not to rest your weight on the pedal when driving ('riding the clutch').

The *accelerator* (often called the 'gas') plays a major role in the regulation of vehicle speed. It works by the pedal operating a petrol/air valve, which in turn regulates the power and speed of the engine. The accelerator is operated by the right foot. Any pedal movement and changes in pressure should be progressive. The response to pedal movement is more pronounced in the low gears.

The *footbrake* also plays a major role in the regulation of the vehicle's speed. The footbrake pedal is operated by the right foot. It operates a hydraulic system that presses high friction material against a rotating wheel disc or drum (similar in principle to a bicycle brake). Any changes in pressure should be progressive. The response to pressure changes on the pedal is immediate. Pressure can be varied between the barely perceptible up to the point at which the wheels lock. Braking pressure on bends and corners should be minimized or avoided. Use of the brake should be preceded by mirror checks. When the brake is applied, warning lights on the rear of the vehicle are automatically activated.

The starter controls

Ignition switch key: a safety and anti-theft device. This activates the engine electrical circuits essential to its operation. It includes an engine cutout system when it is switched off. It also activates a number of warning and other electrical circuits. When the key is removed this usually activates a steering lock.

The *starter* activates the engine via the starter motor. It is usually incorporated into the ignition switch as the final position to which the key is turned. The starter motor should not normally be activated for periods in excess of five to eight seconds. The key should be released as soon as the engine fires. (Some vehicles are fitted with a protection device that will only allow one operation of the starter motor without switching the ignition off.) Before activating the starter circuits, the normal safety checks should be made; that is, handbrake on and gear level in neutral.

The *choke* is used for starting cold engines and during a preliminary 'warm-up' period. To operate, pull out fully, operate the starter and switch the engine on. Push the choke back halfway after the first few seconds. Drive off when safe. Return choke fully after the initial 'warm-up' period. There are three main factors that influence the initial warm-up period: the temperature of the engine, the external air temperature and the maintenance of the engine. On a cold winter morning the maximum warm-up period should normally be no more than four or five minutes. In warm weather this may be only a few seconds. Most vehicles nowadays have an automatic choke. For details refer to the manufacturer's handbook.

Driving aids

Mirrors: interior and exterior mirrors should be clean and adjusted so as to maximize visibility to the rear and minimize unnatural or unnecessary head movements. Even with the most desirable combination of a large interior and two door-mounted exterior mirrors, there will still be areas to the rear and sides of the car not covered by the mirrors' 'fields of vision'. Before making certain types of manoeuvre these 'blind spots' need to be checked; for example, before moving away from the kerb.

The mirrors should be used at frequent intervals on a continuous and systematic basis to take full advantage of the views afforded by side mirrors. They should be used particularly before any manoeuvre involving a change in speed or direction; and specifically well before moving off, signalling, changing lane or direction, stopping and overtaking.

Excessively long or staring looks at the mirror should be avoided, as these are likely to cause problems with both the steering and forward planning. Sensible use of the mirrors involves demonstrating an awareness and sympathy for the speed, distance, actions and movement of other road users.

Direction indicators play an important part in the system of communication between road users. They are operated by the fingertips, but without losing total hand contact with the steering wheel. They are frequently required for moving off, stopping, moving to the left or right, and turning to the left or right at junctions. Generally they should be used in good time, but some traffic situations require special consideration in the timing of them. They must be correct for the situation and cancelled after use. (Automatic self-cancelling mechanisms are not infallible and it is the driver's overall responsibility to reapply prematurely cancelled signals and to ensure that indicators are switched off after a manoeuvre is completed.)

Windscreen, windows, wipers, washers, demisters, defrosters and rear screen heaters all help to maintain good all-round visibility for the driver. The controls vary from car to car (consult the manufacturer's handbook). Avoid using windscreen wipers on dry glass and wiping the insides of windows with bare hands (rings can scratch!). Avoid leaving rear screen heaters on continually when not required. Keep wipers in good condition and the washer bottle topped up with water/ solvent. Keep windows clean at all times. Plenty of fresh air inside the car will help to prevent windows misting up. Familiarize yourself with these controls while the vehicle is stationary.

Lights help the driver to see and be seen by other road users. Controls vary considerably from car to car (consult the manufacturer's handbook). Sidelights must be used when parked outside a 30 mph limit or in a specified parking area that is within 10 metres of a road junction at night. Dipped headlights should be used where visibility is reduced by fog, snow or other extreme conditions. High-density rear fog lamps should be used in adverse weather conditions when the driver of a following car might not otherwise see your car. Front fog lights should only be used when visibility is reduced to below 100 metres.

Horn and flashing headlights warn and inform other road users of your presence. Controls vary from car to car (consult the manufacturer's handbook). Use of the horn is not permitted between 11.30 pm and 7.00 am in a built-up area or when stationary (except where there is danger from another moving vehicle). It should be used sensibly to warn others and not as a rebuke. Try to avoid long 'blasts' of the horn in close proximity to pedestrians, but use longer blasts for drivers in motor vehicles. On fast roads, such as motorways, headlamps may be more effective than the horn.

Instrumentation

This group of controls, dials and displays provides the driver with the necessary information on how the vehicle is performing and functioning. Information displays are becoming increasingly more comprehensive. Most of the information is of great assistance to the driver, but some available equipment has yet to be proved useful and may even be found to be counter-productive by causing unnecessary distractions to the driver. This section deals with the essential information that can be justified as necessary to the safe and sympathetic use of a motor car.

Speedometer. This is legally required to be in working order and should be accurate to an error of no more than 10 per cent. It is an offence to make the mileage recorder read fewer miles than the car has actually travelled. Speedometers are usually marked in graduated scales showing both miles and kilometres per hour. They sometimes incorporate a trip recorder switch that can be set and used to record journey mileages or to calculate fuel consumption. Avoid long staring looks at the speedometer when checking your speed, but where necessary take frequent glances to establish legal status concerning speed limits.

Fuel gauge. Check the fuel level at the start of a journey, remembering some gauges may not be fully reliable. Avoid running on less than a quarter tank of fuel if possible. Ensure that, when topping up the tank, only the correct type of fuel is used. Some vehicles are fitted with dual tanks or reserve systems that include 'changeover' switches.

Vehicles fitted with fuel injection systems normally operate more efficiently and return improved performance.

Unleaded fuel causes less pollution, and is generally cheaper than leaded, but consumption can be slightly higher. Petrol engined vehicles can be converted to run on liquid petroleum gas, which requires the fitting of special tanks. When converted, these can run on either petrol or gas. Where a diesel engine is fitted, do not put petrol into the tank, or allow the fuel to run dry, or it may not restart without professional assistance.

If a spare can of fuel is kept for emergencies, it must be suitably marked and have no leaks.

Engine temperature gauge. An internal combustion engine produces mechanical power from controlled explosions (rapid expansion of burning gases) inside the engine cylinders. At precisely the correct time, vaporized petrol gases are ignited by the spark plugs. The force of these expanding gases pushes pistons up and down inside the cylinders. There are usually four of these cylinders, each working in rapid succession and adding continuously to the mechanical power produced by the others.

At a speed of only 30 mph these controlled explosions can be occurring 60 times every second. This generates a tremendous amount of heat which, if allowed to build up inside the engine, would melt the pistons and heat other moving parts until they became one solid mass of scrap metal. These high temperatures require an efficient cooling system if the engine is to operate satisfactorily. Most engines are cooled by water. This is pumped through special channels cut into the engine block to carry the heat away to the radiator, where it is then cooled before recirculation.

The driver requires confirmation that this system is functioning normally. The temperature gauge that indicates the normal operating range of temperature provides this. This may sometimes incorporate a separate warning light to provide more visual impact for the driver if the system overheats.

Where an excessive temperature is indicated, the driver should stop and either obtain assistance or rectify the problem before continuing with the journey. The most common causes of overheating are:

- *Broken fan belt:* this normally operates the radiator fan and water pump.
- *Lack of coolant:* water can boil and leak away. Unless the level is checked regularly it may become critical to the cooling system. Also check hoses for leaks and wear.
- *Blocked radiator:* water freezes and will block the radiator with ice during the winter months unless an antifreeze solution is present in the cooling system. Ice also expands and can crack the engine cylinder block during severe conditions. During the normal course of running, lime scale from hard water sometimes builds up inside the radiator and blocks the water channels.

Oil pressure gauge. Without lubrication, an engine can tear itself apart within minutes of driving off. Lubricating oil is forced, under high pressure, along a series of pipes and oilways to all the moving parts. Under extreme pressure, the oil is squeezed between the moving metal-to-metal parts, preventing this damaging contact.

An oil pressure failure light and/or an oil pressure gauge provide information about oil pressure. In the event of a drop in oil pressure, pull up as soon as possible and when safe, to check it. Switch off the engine. Obtain assistance or rectify the problem before continuing with the journey.

Before starting an engine, check that the oil pressure warning system is operational. This can be done by switching on the ignition and ensuring the oil pressure warning light activates. The light should switch off within two or three seconds of starting the engine. Oil pressure gauges give a more precise indication of oil pressure when the engine is running, and sometimes help to pinpoint a problem before it reaches a critical level.

Low oil pressure can be caused by *lack of oil, burst oil pipes, inoperative pump*, or a *very worn engine*. Check oil levels regularly, and look for leaks under the car first thing in the morning. Remember too, most cars will use some oil and require topping up between normal servicing.

Brake system malfunction. Vehicles are now being fitted with various different kinds of brake warning systems. These can inform the driver of low fluid levels in the system, of uneven pressure in dual-lined braking systems and of worn brake pads. Check these with the vehicle handbook and remember, if the warning systems activate, *stop immediately and obtain assistance.*

Handbrake and choke warning lights. These indicate that the controls are on and in an operating condition. They are intended as a gentle reminder.

Ignition warning light. The ignition warning light is activated when the engine electrical circuits are switched on. Before starting the engine, the system should be checked. This can be done by ensuring that the ignition warning light is illuminated when the circuits are switched on and before the starter motor is activated. As soon as the engine starts, the alternator should generate its own electrical supply and the light should switch off.

The alternator is operated by the fan belt. If this fails, the alternator will cease to provide the electrical requirements for the engine and the vehicle will then be running on battery power alone. In this condition the ignition warning light should activate.

A broken fan belt will also cause the engine to overheat (see 'The cooling system' on pages 209 to 210). Other causes of the ignition light switching on are *loose wires, burnt out brushes or diodes on the alternator,* and/or *malfunctions in the voltage regulator.* This does not normally cause any lasting or serious damage to the vehicle, but the journey time will be limited by battery power alone. However, there are safety factors that must be taken into account particularly at night and in cold or wet conditions.

Door and seat belt warning/reminders. Visual/audible warning systems are sometimes fitted to remind the driver that doors are not properly closed and/or the seat belt is not fastened.

Main beam/sidelights/high-intensity rear lights. Warning systems are fitted to remind drivers when these aids are operating.

Rear screen heater. A warning system usually reminds the driver that the screen heater is on. Rear screen heaters consume a fairly large amount of electrical power and can cause a heavy drain on the battery during prolonged periods at tickover speeds.

Direction indicators and hazard flashers. These are usually fitted with both visual and audible reminders when the aids are in the operating mode. Hazard flashers should not be used on a moving vehicle.

Automatic transmission

A vehicle fitted with automatic transmission should be a safer car to drive than one with manual change, for the following reasons:

- Both hands are free for the steering of the vehicle most of the time.
- Driving an automatic is less tiring, particularly in heavy and slow-moving traffic.
- Because of the human error factor in driving, to which we are all susceptible, automatic transmission reduces the chances of making an error with a gear or the clutch.

Driving a car with automatic transmission

One of the problems experienced by people wanting to learn on automatics is that there are not widespread facilities available for tuition, with the result that they are not used to their full potential. Driven correctly, automatic cars provide drivers with as much control over the gears as manual-change vehicles. There are certain aspects of driving automatics, however, which the instructor must remember when giving instruction:

- The *handbrake* is generally needed more often and applied more firmly. This is because automatic transmission systems are designed so that the car 'creeps' slowly at tickover speeds on level ground.
- The *footbrake* should be firmly applied before starting some variomatic transmissions, fitted for example to Volvo cars, where the manufacturer recommends that they should be started in gear. This is particularly true when they are 'on choke'. The footbrake should be firmly applied on other makes of automatic transmissions when they are 'on choke' and before drive or reverse gears are selected.
- The *accelerator* must not be depressed when engaging drive or reverse gears.
- *Right foot only!* It is advisable to use the right foot only for both the footbrake and accelerator. There may be some occasions where it is advantageous to use the left foot for the brake, however – in some low-speed manoeuvring exercises, particularly if the transmission is not very progressive at low speeds.

Disabled drivers

Where the driver has a right-leg disability, the left foot may be used for both accelerator and brake, but the vehicle may need to be suitably converted. An automatic gearbox is a tremendous help to disabled clients and older people – or in fact anyone finding it difficult to drive a manual gear-change car.

The driving test

Someone who passes the driving test in a car with automatic transmission is issued with a driving licence only for that vehicle category.

Types of automatic transmission

Fully automatic with gear hold position: these have selector positions for forward and reverse with a gear hold for low-speed driving and/or driving downhill.

Variomatic transmission: this type of transmission system is fitted with a hold device that offers a greater degree of engine braking on downhill gradients.

Multi-hold systems: these can retain any particular gear, and are fitted to many makes of vehicle from a Mini to a Rolls-Royce.

Semi-automatic: this generally means the vehicle is fitted with a normal gearbox and clutch but without the clutch pedal. The clutch is engaged or disengaged by the movement of the hand on the gear lever.

Pre-selector systems: on these the gear is pre-selected before it is required. The gear is later engaged by means of a foot pedal in place of the clutch.

Kick down: this is a mechanism fitted to many automatics whereby it is possible to change down quickly to a lower gear ratio, usually for overtaking. A sharp depression of the accelerator pedal past the full throttle opening will override the normal gear control system.

Using the accelerator: with manual transmission any fidgeting on and erratic or excessive use of the accelerator burns fuel wastefully in any car, but in an automatic it will lead to changing up and down gears according to changes in this pressure. This causes unnecessary wear and tear on the mechanisms involved, and should be avoided.

VEHICLE REGULATIONS

There are many laws that specify the way in which cars are to be manufactured, what equipment they must have and the condition of vehicles when used on the roads. Most of these are contained in the Motor Vehicles (Construction and Use) Regulations. Some of the rules apply only to cars first registered after a specified date; older vehicles may therefore not have to include some of the items of equipment mentioned.

Some of the basic rules apply to vehicles of any age. These include the strict rules relating to brakes and steering gear – each part of the braking system and all steering gear must be maintained in good and efficient working order at all times when the vehicle is being used on the road.

The car must be roadworthy. It is sometimes thought the MOT test certificate is a certificate of roadworthiness, but this is not so. The test system looks at the condition of certain main components, but does not necessarily consider the overall roadworthiness of the car.

The regulations contain rules about the dimensions of cars, and about the maximum overhang. The car must have wings or mudguards. The speedometer must work to within an accuracy of plus or minus 10 per cent. Driving mirrors must be fitted, and other compulsory items include safety glass, windscreen wipers, horn, silencer, seat belts and direction indicators.

Lighting

The regulations require that lights and reflectors be kept clean and in good working order. They must be maintained so that the vehicle may be driven during the hours of darkness without contravening the regulations. This chapter includes only a summary of the main requirements, as the original equipment fitted to a modern vehicle will usually comply with the specifications.

Headlamps must be permanently fitted and must have a minimum rating of 30 watts, displaying a white or yellow beam. The lamps must be matched and the beam must be capable of being deflected to the near side so as not to dazzle oncoming traffic.

Sidelamps must be fitted at the front of the vehicle. The two lamps must have a maximum power of 7 watts each (or they may be diffused).

Rear lamps must be visible from a reasonable distance to the rear of the car. There must be at least two lamps, each with a minimum power of 5 watts. Reflectors are also required.

Rear number plate lamp: the plate must be illuminated so that the letters and figures are easily legible from a distance of 60 feet.

Direction indicators on cars registered after 1965 must be the amber flashing type. On older cars they may be either flashing or semaphore arm, and may be white at the front and red at the rear. Flashing indicators must wink at the rate of 60 to 120 flashes a minute. The indicators on both sides of the car must be operated by the same switch, and there must be a warning light or audible warning inside the car to show that the indicators are working.

Reversing lamps may be fitted using one or two lamps of not more than 24 watts each. The beam produced must not dazzle anyone 25 feet away at an eye level of 3½ feet from the ground, and must only be used when the car is reversing. The lights may be operated automatically when reverse gear is selected, or may have a separate switch that includes a warning light.

Fog lamps are to be used as two front fog lamps (or one fog lamp and one headlamp) in darkness and fog, falling snow or conditions of poor visibility. The lights must be placed symmetrically and must be placed more than two feet from the ground unless they are to be used only in fog and falling snow.

Rear fog lamps are obligatory on cars first used on or after 1 April 1980. If one lamp is fitted it must be positioned on the offside of the car, and if two are fitted they must be symmetrical. Rear fog lamps may only be used during adverse weather conditions and when the vehicle is in motion, or during an enforced stoppage.

Stop lamps are compulsory on cars built since 1971. The lamps must be matched and placed symmetrically at the rear of the car. They must operate automatically when the footbrakes are applied, and show a steady red light visible from the rear.

During the hours of darkness a vehicle must display:

- two headlamps (when the vehicle is driven on unlit roads);
- two side lamps;
- two rear lamps;
- two red rear reflectors;
- one or two rear fog lamps (for vehicles first used after 1 April 1980).

Headlamps must be used when the vehicle is being driven on unlit roads (that is, roads where there are no street lights or where the street lamps are not at regular intervals). Headlamps must be switched off when the vehicle is stationary (except traffic stops). During daylight hours headlamps must be used when travelling in conditions of poor visibility such as fog, smoke, heavy rain, spray or snow. If matching fog or spotlights are fitted, these may be used in the place of headlights.

Parking lights at night: a car or light goods vehicle may park at night without lights if the following conditions apply:

- The vehicle is parked on a road with a speed limit not exceeding 30 mph.
- No part of the vehicle is within 10 metres of a junction.
- The vehicle is parked with its nearside close to, and parallel with, the kerb, except in a one-way street.

The lighting regulations also permit a vehicle to park without lights in a recognized parking area, and within the confines of an area outlined by lamps or traffic signs. If these conditions are not met, lights must be shown (that is, side and rear lights).

Dim-dip lights: new vehicles registered from 1 April 1987 must be fitted with a dim-dip device which causes 10 or 15 per cent of the dipped beam intensity to show when the engine is running (or the ignition is switched on) and the sidelights are on.

Hazard warning lights may be used only when the vehicle is stationary for the purpose of warning other road users that the vehicle is temporarily causing an obstruction, or to warn following drivers on a motorway that there is a hazard ahead.

Parking

Common law states that a public highway is specifically for the free passage of the general public and vehicles, and there is no legal right to park on the road except in specially designated parking places or with the express permission of a police officer or traffic warden. There is no legal right even to park outside your own home. A stationary vehicle in the road or on the grass verge is technically an obstruction, even where no other road user is inconvenienced.

It is a more serious offence to park a vehicle in a position where it might constitute a danger to others (see the *Highway Code* for examples of what might be considered dangerous parking). Parking within the zigzag lines at a pedestrian crossing is an offence punishable by an endorsement. It is illegal to park on an urban clearway at the stipulated times, and on a rural clearway and motorway at any time.

Parking in controlled zones

A controlled parking zone is indicated by waiting restriction signs situated on all entrances, and is marked with yellow lines along the kerb. Restriction times vary from town to town and care should be taken always to read the signs. Parking meter zones are marked with signs 'Meter zone' and 'Zone ends'. It is an offence to park at a meter without paying or to overstay the time paid for, or to feed the meter on return for an extended period.

Use of horn and flashing headlamps

Motor vehicles must be fitted with an instrument capable of giving audible warnings of approach. The tone of the horn must be continuous and uniform, with the exception of emergency service vehicles, which may use a two-tone horn, siren or bell. Some goods vehicles are permitted to use an instrument to announce goods for sale, but the vehicle must also carry the standard audible warning device.

The horn should be regarded as a warning instrument. It should not be used in order to assert a right of way, and should not be used aggressively. There are some legal responsibilities regarding the use of the horn. It must not be used when the vehicle is stationary on the road, except to avoid danger due to another vehicle moving, and may not be used in a built-up area between the hours of 11.30 pm and 7.00 am.

The flashing of headlamps has the same meaning as the horn. It is an indication of your presence to other road users. The lamps should not be used to tell other people what you intend to do, or to tell them what to do. Flashing headlamps can be useful in certain driving conditions – high-speed roads and where there is a high level of noise – but should not be regarded as an indication of another driver's intentions. The signal may be directed not to you but to someone else.

Noise and smoke

There are very detailed rules regarding the maximum number of decibels that may be emitted from a car, and it is an offence to drive a car which does not conform to those rules, or to cause a nuisance by making unnecessary noise. It is also an offence to use a motor vehicle that produces smoke, vapour or sparks which may damage or affect other road users and property. Smoke that affects the visibility of other road users is regarded as excessive.

Seat belts

The law requires that seat belts are fitted to all the seats of new motor cars, that they should be maintained in good order, and that they conform to the regulations. The use of seat belts may be an important factor in the assessment of compensation by a court. Recent cases have shown a reduction in the amount of compensation awarded to non-users of seat belts.

Front seat belts are compulsory on cars and three-wheeled vehicles made after 30 June 1964 and first registered after 31 December 1964, and on light vans made after 31 August 1966 and first registered on or after 31 March 1967. Rear seat belts must also be used.

The use of seat belts by drivers and passengers is compulsory. The maximum penalty for failing to wear a seat belt is £500. Drivers are not responsible in law for the non-use of belts by adult passengers.

There are several exemptions provided in the regulations. For example you do not have to wear one under the following circumstances:

- When driving and carrying out a manoeuvre which includes reversing.
- If you are the holder of a valid medical exemption certificate.
- When you are making a local delivery or collection round using a specially constructed or adapted vehicle.
- If a seat belt has become defective on a journey, or previously, and arrangements have been made for the belt to be repaired.
- If an inertia reel belt has temporarily locked because the vehicle is on, or has been on, a steep incline. The belt must be put on as soon as the mechanism has unlocked.
- If you are an instructor supervising a learner who is carrying out a manoeuvre including reversing.
- Driving test examiners need not wear a seat belt if they feel that the wearing of a belt would endanger them or someone else.
- When driving a taxi during normal taxi work, so long as the vehicle displays a plate showing it is licensed as a taxi.

- While driving a private hire vehicle displaying a plate showing it is licensed as such, or that it is licensed at the Hackney Carriage rate and while used for that purpose.
- If you are driving or riding a vehicle displaying trade plates and you are looking into or repairing a mechanical fault.

Other exemptions apply to people in special jobs and in certain circumstances, for example the police.

Children under the age of 14 travelling in the rear of cars should be restrained where an approved restraint is available. The essential point is that the seat belt or restraint should be appropriate for the age and weight of the child. The law does not require that all children in the rear of cars should be restrained, only that if an appropriate device is available it should be used. An appropriate child restraint is deemed available if carried in or on the vehicle, where there is space for it to be fitted without the aid of tools. Children can be exempt from the regulations on medical grounds.

Seat belt pre-tensioner

The front seat pre-tensioner seat belt works together with the seat belt retractor. It helps to tighten the seat belt when the vehicle is involved in certain types of frontal collisions. The front seats are fitted with a sensor that, in the event of an accident or rapid deceleration, will activate an explosive device to retract the seat belt, providing greater support for the front seat occupants.

Supplementary restraint system (airbag)

Many vehicles now have airbags for passengers as well as for the driver. The driver's airbag is designed to supplement the accident protection provided by the seat belt and to reduce the possibility of injury to the head or upper torso in the event of a frontal collision. The seat belt should be worn correctly and the driver should be seated a suitable distance from the steering wheel to enable the system to function effectively.

The airbag is located in the centre of the steering wheel, and will deploy under a moderate to severe frontal collision; minor frontal, side, rear impact or the vehicle overturning will not activate the airbag. When the airbag system receives a signal from a G-sensor, the airbag inflates as a result of the combustion of a fuel tablet that generates nitrogen gas. The airbag absorbs the impact of the driver's head on the steering wheel and then deflates at a controlled rate. Since the airbag deploys quickly in order to protect the driver, the force of the airbag deploying can increase the risk of injury if the driver is too close to or against the steering wheel during deployment.

A self-diagnosis system monitors the entire system. If a fault occurs, the self-diagnosis system switches on an SRS function light (red) on the instrument panel

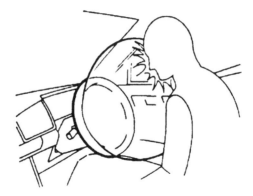

Figure 7.15 The airbag

or steering wheel. It is absolutely forbidden for unauthorized persons to tamper with, or attempt repairs to, the airbag system.

Mirrors

All new motor cars must be fitted with two rear view driving mirrors – one inside, the other mounted on the exterior offside. Most new vehicles now also have a nearside door mirror. Interior mirrors must have protective edges to minimize the risk of injury in the event of an accident. This regulation also applies to the dual mirrors used by driving instructors.

Windscreen washers and wipers

The law requires that all windows are kept clean so that the driver has an unobscured view of the road. This includes keeping the windscreen free of stickers, novelties and mascots. There is a legal requirement for automatic windscreen wipers capable of efficiently cleaning the screen. The driver must have an adequate view of the road in front of the vehicle, and in front of the nearside and offside of the vehicle.

There must also be windscreen washers that work in conjunction with the wipers.

Vehicle defects

Under the Vehicle Defect Rectification Scheme (VDRS) some minor vehicle defects such as lights, wipers, speedometer, silencer may not result in a prosecution if the driver agrees to participate in the following procedure:

1. A VDRS notice is issued.
2. The defect must be rectified within a limited time.
3. The repaired vehicle and the VDRS notice are presented at an MOT garage.

4. The MOT garage issues a certification that the defects have been rectified.
5. The certificate is then sent to a local Central Ticket Office.

Failure to follow the correct procedure will normally result in a prosecution.

DOCUMENTS

Registration document

A motor vehicle must not be used on the road until it has been registered by the Driver and Vehicle Licensing Authority (DVLA). When a vehicle is first registered, a registration document (form V5 – occasionally called a 'log book') is issued in which the appropriate details are listed. The DVLA will also issue a 'registration mark' for use on the number plates of the vehicle.

The document should normally be kept in a secure place away from the vehicle. The registration document is not in itself an indication of the ownership of the vehicle. It is issued to the 'registered keeper' of the vehicle. Should a registration document be accidentally lost, destroyed or defaced, application for a duplicate can be made to the DVLA, Swansea, for a fee of £19. Any alterations to the registered particulars of the vehicle should be notified immediately.

Number plates and registration marks

Number plates are now made up of seven characters. There are three parts to the registration mark, each with a separate meaning.

- The first two letters show where the vehicle was registered – the *local memory tag*. The first letter of the memory tag represents the region. The second letter relates to a local DVLA office.
- The two numbers indicate the age of the vehicle – the *age identifier*. The age identifier changes twice yearly, in March and September. In the example given, '55' represents the six-month period from September 2005 to February 2006. Vehicles registered between 1 March 2006 and 31 August 2006 will have '06' on the plate.
- The last three letters give a unique identity to the vehicle – the *random letters*. The random letters will combine to make each registration mark unique. A new car purchaser may opt to select these three letters. However,

Figure 7.16   The number plate format

the letters 'I' and 'Q' are to be excluded along with any letter combinations that may be considered offensive. The letter 'Z' may be selected.

The complete list of local identifiers is shown as Figure 7.17.

Vehicle excise licence (tax disc)

Application for vehicle excise licences can be made to the DVLA, Swansea, or to the local vehicle licensing office in whose area the vehicle is normally kept. Vehicles can be licenced for either 12 months or 6 months. A variable rate, based on carbon dioxide emissions, is now in place for newer vehicles (see page 242). Renewals can be made online at www.direct.gov.uk/taxdisc, by telephone on 0870 850 4444 or at a DVLA local office and most main post offices.

Duty must be paid if you 'keep' your vehicle on a highway, even if the car is never driven. If you do not tax your vehicle on time you will be liable to a financial penalty, which can rise to £1,000 if the vehicle continues to be driven on the roads. The DVLA now carries out monthly checks on its computer for untaxed vehicles.

You must renew the licence before it expires. A reminder is usually sent by the DVLA when the current licence is due to expire, and this reminder may be used as an application form so long as all the particulars shown on the registration document are still correct. When applying for a new licence, in addition to the registration document and the appropriate fee you must provide a valid certificate of insurance and the Department of Transport test certificate (if the car is more than three years old).

Where the vehicle is kept on a public road, application for renewal of the excise licence must be made before the expiry of the old one. A vehicle must not be used or kept on the road after expiry unless an application was made before the expiry date of the old excise licence. Renewals may be made at main post offices. When the licence disc has been issued, it should be displayed on the nearside of the windscreen so that all particulars are clearly visible from that side of the road.

A licence may be surrendered for any complete months unexpired and must be posted to the DVLA before the beginning of the month for which the refund is being requested. There is no refund for parts of a month.

The keeper named on the Vehicle Registration Certificate – the 'log book' – is now legally responsible for taxing the vehicle until the DVLA has been notified that it is off the road or has been sold, transferred, scrapped or exported. If you are the keeper of a vehicle but are not using or keeping it on public roads, you must make a statutory off road notification (SORN). If you don't, you will receive a penalty of £80.

When you sell, transfer, scrap or export a vehicle, you must notify the DVLA. If you do not, you will continue to be liable for taxing the vehicle and for any other offences committed in the vehicle. When you notify the DVLA it will send confirmation that you are no longer responsible for the vehicle.

Table 7.1 Rates of vehicle duty

Private and light goods vehicles first registered before 1st March 2001:

	12 months	6 months
over 1549 cc	£175	£96.25
not over 1549 cc	£110	£60.50

Private vehicles registered on or after 1st March 2001:

Band	CO2 emission (g/km)	Diesel car TC 49 12 months £	6 months £	Petrol car TC 48 12 months £	6 months £	Alternative fuel car TC 59 12 months £	6 months £
A	Up to 100	0.00	–	0.00	–	0.00	–
B	101–120	50.00	–	40.00	–	30.00	–
C	121–150	110.00	60.50	100.00	55.00	90.00	49.50
D	151–165	135.00	74.25	125.00	68.75	115.00	63.25
E	166–185	160.00	88.00	150.00	82.50	140.00	77.00
F	Over 185	195.00	107.25	190.00	104.50	180.00	99.00

Vehicles registered on or after 23rd March 2006

G	Over 225	215.00	118.25	210.00	115.50	200.00	110.00

MOT test

Most small cars, small goods vehicles and passenger vehicles are subject to an annual test starting three years after the date of the original registration. The car may be taken for test within a month before a certificate is required. If a certificate has expired, the car may be driven to and from a test appointment without a certificate provided that it does not have a serious fault that would contravene the Construction and Use Regulations.

Testing is carried out at designated garages that display the sign of three white triangles on a blue background. The test requirements include brakes, lights, steering, stop lamps, tyres, seat belts (correct fitting, condition and anchorage points), direction indicators, windscreens, windscreen wipers and washers, exhaust systems, audible warning instruments, bodywork and suspension (in relation to braking and steering). A vehicle that passes the test is issued with a test certificate that is valid for one year.

A vehicle failing the annual test but that is left at the testing station for rectification of the faults does not incur a further fee for a re-test. A fee of half the original is charged when the vehicle is removed and then returned for the necessary repairs to be carried out within 14 days of the original examination.

The certificate must be produced, along with the other necessary documents, when applying for a vehicle licence, and on the request of a police officer.

Motor vehicle insurance

Any vehicle being used on public roads must be covered by insurance. For details, see pages 191 to 194.

Local Memory Tag	DVLA office	Local Identifier
A	Peterborough	A B C D E F G H J K L M N
	Norwich	O P R S T U
	Ipswich	V W X Y
B	Birmingham	A - Y
C	Cardiff	A B C D E F G H J K L M N O
	Swansea	P R S T U V
	Bangor	W X Y
D	Chester	A B C D E F G H J K
	Shrewsbury	L M N O P R S T U V W X Y
E	Chelmsford	A - Y
F	Nottingham	A B C D E F G H J K L M N P
	Lincoln	R S T V W X Y
G	Maidstone	A B C D E F G H J K L M N O
	Brighton	P R S T U V W X Y
H	Bournemouth	A B C D E F G H J
	Portsmouth	K L M N O P R S T U V W X Y
		HW Reserved for the Isle of Wight
K	Luton	A B C D E F G H J K L
	Northampton	M N O P R S T U V W X Y
L	Wimbledon	A B C D E F G H J
	Stanmore	K L M N O P R S T
	Sidcup	U V W X Y
M	Manchester	A - Y
N	Newcastle	A B C D E G H J K L M N O
	Stockton	P R S T U V W X Y
O	Oxford	A - Y
P	Preston	A B C D E F G H J K L M N O P R S T
	Carlisle	U V W X Y
R	Reading	A - Y
S	Glasgow	A B C D E F G H J
	Edinburgh	K L M N O
	Dundee	P R S T
	Aberdeen	U V W
	Inverness	X Y
V	Worcester	A - Y
W	Exeter	A B C D E F G H J
	Truro	K L
	Bristol	M N O P R S T U V W X Y
Y	Leeds	A B C D E F G H J K
	Sheffield	L M N O P R S T U
	Beverley	V W X Y

Figure 7.17   Local identifiers

8

Driver Training

This chapter deals with the main elements involved in the complex task of teaching people to drive. They include:

- methods of learning;
- teaching and learning;
- skill training;
- structuring the learning;
- syllabus for driver training;
- instructions and terminology;
- adapting your instruction;
- assessing progress;
- 'L' driver errors;
- developing safe attitudes.

METHODS OF LEARNING

The basic requirements for any effective learning to take place are:

- attention;
- activity;
- involvement.

Attention

This is not a completely conscious activity. Long periods of undivided concentration are difficult to maintain without a break, or at least a change in the type of activity. Periods of concentration, therefore, will need to be shorter in the earlier stages of learning.

Activity and involvement

These elements are vital if the pupil is going to learn efficiently and effectively. Activity should not only be thought of as physical. For example, although learning to drive a car involves a large degree of physical activity, mental involvement is also necessary to initiate the physical responses.

A saying often used in general education and one that is particularly relevant to driver training is:

What I hear, I forget. What I see, I remember. What I do, I understand!

Keeping the novice actively involved in the learning experience will normally result in more being remembered. However, physical activity alone is not sufficient; learners should also be encouraged to think about what they are doing and why!

Learning by repetition (rote)

Learning by rote, or repetition, is the traditional approach and consists of nothing more than memorizing lists, numbers, facts and formulae and so on, without requiring any understanding. For example, you probably remember learning your multiplication tables by reciting them over and over again.

Most of us have the ability to memorize information 'parrot fashion'. However, the information can only normally be recalled in the order in which it was learnt. Can you say, without thinking about it, which letter of the alphabet comes before the letter 'R'? You will probably have to break into the alphabet a few letters before the 'R' to answer the question.

Rote is the lowest form of learning, and is really only a foundation on which to add more information to give a greater meaning. Some driving skills, such as changing gear, are learnt by rote or repetition – that is, carrying out the physical actions over and over again until they are perfected. These are often referred to in teaching as psychomotor skills – because they involve mainly physical actions.

Learning by understanding (Gestalt)

Learning by the Gestalt method is based on understanding. Understanding can be defined as being able to attach meaning to information. Learning to drive involves combining physical actions with knowledge of the rules and regulations, and is therefore learnt through the Gestalt method and classed as an intellectual or cognitive skill. Effective question and answer (Q&A) routines and feedback techniques will normally be useful tools in the teaching/learning process.

The need for rote and Gestalt

Both methods of learning are important for retaining new information. You may need to teach some basic facts or skills in a rote (memorizing) manner in order to help the learner to acquire the basic competence to handle the car. When these basic skills are mastered, you then need to encourage your pupils to extend their knowledge and understanding by analysing the effect their actions have on the vehicle.

What started out as a memorized list of actions begins to take on some meaning. However, it does not imply that this initial 'meaning' will automatically result in an understanding of how to apply the same information to a new situation. You will therefore have to teach the learner how to adapt the skills for moving off, which were initially learnt by rote, in a wide variety of situations; for example, moving off uphill, downhill and from behind parked vehicles.

As an instructor, you will discover that a mixture of the two methods of learning will be required in most situations. It is poor teaching to over-emphasize the traditional rote learning method without encouraging learners to understand how and why actions need to be taken. It would be equally as bad to over-emphasize progressive learning by allowing them to make and act on their own interpretations of situations before they have an adequate knowledge of the essential rules and skills.

Developing safe attitudes

As a teacher, it will be your responsibility to ensure that the new drivers you are putting on to our roads have the correct attitude towards their vehicle, themselves and other road users. To achieve this, you will need to develop an understanding of the effect their actions have. This type of teaching and learning is called 'affective' because you will be developing safe attitudes through an understanding of the effect that their actions, or lack of them, have on others.

Defensive driving is becoming a necessity on our roads and it is important, if you are to achieve this to any great degree, that your learners understand the need to keep themselves safe at all times.

Learning to drive the car safely and considerately is classed as an attitudinal skill because the phrase 'safely and considerately' describes the attitude of the learner. This makes the difference between merely learning to handle the car (a psychomotor skill) and following the rules of the road (an intellectual skill).

Attitude and behaviour

The attitude of drivers will normally influence their behaviour, and attitudes are formed through personal experiences from birth onwards. Reckless or unsafe driver behaviour is frequently attributed to negative attitudes. These are often inherent in the person who has always 'done his own thing' without a thought for the consequences on other people, or who has been influenced by sitting for many years next to an inconsiderate driver.

Those with a positive attitude, who have learnt to be more thoughtful towards others, will normally respond favourably as their understanding of correct behaviour and of the consequences of bad driving develops. For example, the person who drives at 30 mph down a busy shopping street, where there are parked vehicles on both sides, with a high volume of pedestrian activity, has a negative attitude. Someone who doesn't understand the risks involved, or simply does not care, may drive in this unsafe manner.

Knowing and understanding the risks may still not have the effect of slowing the driver down if a negative attitude is present. The driver with a positive attitude, however, will normally listen to your reasoning, analyse the effects of the reckless behaviour and work on correcting it.

Road user error

The design of our roads (and sometimes the individual driver's local knowledge) allows for a certain degree of road-user error. This may reinforce wrong actions because drivers with a negative attitude get away with deficient behaviour. It may encourage the development of a feeling of immunity, and eventually result in changing the individual's attitude towards the degree of risk he or she is willing to take. Let's take an example.

A driver who lives on a quiet estate may emerge from a junction without taking effective observations because there is usually no other traffic about at that time of the day. No other road user is present and therefore nothing happens. This gives the driver a false sense of security. The same situation may recur a number of times, thus reinforcing this 'safe' feeling. Eventually, and inevitably, other road users will be present and an accident will happen.

It will be your responsibility to try to change negative attitudes. This can be done by:

- explaining the risks involved in any given situation;
- persuading the driver to act safely in order to protect other road users as well as themselves;
- setting a personal example.

You may find that some of your pupils will resent your efforts to change their views, remaining subjective and even offering excuses for not complying. Those with a positive attitude will however normally listen to your reasoning and become more objective and flexible when they understand the consequences of their actions.

You should recognize that all human beings have their limitations. Try to remember that a driver who is normally patient and tolerant may sometimes, for a variety of personal reasons, such as emotional problems, become hostile. Explain how conflict with others can be avoided if a little time is taken to relax and regain composure.

At the end of their course of training, new drivers should be able to:

- recognize features in the road and traffic environment where accidents are most likely to occur;
- identify the causes of accidents and assess their personal risk of becoming involved in them;
- recognize their own capabilities and limitations;

- apply defensive techniques to minimize the risk of becoming involved in potentially dangerous situations.

Transfer of learning

It is unusual these days for people to present themselves for driving lessons without having some of the basic knowledge or skills required. For example:

- all of your pupils will have been pedestrians and have learnt how to cross busy roads successfully;
- most will have been passengers in cars;
- many of them will have ridden a bicycle;
- some will have had some experience on motorbikes.

Most of them will therefore have developed some skills in the judgement of speed, distance and timing of traffic. As these are among the most essential skills involved in driving, you should be able to take advantage of this knowledge and transfer it to driving.

There are numerous other associations through which you will be able to help your learners relate or transfer existing skills and knowledge to driving.

Interference in learning

Previous learning can sometimes work the other way round and interfere with learning a new skill. For example, where people have been passengers over a number of years, they will have probably developed a 'partial sense of speed'. They will have subconsciously learnt an impression of the speed norm of experienced drivers, and this can cause problems if they try to copy them. By driving at what they have learnt to accept as the normal speed, this 'previous learning' can interfere with progress, as, in the early stages, the basic car control skills need to be carried out at slower than normal speeds.

The following are examples of interference of learning:

- Always change up through the gears as soon as you have moved off.
- Always change down progressively using all of the gears when you are slowing down or stopping.
- Always signal for moving off, passing parked cars and stopping.

If pupils have been previously indoctrinated with certain views, it is likely to cause conflict with the new information you are giving. You must recognize that your pupils are not learning in a vacuum, and will therefore be subject to all kinds of conflicting pressures from others.

Where this type of interference occurs, you must be tolerant and show an understanding of your pupils' problems during any difficult periods of 'unlearning'. You must also try to avoid saying that the information they have been given is totally wrong.

Motivation

This describes the personal needs and desires of the individual. The fact that someone is prepared to pay for a course of lessons will normally show that he or she is motivated by a desire to learn. The student will normally be alert and keen at the beginning of the course, with a willingness to follow instructions in eager anticipation of the next session. This initial enthusiasm, however, may not always be enough to maintain full interest and attention throughout the entire course, particularly if difficult patches are experienced where very slow progress is achieved.

An important part of your work as a teacher will be to try to maintain pupils' motivation. Help them over any difficult periods by maintaining your enthusiasm and showing that you are interested in their progress. Motivation and interest can be stimulated through success. Even small successes are important to a pupil who is finding the learning hard work.

By creating the right conditions, you can do much to ensure success. This can be done by properly grading the tuition in short, progressive steps. You should then try to maintain this interest by giving suitable encouragement and approval for effort.

Traditional methods of driving instruction mean students are often learning in total isolation from others, and this can frequently cause problems for both the instructor and student. While 'individual' tuition is advantageous, it does limit contact and comparisons with other students. Deprived of the group learning situation, students are unable to measure their progress against that of others. More importantly, if they have no means of assessing their own progress and improvement, they may often feel they are making no progress at all. This may be a result of their instructor not giving sufficient feedback on where improvements have taken place.

If students feel they are making slow progress, encouragement alone from the teacher may not be sufficient to allay their fears of inability. Emphasis needs to be placed on where progress has been achieved, and excess criticism in other areas should be avoided. An unsympathetic teacher may cause students to feel so discouraged, isolated and incompetent, that they become completely demoralized and may even give up the idea of learning to drive.

If you set up easily attainable, intermediate targets, you will help to reinforce your students' feelings of achievement. Intermediate goals also help to organize the learning situation, and do much to prevent pupils from being 'thrown in at the deep end before they can swim'.

One of the first goals to achieve in learning to drive is clutch control. It's important to remember that many of the driving skills are conditioned responses. That is, they not only require the correct system for them to be learnt properly, but they also need continual repetition in order to master them. This basic goal should be attained before students are asked to deal with difficult uphill junctions.

The confidence of some learners is destroyed because they are taken into situations that require good clutch control before they have mastered the basic skill.

Imagine how you would feel if you were sitting at a red traffic light on your first driving lesson and you stalled the engine a couple of times!

Clutch control should initially be developed by full talk-through instruction to ensure that confidence is built up. However, in the final analysis, it is only by practice and success that the skill will become 'second nature' as the pupil learns to control it correctly in all situations.

Everyone learns at a different rate. It is therefore important that pupils are allowed to develop at their own individual pace, and setting intermediate goals should ensure that they progress with confidence. This, in turn, will keep the motivation at a good level.

TEACHING AND LEARNING

You should know from your own experiences that learning is an inconsistent process over which there is little reliable control. Teachers have no mystical power by which to pour knowledge into the minds of their learners, so whatever students learn (whether it is a psychomotor or an intellectual skill), they must learn for themselves. You will merely be providing the circumstances from which learning may occur. These 'learning conditions' may be in the form of practical driving lessons, lectures or discussion; or some other teaching or instructional method.

Your role will essentially be one of establishing the quality of the teaching and of planning and organizing the conditions in which learning can take place. Teachers manage the learning experience by:

- preparing the material;
- organizing the material;
- presenting the experience to the student;
- creating opportunities to practise;
- observing the student's reactions;
- assessing progress.

No matter how carefully prepared and presented the lesson may be, success can be judged only by how much knowledge or skill the learner gains from it.

Teaching driving

The complete experience in learning to drive involves the car, the classroom, or some other location, and the personality and teaching methods of the instructor. It will also be dependent on the attitude, knowledge and skill of the student. Whatever natural abilities and aptitude your pupils have, they will only gain the full benefit of learning if they are actively involved and are attentive. Motivation is vital to students' willingness to learn. You must motivate your students and create an environment and situations from which they can learn.

You should think of yourself as a manager of the learning experience, with responsibilities extending far beyond the act of teaching. You should always be aware that what you are teaching – or are neglecting to teach – could at some time in the future be a matter of life or death to your students.

Apart from the quality and content of your lessons, your responsibilities will range from the organization of the course to the final assessments you will need to make before your students take their driving tests.

The key to the successful management of learning will be your ability to present, adapt and adjust the same basic knowledge and skills for the wide range of learning abilities of the different pupils you will be teaching. You should not only be master of your craft and skills, but you should also have at your command an infinitely variable range of instructional techniques to call on as and when the situation, or your pupils' needs, demand it. Teaching driving is a challenging task that requires thorough training. Make sure you are prepared for it properly.

THE LEARNER'S NEEDS

The most successful instructors are those who have a concern for their students and are most sensitive to their learning requirements. The needs of the learner driver are as varied and complex as the differences between the students themselves. Avoid grouping people into preconceived categories such as young and old, or quick and slow to learn. Making this type of pre-judgement before you get to know pupils may prevent you from treating them as individuals, and might also prevent you from seeing them with 'open' and 'more sensitive' eyes.

One of your first priorities will be to create a good working relationship with your students. A good test of this will be the rapport that develops between you; and, perhaps more significantly, the level of communication. For example, if a good relationship develops:

- pupils should feel they can readily admit their mistakes without the risk of feeling inadequate;
- they should be able to discuss freely with you their fears and anxieties about their progress;
- you should be able to laugh together about silly mistakes.

In order to develop students' ability and confidence, learning should be founded on mutual cooperation. You can encourage this by structuring the learning so that they are asked only to carry out tasks that can be achieved with some degree of success.

Points to remember about teaching and learning
- Begin with what the learner already knows or can do and build on this.
- Structure the learning in short progressive steps.
- Be consistent with your instructions and terminology.
- Make sure that your terminology is fully understood.
- Keep your explanations short and simple.

- Emphasize the key points.
- Ensure that your instructions are positive: indicate what to do rather than what not to do.
- Explain the purpose of any demonstration before carrying it out.
- Carry out demonstrations at the correct level according to the ability of the learner.
- Keep initial explanations and demonstration commentaries simple – too many variables will confuse.
- Allow for plenty of practice – people learn by doing things for themselves.
- Ensure that the learner is in no doubt about what is expected.
- Success will stimulate interest and involvement, so try to ensure that initial practice is successful.
- Give praise and encouragement to help stimulate progress – excessive criticism may destroy motivation.
- Give continuous feedback of progress.
- Correct errors positively before they become habitual.
- Positive correction should be made to improve learners' performance.
- Confirmation of minor successes is important to those who may be finding the going difficult.
- Be patient; lack of sympathy for someone who feels he or she is not making progress may demoralize that person.
- Reassure pupils that periods of slow learning are quite natural and common.
- Avoid comparing learners with other students.
- Setting easy-to-achieve intermediate goals may help to promote progress.
- Allow students to learn at their own pace.
- Changes in activity may help sustain interest, so avoid excessive repetition.
- Allow longer periods of training for more mature students.
- Give reassurance and emotional encouragement to avoid the fear of failure.
- Select routes that will ensure, as far as possible, that the learner can cope with the conditions.
- Be prepared to vary your methods of instruction.
- Avoid attempting to expand on variables before the pupil has grasped the key points of a new topic.
- 'Nothing has been taught until something is learnt.'

SKILL TRAINING

The term 'skill' describes an activity in which the performance should be economical and effective in order to achieve a consistent and satisfactory result. Although it is relatively easy to recognize the skilled performance of an expert driver, it is considerably more difficult to define why it is so. It is even more difficult to analyse (and to give a valid explanation of) the many skills involved in the complete task.

Driving instructors are obviously highly skilled drivers. Many drivers are unaware of the numerous individual tasks they are putting into practice because, with experience, these have mostly become subconscious actions. As an instructor you need to be able to analyse each of the skills in detail before being able to teach the complex tasks involved in the process of learning to drive.

As a driver you have to obtain relevant information from the environment, process it, then respond by making decisions and executing the appropriate car control skills. The driving task involves attending to, perceiving and responding safely to driving-related stimuli. The activities involved relate to three different areas:

- psychomotor (or physical skills);
- cognitive (or knowledge-related skills);
- affective skills (or attitude).

When driving, you allocate attention by using your senses to gather information about the performance of your vehicle and also the conditions of the road and traffic environment. You must process the information by comparing it with existing knowledge, memories and previous experiences. You then assess its relevance and either ignore it and do nothing, or decide on a particular response or course of action to be taken to maintain a safe environment.

As an instructor you will have to recognize all of these different aspects and teach your pupils how to drive safely in order to survive.

Analysing the learning task

To assist your pupils in the acquisition of new skills you need to be able to identify key learning points and to isolate any areas of weakness. To do this you will need to identify the elements of knowledge, attitude and skill involved in a particular learning task.

Essential elements: knowledge

This describes what you know. It has been found that knowledge influences attitude and assists in the acquisition of skills. Driving involves considerable knowledge of the *Highway Code*, traffic law and the principles of safe procedures. Certain aspects can be learnt more effectively in a classroom or at home rather than in the hustle and bustle of today's road and traffic conditions.

Knowledge, however, is only a basis for 'real' learning. Although it may influence attitudes, in practice knowledge alone is not always sufficient to ensure we have the will or skill needed to behave safely. For example, although most drivers know about speed limits, this doesn't always prevent them from driving at excessive or inappropriate speeds. Legislation and the consequences of being caught, however, place incentives on drivers not to break the law.

Other incentives include the consequences of accident involvement. This knowledge may also help influence our attitude towards alcohol and driving. On this basis, the more we know, the better equipped we are to make our decisions.

Essential elements: attitude

This describes what we really think, and it usually influences our behaviour. Attitudes are formed over a lifetime of experience and learning. They will not normally be changed overnight! Unsympathetic attitudes towards others, and towards the established principles of road safety, can be contributory factors in causing many road accidents.

You should encourage your pupils to develop safe attitudes towards others. You can do this by constantly persuading and providing them with good examples.

In addition to knowledge, an attitude has motivational and emotional elements that influence behaviour. These elements can be so powerful that we may sometimes lose control of our actions. Uncontrolled aggression and love are two extreme examples of this.

Essential elements: skill

This describes what we can do! There are two main types of skill: *manipulative skills* are physical actions such as turning the steering wheel, pressing the footbrake or operating the clutch pedal, and *perceptive skills* are skills associated with awareness, thinking, reasoning and making decisions. They are the predominant skills used in the overall driving task, and rely heavily on visual sense. They include the judgement of:

- reductions in speed caused by differing amounts of braking pressure;
- detecting changes in direction when steering;
- awareness – the general state of mind involving hazard recognition and comparisons with previous experience;
- assessing and predicting risk and making decisions.

Making the driving effective involves the following skills:

- attention – staying alert and concentrating;
- visual search – a systematic scanning of the road and traffic scene;
- responding to situations and taking the appropriate action to control the car;
- using the car's controls smoothly and efficiently.

To make the learning and the driving effective, organize lessons into short progressive steps and let your pupils work through them at their own pace. As aptitudes and abilities vary, you will need to adapt the pace of your instruction to the ability of each individual.

Build on what the pupil already knows and can do, then move on one step at a time. Before attempting a new skill, the pupil will require some basic knowledge upon which to build.

Each physical action has a 'get set' position from which the actual skill commences. This involves preliminary movements and positioning of the hands and/or feet in anticipation of carrying out the skill or sub-skill. This 'get set' position is important for ensuring the efficient and smooth execution of the overall task. For example:

- siting the hand over the gear lever in anticipation of a change, while:
- positioning the foot over the clutch pedal;
- extending the fingers ready to use a signal;
- raising the appropriate hand ready for the first pull movement on the steering wheel.

Teaching a skill

Before you can teach a new skill you have to establish the present standard and abilities of your pupil. You can then decide on the level at which the skill should be introduced, demonstrated and practised. Be prepared to adjust this level, up or down, depending on the pupil's responses and performance.

At the beginning of each session, explain to your pupils what they are going to do and why. They should understand how the skill is to be performed and what is expected of them. Relate the subject matter to what they already know and can do, so that they feel the task in hand is attainable. It may be necessary to break some skills down into their component sub-skills to ensure success is achieved.

The generally accepted pattern of skill training is:

- **explanation**;
- **demonstration**;
- **practice**.

The explanation

Introduce the topic for instruction and include an indication of:

- what the topic involves;
- why this particular aspect is important;
- when and where it is carried out;
- how it is to be carried out.

Keep explanations short and to the point. They should be appropriate to each pupil's ability. For example, it would be pointless to go into lengthy explanations on how to exercise clutch control at busy uphill junctions if the pupil cannot move away under control on a level road. Establish and consolidate the main principles of the subject before introducing the finer points and variables. Once basic rules and procedures are established, it will be easier for the pupil to understand and retain additional information given at a later date.

There are three main constituent parts to most explanations. These include details and information concerning:

- *control* – of the vehicle's speed;
- *observation* – of hazards and general attitudes towards them;
- *positioning* – of the vehicle by using the steering.

Control

Explanations should include the general control of the vehicle for dealing with hazards. Control is mainly a manipulative skill, for example:

- coordination of the car's controls when moving off;
- low-speed clutch control for manoeuvring;
- smooth, gradual use of the steering wheel;
- smooth and progressive use of the accelerator and gears;
- smooth and progressive use of the brakes for slowing down and stopping;
- securing the car when stationary.

Observation

Explain about the visual search required to deal safely with any hazard or to maintain safety when manoeuvring. The use of any necessary signals should be included, and any special danger clues the pupil should be looking for.

It is your responsibility to encourage safe attitudes and you should include information on the perceptive skills and safety margins. Explain about the decision-making process required to respond correctly.

Positioning

Explanations should include:

- the rules relating to positioning and when to adjust to suit the situation;
- steering – the physical use of the steering wheel;
- maintaining general accuracy throughout the required course;
- lane discipline where appropriate.

Points to remember

A general guide for lessons is to:

- tell your pupils what they will be doing during the current session;
- explain how to do it;
- allow plenty of time for practising.

It can prove to be totally unproductive to introduce complex procedures until basic car control skills have been adequately developed. Do it with a 'KISS':

Keep It Short and Simple

- Keep explanations as brief as you can for the subject.
- Get straight to the point.
- Use terminology that is straightforward and understandable.
- Use visual aids where they will help your pupil understand what you mean.
- To validate points, refer to official publications such as the *Highway Code* and *The Official DSA Guide to Driving: The essential skills*.
- Emphasize the key points – leaving out any unnecessary detail.

The demonstration

The demonstration has a number of applications. It can be used to:

- show pupils how an expert would carry out a manoeuvre or procedure;
- emphasize or reinforce individual components of any skill;
- show the key elements of a manoeuvre prior to giving a fuller explanation;
- dispel the pupils' apprehension.

To obtain maximum effect from a demonstration it must be preceded by a briefing. You can then emphasize the key points as you give the demonstration by talking yourself through the procedures. Conclude the demonstration with a summary of the key points, then if necessary give a more in-depth explanation.

Consolidate the explanation and demonstration by giving your pupil plenty of practice under controlled conditions.

Quite often new drivers are genuinely unaware of the mistakes they are making and cannot visualize the correct procedure. A demonstration may help them to 'see' exactly what you mean. This particularly applies where safety margins, hold-back positions and also the use of speed when approaching hazards are concerned. Because of inexperience, pupils can fail to recognize the dangers involved. If you demonstrate safer clearances and speeds, it may result in a better understanding of the problems.

You can tell a pupil to slow down more before a corner and get no result whatsoever. This can mean that the pupil's concept of the word 'slow' is different from your own. Under such circumstances, a demonstration can be invaluable, but use it as part of your explanation and not as a substitute for it.

Points to remember about the demonstration

- It should be at an appropriate level for the pupil's ability.
- It should follow an explanation of the subject.
- It should be a perfect example of the skill or procedure carried out at near normal speed. (Slightly less than normal may be advantageous at times, but it should not be so slow as to become unreal.)
- Commentary should be restricted to the main points using key words (too many variables may confuse).
- It must be consolidated with plenty of practice in controlled conditions.

Pupils' practice

Your pupils can only learn practical skills by carrying them out! The practice should, however, be structured and follow a pattern of:

- controlled;
- prompted;
- transferred responsibility; and
- distributed practice.

Controlled practice and talk through

As far as possible try to ensure your pupils 'get it right first time'. Talk them through each action and stage of the operation, skill or exercise until they develop the ability and confidence to do it for themselves. This 'talk-through' technique enables initial practice of new skills or procedures to take place realistically and in relative safety. It also helps to prevent vehicle abuse and inconvenience to other road users. The need for the full 'talk through' is greatest in the early stages when terminology is least familiar and pupils are more likely to misunderstand the instructions given.

Make sure that pupils are familiar with your terminology and can carry out your instructions before they move away. Instructions should be clear and should be given so that the pupil has plenty of time to interpret and execute them comfortably.

In order to build up confidence, it is essential that initial practice of a new skill should be successful. The 'talk through' ensures, as far as possible, that nothing goes wrong at this early stage.

While this method of instruction is usually successful for introducing pupils to the basic skills, it does have some complications. Due to the limitations of speech, the timing of some skills is slightly artificial. We can only speak, or give instructions, in a specific order – one at a time. Some skills require perfectly coordinated use of different controls at the same time. It is therefore impossible to give instructions exactly as they should be carried out.

Another problem lies in pupils' speed of interpreting and then carrying out the instruction. There will be a delay of varying lengths for different pupils. They may also temporarily become confused over an instruction, causing even more delay.

There are no real alternatives to this method of instruction during the initial stages of training. The driving simulator is perhaps a safe alternative, but it falls a long way short of being ideal. This is because there is normally no sensation of movement, direction or change of speed.

New skills should normally begin to develop after two or three talk-through exercises. When you can see that some progress is taking place, encourage your pupils to take some personal responsibility for their actions. There are a number of ways in which development of this responsibility can be encouraged:

- Ask pupils to talk themselves through the sequence. This gives them the responsibility but it may also give you forewarning of any errors. You can then verbally rectify these before they are actually committed.
- Break the sequence into three parts (preparation, observation, and action), and get pupils to talk themselves through each. If pupils become confused with the unfamiliar terminology it is not important as long as they understand what is required. Don't be too particular about making the pupil use your precise phrasing. This may result in them feeling inadequate and inhibit their performance of the skill.

- If pupils 'dry up', give a cue or prompt, then let them continue. Practise until the whole sequence can be completed unaided.
- Insist that previously learnt routines are carried out properly, and correct any errors before they become habitual. Excessive criticism, however, should be avoided as it can destroy confidence.
- Encourage improvement by pointing out progress. Identify weaknesses and help pupils overcome them.
- Devise simple exercises to help with any problems.
- Experiment and be prepared to vary your methods of instruction if problems persist.
- Your students should feel that they can approach you without feeling foolish or incompetent. If problems persist, try something new for a while and go back to the subject later.
- Reassure those who find things difficult. Let them know that periods of slow progress are quite common.

At the end of practice sessions, decide if the objectives have been achieved. Ask questions to ensure that the subject has been clearly understood before you proceed to the next. Practice sessions should finish not only with a review of what has been achieved, but also a look forward to what will be covered in the next lesson.

At the beginning of each lesson, revise and reinforce the points learnt in the previous one before going on to new subject matter.

Prompted practice

Some pupils may become very good at following instructions, but when left to carry out a skill unaided they are unable to do so. Others who find it more difficult to follow individual instructions are often far more advanced when they are allowed to work on their own initiative. While controlled practice is an essential part of basic training in new skills, it should gradually be phased out when you feel pupils can cope for themselves. Some pupils will require lots of encouragement to act and think for themselves.

Prompting, where required, is perhaps the natural progression from the controlled practice or talk through. The amount of prompting required will largely depend on the ability and willingness of pupils to make decisions for themselves. The type of decision required is also significant. For example, if the conditions become too busy for the pupils' ability, there will be a tendency for them to refrain from making any decisions at all. Where these situations arise, you must be prepared to prompt as required. The ultimate objective is to get pupils to carry out all of the skills under normal traffic conditions without any prompting at all.

Revision is important and it requires continuous consideration, particularly in the early stages of establishing a new skill. A true and wholly accurate assessment cannot be made of the driving skill where it is still necessary to prompt.

The use of detailed instructions should be reduced as the pupil's ability increases. For example, at the beginning of a lesson, a pupil hesitates and shows minor signs of distress on being asked to move off. You know that this pupil can carry out the procedure without any assistance, so all you may need to do is give a simple cue such as 'Select first gear'. Normally this will trigger the actions required as the sequence is remembered.

Remember that a simple cue like this is often sufficient to bring back a whole sequence of complicated actions without further instruction. Try not to help too much by giving all the necessary information. If capable, the pupil needs to be given the opportunity of achieving some success independently.

Practice will be required to build consistency, stamina and to reduce the time taken to complete any sequence. When the skill becomes consistent and is carried out in a reasonable length of time, other important aspects can be introduced, with more emphasis being placed on the visual search and timing.

Skills must be applied and practised progressively in more difficult traffic situations: for example, moving off from junctions and traffic lights; moving off and maintaining low-speed control in conjunction with steering.

Transferred responsibility

There comes a time when you must hand over to your pupils the responsibility for making their own decisions and acting on them. As control skills develop and confidence grows, you should place more emphasis on the development of perceptive and hazard recognition skills. Point out what pupils should be looking for and where to expect it. Explain the dangers involved and why particular responses are called for.

Encourage pupils to think and to make decisions. Get them to look for information, and encourage them to use their knowledge of the rules and previous experience in order to assess each situation. Build the confidence they need in order to make decisions and to act for themselves.

The Q&A technique becomes very useful in this stage of training. By asking questions relevant to the traffic situation, you can find out what pupils are thinking. How they respond will give you an indication of areas where misunderstandings are occurring and you can then make the necessary corrections.

Distributed practice

No matter what skills are being learnt, there is no substitute for practice and this should be organized sensibly. 'Cramming' everything into a few marathon sessions is not an efficient way of learning. 'A little and often' is a more efficient strategy.

Carefully distributed practice, divided evenly over four or five weeks, is more efficient than working for the same amount of hours during an intensive one-week course. For example, one hour of training a day is considerably more efficient than:

- one hour of training twice a day;
- two hours' training once a day;
- two hours' training twice a day.

The general learning curve

You will be able to see the manipulative aspects of the driving task improving by simply watching your pupils execute them. However, prompts and verbal guidance during the early stages of learning will still be necessary. When the skill is sufficiently developed, hints and reassurance should be all that is required. Pupils' progress will vary depending on the type of skill being learnt.

With the learning of some skills, pupils often reach a stage that is referred to as 'the plateau of learning' and progress appears to come to a halt. However, this is not normally the limit of their potential and is usually very short-lived. After a brief while most pupils will overcome the problem and progress to their own personal limits.

STRUCTURING THE LEARNING

There are nine main principles involved in structuring any course of training or instruction. As there is a good deal of common sense involved in teaching a practical skill, most good instructors follow these principles intuitively:

1 The aims and objectives of a course of lessons, and each part of it, should be clearly specified in advance in terms of observable behaviour

Objectives are written statements that describe what your pupil is expected to be able to do at the completion of a lesson or a course of lessons. They are normally

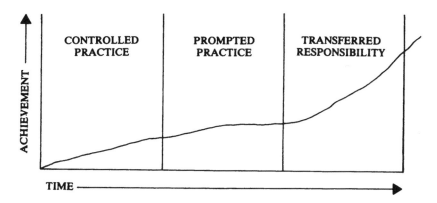

Figure 8.1   The general learning curve

phrased in terms of observable behaviour. Pupils should be made aware of the new skills they are expected to be able to carry out, or what knowledge they are expected to have gained by the end of the session or each section of learning.

The DSA has published a comprehensive set of objectives in its syllabus for learning to drive, but you will probably want to produce your own supplementary objectives – particularly for the earlier stages of learning.

2   The subject matter to be learnt, and the training routes used, should be appropriate to achieving the specified aims and objectives

The content of each lesson, together with your support materials and the training routes used, should ensure that the aims and objectives are achievable by the pupil. You should classify the matter to be learnt in order of importance as follows:

- *essential material* – what the learner *must* cover in order to achieve the course objectives;
- *desirable material* – what the learner *should* cover, but is not absolutely essential to achieve the objectives;
- *useful material* – what the learner *could* cover, but it is not completely relevant to the objectives.

3   The course content, and individual lessons, should be organized in short progressive steps that follow a logical sequence

Intermediate targets will help to stimulate interest and progress. They can help to reinforce learning by providing positive evidence of progress through each section and also organize the learning situation.

Considered as a whole, driving is a complex task. It is made up of many sub-skills such as moving off, steering and stopping. The whole should be analysed and organized into short progressive units of instruction taking the acquisition of these sub-skills into consideration.

A course of driving lessons should be structured to proceed from:

the known to the unknown

the simple to the complex

basic rules to the variations

concrete observations to abstract reasoning.

Once pupils have grasped the basic rules and concepts, it becomes easier for them to develop new skills and understand the variables.

4   The content of lessons, and the routes selected, should be graded in difficulty so that your pupils will make as few mistakes as possible, especially in the early stages.

Make sure students experience success during the early stages of their training. To do this, avoid setting standards that are too high. Be prepared to accept some technical inaccuracies and deficiencies until they have developed more confidence in their ability. Initial failure may deter pupils and inhibit progress. Build confidence and understanding on a firm foundation of practical skills.

Progress from what students know and can do, working up to the unknown and the new. Simple skills should be taught before complex procedures are introduced. For example, it is unreasonable to expect pupils to deal with right turns at busy traffic-light controlled junctions before they can control the vehicle properly.

5   Your pupils should be introduced to new materials and skills at a level of difficulty that relates to their ability, previous experience and attainments

There are considerable variations in the rate at which students learn. This should cause few problems when giving one-to-one tuition because the course can be tailored to suit the needs of each individual. Pupils should be allowed to work through each unit of learning at their own pace. New skills and techniques can then be introduced at a level commensurate with ability, knowledge and achievement.

One of your first tasks when meeting new students is to find out what previous experience they may have had, and how much they know and can do. In order to plan the level of training, it is necessary to establish the pupil's current knowledge and ability. Use Q&A with pupils to find out what they already know, then encourage them to take some responsibility for the decisions you will be making together.

As skills develop, and mastery of the controls is attained, keep pupils informed of what they are doing and why. They should never be left confused or in doubt. However, some of the basic skills must be taught as simple conditioned reflex procedures. Initially, it is more important for pupils to respond correctly to an emergency than to understand why the particular response was required.

6   Pupils should be allowed to proceed through the course at their own pace

The amount of time devoted to each element of training will vary from one pupil to another. Learning is more efficient when pupils are allowed to proceed at their own pace, as slowly or as quickly as they are able. This allows the learning to be most effective.

7 Keep pupils 'actively' involved in the learning process

Keep your pupils physically and/or mentally involved in the learning experience. Whatever the task under instruction, learning can only be achieved by pupils thinking and doing things for themselves. Activity will help to hold pupils' attention.

Where students may be sitting passively in a classroom, supposedly listening to a necessary, but boring, lecture, it is easy to see how they may become 'switched off'. This may happen where the students do not think the content of the lecture is particularly relevant to their personal needs.

Observing the physical activity of the pupil is relatively straightforward. Recognizing what the pupil is thinking, however, is a rather more difficult problem. An active mind on the part of the pupil is essential to learning and is an important part of driving.

For example, driving at 40 mph along a quiet road with relatively little traffic requires little physical activity other than controlling the steering. The problem in this situation is that there is very little to occupy the mind, so it may not be involved in the driving at all. These situations provide ideal conditions for you to develop the pupil's visual search and observational skills and to relate them to the decisions of an experienced driver.

In the earlier stages of learning a task, keep the pupil's mind active – ask questions about the relevant road features, or of any intended actions. For example, if you see a bus with a left signal on, you could ask what the pupil expects it to do. However, when using this technique, make sure the questions are not too technical and likely to distract the pupil's concentration.

8 Give your pupils continuous feedback of progress

Learning should be reinforced through feedback of progress, helpful comments and a balance of constructive criticism and encouragement. Active involvement facilitates learning. However, this does not ensure that the learning is of the right kind, or that the pupil is making progress towards the final performance as stated in the objectives.

Make sure that pupils are not just perfecting existing faults. Reinforce learning and improve performance, by giving continuous information on progress. Feedback should occur as soon as possible after an event, or between each step in an exercise or manoeuvre. This will help prevent further faults appearing. Comments such as 'good' or 'well done' may be useful as an indication of progress where there is insufficient time to give more detailed information. These comments do not, however, tell the pupil anything about the actual performance. Comments such as the following are all more helpful because they give information on the actual performance:

Our position was a little wide on the approach to the turn.

The gear change was left a little late.

The approach speed needs to be a little slower.

Positive comments that indicate what action must be taken to correct an error are even more beneficial. For example:

Position about a metre from the kerb when turning left.

Slow down earlier before reaching the corner.

Change down to second a little sooner next time.

Short comments and corrections made on the move will be of great value in improving your pupil's performance. However, avoid giving detailed verbal corrections on the move. When they are required, give them as soon as practicable after the incident when a suitable parking position is found.

9   Pupils should master each skill and section of the course before you go on to the next stage

There is sometimes confusion over what is meant by 'complete mastery', and some instructors argue that this cannot be attained until a very advanced stage is reached. Do not expect 'total mastery of the full task' during the intermediate stages. Reduce the demands placed on your pupils by setting properly structured objectives and choosing your routes carefully.

If a course is properly structured, mastery can, and should, be attained in each sub-skill, technique or procedure before introducing new and progressively more complicated variables.

Consistency is an essential feature of good driving. To achieve it, each skill or task should be 'over-learnt' before proceeding to the next. Progress based on mastery of each phase of learning will do much to develop a sense of achievement and confidence. Staging the course into a number of progressive learning units also helps to increase pupils' motivation to learn by sustaining a continuous sense of urgency.

DRIVER TRAINING SYLLABUS

The DSA officially recommended syllabus (which you will find in its publication *The Official Guide to Learning to Drive*) covers the complete range of driving skills and is not restricted simply to 'learning to pass the "L" test'. The syllabus therefore provides a basis for structuring courses for:

- pre-driver training;
- learner driver training;
- post-test training under the Pass Plus scheme;
- advanced/defensive/fleet training.

The main elements of the syllabus include:

- legal requirements;
- car controls, equipment and components;

- road user behaviour;
- vehicle characteristics;
- road and weather conditions;
- traffic signs, rules and regulations;
- car control and road procedure;
- motorway driving;
- riding mopeds and motorcycles;
- towing larger trailers or caravans.

When structuring your own course you should use this syllabus in conjunction with *The Official DSA Guide to Driving: The essential skills*, the *Highway Code*, and any other material that will help develop and reinforce safe procedures and attitudes.

As well as the skills in which your pupils must achieve basic competence in order to pass the driving test, they must also have a thorough knowledge of the *Highway Code* and the motoring laws, and understanding of the driver's responsibilities. It is your responsibility to influence safe attitudes. You must teach your pupils to have real concern, not just for their own safety, but for the safety of all road users, including pedestrians.

You should be able to teach your pupils most of the subjects listed in the DSA syllabus during their practical on-road lessons. However, some may be difficult for you to cover because of the road and traffic conditions in your area. You may not, for example, be able to give practical experience at dealing with level crossings, floods or dual carriageways, because these situations do not exist locally. However, it remains your responsibility to ensure your pupils have sufficient knowledge on all of the subjects. You can do this by various means. Some of these are:

- teaching pupils in groups;
- spending time in the car going over the rules and procedures;
- setting homework based on the official publications and asking relevant questions on subsequent lessons.

The four phases of skill development

New drivers normally progress through four phases of learning before reaching a competent standard.

1 Dissociated passive

This phase of learning is very superficial. Pupils are only passively attending to the driving task, while you will be playing a dominant role in talking them through the basic routines and procedures. Novice drivers are usually visually inactive, slow to respond, and hesitant, with a tendency to make sudden unexpected moves. You will need to use the basic principles of 'controlled practice' outlined earlier in this chapter and give pupils full instruction through each routine or skill.

'*Controlled practice.*' During this phase of giving full instruction through each routine or skill, tuition should be restricted to developing car control skills. Although the carrying out of the routines may be superficial at this stage, you can still try to develop good habits such as the M–S–M sequence.

The aim of the first lesson is to familiarize pupils with the car's controls. It will also give them an opportunity to get a feel for these by practising some simple exercises while stationary. When you have explained the terminology you will be using, make sure your pupils understand, and are able to carry out, basic instructions before moving away. For example:

Handbrake ready.

Cover the clutch.

Clutch down.

Set the gas.

Find the holding point.

Cover the brake.

In order to develop pupils' car control and steering skills, talk them through the routines and allow plenty of practice on the nursery routes. You will need to tell them exactly what to do and when to do it. This should help them to get things right first time and build up their confidence. Let them practise each step of each exercise separately until they have mastered it reasonably well. Keeping to the quiet routes, use step-by-step exercises to encourage your pupils to do more for themselves.

2 Dissociated active

At this stage your pupils will become more 'active' in the manipulative skills but will still be visually inactive, with slow perceptive responses. You will often need to prompt them into action. (For future reference this phase is referred to as 'prompted practice'.) Near misses, sudden unusual manoeuvres and late over-reactions tend to be the norm, and pupils seem to actively take risks. During this phase you need to use the 'prompted practice' routines described earlier in this chapter.

Your pupils will initially require considerable prompting. Progression through the phase should be structured within their capabilities. First teach them to deal with static hazards. The circumstances of routes and movement of pedestrians and traffic, however, will sometimes create unforeseen situations with which they are unable to cope. When this happens, reassure the pupil and talk him or her through the situation.

To develop skills, use quiet estates with wide roads, rounded corners and as few parked cars as possible. Practise simple M–S–M routines, turning left and right into side roads. Once pupils have mastered this, practise the system approaching and emerging from roads. At first, only practise on junctions that provide clear views into the main road.

When pupils can cope with the quiet estates, give them the opportunity to practise on sharper corners and major roads with more traffic. Avoid very busy junctions and those on uphill gradients. As mastery of the system of car control is achieved at basic junctions, and confidence increases, practise on busier roads, uphill junctions, and those with restricted sightlines.

Introduce the manoeuvring and parking exercise when control skills are adequately developed to ensure initial success. As pupils improve towards the end of this phase, encourage them to assess situations, take on more responsibility for themselves and begin to make their own decisions.

3   *Injudicious*

Your pupils will now start to become 'visually aware', developing perceptive responses and actively attending to driving the car. They should become more responsible for their own actions. (For future reference this phase is referred to as 'transferred responsibility'.)

At this stage pupils will:

- make some false assumptions;
- be prepared to take risks;
- make occasional misjudgements;
- suffer near misses;
- still make some unusual manoeuvres.

This phase will usually involve some 'transferred responsibility'. Once pupils have mastered the car control skills and the basic rules and routine procedures, give them some experience on busier roads and in traffic. Try to keep them calm and build their confidence in these conditions by giving them plenty of practice. Provide them with plenty of experience on a wide variety of roads and junctions, for example:

- in laned traffic;
- on one-way streets;
- turning on to and off dual carriageways;
- negotiating roundabouts;
- turning right at busy traffic-light controlled crossroads.

Avoid heavy, fast-moving traffic and multi-lane roads containing combinations of parked vehicles, pedestrians and complex junctions until the final stages of training, when they will be able to cope with these situations.

Remember, excessive criticism will destroy pupils' confidence. A little praise will encourage them to do better next time. Tell them when they carry out procedures well, commend them for making good decisions, and flatter them for their concentration and effort.

4   Independent

By the time your pupils reach this phase of learning they should be more visually active and aware. They should be developing a quick perceptive response to recognized risks and be able to react in an unhurried and skilful manner. There should no longer be any near misses or unusual reactions. It is your responsibility to teach pupils to recognize and accept that other road users make mistakes. They can be taught to avoid accidents by compensating for other people's mistakes.

Carrying out assessments and mock tests at this stage should be constructive. They should help to provide your pupils with evidence of progress as well as any weaknesses still to be worked on. Before presenting pupils for the test, ensure, as far as you possibly can, that they are able to cope with busy road and traffic conditions. It is not sufficient for them merely to satisfy the minimum standard required by the examiner.

You will find more detail about these phases in *Practical Teaching Skills for Driving Instructors*. The book *Learn to Drive in 10 Easy Stages* also follows the same phases, and contains a systematic programme designed to support professional instruction. Each stage contains a special chart linked to DSA requirements. This can be used to identify areas of weakness and organize appropriate revision exercises. The book guides the reader through the various stages of learning to the point where knowledge, skill and understanding are combined and assessed to confirm strengths and to highlight any weaknesses. It is based on the four phases of skill development and follows the principles detailed in this chapter.

ROUTE PLANNING

Route planning is an essential element of lesson preparation. It requires a thorough knowledge of local geography and traffic conditions. When planning routes you must take into consideration any specific driving skill or procedure that is to be practised. An inappropriate route can have disastrous consequences when novices are unnecessarily exposed to conditions with which they are unable to cope. In extreme cases, and with particularly nervous pupils, it may even make them give up the idea of learning to drive at all.

Ideally, a fairly wide selection of planned routes containing various types of traffic hazards and conditions will be required. You should not consider them as being rigidly fixed routes from which there must be no deviation.

Flexibility is an important consideration when planning a route, because it allows for changes to be made midway through a lesson. This may become necessary to allow more time to be spent on an area of driving which may be proving unexpectedly troublesome, and yet still allow the lesson to be completed on time for your next appointment.

Excessive repetition over the same routes will often prove counter-productive. It frequently leads to a reduction in the pupil's interest. This in turn may result in boredom and slow progress. Some repetition, however, can be helpful at times when carried out deliberately for a specific purpose relevant to the lesson. For example, practising control skills on the approach to uphill junctions might need to be restricted to a localized area where the same junctions might have to be used several times. This will give pupils more opportunity to practise the skills.

Training routes and areas fall loosely into three groups:

- nursery routes;
- intermediate;
- advanced.

There is no definite dividing line between these groups, and there may frequently be considerable overlap between them. On occasions there is justification for incorporating all kinds of route on one lesson: for instance, when making an initial assessment of a new client with previous driving experience.

Starting with the nursery routes, introduce new traffic situations at a controlled rate that is sensitive to the needs of your pupils and sympathetic to their ability. However, in reality, the nature of traffic conditions can be very erratic. Even the most carefully planned route may suddenly prove unsuitable, and the pupil will be faced with new situations he or she cannot yet cope with. Route preparation will, however, help keep these incidents down to a fairly isolated and acceptable level.

Training routes are often a compromise between the ideal and the reality of local geography and traffic conditions. In general, instructors working near the centre of a large city may experience difficulty in finding suitable nursery routes. However, their counterparts, operating in isolated rural areas, may experience problems in finding suitably varied conditions for the advanced routes. Extending the length of some lessons may be a satisfactory answer in both instances, by allowing more travelling time to training areas that are more suitable to the needs of the pupil.

Nursery routes

Various kinds of roads are required, but in general, 'nursery' routes should avoid areas with a high proportion of turns and junctions. Remember too, that apart from not wanting to worry your pupil, you are your own best advert – select routes to allow minimum interference with the flow of traffic and inconvenience to other drivers.

You should progressively use routes that incorporate:

- fairly straight, wide roads that are long enough to allow uninterrupted progression through the gears;
- quiet, fairly wide roads on up/down/level gradients on which to practise the manipulative skills;
- roads containing right/left-hand bends, allowing practice at slowing down, using the gears and steering;
- simple left turns from main into side roads;

- simple left turns into main roads;
- right turns from main into side roads and right turns into main roads;
- some routes containing parked vehicles will be necessary towards the end of the initial stages.

As far as possible avoid:

- busy roads;
- areas where there are lots of parked vehicles;
- pedestrian crossings;
- traffic lights;
- busy roundabouts.

Intermediate routes

There will be some overlap between these routes and the more advanced nursery routes. They should include:

- junctions with 'Give way' and 'Stop' controls;
- all types of basic rule crossroads;
- uphill 'Give way' junctions at which to practise first gear hold and control;
- traffic-light controlled junctions;
- roundabouts that conform to basic rules.

Roads selected for the initial practice of the turn in the road and reversing exercises should be reasonably traffic-free, and roadside furniture such as post boxes and telegraph poles should be avoided.

Routes should, wherever possible, be planned to avoid:

- dual carriageways;
- multi-lane roads;
- one-way streets;
- junctions that do not conform to basic rules;
- right turns on to very busy main roads;
- any other particularly difficult situations;
- driving test routes.

Because of the length of the tuition periods, you should take into account any special features of local geography and road design. If complicated situations cannot be avoided, you may either have to drive pupils to more suitable areas, or give them full instruction and talk through.

Advanced routes

These will incorporate most of the intermediate routes. They should be progressively extended to include as many variations to the basic rules as possible. Where possible include:

- dual carriageways;
- multi-lane roads;
- one-way streets;
- level crossings;
- busy shopping streets;
- all types of pedestrian crossing;
- rural roads providing an opportunity to practise overtaking.

Advanced routes will provide an opportunity for you to conduct 'mock' tests in conditions similar to those used for the driving test. It is stressed, however, that you should avoid actual test routes.

Points to remember

When selecting routes, you should give consideration to:

- the standard and ability of the pupil;
- disruption and inconvenience to other traffic;
- what specific skills you wish to practise;
- which particular hazards you wish to include or avoid;
- how much time is available;
- what danger or inconvenience might be caused to other road users;
- whether any excessive nuisance is likely to be caused to local residents;
- excessive repetition of routes causing boredom;
- test routes and areas used by driving examiners for manoeuvre exercises during their testing hours.

Giving route directions

The quality of a pupil's performance can be totally destroyed if you give late or unclear directions. You must give pupils sufficient time to interpret and respond to any request. You should also bear in mind that inexperienced pupils will take a long time to react to your instructions.

Instructions must be given clearly and concisely. Most directional instructions contain three basic ingredients. These are:

- Alert – draw your pupil's attention to the imminent request.
- Direct – the instruction to turn or pull up.
- Identify – confirm where the instruction is to be carried out.

Examples:

Alert:	I would like you to …
Direct:	… turn left …
Identify:	…at the junction ahead.

Alert:	Would you …
Direct:	… take the second road on the right …
Identify:	… this one being the first.

Alert:	At the roundabout, I'd like you to …
Direct:	… take the road leading off to the right …
Identify:	… That is, the third exit.

Alert:	I want you to…
Direct:	… take the next road on the left, please.
Identify:	It's the one where the pillar box is.

Confirmation can be given where required by adding further information such as 'It's just out of sight around the bend' or 'It's just before the telephone box, bus stop'.

INSTRUCTIONS AND TERMINOLOGY

General instructions

Be consistent and standardize your instructions. If you use terminology similar to that used by DSA driving examiners, your pupils will be familiar with it when they take their test. The following are general instructions for normal driving and special manoeuvre exercises:

General route brief

I want you to follow the road ahead unless otherwise directed by road signs or markings.

When I want you to turn, I will ask you in good time.

Drive on when you are ready, please.

Stopping – parking – angled start – moving off

I want you to pull up and park on the left at the next convenient place, please.

I want you to pull up just behind the stationary vehicle, but leaving yourself sufficient room to move out again.

Drive on when you are ready.

Emergency stop

Shortly, I will ask you to stop the vehicle as in an emergency. The signal will be 'Stop'. When I give this signal, stop immediately and under full control, as though a child has run off the pavement.

After the exercise is completed, let the pupil know exactly what is happening next by saying:

Thank you! I won't/will be asking you to do that exercise again.

Drive on when you are ready, please.

Left-hand reverse exercise

The road on the left is the one I want you to reverse into. Drive past it and stop, reverse in and continue back for some distance into the side road. Keep reasonably close to the kerb.

Right reverse

The road on the right is the one I want you to reverse into. Drive on the left until you have passed it, then move across to the right and stop. Reverse in and continue back for some distance down the side road, keeping reasonably close to the right-hand kerb.

Turn in the road

I want you to turn the car round by means of forward and reverse gears. Try not to touch the kerb while turning.

Reverse parking

Pull up on the left in a convenient place, please. This is the parallel parking exercise. Will you drive forward and stop alongside the vehicle ahead. Then reverse in and park reasonably close to, and parallel with, the kerb. Try to complete the exercise within about two car lengths from the vehicle.

Lane selection

Wherever possible you should encourage your pupils to make lane selection decisions for themselves. During early practice in new situations, however, and at more complex junctions, assistance may still be required. For example:

Approach in and maintain the left-hand lane through the roundabout.

Select and maintain the centre/right lane.

Route confirmation

When confirming a straight-ahead direction, use the phrase, 'Follow the road ahead' at a junction or roundabout. Avoid terms such as 'Go straight on' or 'Carry straight on' as they may be taken literally resulting in the pupil ignoring traffic signs, give way markings, or stop rules.

Directional errors

Giving clear directions in good time may not always guarantee the correct response. People are often confused between left and right, particularly when under stress, and this problem can be embarrassing for them. Providing no danger or inconvenience is caused to other road users, if a pupil is not going where you have asked, it may be advisable to let him or her continue in the chosen direction – as long as he or she is signalling to go that way. Try not to over-emphasize the problem as this will only make the pupil feel more foolish.

Obviously you should try to cure this problem as soon as possible. One way of helping a pupil who is right-handed is by saying 'I write with my right and what's left is my left.' Another is that most people wear their watch on the left wrist; similarly, wedding and engagement rings are worn on the left, so this could also be used as a point of reference.

Although candidates are not tested on their ability to distinguish between left and right, excessive errors of this nature could prove very difficult for the examiner.

Encouraging independence

When giving directional instructions to pupils who are near test standard, it is important that these are as neutral as the circumstances allow. While they should always be clear and precise, guard against giving pupils too many reminders of what they should be observing for themselves. For example, telling an advanced pupil to turn left where there is a sign giving this order will not encourage independence, nor will it test his or her observation, knowledge or planning.

Extra information, however, may be justified in special circumstances at a particularly complex junction. In certain areas it may be virtually impossible to ascertain which lane will subsequently be required without some knowledge of the area. Under such circumstances you may have to tell your pupil which lane to select and give a reason for doing so.

Points to remember

- Late instructions are likely to cause:
    - rash, hurried decisions;
    - poor control;
    - poor observations;
    - erratic steering;
    - lack of confidence;
    - difficult/dangerous situations arising;
    - over-use of the dual controls.
- Avoid using the word 'Stop', except in an emergency. This could result in the pupil stopping in a dangerous position. If you want the pupil to hold back, or avoid moving away unsafely, the word 'Wait' can be used quite effectively.
- Avoid beginning an instruction with the words: 'Turn' or 'Pull up'. You could get an immediate and incorrect response.
- Try not to use the word 'right' for anything other than a directional change. For example, using the instruction 'Right, turn left at the crossroads please' could cause obvious confusion; as could saying 'That's right!' when in fact you mean 'That's correct!'

Giving instructions and using terminology

Any instructions you give while the vehicle is in motion should be firm, concise and clearly understood. Your terminology should be consistent, particularly in the early stages of tuition. For example, if, after mostly referring to the 'holding point', you change your wording to the 'biting point', there is a possibility of confusion.

Similarly, if, after giving frequent instructions to 'signal' right or left, you change your terminology to 'indicate', it could lead to momentary hesitation, which could lead to serious consequences if there are other road users about. If you wish to instigate correct and immediate response, your pupils must be able to recognize and interpret your terminology.

The need for most instructional jargon is at its highest during the early stages of tuition. However, this is when pupils are least familiar with it. A new pupil should, however, in a short time, become accustomed to your style of terminology.

Pupils who come to you after having had lessons with another ADI may be used to a completely different style of instructional language. In order to make life easier for them, it may help if you can adapt to the difference rather than expect them to learn new vocabulary. This is not always easy, or successful, but it should help you appreciate the difficulties caused by using unfamiliar phraseology.

Terminology

'Koplings' – 'Bremse' – 'Girkasse'

Unless you are familiar with Norwegian, these words for three of the car's controls will be strange to you. When talking to an absolute novice about the clutch, brake or gearbox, you might as well be speaking in a foreign language, so when you introduce these controls, give your pupils sufficient time to assimilate the new words.

Wherever possible, your terminology should be in simple and consistent language that will be easily recognized and clearly understood.

Standard instructions

The following instructions can be used to instigate set responses from your pupils. Make sure you give adequate explanation and practice at using them before expecting pupils to remember them. In most cases the basic responses can be practised while the car is stationary.

Get to know your pupils and vary the tone of your voice according to their personality and the nature or speed of the response required. For example a short, firm 'Brake harder' is far more likely to achieve a positive effect than the same instruction given in a very quiet and slow manner.

Make sure your pupils can understand and carry out the following instructions before attempting to move off:

The instruction	*What it means*
'Handbrake ready.'	Hand on the handbrake, ready to release it.
'Set the gas.'	Increase the engine speed to a faster tickover.
'Find the holding point.'	Clutch up until the engine is slowed down at the point of clutch take-up. This is often called the 'biting point'.
'Cover the clutch.'	Foot over the clutch pedal.
'Cover the brake.'	Foot over the brake pedal.

Instructions used for moving off and increasing speed

Make an initial check all around.

Clutch down; hand on gear lever, palm towards me, and select first gear.

Set the gas.

Find the holding point and keep your feet still.

Check the interior and door mirrors.

Look over your right shoulder to check the blind spot.

Signal if helpful to warn or inform others.

Handbrake off; hand back to the wheel.

Increase the gas slightly; and slowly raise the clutch.

Cancel the signal (if used).

Instructions used for changing up the gears

Hold the wheel firmly with your right hand and cover the clutch.

Hand on gear lever, palm towards me.

Push the clutch down and come off the gas.

Move the gear lever into second.

Clutch up smoothly; increase the gas gently.

Hand back to the wheel; rest your left foot.

For changing into third and fourth use the same instruction. If the palming method of gear selection is used, you should say 'palm to you'.

Instructions used to change down the gears

Keep both hands on the wheel; off the gas and cover the brake.

Brake gently; off the brake but keep it covered.

Hold the wheel firmly with your right hand and cover the clutch.

Hand on gear lever, palm towards (whichever direction is appropriate for the gear).

Push the clutch down.

Move the gear lever into ... gear.

Clutch up smoothly.

Further instructions will then depend on whether you wish the pupil to keep slowing down or to speed up again. For slowing down more, it would be:

Keep the brake covered; clutch down, etc.

For building up the speed again, it would be:

Increase the gas so that we can change up again.

After any gear change, make sure the left foot is clear of the clutch and the hand returned to the wheel.

Instructions used in normal driving

Hold the wheel firmly.

Look well ahead; look where you want to steer.

Prepare to turn the wheel left/right.

Check the mirrors.

Signal left/right.

Increase the gas/off the gas.

Brake gently/brake harder/ease off the brake.

Clutch down.

Handbrake on and select neutral.

Instructions and prompts used to alert drivers to risks and hazards

Look for pedestrians/cyclists/animals/vehicles moving into/across your path.

Look for and act on things which restrict your view, such as parked cars.

Look for and act on signs/signals/road markings.

Look for and act on bends/junctions/obstructions.

Look, and keep looking both ways.

Instructions to reduce speed

Hold back for ...

Once explained and demonstrated, the 'hold back' procedure provides a usefully abbreviated expression. It can be used to replace abstract instructions relating to braking pressure. It also involves the pupil in learning how to judge speed and timing, and helps to develop accelerator sense. It does, however, require considerable practice.

The procedure involves slowing down early enough in order to give the situation more time to clear. Thus it reduces the likelihood of having to bring the car to a complete stop. Once understood, this procedure will give your pupils more freedom and help them develop a sense of responsibility for their own actions in good time to avoid last-minute decisions.

The hold-back position describes that in which drivers would normally:

- wait behind parked vehicles or other obstructions for oncoming traffic;
- follow behind cyclists when waiting for oncoming traffic to clear.

The following are positive commands that should leave pupils in no doubt as to the action that you require of them:

Slow down for …

Give way to …

Both of these instructions should encourage pupils to take some responsibility for their own actions in order to avoid unnecessary stops.

The command 'Stop!' should only be used in an emergency. It is the verbal equivalent of using the dual controls. The tone of your command will normally affect how pupils respond. Used in a careless manner, this command could result in an emergency stop, particularly if the learner is under stress.

Instructions and prompts used to stimulate thought

New drivers, because of their inexperience, often fail to recognize or anticipate danger in many common 'high risk' situations. Short comments or questions, directed at drawing their attention to the danger, can help to improve anticipation and responses. Provided that the prompts are used in plenty of time for pupils to respond, this technique helps to make them think about and consider the consequences of their own inaction. For example:

I would approach much slower than this.

I would give way to the oncoming driver!

Are you ready to move away when it's clear?

What's happening behind?

Is it safe to go yet?

Can you see properly?

How far can you see?

Is it clear?

Do you need to signal?

Do you know how much clearance you should give to a parked car?

Can you tell me what the normal driving position is?

What's the speed limit on this road?

Approaching a row of parked vehicles at an excessive speed, ask:

What will you do if a child runs out?

What will you do if a car moves out?

What will you do if a car door opens?

What will you do if the cyclist pulls out?

What will you do if the oncoming car keeps coming?

Approaching a pedestrian crossing at excessive speed, ask:

What will you do if that pedestrian steps onto the crossing?

Do you know what's behind us?

Driving too close to the vehicle ahead, ask:

What will you do if the car in front has to stop quickly?

Do you know how close the car behind is?

What is the stopping distance at x mph?

Approaching a bend or corner at excessive speed, ask:

What will you do if there is a car parked just around the bend?

What will you do if there is a pedestrian crossing the side road?

CORRECTIONS ON THE MOVE

Under normal circumstances, detailed explanations should be avoided while the vehicle is in motion. This applies particularly if your pupil is concentrating on something else, such as when emerging from a junction or waiting at red traffic lights.

However, most incidents involving minor errors may not be recognized by the learner at the time they are committed and 10 minutes later, those that were recognized will have been forgotten. Some brief feedback, therefore, should be given at the time errors are committed, or as soon as possible afterwards. This will draw attention to them, making incidents easier to recall when later referred to and corrected in detail.

You can use short comments as cues to help pupils deal with difficult situations, or as minor rebukes for errors that may have been committed. Where corrections are made, they should be of a positive nature and ideally state the action that is required to cure the error. For example, it is better to say 'Hold the clutch still' rather than 'Don't let the clutch up', or 'Drive about two or three feet from the kerb' rather than 'Don't drive in the gutter'.

Serious errors, or repeated minor ones that appear to involve misunderstandings, should be corrected as soon as reasonably possible after they have occurred, when a suitable parking place has been found.

DUAL CONTROLS

Because of their inexperience, new drivers lack anticipation and will fail to recognize or respond to potentially dangerous traffic situations. You should never completely trust them to follow your instructions or to do the correct thing.

Make sure they are aware of their legal responsibilities. Remember too that you could be prosecuted for aiding and abetting offences committed by them. You must sometimes be firm and take whatever action necessary to protect your pupil, the car and other road users. Look, think and plan well ahead. Get to know individual pupils and watch them. You will soon learn to predict how they are likely to respond in given situations.

You must anticipate changes in the traffic situation and give instructions early enough for pupils to react. If anticipated early enough, most awkward situations can be avoided by giving verbal commands or, if it becomes necessary, taking action with the dual controls. Uncorrected errors will lead to the development of potentially dangerous and frightening situations.

There are four main reasons that you should intervene:

- to prevent risk of injury or damage to persons or property;
- to prevent an offence against the law;
- to prevent excessive stress to the learner in certain unplanned circumstances;
- to prevent mechanical damage to the vehicle.

A verbal command is often sufficient if given in time. However, if your pupil does not react to this, you will need to act. For example, you might:

- sound the horn;
- turn the wheel;
- switch off the engine;
- select a missed gear;
- release a partially engaged handbrake;
- prevent an unsympathetic gear change by covering the lever.

If it becomes necessary, you must be ready to use the dual controls. However, they should not be used as a matter of routine and when you do use them, tell the pupil afterwards what the reason was.

Continual steering corrections and excessive use of the duals does little to build pupils' faith in their instructor. It could also lead to resentment, particularly if they do not understand why you used them.

There are various ways in which you can maintain a safe learning environment:

Verbal intervention

The verbal command is the most common form of intervention. It will usually work if you are concentrating properly, planning well ahead and giving instructions early enough for your pupil to respond. Commands range from a mild memory prompt to a more positive command for a specific and immediate action.

The prompt is usually associated more with the earlier lessons, but may be extended to more positive instructions such as:

Use the mirrors before changing direction.

Brake harder (or, Ease the brake off).

Clutch down (or, Hold the clutch still).

Increase the gas (or, Off the gas).

The more positive commands needed to relieve potentially dangerous traffic situations are usually those needed when you want your pupil to slow down earlier on the approach to hazards. 'Hold back' or 'Give way' are positive commands requiring a specific reaction, but these also leave the pupil with some freedom of judgement.

'Stop' is the final and absolute command. It should generally only be used in a situation that is fast getting out of control and/or where other instructions have been ignored or are unlikely to achieve the desired response.

Physical intervention

Physical intervention should normally be restricted to situations when it is necessary to avoid danger. This occurs when verbal intervention has not worked or where there is insufficient time to give it. The main methods of physical intervention are use of the dual footbrake, and steering corrections.

In any situation you will need to consider the method of intervention best suited to correcting the problem. There are occasions when both steering and braking corrections may be required. For example, you may need to control the steering wheel while using the dual footbrake. This is to resist the tendency the pupil may have to swing on the wheel. In order to generate more time for you to intervene and turn the wheel it may be necessary for you to control the speed of the car with the dual brake, particularly if the pupil has 'frozen' on the accelerator.

Using the dual footbrake

The procedure is as follows:

- Keep your foot near the brake to allow for its use with the minimum amount of movement.
- If you see a potential need for using the brake, have your foot ready over the pedal.
- Avoid fidgeting with the brake – this is likely to unnerve the pupil.

- If your pupil becomes frozen on the accelerator, it is generally not advisable to use the dual clutch as well as the brake. This could result in a 'blown' engine.
- Sometimes when pupils see a sudden movement towards the pedal, or where they feel a pressure change on theirs, they may react instinctively by braking harder. This double pressure can be dangerous to following traffic or may possibly lock the wheels. Be aware of this possible reaction.
- Before using your brake, check on what's happening behind.
- After using the dual controls, explain to the pupil why it was necessary.
- Reducing the speed with the dual brake sometimes allows pupils more time to turn the wheel.

The steering wheel – points to remember

- Turning the wheel from the passenger seat is generally more difficult than using the dual footbrake, and in certain circumstances it may be the only safe or practical method of intervention.
- The need for your taking the wheel can be kept to an acceptable minimum by ensuring that the route and conditions are suitable and appropriate for your pupil's ability.
- Other than for minor course corrections, if you intend turning the wheel left, go for an initially high position – this will give more leverage. For turning it right, go for a lower position which is more suitable for pushing the wheel.
- When turning the wheel, try to avoid physical contact with the pupil, though circumstances may make contact with the hands or arms inevitable.
- When 'frozen' on the wheel, even a very frail person can become immensely strong and may resist any attempt you make to turn it.
- Minor corrections with the steering to adjust the course are frequently more practical and safer alternatives to using the dual footbrake: for example, if a pupil is steering towards the kerb or too close to oncoming traffic, parked vehicles, cyclists or pedestrians.
- Use the top of the steering wheel to help maintain a steady course, particularly if the pupil has made an incorrect decision to proceed through a narrowing gap.

The dual clutch

Assisting pupils by using the dual clutch should be done sparingly. It should, of course, be used where there is potential danger or risk of damage, but try to avoid over-use as it can lead pupils to think that they have better control than they really do.

The dual clutch could also be used in relatively extreme circumstances when it is necessary to get away from a situation with which the pupil cannot cope. Covering the clutch so as to avoid an unexpected and potentially dangerous move off is one of the more important 'uses' of the dual clutch.

The dual accelerator

Dual accelerators are not normally fitted to driving instruction cars. If one is fitted, it must be removed while the vehicle is being used for a driving test. This is for safety reasons, so that the examiner does not use this pedal by mistake.

Its main use is to accelerate out of danger.

The horn

This should be used sensibly. It is better to remove a danger at source by giving a warning, than to find later that more drastic intervention has become necessary.

Other forms of intervention

- Engage a missed gear at a critical time or place.
- Switch off the engine – as long as you can reach the key.
- Put on or cancel an indicator at times when the pupil is unable to attend to it.
- Correct a mistake in the use of the handbrake, for instance by releasing it properly or applying it when needed.
- Prevent unsympathetic gear changes by covering the lever until the appropriate speed has been reached.

Dual eye mirrors

The importance of the extra mirrors should be obvious. While the extra rear view mirror will help you to keep in constant touch with the all-round traffic situation, the dual eye mirror, strategically placed and focused on the pupil's eyes, will enable you to monitor his or her mirror use.

Mirrors should be placed fairly high on the windscreen so as not to impede the pupil's view, but low enough to provide you with an adequate view to the rear. They should be correctly adjusted and perfectly directed for you to check just as you would adjust your driving mirror. They should give maximum vision with the minimum of movement.

Some instructors use nearside door mirrors for their own convenience. This can be counter-productive and defeats the commonsense purpose of encouraging pupils to make all-round observations.

Avoiding problems

Safety is no accident! It is your responsibility to maintain a safe learning environment by:

- planning routes to suit each pupil's level of ability;
- looking and planning ahead and concentrating on the traffic situation all around;

- being alert to, and anticipating, pupils' actions and reactions in response to moving traffic situations;
- giving directions and instructions clearly and in good time to encourage pupils to think, respond and act accordingly.

Popular belief is that learner drivers are far more likely to have accidents than experienced motorists. However, the novice who is learning in a dual-controlled car under professional supervision is far less likely to have one.

If a driving school car is involved in an accident it is most likely to be a 'rear end shunt'. There are two main reasons for this. First, most novices are reluctant to slow down, give way or stop because of their inexperience at hazard recognition, and because for them, it's easier to keep moving. This initial reluctance to deal with a hazard may subsequently develop into an emergency. Where the situation is allowed to reach this critical level, there are two possible unwanted reactions from the learner:

- do nothing, remain frozen on the controls and proceed on a collision course;
- over-reaction – this can often result in harsh unregulated braking, that will usually bring the car to an uncontrolled and abrupt stop some distance before it's necessary.

Whether it is the instructor or pupil who stops the car under these circumstances, the result is likely to be the same if the driver behind is not concentrating or is following too closely!

The second reason is the 'false start', or 'stall' when moving into a roundabout or pulling out of an 'open' junction. Often, as the learner starts to pull out, the driver behind is looking to the right while moving into the space he or she thinks has been vacated. Unfortunately, and without the driver realizing it (usually because of a lack of observation in both directions), when attempting to move, the learner has stopped or stalled the engine (or the instructor may have stopped the car because of approaching traffic). This emphasizes the need for proper route selection according to the student's abilities.

How to avoid rear end collisions

First, keep your distance, slow down earlier and allow the car to run gently to a halt.

Second, act promptly to prevent a pupil from trying to move off at the wrong time. To allow a pupil to move off in this manner, necessitating a stop within a few feet, is potentially dangerous because it also encourages the following driver to move.

Other accident-prone situations

Pay special attention when approaching traffic lights. Because of a lack of understanding of the meaning of the light sequence and colours, some pupils are apt to stop abruptly if the lights change. This can sometimes happen when they have already crossed the stop line.

The right turn at traffic lights is a particularly dangerous manoeuvre, and careful attention should also be paid when emerging from blind junctions, or where parked vehicles or other obstructions restrict visibility. As well as checking on your pupil's observations, look for yourself and be sure it is safe to proceed before allowing the pupil to go.

You must remember that inexperienced learners will not be as quick off the mark as experienced drivers. This can make emerging into busy roads and roundabouts potentially dangerous manoeuvres. Again, choose your routes to match your pupil's ability.

Be ready to compensate for any sudden movement of the car during low-speed manoeuvre exercises. A slight error on the part of your pupil could have disastrous consequences.

When emerging from junctions, pay particular attention to the blind areas behind your pupil's head. At the same time, position yourself so that you do not restrict the pupil's sightlines. Always make sure for yourself that your pupil is emerging safely.

ASSESSMENTS AND STANDARDS

To be able to judge how effective your teaching is, you will need to be able to properly assess your pupils' performance as they progress through the different stages of learning to drive. The elements you will need to be able to assess are:

- knowledge;
- skill;
- attitude;
- personality.

The different methods of assessment needed to keep a check on progress are:

- interviews/oral (Q&A);
- written tests/examinations;
- objective tests;
- aptitude tests;
- practical tests.

As an instructor you will mainly be concerned with assessing the practical skills involved in the driving task. However, because effective driving needs an understanding of the rules and regulations, you will also need to test your pupils' knowledge of the *Highway Code* and other relevant motoring matters, either orally, or by setting written papers at intervals throughout the course.

To assess the effectiveness of your training you will need to:

- ascertain the level of pupils' ability at the beginning of their course;
- state what they should know and be able to do as they progress through each stage, by specifying objectives for each topic;
- test their ability at the end of the course.

Initial assessments

To make an initial assessment of current knowledge and skill, you will need to use a mixture of interview technique and aptitude testing. From information gained, you will then be able to establish a base from which to commence your tuition.

Adapting your instruction

As a driving instructor you need to be able to adapt the style of your teaching methods to suit the ability of the person you are teaching. Your instruction and approach with someone who has never driven before should be totally different from that applied to a driver with years of experience. You should find it much easier to develop efficient skills and safe attitudes in the new learner, than in trying to change the style of the experienced driver who has recently been ordered to take an extended test.

Dealing with new pupils

The first lesson

It can be helpful to find out a little about pupils prior to their first driving lesson, particularly if they have any disabilities that could mean you need to adapt your teaching methods. You can do this by asking a few relevant questions when you are making the booking.

If you are picking up the pupil, it is important that you look professional. Be punctual and make sure your car is clean and tidy.

Use this lesson as an opportunity to get to know each other, establish a form of address (this is often dictated by the age and profession of each pupil), and find out what the pupil already knows and can do. It's important that you use a first meeting to build up pupils' confidence in you and to get them used to your style and terminology. Reassure them that learning to drive can be enjoyable, and motivate them by confirming that driving is an asset, and also that if you work together it will be much easier.

Pupils with no experience

For pupils with no previous experience, drive to a quiet location and explain how to get into the car safely, and about the function and use of the main controls. Depending on the pupil's ability and the length of the lesson, by the end of it the pupil should have had some experience in moving off, stopping and changing gears. This initial success will go a long way to satisfy their expectations.

Pupils with some experience

For those with previous experience, use Q&A to confirm the standard they have reached. However, do not rely entirely on what you are told – some learners are not as good as they think, others understate their ability. It's vital that you make your own assessment by asking a few relevant questions and then select an appropriate route so that you can validate what you have been told. Confirm, and make allowances for, the differences in your car and the one the individual has been driving.

During the drive, be prepared to adapt your terminology if the pupil appears not to understand you. Only when you have carried out this process can you establish the level of instruction to be used and the point in your syllabus at which to begin.

Dealing with full licence holders

When assessing or training experienced drivers you need to exercise a great deal of tact and diplomacy. Do not make the mistake of treating them as learners – treat them as equals. For example, if habits such as crossing hands on the steering wheel have been practised for 20 years, you should not expect to completely eradicate this style. As long as the car is under control, and is in the correct position on the road, try not to over-emphasize the fault. You may find the driver feels you are 'nit-picking'. This could result in resentment to the point where no learning or improvement takes place in more important areas such as forward planning, hazard awareness and anticipation.

Where weaknesses in style of driving and knowledge are apparent, advise and give valid reasons for adapting and changing. A very common example is where drivers change down through all of the gears because this is how they were originally taught. Give them a few reasons for 'selective' gear changing, such as:

- it involves less work using the controls, which allows more attention to be paid to the all-round situation;
- your hands are on the wheel longer, especially when braking;
- it saves wear and tear on the clutch and gearbox;
- it's better for fuel economy.

You should find that reasoning is a more positive way of changing attitudes!

Licence and eyesight check

No matter what the level of experience of your client, it's your responsibility to ensure that he or she is legally entitled to drive your car. Check the licence details. If a pupil does not produce his or her licence for any reason, ask for it to be brought on the next lesson. If you are in any doubt, it may be advisable to postpone the lesson.

You should also check for yourself that the pupil can read a number plate at the prescribed distance. If he or she cannot read it, or has problems with some letters or numbers, try several plates. If difficulties persist and you are not satisfied, postpone the lesson and advise the pupil to get his or her eyes tested professionally.

Getting to know your new pupil

During the drive to a suitable training area, establish previous experience and other details. Avoid long periods of silence as these can increase tension, particularly if the pupil is already feeling a little apprehensive. An informal chat will help to relax him or her, and it can also:

- help break the ice by relieving initial tension;
- help keep the pupil's mind occupied if he or she is anxious;
- provide you with some outline information on which to base your objectives.

Do not press too hard if pupils are reluctant to talk about themselves. Other opportunities will arise later. On the other hand, some pupils will be more talkative – this could be to cover up anxiety on their part. In any case, keep the conversation professional, polite and sympathetic.

Try to keep your questions relevant. You could include:

- Are you still at school or college?
- What kind of work do you do?
- What interests or hobbies do you have?
- Why do you want to learn to drive?
- Do you have any previous experience in driving a car, riding a bicycle or motorcycle?
- Do you have any particular worries about learning?

Outline the course objectives

Outline the progressive stages of learning to drive. Explain that everyone is different and reassure your pupil that the course will be structured to suit their own capabilities.

Selecting a suitable route

When choosing a route for initial assessments, as far as local geography will allow, the following should be taken into consideration.

- It should be suitable for the absolute novice.
- It should be flexible enough to allow for progression to intermediate routes where pupils' ability to cope is satisfactory.
- For those with previous experience, the route should begin in a quiet area, affording the opportunity of familiarizing them with your car. It should then become progressively more difficult. Make sure, however, that it is possible to escape from the more difficult areas if the pupil is unable to cope.

DRIVER'S RECORD

As the driver training industry becomes more regulated, it is increasingly important to keep accurate records of pupils' progress and achievements in line with the industry code of practice. For this reason, the DSA has introduced a 'Driver's Record' system. The Driver's Record has been designed and produced by the DSA to help instructors and pupils keep a check on progress during a course of training, and to provide an accurate record of the pupil's level of ability.

The system is based on the official syllabus for learning to drive. It lists all the skills required for safe driving, and should be completed by instructor and pupil on each lesson. A personalized booklet for the pupil and a set of record sheets for the instructor are included. Additionally, the instructor is provided with a set of guidance notes and details of the competencies required for each item in the syllabus.

The pupil's part of the Record is issued to all new learners with their provisional licence. Copies are available from test centres, or may be downloaded from www.driving-tests.co.uk. An integral part of the Record allows the pupil and instructor to monitor progress on each topic through the various stages of learning:

- topic introduced;
- pupil under full instruction;
- prompted practice;
- seldom prompted;
- independent.

The main advantages of a Driver's Record (or 'log book') include:

- It enables a structured approach to training and skill development through a written record.
- Both the instructor and the pupil are focused on the need to combine structured formal training and private practice where appropriate.
- Pupils and instructors are encouraged to expand on the learning process beyond the requirements of the 'L' test.
- Pupils are encouraged to gain experience in a wide variety of road and traffic conditions until each part of the syllabus has been achieved.

The inclusion of a 'declaration of test readiness' raises the pupil's awareness of the need to be fully prepared before taking the test.

Patterns of errors

A properly kept progress record will show where any distinct patterns of errors are developing that might otherwise not be so obvious. If allowed to go unchecked, these errors could eventually mean the difference between a pass or a fail of the driving test.

Assessment reports

Where relatives or employers are paying for lessons/assessments you may be required to provide reports. These need not necessarily include detailed information on faults, but they should give a clear and honest outline of the pupil's performance. In certain cases a prospective employer may require a more in-depth assessment before employment is granted.

The following general headings may assist in formulating your reports:

- Knowledge of the *Highway Code* rules and driving procedures.
- Attitude to speed and the safety of other road users.
- Attitude to lessons and the driving test.
- Vehicle control skills.
- Vehicle sympathy.
- Visual and perceptive ability.

PASS PLUS SYLLABUS

Pass Plus consists of six separate training modules covering:

- town driving;
- all-weather driving;
- driving out of town;
- night driving;
- driving on dual carriageways;
- driving on motorways.

Town driving

After an introduction to Pass Plus and an explanation of the aims and objectives of the course, you should include in the practical session:

- observations, judgement and awareness;
- eye contact;
- consideration for vulnerable road users;
- keeping space around your car.

All-weather driving

This section should include:

- correct speed;
- safe stopping distances;
- seeing and being seen in:
    - rain
    - sleet, snow and ice

- mist and fog
- bright sunshine;
- skidding:
  - causes and prevention
  - correcting slow-speed skids
  - braking on poor surfaces
  - aquaplaning.

Driving out of town

This module, which would be on country roads, will deal with the main differences between town and country driving including:

- observation of the road ahead;
- making progress safely;
- bends, hills, uneven roads, dead ground;
- keeping a safe distance from the vehicle ahead;
- overtaking safely;
- being aware of and showing consideration for:
  - pedestrians, horse riders and animals in the road
  - farm entrances
  - slow-moving vehicles.

Night driving

For this section of the syllabus, you need to cover the main aspects of driving at dawn and dusk, as well as in the dark, and in particular:

- the importance of the correct use of headlights;
- adjusting to dark conditions;
- judging speed and distances;
- correct use and care of lights;
- dealing with dazzle;
- road users who can be difficult to see;
- parking.

Driving on dual carriageways

Driving on this type of road requires particular skills:

- effective observations;
- use of mirrors and checking blind areas;
- judgement and planning well ahead;
- safe separation distances;
- joining and leaving dual carriageways;
- lane discipline;

- overtaking;
- correct use of speed.

Driving on motorways

Ideally, this module should be a practical session on a motorway. If this is not possible, then a theory lesson is acceptable, but the pupil should have a motorway drive as soon as practicable so as to put the theory into practice.

Either way, the training should include:

- planning journeys in advance;
- joining and leaving motorways;
- using slip roads properly and effectively;
- safe speeds for varying circumstances;
- effective all-round observations;
- signs, signals and markings;
- overtaking and lane discipline;
- courtesy towards other road users;
- motorway fatigue;
- breakdown procedures;
- use of lights and hazard warning lights;
- debris on the carriageway;
- crosswinds.

Pupils are allowed to take Pass Plus within a year of passing the driving test to qualify for reduced rates of motor insurance from several companies.

For details of the Pass Plus scheme, see page 24.

'L' DRIVER ERRORS

Driving errors range from those with sometimes very simple causes, to those caused by the pressures and stress built up by driving in complex traffic conditions. Simple causes can range from unsuitable shoes being worn to an incorrect seating position. Both of these could make control of the pedals extremely difficult and result in loss of concentration. Make sure your pupils seat themselves correctly when they get into the car.

The tensions caused by driving in difficult conditions can sometimes result in unusual and possibly dangerous decisions or actions being taken. Avoiding road and traffic situations with which pupils are not yet able to cope should, in most cases, solve this problem.

Poorly developed perceptive skills frequently result in inexperienced drivers approaching hazards at excessive speed. This usually results in rushed actions when carrying out the manipulative skills, and this in turn will result in errors in vehicle control. This problem can be avoided by your giving your instructions early enough for pupils to respond, and encouraging them to slow down sufficiently to maintain control.

The types of errors committed vary considerably according to the particular stage of learning reached. The aptitude and attitudes of pupils also influence the mistakes made. Most errors in the early stages of learning cannot seriously be considered as driving faults as they are usually caused through lack of knowledge or practice. However, unless nipped in the bud, they may well develop into driving faults.

A lack of understanding of new information may also cause errors. Many such problems are intensified by lack of sufficient practice in basic car control skills. This initial 'familiarization' should be carried out in relatively safe surroundings on suitably quiet routes.

You must remain acutely alert for any unusual, sudden or excessive movements with the steering or other controls, particularly during the initial stages of learning. No matter how good your instructions may be, you should not assume that the pupil will carry them out. Initially, most learners have difficulty in coordinating their hands, feet, steering and observations. You must allow for this and give full talk-through until these skills develop.

Some of the main causes of basic driver error are:

- lack of knowledge;
- conflicting knowledge;
- underdeveloped perceptive skills;
- lack of or inadequate observations and/or misinterpretation of visual information;
- deficiencies in the basic manipulative (car control) skills;
- deficiencies in behaviour caused by timidity or aggressive and irresponsible attitudes;
- poor health, fatigue, drink, drugs, emotional stress.

Note: the learner driver may often be subject to considerable pressure when having to interpret verbal directions while, at the same time, attempting to assimilate other instructions on the move. Do not overload the pupil with too much information, as this can result in lack of attention to the task in general.

General errors

Poor car control

Inadequate car control can usually be traced to insufficient practice at a basic skill, incorrect training and the interference of previous knowledge or practice, lack of knowledge, poor coordination, hurried movements, and excessive speed.

Persistent excessive use of speed

Excessive speed is often attributable to an unsafe attitude, incorrect use of the footbrake, lack of awareness of potential or actual danger, or poor perception of speed.

Lack of awareness of potential or actual danger

This fault is very common and generally caused by a lack of experience, knowledge, imagination or visual scanning. If a pupil is passively observing a traffic scene, it does not imply that he or she will take any action on a developing traffic hazard.

Indecision

This can be associated with lack of confidence, poor control skills, lack of knowledge, timidity or the conditions being too busy for the pupil's ability. Indecision and/or an unwillingness to give way, slow down or stop for a hazard is often caused because pupils lack confidence in their basic ability to move off again. They often fail to recognize that slowing down early will alleviate the situation by creating more time for it to clear, thereby often reducing the need to stop.

As a driving instructor, it is your responsibility to ensure that your pupils attain as high a standard as possible, taking into consideration their own individual abilities. You need to aim for a high standard of driving at all times and at all levels. Try to offer as wide a scope of driver education as possible. This will mean that your work is more interesting, varied and satisfying.

ASSESSING PROGRESS

Question and answer (Q&A) technique

It is your responsibility to produce thinking drivers who will be able to cope safely and effectively with today's complex road and traffic conditions – and also to share the road with all of us. To do this you will need to learn how to use the Q&A technique to encourage pupils to look and plan well ahead, and respond early to developing situations.

Teaching usually involves a progression from the known to the unknown. At the beginning of each lesson recap on what a pupil already knows and can do, then introduce new information at a level to suit his or her knowledge and ability. By asking relevant questions throughout their training, you will discover whether pupils are learning the appropriate rules and procedures outlined in the *Highway Code* and other official publications.

Questions should be short, to the point and phrased in a way that encourages the required response. Begin questions with 'How', 'Why', 'What if', 'When', 'Where' or 'Which'. Sometimes questions will only have one correct answer. If this is the case, make sure the question is phrased so as not to mislead. The following questions could be ambiguous:

'Do you know the main causes of skidding?' A correct response could be either 'Yes' or 'No'.

'What do you know about correcting skids?' This could result in the pupil saying 'Nothing'.

Neither of these responses would be what you were looking for. The questions would have been more direct if phrased as follows:

What is the main cause of skidding?

How would you correct a skid where the rear of the car is sliding to the left?

Allow pupils time to think when using more open-ended questions, such as 'When driving along, what kind of things should you be looking out for about four seconds ahead?' Don't worry about short silences – your pupil will need time to interpret the question, search for the answer and then find the words with which to express the answer.

If the pupil is having obvious difficulty in responding, phrase the question differently or give some clues about what you are looking for. For example you might add, 'Think about the movement of other road users' or 'What about the restrictions to your sightlines?'

Listen carefully to what the pupil is trying to say and make the most out of incorrect answers! Give a little praise for partially correct or thoughtful answers before providing the correct information.

Avoid questions that go far beyond what the pupil is likely to know. You could easily cause embarrassment if he or she is never able to give you a correct answer.

The timing of questions can be as important as the wording. While the car is on the move, avoid asking questions that need a lot of thought. This can be a distraction and cause the pupil to lose concentration on the driving task.

If you want to find out what your pupil is thinking about a particular situation, keep your questions simple. For example, if you see a dog wandering about near the pavement edge you could ask, 'What can you expect that dog to do?'

Each learning session should conclude with a few questions to ensure the student understands the main points. Q&A can be very effective for a 'recap' at the end of the lesson. It can also be useful as revision on subsequent lessons.

Throughout their training, students should be encouraged to ask you questions relevant to the points under instruction. If irrelevant ones are asked, rather than giving no response at all, answer them simply and confirm that you will cover this subject in detail at a more appropriate time.

Answering questions with questions

Socrates, the Greek philosopher, is famous for his inductive technique of answering questions with questions to reach new definitions. This 'Socratic method' is probably one of the most effective ways of teaching. It allows pupils to acquire knowledge through their own personal involvement and effort. For example, if a pupil asks you, 'What shall I do about the bus that is signalling to move away from the bus stop?' you could respond with, 'What will you do if it starts moving?'

Highway Code and driving-related questions

New drivers generally need some kind of motivation to get them to read the official publications. Continually verbally emphasizing the importance of the *Highway Code* and other publications and their relevance is not always enough. Asking questions that relate directly to the topic under instruction can do much to change attitudes towards learning the rules and procedures. Explaining what should be done and, most importantly, why it should be done, will encourage a better understanding.

A few simple questions and words of encouragement will also help to arouse a degree of interest and a willingness to work with you. You could organize between-lesson projects and provide self-test exercises consisting of multiple-choice objective questions. Supply an answer code to enable students to check their scores.

Objective questions

These are designed so that pupils have to select a response from several answers. For example:

1. Triangular signs usually give:
   (a) orders
   (b) warnings
   (c) information

2. Tyres must have a minimum legal tread depth of:
   (a) 1 mm
   (b) 2 mm
   (c) 1.6 mm

Short-answer questions

These require a specific answer and can be used to reinforce particular learning points. For example:

3. Give reasons for each of the following. Drivers:
   (a) must allow adequate clearance for parked cars
   (b) should reduce speeds in busy shopping areas
   (c) should take extra care on country roads without footpaths

Examples of questions more commonly used in driving instruction and testing are:

What is the stopping distance when driving at 30 mph in good conditions?

Give six examples of places unsuitable for parking.

What are the characteristics of a safe parking position?

Designing questions

Questions should be written simply, so as not to mislead. For example, 'What must you not do before turning right?' is a negative question. After considering this question, you should find two basic flaws which could prove counter-productive if put to a novice:

- Because the question asks what not to do, the learner will probably go up a number of 'blind alleys' prior to reaching the correct answer. There are literally dozens of correct and sensible answers. While occasionally there may be justification for this type of question, it is normally far better to use questions that require a positive and constructive response.
- Changing the question to 'What must you do before turning right?' narrows down the field of correct answers. Remember, while this is a better question, the word 'what' still implies that a specific answer is required. However, there is not one specific answer as the full procedure for turning right involves several actions.

If you require a short, exact response then more information should be included in the question. For example:

What must you do before signalling to turn right?

When turning right into a side road, what must you particularly look out for just before turning?

What position should you be in for turning right on a wide road?

If a more general answer is required, the question could be phrased as follows:

Outline the basic procedure for turning right into a side road.

While this kind of question may frequently be necessary, one of the problems is that it also puts on trial a pupil's ability to communicate. The procedure may be understood but the pupil may have difficulty in explaining the details. Patience and understanding should be exercised, and where necessary, give further help by asking different questions of a more specific nature.

Practical assessments

To assess progress, you need to take pupils into traffic conditions appropriate to their experience and then observe their behaviour. This type of assessment is mainly of a visual nature and consists of watching the pupils' actions in the car. You need to constantly be monitoring their use of the controls, instrumentation, mirrors and ancillary equipment, and behaviour towards the external traffic situation.

You should guard against watching the pupil too intently, as this may result in your missing important changes in the situation to which your pupil should be responding; and against watching the road and traffic too intently, as you may miss faults of a physical nature inside the car, such as an incorrect signal being given, riding the clutch, poor mirror use, or attempting to select a gear with the clutch engaged.

You will need to divide your attention over a wide range of your pupil's activities in fairly rapid succession, and in order to maintain safety, you also need to be reading the road and traffic conditions.

There are some areas where prolonged observation of the pupil will be required so that a thorough assessment may be made. These are observation of his or her use of all mirrors, and the pupil's pattern of observations on the approach to, and emerging from, different types of road junctions. In order to limit the time required to check on mirror use, and also to leave you with more time to keep in touch with the all-round traffic situation, an additional mirror can be discreetly focused on to the pupil's eyes. This extra mirror does away with the need to look directly at pupils at appropriate times when a check would be required.

Looking at pupils often serves as a prompt for them to check the mirror when they might otherwise have forgotten to do so. Reducing these prompts will allow you to make an entirely objective assessment. Similarly, unless they are intended to be prompts, you need to be extremely discreet with your observations of the road and traffic situation at junctions and during any of the manoeuvre exercises.

Intermediate assessments and tests of students' knowledge and ability are an integral part of a teacher's work, and a considerable amount of your time will be involved directly in this ongoing process.

Mock tests

An objective assessment is one that measures a learner's actual performance against a pre-fixed standard. For the ADI, this pre-fixed standard is the 'perfect driver'. It is a satisfactory yardstick by which any level of driving can be measured.

The perfect driver can be defined as one who:

- is in complete harmony with the vehicle and traffic conditions;
- is always in the correct position on the road;
- is travelling at a safe speed for the conditions and visibility;
- has the ideal gear engaged to suit the varying speed and power requirements.

This 'perfect' driver is totally aware of the surroundings and shows consideration for the rights of other road users. Technically, anything that detracts from this perfection is an error. However, perfection to this degree is extremely rare, even in an experienced driver and it would be unrealistic to expect an inexperienced learner to achieve this standard. It is therefore necessary to devise some means of grading faults whereby significantly more importance is attached to serious and dangerous faults than to those of a minor nature.

You should try not to class driving errors as either 'black' or 'white'. There are many shades of grey, and when assessing the seriousness of a fault, you need to bear in mind that an error can involve varying degrees of importance, and that some errors are of a more serious nature and can result in more severe consequences than others.

Continuous assessment

This type of assessment is more sensitive to the needs of the learner progressing through a course of lessons, than is the more decisive objective assessment previously discussed. During the early stages of learning, it is unreasonable to compare the performance of the novice with the 'perfect driver'. Although assessments should be objective, they should also take account of previous experience, practice and general progress, as well as the learner's capability. They should take into consideration the reasons that faults may be occurring.

Continually look for ways to correct faults and encourage your pupils to have a greater understanding of their causes. If you do this, the pupil's overall knowledge and driving performance should improve.

When a learner makes a mistake there is usually a valid reason for it: for instance there may be a basic misunderstanding of what is required. If there is a recurrence of errors you will need to cure them at source rather than superficially treat the symptoms.

There are literally hundreds of different errors waiting to be committed by the learner. Their causes are fewer. If you concentrate therefore on curing the cause, improvement should result in other areas where similar mistakes may be occurring. For example, if a pupil is having difficulty steering around a corner because of lack of time, it is the speed on approach that needs to be worked on.

The 'halo effect'

It isn't possible to remove the human element from driver assessments! If you develop a particular regard for a pupil with whom you get on well, it's possible to subconsciously ignore minor errors. You may even gloss over those of a more serious nature. Without realizing it, you may even select an easier route for the pupil by avoiding some of the more difficult situations. Acceptance that this phenomenon, known as the 'halo effect', exists is in most cases sufficient to guard against it. Try to remain objective, otherwise your pupils may suffer in the long term.

To a certain extent the opposite can also occur with an unpopular client. In this case you may subconsciously treat relatively minor errors as more serious ones; and perhaps fail to notice improvements in performance and give credit where it's due.

9

Disabilities and Impairments

This chapter outlines some of the things to consider when teaching driving to people who have disabilities. It covers topics such as making preliminary assessments, vehicle modifications and adaptations, methods of teaching, notes on some disabilities, how to apply for the driving test, how the test differs, and driver licensing.

We also deal with factors that might affect the driver's performance, including learning difficulties, physical stature, ill health, drugs, stress, illness and ageing.

ASSESSING THE NEEDS

Many thousands of people with disabilities have passed the driving test and are regular, safe and competent drivers. Teaching driving to people who have disabilities is essentially the same as teaching anyone else. The subject matter is exactly the same – you merely have to adapt how you teach it, and take into consideration each individual pupil's needs.

This type of driving instruction can be extremely rewarding. Very often pupils with some form of disability are much more highly motivated to do well and gain their independence.

You will need to assess your pupil's personal requirements with regard to any necessary vehicle adaptations. For many, all that may be required to control the car effectively could be:

- a car with automatic transmission;
- a steering ball on the wheel;
- power-assisted steering;
- left-foot accelerator.

For those with more severe disabilities, a range of more complex adaptations may need to be considered. Recent developments in technology, such as joystick steering and remote control devices, have given the freedom of driving to those with little movement or strength.

Preliminary assessments

There are many centres in the UK offering advice, information and assessments. A list of these is given in the 'Useful Addresses' section of this book. They offer advice on the different vehicle adaptations available to compensate for physical limitations.

Minor adaptations may be all that are required for people with disabilities such as arthritis or those caused through spinal injuries. However, if there is a possible difficulty with a person's learning capability or ability to cope with the cognitive demands of driving, then a more comprehensive assessment will be required. This type of assessment may be particularly appropriate for those with:

- stroke;
- hydrocephalus;
- cerebral palsy;
- head injuries;
- marked general learning difficulties (even in the absence of physical disability).

Specialist assessment centres around the country offer 'medical fitness to drive' assessments.

This type of assessment forms an invaluable information resource for the pupil and the instructor, providing information on relevant aspects to be especially aware of during tuition.

Most centres offer a free advice service; however, there is normally a charge for the assessments. This will depend on the scope of service and facilities required. It is sometimes possible to obtain a subsidy for these fees from an appropriate disability group, for example ASBAH (Association for Spina Bifida and Hydrocephalus). The Department of Social Services, or a local fundraising organization such as the Rotary Club, may also be able to help.

It is certainly sensible to invest in a professional assessment as to the probabilities of driving, prior to investing large sums of money in a vehicle and adaptations.

An assessment centre should provide information on:

- eligibility to apply/reapply for a provisional or full driving licence;
- possible learning or other difficulties during the learning/retraining period;
- suitable cars and adaptations;
- conversion specialists and local driving instructors registered to teach those with disabilities.

NOTES ON DISABILITIES

Cerebral palsy This condition, present from birth, can be caused by birth injury or by the baby and mother having incompatible blood groups. It leads to stiffness, clumsy movement and difficulty with walking and speech. Speech problems sometimes mask an alert and lively intelligence. Extra work may be needed in practising coordination of car controls.

Spina bifida   This is a failure of the spine to form normally, and involves the spinal cord. At its most severe it can mean deformity of the spine, loss of feeling from the waist downwards and inability to control the bladder and bowels. Gaining independence as a driver may involve the need for assessment at a specialist mobility centre for advice on transferring into the vehicle and wheelchair stowage methods. Sitting height and sitting balance may need attention. Reduced sitting balance can affect coordination of the controls.

Hydrocephalus   This means 'water on the brain' and may be associated with spina bifida. It will have been treated medically by the time people are mature enough to drive. It sometimes leads to damage to parts of the brain dealing with concentration, memory and perception, which may make learning slower and more difficult.

Stroke   This is caused by a bleed or clot in the brain that interrupts the blood supply to part of the brain. It is common to assume that the resulting physical paralysis of one side of the body is the only problem. The brain damage causing the paralysis can also cause visual perceptual disturbance (affecting vehicle positioning skills) and information processing difficulties (affecting quick thinking and decision making). Loss of visual field can cause lack of visual awareness on one side. Expert assessment is needed to ensure that the legal standards for driving are met. An assessment at a specialist mobility centre prior to rehabilitative tuition is recommended.

Paraplegia   This affects the lower half of the body. It is nearly always caused by damage to the spinal cord from an accident. The level of the injury determines the amount of weakness and whether the result will be a spastic (stiff) or flaccid (floppy) weakness. Transfer methods, sitting balance, pressure care and wheelchair loading as well as the choice of hand control styles will need attention.

Parkinson's disease   Reduced coordination and ability to use the car controls efficiently is the presenting problem. Initiating a movement is often difficult, making reaction times too slow. Later in the course of the disease, thinking processes can become slow and some dementia-like changes can occur. The involuntary movements of Parkinsonism can be controlled with medication, but it is imperative that the driver takes the medication at the correct time as physical performance can deteriorate immediately prior to a dose being due. Reducing the physical coordination required by selecting a car with automatic gears and driving it with only the right hand (on a steering aid) and the right foot on pedals can help someone with Parkinson's disease to maintain control more easily.

Cerebellar disease This leads to problems with coordination: patients may stagger and lurch when walking, have difficulty in speaking and are clumsy in movement. It is caused by a problem in the cerebellum such as a tumour, or can result from conditions such as multiple sclerosis.

Multiple sclerosis This is a condition in which the insulating cover of the nerves of the central nervous system and brain is damaged. Once the cover (myelin sheath) is destroyed, conduction down the nerve is impaired. It can cause alteration of feeling, loss of balance, difficulty in vision and, in the later stages, deterioration of the mental processes. It is a disease that 'comes and goes', so thorough and frequent assessment is needed for driving. MS can cause loss of position sense in a limb. It is common for the driver to have good sensation and action in the feet, but to have trouble in finding the pedals accurately. Coordinating feet and hands on the controls can be an issue. Nystagmus (eye wobble) can cause intermittent blurring of vision. Optic neuritis (inflammation of the optic nerve) can cause other temporary visual problems. Some people experience cognitive problems affecting speed of thinking and decision making. Denial of symptoms is a common coping strategy, making tuition more difficult.

Arthritis This means inflammation of the joints, and there are two common forms. Osteoarthritis implies premature ageing and degeneration of the joints which may be precipitated by an injury in earlier life. In rheumatoid arthritis the lining of the joints and other tissues deteriorates with specific injury. There are many conditions allied to, though not identical with, rheumatoid arthritis. It is important to preserve the joints by not straining them at all. If the hands are affected all controls should have chunky grips and easy operation. Parking brake and gearshift releases are advised. Lightened power steering can help.

Myopathies This means disease of the muscles, and covers conditions in which there is progressive weakness. Most of these conditions are inherited. Often there is weakness round the shoulder and hips, so aids such as power-assisted steering may be needed. Frequent checks are needed to make sure a person has not become unfit to drive. There are not usually learning problems with this disability.

VEHICLE ADAPTATIONS

A wide range of modifications is available for drivers with disabilities. In all instances, selecting the correct adaptation to suit the particular qualities of the physical limitation is a specialist exercise. A referral to an assessment centre such as the Queen Elizabeth's Foundation Mobility Centre at Carshalton is strongly recommended. Mobility centres are able to offer advice on where to purchase the correct products. The controls available have been categorized under headings to explain the use of these controls. The majority of adaptations, however, will need to be fitted to automatic cars.

Steering

Power-assisted steering can be tailor-made to match the strength of the driver of the particular car. Most pupils who use one hand to steer need standard power-assisted steering to help them in various exercises, for example, turning the car round in the road or reversing.

If only one hand is used for steering, various modifications are available. Remember that the one hand must also operate secondary controls, so a steering aid alone is insufficient for the one-handed driver. (See 'Secondary controls' on page 307.)

Steering ball for either right or left hand. This is usually placed at 10 o'clock for the left hand or 2 o'clock for the right hand, but it can vary, depending on the pupil's sitting position.

Steering aids come in various shapes and sizes to suit the pupil's disability, such as:

- mushroom grip – this has a broader flat top;
- steering peg;
- quad grip – this is used by pupils who do not have any finger grip, but have sufficient strength in their wrists to turn a steering wheel.
- glove peg – this is used where gripping the steering wheel is not possible;
- T bar – this is often useful for drivers with cerebral palsy who have high muscle tone and flexed wrists. They can comfortably hold the grip with the back of the hand towards the steering wheel.

A joystick system may be fitted to an automatic vehicle if a pupil is unable to turn the steering wheel. This can be fitted either to the right or left side of the steering column, and will turn the steering wheel without actually touching it.

Foot steering may be used by pupils who have no useful function in their arms, but have full use of both legs. Shoulder or foot steering can steer the vehicle. The size and angle at which the steering wheel is placed can also be altered to suit.

Brake and accelerator modifications

Foot pedals　For those who cannot use the right foot on the accelerator/brake pedals, the accelerator may be moved over to the left of the footbrake on a car with automatic transmission. The use of flip-up pedals or bayonet or wing nut fitting allows the accelerator to be switched back to the right for normal use. Both the accelerator and the brake pedal can be levelled to make operation easier; or the pedals can have raised edges to keep the feet in place if using one foot over the brake and one over the accelerator. Foot pedals can be extended for a driver of short stature. A floor raise is required. For a driver who is used to driving a manual car, the left-foot clutch reflex causes the potential danger of pressing the left accelerator pedal when intending to press the brake pedal to slow down or stop. Several hours of tuition with a considerable amount of manoeuvring are needed to retrain the driver.

Knee controls If the feet are not reliable, but the hip and knee joints are functional, adaptations can be fitted to allow a driver to operate the accelerator/brake controls with the in and out movement of the thigh.

Hand controls If the lower limbs cannot be used to accelerate/brake, then either hand can be used. The most popular modification is the single combined lever for accelerator/brake. This is placed near the steering wheel and the hand normally pushes away to brake, using the driver's body weight. The accelerator is controlled by pulling towards the steering wheel. There are, however, various types of hand control which include a split control, where the driver pulls the separate levers towards the steering wheel for accelerating and braking.

Another system is the radial servo vacuum unit in which the driver pushes down towards the floor to brake and pulls up to accelerate. The last two systems mentioned have power-assisted braking. Accelerator ring, automatic clutch button on the gearshift and right-hand push brake are other alternatives.

Joystick A joystick can also be placed either side of the steering wheel, if the driver is unable to use other methods mentioned for accelerating/braking. There is also a four-way joystick system for use in an automatic vehicle, which enables a disabled pupil with only one usable limb to drive. The joystick can be placed either side of the steering wheel, and the driver pushes the stick to the right or left for steering and pushes forward and backwards for the accelerator/brake.

Tiller This system combines steering, accelerating and braking. The steering wheel is replaced by two handles either side of the steering column, and is steered like a motorcycle. Acceleration is achieved by twisting one of the handles, and braking is achieved by pushing the whole steering unit downwards.

Gear selector This can be modified to suit a driver's restricted movement, either by extending the lever, removing the depressant button or lightening the tension required to move the lever. If this is not possible, an electric system can normally be fitted anywhere in the vehicle.

Handbrake This can be moved to the right-hand side of the vehicle if the left hand cannot be used. If the left hand can reach the handbrake, but the button cannot be depressed, various aids can be fitted to assist with this.

There is a handbrake which is like a stick without a button. This is called a CAM handbrake. It is pushed forward to release or pulled back to secure. Electric handbrakes are available and can be placed anywhere within the car. An extension to the handbrake can be made for convenient use. A foot-operated parking brake can also be fitted to suit the driver.

Secondary controls

Indicators The driver must, of course, be in complete control of the car and must be able to operate all secondary controls while maintaining efficient, coordinated control of the primary controls.

The minimum requirement, when using the single combined lever hand control, is a trafficator thumb switch attached to the top of it. Some drivers also have the horn and headlamp beam control fitted.

For the one-handed driver, an infrared or radio-controlled switch panel attached to the steering aid is essential. Up to nine secondary functions can be operated using press buttons or flick switches on the panel while still holding the steering wheel aid.

Both of the above systems are very important from the driving instructor's point of view, as they enable the driver to indicate correctly and in good time. All secondary controls, however, can be placed anywhere in the car to suit the driver's disability, including using the head.

Mirrors

Additional mirrors can be placed in or on the vehicle to suit a pupil who has a neck restriction. A panoramic mirror is most frequently used. This is fitted over the normal rear view mirror and gives more visibility, especially when reversing. This mirror, used properly in conjunction with the two side mirrors, will satisfy safety standards. Other mirrors can be mounted internally or externally to enable safe observation at various types of junction and blind spot areas.

IMPAIRED VISION

Distance vision

A person must be able to read an old-style number plate from a distance of 20.5 metres, or a new-style plate from 20 metres. If a person has a defective or lazy (amblyopic) eye, at no time should they attempt to drive with their good eye covered (occluded).

When assessing whether a driver can read a standard number plate, it is advisable to note the following:

1. Whether his or her eyes are being screwed up noticeably. If so, this may indicate the need for glasses or a change of lenses. The driver should be referred to an optician. If glasses cannot bring the vision up to the required standard, sometimes contact lenses can.
2. Whether the driver is adopting a noticeable head posture, which may be:

    (a) chin elevation or depression;
    (b) face turned to one side;
    (c) head tilted to one side.

A head posture may be adopted for the following reasons:

(a) to help overcome double vision (diplopia);
(b) to bring a reduced field of vision to the central position;
(c) to steady a fine wobble in the eye (nystagmus) if this reduces the vision;
(d) to try to improve vision when incorrect glasses are worn.

If the head posture is significant, it is advisable to suggest that the driver seeks the advice of an ophthalmologist regarding the cause and possible treatment.

3. Whether there is a tendency to close one eye. This may indicate diplopia (double vision). If so, and treatment cannot be given to eliminate it, the driver is permitted to cover one eye, provided the visual field in the uncovered eye is sufficient. For driving in the UK, we advise covering the left eye when the vision in the right eye is satisfactory, as the field of vision to the right is the most useful.

Sometimes only partial occlusion of one lens is all that is needed, but the advice of an ophthalmologist should be sought. The presence of a squint does not necessarily mean that diplopia is likely to be a problem.

Squints These present no problem to driving, provided that a person sees adequately and that there is no double vision (diplopia).

Double vision There are varying degrees of diplopia depending on the level of vision in each eye and the separation of the images. Diplopia is usually at its worst when drivers are tired and therefore, if control of the diplopia is possible, they should be instructed when feeling least tired. Prisms are often used to correct this, and if recently given, the driver may need a little time to get used to them. In all cases with constant diplopia, one eye must be covered (occluded) for driving.

Colour vision Defective colour vision is no bar to driving in most countries. However, it is always advisable to check that a person can assess traffic lights correctly by the position of the colours. Particular attention should be paid to *Highway Code* studies so that all types of signs can be recognized.

Visual fields People with constricted vision may drive, provided that there is at least 120° in the horizontal field and that it spans the central area. No one may drive with homonymous hemianopia (half the field missing with a vertical or horizontal cut off through the centre of the field), or with a total quadrant loss (quarter missing).

Monocular vision These drivers have no depth perception (stereopsis). Forty degrees of their visual fields will be missing on one side and night-time driving may prove more difficult. They may also find it difficult to judge the speed of approaching vehicles.

IMPAIRED HEARING

Deafness is not classed as a driver disability. No restrictions are placed on a full licence when a deaf driver passes the driving test.

It will be of benefit for those with any hearing problems, especially the profoundly deaf, to disclose this on the Driving Test Application form (DL26). This will ensure that the driving examiner is properly prepared.

OTHER IMPAIRMENTS AND DISTRACTIONS

Illiteracy, dyslexia and non-English-speaking pupils

Some pupils have difficulty in reading – some may not be able to read at all. This is not a disability and does not necessarily mean that they will have difficulty in learning to drive.

There are various ways in which you can help these pupils and these are discussed in the 'Methods of teaching' section of this chapter.

Autism

There is a range of disorders in this spectrum. Symptoms can include difficulty communicating and relating to other people. There is often a tendency to work by rules and an inability to work out the more abstract concepts of driving, making it difficult for such pupils to deal with unusual driving situations. This might include situations where the *Highway Code* rules need to be supplemented with situational analysis and a reading of other drivers' non-verbal responses or possibly an unusual response, for example when cars from all directions meet simultaneously at a mini-roundabout.

Physical stature and ill health

Physical discomfort such as toothache, cramp and natural functions can distract drivers. The performance of even the most skilful of drivers can deteriorate when they are feeling unwell. Alcohol and drugs affect every aspect of the driver's physical and perceptive processes, and some simple cold cures contain drugs that affect driving performance. Some common drugs to be avoided while driving are:

Sleeping pills	Tranquillizers	Antihistamines
Anti-depressants	Pain killers	Opiates
Amphetamines	Belladonna	

Drivers suffering from the following may be taking the above drugs:

Anxiety	Depression	Insomnia
Toothache	Indigestion	Headaches
Colds/flu	Hay fever	Asthma
Period pains and premenstrual tension		

One of the difficulties in helping clients with some of the less obvious problems is that they can often go unnoticed for a long time, throughout which period the learners simply struggle on as best they can. Some people suffering from a minor disability may be embarrassed by it and so don't mention it. Others may not admit to having one through ill-founded fears that the instructor might be reluctant to take them on. Tact and understanding must be used when dealing with these problems.

In some cases a properly secured cushion may be all that is required. Pedal extensions can be used for people with short legs or small feet. The floor of the car can be easily raised, by placing a board (or similar object) under the carpet or mat.

Mirrors can often compensate for trunk and neck restrictions of movement.

None of us feel well all the time, and your pupils will be no exception. Women in particular may feel less well one week in every four due to the menstrual cycle.

Mothers-to-be are not invalids and most of them will not appreciate being treated as such. However, they must be given some consideration, particularly with regard to ensuring the happy event does not occur during the driving test (or, for that matter, during a lesson!). Plan the lessons and test sensibly. Opinions in this respect vary considerably, and the final discretion must be exercised jointly by the instructor and pupil in relation to both lessons and test. Where there is any doubt, the client should seek her doctor's advice.

Alcohol

Alcohol is a drug and is a contributory factor in over 30 per cent of road accidents. After just one drink a driver is less able to make decisions quickly or react promptly in an emergency.

After the second drink a driver will become more relaxed, with less concern for normal restraint and attention to detail. There is a further deterioration in mental responses and physical reactions, combined with a slight degeneration in coordination and the execution of manipulative skills.

After the third drink a driver's emotions become more extreme and behaviour exaggerated. The driver becomes more confident, talkative, noisy or morose and there is a further deterioration in reactions, coordination and manipulative skill. Perceptive responses become slower and impossible feats are far more likely to be attempted.

Following the fourth drink there is still further deterioration in coordination to the point of clumsiness. Confidence continues to increase while perceptive skills are unknowingly deteriorating. The driver's levels of attention and powers of discrimination and normal restraint are rapidly disappearing. Impossible feats are even more likely to be attempted.

After the fifth drink normal perception of moving and static objects becomes blurred. It takes longer for the eyes to focus, and speeds and distances are severely misjudged. The driver's ability to make sensible decisions, and react promptly, is totally unreliable, resulting in high-accident-risk manoeuvres being unknowingly attempted.

Prescription and non-prescription drugs

Drugs impair driving ability by reducing attention levels, the perception of risk, and the ability to make sound decisions quickly and respond promptly to the road and traffic scene. Studies in the United States show that about 10 per cent of drivers involved in accidents take non-alcoholic drugs of some kind.

Instructors should be particularly cautious when clients are suffering from some temporary illness for which they may be taking drugs. They should be advised to ask their doctors whether any prescribed drug will affect driving ability. They should carefully read instructions on the labels of non-prescribed drugs. It may also be appropriate to offer advice on the use of illegal drugs and their effect on driving.

Amphetamines speed up the nervous system and help users to keep going. While taking this type of drug, users may feel more alert and confident, but when the effect wears off they are likely to feel very tired and depressed.

Barbiturates are used to calm the nerves. They have an effect similar to that of alcohol, but when the effect wears off depression may follow. A combination of barbiturates and alcohol can cause severe depression. Tranquillizers are used by people with nervous and emotional conditions. They cause drowsiness, and the people who take them often combine their use with alcohol, with the likelihood of severe or even fatal consequences.

Marijuana is an hallucinogen which can act as either a stimulant or depressant. It slows mental responses and physical reactions, affects the judgement of time and space, and limits the ability to concentrate on more than one thing at a time.

Fatigue

Fatigue is a temporary condition that impairs the ability of all drivers. It reduces the ability to concentrate, impairs vision and the other senses, makes decisions more difficult, and makes drivers more irritable and so less tolerant with other road users.

It can be caused by hard work, lack of rest, emotional stress, boredom or carbon monoxide poisoning. Contributory factors may include illness, overeating, an overheated car, driving for long distances without rest, bright sunlight or glare from oncoming headlights.

Fatigue of physical action and of thinking skills can occur in many neurological conditions, particularly in a driver with multiple sclerosis. Carbon monoxide is discharged by the car's exhaust system. If this is leaking, or if boot seals are not effective, or if the tailgate of an estate or hatchback car is not fully closed, carbon monoxide may find its way into the passenger compartment. It is colourless, odourless, tasteless and poisonous. Keep plenty of fresh air circulating through the car.

The effects of fatigue on driving performance are not always obvious to the driver. They are:

- concentration becoming more difficult;
- the eyes becoming inactive;
- increased thinking time;
- a slowing of physical reactions;
- increasing difficulty in making decisions.

Symptoms for the instructor to be aware of are:

- consistent late braking;
- slow or erratic decision making;
- reduced hazard awareness and anticipation;
- a general impression of the driver driving on the brake lights of the vehicle in front.

Emotions and stress

Extremes of emotions, such as fear or anger, affect attention levels, perception and response to everyday traffic situations. They limit the driver's ability to reason quickly and logically.

Some medical conditions such as a brain injury have effects on personality, mood and emotional control. Aggression, impulsivity or a volatile nature can be symptomatic. Lack of appreciation of danger is common. Driving is in itself a stressful activity. High levels of frustration or stress can be created by the vehicle and traffic environment. Stress can cause excessive over-reaction, and this adds even more fuel to the fire. On the other hand, these overreactions may (particularly in the case of new drivers in situations they are not yet competent to deal with) be associated with poorly developed hazard recognition skills, resulting in additional stresses due to late reactions and lack of confidence due to deficient car control skills.

Aggression is characterized by the hostile feelings or behaviour that some drivers display towards others. Normal mentally healthy people are able to tolerate a degree of aggression towards themselves without retaliation. Some experts claim aggression is linked to an individual's desire to dominate another and to compensate for feelings of inferiority or inadequacy. Others describe it as a surge of destructive feeling provoked by frustration. It is unlikely that aggression can be completely suppressed, and when it manifests itself in new drivers, instructors should direct it towards the driver error rather than the person committing it.

After brain injury, it can be a contraindication to driving. A specialist assessment is recommended. Young people are generally more at risk because they are less able to control hostile feelings. However, aggressive behaviour is not restricted to any particular age group or gender if drivers are pushed beyond their limits.

Anxiety

Most normal people get upset and anxious from time to time, particularly when faced with a threat of some kind. Anxiety describes the psychological disturbance characterized by feelings of apprehension. Some people are more susceptible to anxiety than others. This may be due to feeling helpless and alone, or experiencing a deep sense of inadequacy.

These feelings are all normal in themselves but they have become over-obtrusive. Anxiety ranges in intensity from a vague restlessness to extreme uneasiness, and is usually accompanied by some kind of physical distress such as a tightness of the chest, dryness of the throat, sweating, trembling or tears. Anxiety can be caused by financial or business difficulties, uncertainty about how to behave in some circumstances, fear of failure or fear of the consequences of an action.

Intense anxiety can sometimes result from seemingly insignificant matters: for example, having dirt on one's shirt or blouse when meeting a stranger. Such exaggerated cases may indicate some subconscious cause relating to forgotten experiences.

Anxiety makes it difficult for learners to think, reason or make judgements. It reduces their level of awareness and makes it difficult for them to concentrate on driving or any point under instruction. It results in a low level of retention of new information and skills, panic, reduced physical coordination, forced errors and a high degree of risk taking (to flee the situation). Instructors can assist over-anxious students by:

- creating a confident but relaxed and caring atmosphere;
- giving more reassurance and encouragement;
- using common sense over the task demands to help build up confidence – for example, letting them drive more slowly on routes with reduced task demands until confidence grows;
- seeing if shorter training periods and frequent breaks help;
- ensuring students understand what is expected and why;
- following the structure in Chapter 8 under the heading 'Structuring the learning';
- demonstrating and presenting information as graphically as possible.

Illness

From time to time, everyone suffers from a temporary minor illness such as colds, toothache, headache or stomach upsets. Any of these can reduce the attention, impair vision and upset judgement, timing and coordination.

Ageing

Ageing can reduce perception. Thinking processes are slower and manipulative coordination can be impaired. Older people are more set in their ways and will generally find learning to drive more difficult. They tend to be more anxious and their reactions are generally slower. Instructors should not place them under too much pressure or compare their progress with that of younger learners.

Regular eyesight tests are necessary, as deteriorating visual acuity can be so gradual that the driver does not notice. Difficulty dealing with headlight glare at night is common in the older driver, and many give up driving at night as a coping strategy. Choosing quieter times of the day to drive and avoiding right turns are other common strategies for continuing to drive safely up to an older age.

METHODS OF TEACHING

The rules, regulations and subject matter of driving remain the same. However, you will need to adapt your teaching methods and lesson programmes to suit the needs of each of your pupils.

Physical disabilities

For those with a severe disability, you may need to allow extra time for getting into and out of the car, and for finding the most comfortable driving position.

Some conditions cause people to tire during the day. It is important for you to discuss this with your pupil and arrange lessons at times of the day when he or she is likely to achieve the best results. This should also be taken into consideration when you apply for the driving test so that his or her concentration and confidence will be at a peak.

Hearing problems

The following is an extract from *Teaching the Deaf to Drive* and is reproduced with the kind permission of the Institute of Master Tutors of Driving.

As the age of 17 must have been reached before a provisional licence can be issued, deaf youngsters, having received their education mainly in special schools or units, have some speech, although this may be difficult to follow. Usually sign language is used, and in addition they will be able to lip-read to a certain extent.

Lip-reading, however, depends as much on the clarity of the speaker's lip movements as on the ability of the deaf person. Young people may have a reading age much lower than the natural age. Consequently, the ability to read and write may be limited. They can, however, be just as bright and intelligent as their hearing peers, and with understanding and patience from the instructor will assimilate all that has to be learnt to drive a motor vehicle.

The problem for the instructor is to learn the best way to impart the knowledge and the skill to the pupil. The essential is, what is the best way of communication?

You do not need to learn the sign language, but it is necessary to use simple, straightforward words, which only have one meaning. For example, 'Do not hug the middle of the road'. The word 'hug' to the deaf has only the literal meaning of someone putting arms round another. Again, 'traffic jam' would not be understood; 'jam' is something one spreads on bread and butter.

It is essential to speak slowly and distinctly, and move the lips to form each word. Do not talk through your teeth. It will be appreciated that this approach means it has to be a face-to-face conversation and can therefore only be utilized in a stationary situation. Never shout – the pupil is deaf.

Due to the lack of hearing, it is vital that all 'conversations' be reinforced by demonstrations. Always be patient. Unsatisfactory response is likely to be the fault of the teacher rather than the pupil.

People who are deaf can normally speak, but it is not always easy for the hearing to understand what they are saying. It is difficult for them to make the sounds which we are used to, as they are unable to hear their own voices. Always have a writing pad ready to hand, and ask the student to write down questions.

Learning the *Highway Code* can be helped if you simplify your language. Formulate questions in written form and have the answers following in the same easy wording.

You may benefit from getting in touch with local associations for deaf people or the Royal National Institute for Deaf People (RNID), 19–23 Featherstone Street, London EC1Y 8SL (tel: 020 7296 8000). They are always very ready to help with any problems which may arise.

Reading and understanding problems

If you have any pupils with problems such as dyslexia, or pupils who are non-English speaking, there are various ways in which you can help.

Making more use of visual aids during in-car training sessions will help pupils to understand when introducing new topics. Showing them pictures of road signs and markings and explaining their meaning should also help. They will understand the *Highway Code* rules better if they can apply them to on-road situations as soon after learning them as possible.

It can be helpful to discuss with family or close friends the subjects currently under instruction, and encourage them to help the pupil by giving some in-between lesson revision and learning exercises.

If a student's command of English is inadequate for both training and testing purposes, try to develop some comprehension of the 'key words' described in Chapter 8. Keep your terminology as simple as possible, and to avoid confusion, make sure you are consistent with the words and phrases you use. It may be advisable to obtain the services of someone known to the pupil to act as interpreter. This can be particularly useful during the training stages because, when the pupil attends the driving test, you will not be able to act in this capacity and the person who has already been present on lessons would be familiar with what is required.

You should try to give as much encouragement as possible to all of your pupils, perhaps by emphasizing their successes at the practical skills. In no way should you embarrass them or make them feel inadequate – this will do little to gain their confidence in you.

The book *Learn to Drive in 10 Easy Stages* by Margaret Stacey is ideal in that the learning is organized into short, simple steps. It also reinforces the *Highway Code* rules in relation to the practical topics currently under instruction.

APPLYING FOR TESTS

The procedure outlined in Chapter 10 should be followed when applying for tests for people with disabilities, taking into consideration the following notes. When completing the application form DL26, try to give as much information as possible about the disabilities. If there is not enough room on the form to explain the disability and how the candidate is affected by it, write the extra information out and attach it to the application form. Supplying this information in advance will avoid any possible embarrassment to both pupil and examiner by questions that have to be asked on the day of the test.

If the candidate is dyslexic, supplying this information beforehand will allow a suitable means of communication to be devised. The senior examiner at the test centre should be informed at least two days before a test appointment where any of the following exist:

- impaired hearing;
- minor restrictions are experienced;
- abnormal stature;
- any disabilities not noted on the application form.

Providing such information may explain to an examiner why certain actions are taken by the candidate, and allowances can therefore be made for them. For example, if an examiner knows in advance that a candidate has restricted neck movement, not classed as a disability, and uses the mirrors for making rear observations when manoeuvring, this will be expected and allowed for. If the information is not volunteered, then the examiner can only assume that correct observations are not made and there is no reason for it.

When preparing for the test

By this time you should have ensured that the adaptations used by each individual pupil overcome their disability as far as possible. If they do not, then you should advise on any further adaptations which you think are necessary, allowing plenty of time to get used to them.

The time allotted for testing people with disabilities spans two normal test periods. You should bear this in mind when entering the appointment in your diary.

Attending for the test

Make sure you allow plenty of time for getting to the test centre if the candidate has difficulty getting out of and into the car. Where severe disabilities exist, you may go into the waiting room to inform the examiner that the pupil has arrived.

The content and length of the driving test are the same as for normal driving tests. (See Chapter 10 for the syllabus.) The extra time allotted is to allow:

- for the examiner to establish any extra details about the disability;
- for the examiner to make a note of vehicle adaptations;
- sufficient time to repeat any manoeuvres if the examiner feels this is necessary;
- for the examiner to complete the extra paperwork.

At the beginning of the test, the candidate will be asked if there are any additional disabilities that are not noted on the application form. Encourage your pupils to be frank about this as it will help the examiner to make an effective and objective assessment. The examiner will also ask about the vehicle's adaptations.

Where there are hand adaptations, more emphasis will normally be placed on downhill junctions to check that control is adequate. If a candidate has neck or vertebrae problems, emphasis is normally placed on the ability to make frequent observations at those junctions where sightlines are restricted.

At the end of the test

The examiner has two decisions to make; does the candidate have the ability to drive? And do the adaptations overcome the disabilities? If the examiner is satisfied that the candidate is competent to drive and the vehicle is unadapted, an unrestricted pass certificate for the category of vehicle tested on, and any additional categories covered, will be issued.

If the examiner considers the candidate competent to drive unadapted vehicles of the category tested only, then the pass certificate will be issued for that particular category. The restriction will be noted on the form D255.

If it is considered that automatic transmission entirely overcomes the effects of the disability, the appropriate category letter will be noted. However, if it is considered that this is not the case, the appropriate category letter would be noted and the words 'with controls adapted to suit disability' and, if appropriate, the words 'and with suitably positioned mirrors' will be added.

All candidates, whether they pass or fail, are given a copy of the Driving Test Report Form DL25. If a candidate fails and the examiner feels that some other adaptation might enable him or her to pass, an indication of this may be given.

A pass certificate is not normally restricted solely because of abnormal stature, as this is not considered to be a disability in itself. However, there may be cases where extraordinary size has an effect on the candidate's driving ability. Where adaptations have been made to overcome this, then the words 'with controls adapted to suit disability' would be included in the pass certificate.

The reporting of driving test results

The results of all tests are reported to the DVLA at Swansea. Any restrictions noted by examiners are then itemized on candidates' driving licences.

INSTRUCTOR COURSES

If you are interested in teaching people with disabilities, special training courses are available at Queen Elizabeth's Foundation Mobility Centre, Damson Way, Fountain Drive, Carshalton, Surrey SM5 4NR (tel: 020 8770 1151; fax: 020 8770 1211; website: www.qefd.org/mobilitycentre). For details of other centres, see pages 368–89.

With grateful thanks to Sue Vernon at the Queen Elizabeth's Foundation Mobility Centre for her assistance in updating and revising this chapter.

10

The Driving Test

This chapter contains information on:

The Theory and Hazard Perception Test:

- administration;
- booking;
- syllabus;
- sample questions;
- training;
- pass marks.

The Practical Driving Test:

- administration;
- syllabus;
- applying for tests;
- cancelling and postponing tests;
- DSA Compensation Code;
- attending for a test;
- the marking system;
- the DL25 explained;
- 'L' driver errors;
- at the end of the test.

The Car and Trailer Test:

- test vehicles;
- test syllabus;
- safety questions;
- uncoupling.

The Extended Driving Test.

The 'L' test for new drivers is conducted in two parts – the Theory Test (including hazard perception), followed by the Practical Driving Test. Candidates must pass the theory part before they can apply to take the practical. Both tests have to be passed within a two-year period.

THEORY AND HAZARD PERCEPTION TEST

Administration

An appointed contractor conducts the Theory Test on behalf of the Driving Standards Agency (DSA) at about 150 test centres throughout England, Scotland and Wales. Candidates are allowed to take the test at any centre of their choice.

All test centres in Wales, and some in England, are equipped to conduct the test in Welsh. For candidates with special needs such as dyslexia or reading difficulties there is a facility to listen to the test being read in English. Candidates who are not able to read or understand English or who want to take their test in their first language can listen to the test in one of 20 other languages.

For people who have learning difficulties, arrangements can be made for a showing of an 'on screen' video of the test in British Sign Language. Candidates with any other special needs can apply for more time to complete the multiple-choice part of the test.

Booking the Theory Test

The test can be booked by phone, fax, and post or online.

By post

Application forms are available from test centres or from the DSA. Payment can be made by credit or debit card or with a cheque or postal order. The completed application form should be sent to: DSA, PO Box 148, Salford M5 3JY. It normally takes about 10 days to receive a reply, and there is no guarantee that you will get the date requested.

By fax

The form should be faxed to the DSA on 0870 01 04 372 together with credit or debit card details. Again, the response time is normally about 10 days.

By phone

Applications can be made by phoning the DSA on 0870 01 01 372. If you are ringing on behalf of a pupil, you will need to have their personal details and driver number. If you are using the pupil's card for payment, they must be present when you make the call.

The advantage with this method of booking is that you can discuss alternative dates and times and receive immediate confirmation of the appointment. The disadvantage is that it can sometimes be quite time-consuming to get through the DSA telephone menu system in order to talk to a booking clerk.

Online booking

Log on to www.dsa.gov.uk, www.driving-test.co.uk or www.motoring.gov.uk. This is probably the quickest and easiest method of booking. As with telephone bookings, you will need to have the candidate's personal and card details to hand. Confirmation of the date and time of the test is given immediately.

'Trainer booking'

As a registered driving instructor you can now make your test applications 'online'. To do this, you need to register with the DSA for an 'online profile', indicating which test centres you expect to use and up to five credit or debit cards you will use for payment. The website for bookings is available 24 hours, but you can only assign pupils to a test at times when their licence entitlement can be verified by the DVLA.

To register for this service, visit the DSA website at www.dsa.gov.uk/tests.

Test fees

The current fee (at April 2006) is £21.50.

Cancelling tests

To cancel or postpone a Theory Test, at least three clear working days' notice must be given. This period of notice does not include:

- the day of the test;
- the day that the notice of cancellation or postponement was made;
- Sundays;
- public holidays.

This means that you need to give more than six or seven days' notice if there are weekends and holidays involved.

Attending for the test

Your pupils must produce both parts of their photo card driving licence as visual proof of their identity. In the unlikely event that the pupil has the old-style paper licence instead of a photo card licence, a valid passport must be produced. Pupils should also take with them the appointment card or booking reference details.

The format of the test

The test involves multiple-choice questions, followed by a hazard perception test.

The multiple-choice questions

This part of the test involves answering 35 questions that are displayed on a computer screen. A number of correct and incorrect responses are shown, and the candidate selects his or her choice by touching the screen. To pass, 30 questions must be answered correctly within 40 minutes.

Only one question appears on the screen at a time, and candidates can move backwards or forwards through the questions. This means that they are able to recheck or alter any answers. The system also alerts the candidate if any questions have not been answered.

There is no requirement for the pupil to be computer literate, as members of staff are on hand to assist with any queries or difficulties. A practice session of up to 15 minutes is allowed to enable candidates to familiarize themselves with the system before starting the actual test.

The Theory Test syllabus

The pupil's knowledge of the following subjects is tested:

- *Alertness:* observation, anticipation, concentration, awareness, distraction.
- *Attitude:* consideration, safe distance, courtesy, priority.
- *Safety and the vehicle:* fault detection, defects, safety equipment, emissions, noise, vehicle security.
- *Safety margins:* stopping distances, road surfaces, skidding, weather conditions.
- *Hazard awareness:* anticipation, attention, speed and distance, reaction time, alcohol and drugs, tiredness.
- *Vulnerable road users:* pedestrians, children, elderly drivers, new drivers, people with disabilities, motorcyclists, cyclists, animals, horse riders.
- *Other types of vehicle:* motorcycles, lorries, buses, trams.
- *Vehicle handling:* weather conditions, road conditions, time of day, speed, traffic calming.
- *Motorway rules:* speed limits, lane discipline, stopping, lighting, parking.
- *Rules of the road:* speed limits, parking, lighting.
- *Road and traffic signs:* road signs, speed limits, road markings, regulations.
- *Documents:* licence, insurance, MOT certificate.
- *Accidents:* first aid, warning devices, reporting procedures, safety regulations.
- *Vehicle loading:* stability, towing.

Sample questions

Q **You are the driver of a car carrying two adults and two children, both of whom are under 14 years of age. Who is responsible for ensuring that the children wear seat belts?**

(Select one answer)

a the children

b their parents

c the driver

d the front seat passenger

A The correct answer is
c the driver (*Highway Code* rule number 40)

Q **You are driving towards a zebra crossing. Pedestrians are waiting to cross. You should:**

(Select one answer)

a slow down and prepare to stop

b give way to the elderly and infirm only

c use your headlamps to indicate that they can cross

d wave at them to cross the road

A The correct answer is:
a slow down and prepare to stop (*Highway Code* rule 71 and **The Official DSA Guide to Driving: The essential skills page 109**)

Q **On which three occasions must you stop your vehicle?**

(Select three answers)

a when involved in an accident

b at a red traffic light

c when signalled to do so by a police officer

d at a junction with double broken white lines

e at a pelican crossing when the amber light is flashing and no pedestrians are crossing

A The correct answers are
a, b and c

Hazard perception test

After completing the multiple-choice questions the candidate is given a three-minute break before starting the hazard perception test. The test consists of 14 video clips featuring various types of hazard, with each clip lasting about a minute. The candidate has to respond to each hazard by clicking on a computer mouse as each hazard develops. Up to 5 marks can be scored for each hazard; the earlier a response is made, the higher the score. On this part of the test it is not possible to go back to change a response, as the object is to recognize hazards as early as possible.

The hazards depicted are those that would need a response from the driver such as changing speed or direction, or by taking some other form of action.

Candidates are not penalized for clicking on insignificant hazards – they are only marked on the designated developing ones. However, if too many unnecessary responses are made in a very short space of time, a score of 0 might be allocated for that clip. This is to stop the candidate randomly clicking or guessing.

The pass mark for this part of the test is currently set at 44 out of a possible 75, but the DSA constantly review the results and adjust the requirement.

At the end of the test

Candidates are given the result of both parts of the test within a few minutes of completing the HPT test. Feedback is given on any incorrect answers.

Successful candidates are issued with a pass certificate that is valid for two years. The Practical Test must be passed within this two-year period, otherwise a further Theory Test needs to be taken.

When applying for the Practical Test the Theory pass certificate number should be quoted.

Theory Test training

To prepare for both parts of the Theory Test your pupils will need to study:

- the *Highway Code;*
- *The Official DSA Guide to Driving: The essential skills;*
- *The Official Guide to Learning to Drive;*
- *The Official Theory Test for Car Drivers;*
- *Know Your Traffic Signs.*

For details of these books and other resource material see page 392.

You need to have a thorough knowledge of the contents of all these books to prepare yourself for the ADI Theory Test. You also need to have an understanding of the syllabus and the various topics so that you can help your pupils prepare for their own Theory Test.

Your own knowledge and teaching skills will be even more relevant if you are dealing with pupils who have learning difficulties. In these circumstances you will need to use plenty of encouragement, and might involve the pupil's family or friends to assist.

There are many books and CD ROMs on the market to help with theory training. Some of these materials contain the entire DSA question bank and can be used to aid the learning process. However, you will need to check, by the skilful use of your question and answer technique, your pupils' understanding of the rules and regulations if they are to be able to apply them to the on-the-road situation. Other CDs are aimed at the practical side of the ADI's job, and relate to hazard recognition and awareness.

The DSA has produced programmes for all types of learner, including car, motorcycle, large goods vehicle (LGV) and passenger-carrying vehicle (PCV) drivers. Even if you do not have computer skills or access to a PC yourself, you should make sure that you are able to offer the appropriate CDs to your pupils. Most of them will have these skills and be able to use a computer at home, school or college.

Good instructors will automatically be incorporating hazard perception into their practical training courses. This helps learners to understand how to apply the rules and procedures. After all, how can you teach driving without teaching the rules and regulations and encouraging safe attitudes?

For more information about both parts of the Theory Test, visit the website at www.dsa.gov.uk or phone the DSA on 0870 0101 372.

Preparation for the Theory Test

The DSA book, *The Official Theory Test for Car Drivers*, offers advice on how to prepare for the multiple-choice part of the theory test and recommends that pupils study the various books from which the questions are taken. You should also use the other resource materials as teaching and study aids. These include:

- *The Highway Code.* Contains the laws that apply to all road users and up-to-date advice on road safety.
- *Know your Traffic Signs.* Contains information and explanations of most signs and road markings.
- *The Official DSA Guide to Driving – the essential skills.* Explains the best driving practices in detail.
- *The Official DSA Theory Test CD ROM for Car Drivers.* Contains all the questions and allows your pupils to practise for the multiple-choice part of the theory test.

All of these books and materials can be obtained from The Stationery Office by telephoning 0870 600 5522 or using their website. Other suppliers of books and training materials are listed on page 383.

Remember that the Theory Test questions change from time to time. This can sometimes be as a result of revisions to legislation or because of customer feedback. Make sure that you and your pupils are using the most up-to-date versions of any publications.

Your pupils can also take a mock theory test online at www.theory-tests.co.uk. For a fee of £6.99 (at April 2006) you can practise taking the multiple-choice part of the Theory Test as often as you like within a 30-day period.

PRACTICAL TEST

Administration

This test is administered by the DSA, which is an executive agency of the Department for Transport. The DSA conducts about 1.6 million 'L' tests on cars and motorcycles every year, as well as administering the vocational tests for LGV and PCV drivers. (Vocational tests are dealt with in Chapter 11 of this book.) In Northern Ireland driving tests are conducted by the Driver and Vehicle Testing Authority.

To ensure uniformity in the conduct of Practical Driving Tests, all the DSA's driving examiners are trained at the Training Centre at Cardington, Bedford. They are monitored regularly and are sometimes accompanied on test by a senior member of staff.

The 'L' test syllabus

You will find the test syllabus in full in *The Official Guide to Learning to Drive*, which is available from most good bookshops. Alternatively, it can be purchased in bulk from Desk Top Driving and other suppliers for selling on to pupils. The book describes in detail:

- the requirements of the test;
- the types of vehicle suitable;
- different categories of driver, such as those with disabilities, hearing and speech problems;
- general road procedures;
- the manoeuvring exercises;
- what the examiner will be looking for;
- the recommended syllabus for learning to drive.

The 'L' test syllabus covers the following main points.

Eyesight test

At the start of the test the examiner will ask your pupil to read a car number plate at the prescribed distance. (To avoid problems, make sure by checking that your pupils can do this a few weeks prior to the test and then check again a couple of weeks before.)

Safety questions

Before starting the on-road part of the test the examiner will ask the pupil two vehicle safety questions. The subjects covered in this part of the test include:

- tyres and wheels;
- brakes;
- steering;
- engine oil and cooling fluids;
- lights and reflectors;
- direction indicators; and
- audible warning devices.

One of the questions will be a 'show me' type and the other will be 'tell me'.
Example questions include:

- '*Tell me* how you would check that the engine has sufficient oil.'
  The pupil would need to be able to open the bonnet, identify the oil indicator level or dip stick and describe how to check the oil level against the minimum/maximum marker.
- '*Show me* how you would check that the headlights and taillights are working properly.'
  The pupil should operate the appropriate switches (by turning on the ignition if necessary) and walk round the vehicle.
- '*Tell me* how you would check the tyres to ensure that they have sufficient tread depth and that their general condition is safe to use on the road.'
  The pupil would need to explain to the examiner about 'no cuts or bulges' and about '1.6 millimetres of tread across the central three-quarters of the breadth of the tyre and round the entire circumference'.
- '*Show me* how you would check the parking brake for excessive wear.'
  The pupil would need to demonstrate to the examiner that the brake secures itself when it is applied and that it is not at the end of its working travel.

Safety precautions

Driver checks are carried out including doors, seat, mirrors, seat belts and head restraint. The pupil should adjust these so that he or she is comfortable and can reach all the controls. Before starting the engine, the doors should be shut properly, the handbrake should be on and the gear lever or selector in neutral.

Controls

All the main controls should be handled smoothly. This includes use of the accelerator, clutch, gears, footbrake, handbrake and steering.

Moving away

Moving away safely, under control, on the level, from behind a parked car and, where practicable, on a hill, with correct observations.

Emergency stop

Even and progressive braking is required, avoiding locking the wheels. In wet weather pupils should be aware that it could take twice as long to stop.

Reverse to the left or right

Under full control and with reasonable accuracy. Good all-round observations and correct response to others.

Turn in the road

Smooth control with full all-round observations. Correct responses to other road users.

Reverse parking

Either reversing behind one car, between two cars, or the manoeuvre may be carried out in the test centre car park, reversing into a bay. This exercise may be done at the start, during or at the end of the test.

Use of mirrors

Mirrors should be used regularly and pupils should be aware of the presence of others in their blind spots. Pupils' response to the all-round situation is tested. Early use of mirrors should be made before signalling; changing direction and/or speed; and as part of the mirror–signal–manoeuvre routine.

Signalling

Give signals clearly and in good time to warn other road users of intentions in accordance with the *Highway Code.*

Response to signs and signals

Understand and be able to react to all traffic signs and road markings; check when proceeding through green lights; and respond to signals given by police officers, traffic wardens, school crossing patrols and all other road users.

Use of speed

Safe and reasonable progress should be made according to the road, weather and traffic conditions, the road signs and speed limits. Candidates should always be able to stop within the distance they can see is clear.

Following distance

Maintaining a safe distance from the vehicle ahead in all conditions, including when stopping in traffic queues.

Maintaining progress

Driving at appropriate speeds for the type of road and the speed limit; the type and density of traffic; the weather and visibility. A safe approach to all hazards should be demonstrated without being over-cautious. All safe opportunities to proceed at junctions should be taken.

Junctions

Apply the correct procedure to all types of junctions, including applying the mirror–signal–manoeuvre routine and using the correct lanes. Good all-round observations should be made and safe response to other road users demonstrated.

Judgement

Correct responses when dealing with other road users including overtaking, meeting oncoming traffic and turning across traffic. Other road users should not be made to slow down, swerve or stop.

Positioning

Maintain correct positioning at all times according to the type of road, the direction being taken and the presence of parked vehicles.

Clearance to obstructions

Allow plenty of room when passing stationary vehicles and other obstructions that may be obscuring pedestrians.

Pedestrian crossings

Recognize and respond correctly to the different types of crossing.

Position for normal stops

Choose safe and legal places to stop without causing inconvenience or obstruction to others.

Awareness and planning

Think and plan ahead and anticipate the actions of other road users. Demonstrate safe attitudes when dealing with vulnerable road users such as pedestrians, cyclists, motorcyclists and horse riders.

Ancillary controls

Understand the function of all the controls and switches, especially those that have a bearing on road safety. Appropriate use of indicators, lights, windscreen wipers, demisters and heaters.

Notes:

1   Only two out of three of the manoeuvring tests – reverse, turn in the road and reverse parking – are conducted on the test.
2   The emergency test is conducted randomly on about one test in three.

Applying for the Practical Test

When you feel your pupils have reached a fairly consistent standard, you will need to advise them on applying for their driving test. It is important that you make the decision and the application jointly. This avoids problems arising such as pupils:

- applying independently before they are ready;
- not informing you of the date until it is too late to be postponed;
- being reluctant to delay the test once they have an appointment;
- obtaining an appointment at a time when you may already have another test booked.

Whether or not to apply for the test is one of the most difficult and subjective decisions you may have to make. There are a number of reasons for this:

- From a business point of view, to make sure pupils stay with your school, you may often feel obliged to apply for tests early on during their training.
- Because of pupils' wishes, you may often be put under pressure to apply at the earliest possible date.
- If there is a particularly long waiting list for test appointments in your area, a combination of this with the above two reasons may also affect your decision. However, sometimes an early application might act as an incentive and increased motivation for the pupil.

Where none of these pressures exist to any significant degree, your decision may still not be easy. You must be fair to pupils and not impose standards so high as to absolutely guarantee a pass. It could well mean that pupils feel you are delaying the decision for purely monetary reasons. Apart from this, you can never actually guarantee they will pass!

Pupils will make varying rates of progress at different stages of their training. For example, some make very rapid progress in the early stages, and later, when a higher degree of understanding is required, progress may slow down considerably. Others make very slow progress at first, then make very rapid headway after better understanding is achieved.

Although the DSA try to ensure that tests are usually available within six weeks, the waiting time is occasionally unpredictable in its length. Sometimes, for example if a new examiner is appointed to a centre, you may receive an appointment much more quickly than you anticipated. To ensure that you do not arrange one before the pupil is ready, make sure you specify an earliest date on the application.

It is as well to remember that if you apply for tests too early:

- The test may subsequently have to be postponed. This means extra administration, expense, time and possible ill-feeling, since pupils generally do not like having tests deferred.
- The pupil may not be ready and will probably fail. This may reflect back on you since you were saying, in effect, that when you applied you considered that the pupil was ready for the test.
- Your efficiency record of passes and failures on the DSA statistics will be affected.

If you are applying for a test where there is a long waiting list, you should emphasize to the pupil that the booking is made on the assumption that a reasonable rate of progress will be maintained and that his or her driving will have reached a suitable standard.

Having taken all of this into consideration you can make the application by phone, fax, post or online as shown on pages 320 and 321. Make sure you give your driving school number as this will avoid problems with double-booked appointments. Most pupils and instructors these days prefer to book online, as it is now possible to use a 'trainer booking' facility and the opportunity to book, cancel or change a booking.

The current fees for 'L' tests (at April 2006) are:

| Weekday test | £48.50 |
| Saturdays and weekday evenings | £58.00 |

It is important to keep a record of test applications. For postal applications if an appointment is not received within three weeks, contact the DSA booking clerk to check. Make sure pupils inform you immediately they receive appointments so that the date and time can be entered into your diary and the school car reserved accordingly.

If you are posting the application, it is advisable to accept only cheques and postal orders payable to the Driving Standards Agency. This will ensure that no misunderstanding occurs over the fees paid.

When the appointment card is received you should reserve the time in your diary. It is usual to give pupils a lesson immediately prior to the test. Ensure that on the day they know that payment normally has to cover both the lesson and use of the school car for the test. Some pupils may think that payment of the test application fee also includes your fees.

Application forms (DL26) are available from driving test centres or in bulk from the DSA. Make sure all of the requested information is included to avoid any delays in the allocation of appointments.

The same application form is used when applying for tests for people with disabilities and for drivers who have been ordered to take extended tests. It should be noted that the time for extended tests is double the length of the 'L' test and the fees charged are higher.

For more information on how to apply for tests for people with disabilities see Chapter 9.

Driving test times

Practical tests are normally available at most test centres from 7.30 am to 3.27 pm Monday to Friday. The application form allows you to request preferred days of the week and morning or afternoon appointments. If you apply for an evening or weekend test, make sure that your pupil understands that there is a higher fee.

Cancelling and postponing tests

If you feel that the pupil is not yet ready to take the test, make sure he or she understands that it is in his or her own interests as well as those of other road users that you postpone it. Remember, though, that the booking is a contract between the pupil and the DSA – you should not cancel without the pupil's agreement.

The DSA require at least three clear working days' notice for a cancellation; otherwise the fee is lost. You should advise the pupil of the need to cancel at least two weeks before the day of the test and certainly not less than 10 days before.

The pupil may offer resistance to your advice. Be sympathetic and tactful, but firm. Be objective and give the pupil a realistic 'mock test'. This will usually convince even the most adamant that you are acting in their best interests. If the pupil still insists on going against your advice, then all you are entitled to do is withhold the use of your car.

It should be noted that driving examiners may not use the dual controls to avoid an accident unless there is a risk of danger – and then it may only be a last-second decision. Your car may be at risk! The school car is the 'tool of your trade'. It is imperative, therefore, that it is not off the road for unnecessary repairs because you let someone attend for a test too soon.

There are also other considerations. You are depriving other candidates of an appointment, and, more importantly, your reputation could be at risk if you regularly present candidates for test when they are not up to standard.

When you and your pupil have come to a joint decision to postpone a test, you will need to give three working days' notice to avoid forfeit of the fee. Remember that this period of notice does not include Sundays, public holidays, the day of the test and the day of the cancellation. In practice this means that more than a week's notice has to be given – especially if any public holidays are involved. You may simply defer the test to a later date or you may cancel it. If a cancellation is made by telephone and a further appointment is not required, it must be followed up with a request in writing for a refund of the fee. The fee will be withheld pending receipt of this request, which should be made within one week of the cancellation.

Driving test cancellations: the DSA's Compensation Code

Occasionally tests have to be cancelled by the DSA at short notice: this means with less than three clear working days. The DSA will refund the fee or another test will be arranged at no further cost if the test:

- is cancelled by the DSA;
- is cancelled by the candidate and the above amount of notice is given;
- is cancelled by the candidate for medical reasons and a doctor's letter or certificate is provided;
- does not take place or is not finished for a reason other than the candidate's fault, or the fault of the vehicle, for example bad weather conditions.

Certain expenses incurred on the day of the test will also be refunded to the candidate if the DSA cancels at short notice, unless it is for bad weather or poor light conditions. Reasonable claims for the following will be considered:

- any standard pay or earnings lost through taking unpaid leave (usually for half a day);
- the cost of travelling to and from the test centre if a Theory Test is involved, or the cost of hiring a vehicle for the test, including travelling to and from the test centre if a Practical Test is involved (generally up to one and half hours of vehicle hire).

The DSA will not pay for the cost of driving lessons arranged prior to a particular test appointment, or for extra lessons taken while waiting for a rescheduled appointment.

Application forms, giving full details of the above and how to apply for compensation, are available from the DSA in Nottingham.

Attending for the test

To ensure that everything goes smoothly on your pupil's test day:

- Check that the pupil has a valid, signed driving licence, his or her Theory Test pass certificate and some form of photographic identity if necessary.
- Take the test appointment card in case any errors have been made.
- Make sure your car is clean and tidy and has sufficient fuel.
- Clean the windows, leaving one slightly open if there is a risk of condensation.
- Make sure that the pupil knows where the ancillary controls are and how they work.
- Make sure that your car is:
  - roadworthy and has a current MOT certificate if applicable;
  - fitted with front and rear seat belts in working order, and adjustable head restraints;
  - fully insured for the pupil to drive while on the test;
  - properly taxed with the disc displayed in the correct position;
  - displaying 'L' plates clearly visible to the front and rear;
  - fitted with a rear view mirror for the driving examiner.

The car must meet the minimum test vehicle requirements. For a car first registered after 1 October 2003, this means that it must be capable of reaching 100 kph.

You should leave your ADI Registration Certificate or Trainee Licence in the windscreen when your car is being used for a test.

If any of these points are overlooked, the test may be cancelled and the pupil will lose the fee. As these requirements are your professional responsibility, you will then be obliged to pay for another appointment.

At the test centre

Take your pupil into the waiting room a few minutes prior to the time of the appointment, making allowances for toilet requirements. Try to maintain a relaxed atmosphere by chatting to your pupil.

Documents

The examiner will come in to the waiting room and ask for your pupil by name, request some form of identification and ask the candidate to sign the DSA 'Driving Test Report' form. This signature will serve as a declaration that the vehicle presented for test carries valid motor insurance in accordance with the Road Traffic Act.

A reminder is given to candidates about motor insurance responsibilities on their test appointment card. However, it is sensible to remind your pupils, before they go into the waiting room, that this formality will take place. Confirm with them that your car is properly insured. If, for any reason, the candidate does not sign the declaration, the examiner will refuse to conduct the test and the fee will be forfeited.

Introduction

Examiners are trained to use their discretion about introducing themselves either on the way to, or in, the car. They will also decide whether or not it is appropriate to use first names.

Driving test examiners are sympathetic towards candidates. They understand 'test nerves'. You should realize, however, that while nerves are frequently used as an excuse for failing, they are rarely the real cause. Provided your pupils are properly prepared, and know what to expect, nerves should not be too much of a problem. Conducting a realistic 'mock test', to give pupils an insight into what will happen, can do much to allay these fears.

Eyesight

The eyesight test will be conducted outside the test centre. The legal requirement is for the candidate to be able to read, in good daylight, a car number plate from a distance of 20 metres (or 20.5m for the old-style plates). If the candidate fails this, the test will not be conducted.

Vehicle safety questions

Before starting the on-road part of the test the examiner will ask two questions on vehicle safety. Sample questions are:

Would you show me how you would check that the power-assisted steering is working properly?

Identify where you would check the engine oil level and explain how.

Tell me how you would check that the brake lights are working on this vehicle.

Show me how you would check the handbrake for excessive wear.

The pupil is not expected to physically check fluid levels, or to touch a hot engine, but may be required to open the bonnet to show the location of the various items.

Directional instructions

At the start of the test the examiner will explain to the candidate that he or she should 'follow the road ahead unless directed otherwise'. Any instructions to turn off to the left or right will be given in plenty of time.

Driving Test Report

DL25A
12 / 03 T

S　D/C

I declare that the use of the test vehicle for the purposes of the test is covered by a valid policy of insurance which satisfies the requirements of the relevant legislation.

X

Application Ref.　　　　Dr./No.

Date　　　Time　　　Reg. No.

DTC Code / Authority　　　Staff / Ref. No.

Cat. Type　　Auto　Ext　　1　2　3　4　5　6　7　8　9　0

ADI / Reg　　　　Sup　ADI　Int　Other　　V　C

	Total S D		Total S D		Total S D
1a Eyesight		13 Move off safety		23 Positioning normal driving	
1b H/Code / Safety		control		lane discipline	
2 Controlled Stop promptness		14 Use of mirrors- M/C signalling rear obs.		24 Pedestrian crossings	
control		change direction		25 Position / normal stops	
3 Reverse / Left Reverse with trailer control		change speed		26 Awareness / planning	
observation		15 Signals necessary		27 Ancillary controls	
4 Reverse/ Right control		correctly		28 Spare 1	
observation		timed		29 Spare 2	
5 Reverse Park control		16 Clearance / obstructions		30 Spare 3	
R　C　obs.		17 Response to signs traffic signs / signals		31 Spare 4	
6 Turn in road control		road markings		32 Spare 5	
observation		traffic lights		33	
7 Vehicle checks		traffic controllers		Pass Fail None Total Faults Route No.	
8 Taxi manoeuvre control		other road users			
observation		18 Use of speed			
9 Taxi wheelchair		19 Following distance		ETA V P SN	
10 Uncouple / recouple		20 Progress appropriate speed		Survey A B C D	
11 Precautions		undue hesitation		E F G H	
12 Control accelerator		21 Junctions approach speed		Debrief Activity Code	
clutch		observation			
gears		turning right		I acknowledge receipt of Pass Certificate Number:	
footbrake		turning left			
parking brake / MC front brake		cutting corners			
steering		22 Judgement overtaking			
balance M/C		meeting			
LGV / PCV gear exercise		crossing		**X** Lic. R'cd	
PCV door exercise					

© Crown Copyright 2002　　　DSA – An executive agency of the Department for Transport　　　Form Ref. DL25 FCN17747709

Figure 10.1　The Driving Test Report form

The directions and instructions described in Chapter 8 are general guidelines, and examiners may use slightly different terminology where appropriate to suit a particular candidate.

MARKING SYSTEM

Driving examiners are trained to look for the 'perfect driver'. At the moment of getting into the car every test candidate is considered to be perfect. Any deviations from this perfection are graded into three categories of fault: driving, serious and dangerous.

Faults are graded and recorded on the Driving Test Report form (DL25C), as they occur. Before any minor deviation from perfect is marked on the form, the examiner must consider its significance to the overall performance.

The Driving Test Report explained

Please note that the following is a direct extract from the DL25, using DSA terminology.

1(a) The eyesight test
At the start of the test the examiner asked you to read a vehicle registration number. If you required glasses or contact lenses, you must wear them whenever you drive. If you had problems with the eyesight test, perhaps you should consider consulting an optician.

1(b) *Highway Code*/safety
If you didn't need to take a separate Theory Test, for example to obtain a licence for a tractor or other specialist vehicle, you will have been asked questions on the *Highway Code* and other related motoring matters. You will also have been asked to identify some traffic signs. If you had difficulty with these questions make sure that you study properly by reading as wide a range of publications as you can to increase your understanding. If you have already passed a theory test you will not have been asked *Highway Code* questions at the practical test stage; but you should still have a thorough knowledge of it.

Safety questions (if applicable) – you should know the location of, and be able to operate, safety components such as fire extinguisher, fuel cut-off switch and emergency door.

2 Controlled stop
You will need to be able to display a high level of skill in bringing your vehicle to a stop, safely, promptly and under full control avoiding locking the wheels.

Remember that in wet weather it can take twice as long to stop safely.

3, 4 and 5 Reverse exercises

You will need to display the ability to control the vehicle safely whilst reversing to the left, right, when parking on the road or into a parking bay. You must take good effective all round observation throughout the manoeuvre and show consideration to other road users.

6 Turn in the road

You will need to display the low speed control and observation skills necessary to carry out this exercise safely with due regard for other road users and pedestrians.

7 Vehicle checks

You will need to display to the examiner a basic knowledge of the fundamental safety checks applicable to your vehicle. For example safe fluid levels, lighting and tyre checks.

8 Taxi manoeuvre

You must be able to display the ability to turn your car around by whatever means available, making sure you take effective, all round observation showing consideration to other road users and pedestrians.

You should control your vehicle smoothly making proper use of the clutch, accelerator, brakes and steering.

You should not use a driveway or allow your vehicle to mount the pavement as this could damage your vehicle.

9 Taxi wheelchair

You should be able to

- securely erect wheelchair ramps,
- safely install the wheelchair and an imaginary occupant into your vehicle,
- ensure the wheelchair and occupant are secured in readiness for the journey, and
- reverse the entire process.

10 Vehicle and trailer combinations. Uncoupling /recoupling

You will need to demonstrate the skills necessary when uncoupling and recoupling your vehicle, driving the towing vehicle to a designated position prior to recoupling safely.

11 Precautions

Before you start the engine make sure that you are comfortably seated and all controls can be safely operated.

12 Control

This section covers, where appropriate, the safe and controlled use of accelerator, clutch, gears, footbrake, parking brake and steering.

Additional specific control elements apply to the drivers of different vehicle categories.

Always try and use the vehicle controls as smoothly as possible. This means less wear and tear on your vehicle and a smoother ride for your passengers.

Make proper use of your accelerator and clutch to make a smooth start.

Always depress the clutch just before you stop.

Select the correct gear to match the road and traffic conditions.

Change gear in good time but not too soon before a hazard.

Do not allow the vehicle to coast by running on in neutral or with the clutch depressed.

There should be no need to look down at the gear lever when changing gear.

Use the footbrake smoothly and progressively.

Brake in plenty of time for any hazard.

Make full use of the parking brake whenever it would help you to prevent the car from rolling backwards or forwards, and if you are parking.

Steer the vehicle as smoothly as possible.

Avoid harsh steering, or steering too early or too late as it may cause you to hit the kerb or swing out towards another road user.

If you are riding a motorcycle slowly, maintain a straight line and do not allow the machine to wobble towards other vehicles.

13 Move off

You will need to demonstrate your ability to move off smoothly and safely on the level, on a gradient and at an angle taking the correct precautionary observations.

14 Use of mirrors – rear observations

Use all the mirrors fitted to your vehicle safely and effectively.

You must always check carefully before signalling, changing direction or changing speed.

Use the Mirrors Signal Manoeuvre (MSM) routine effectively.

15 Signals

You must signal clearly to let others know what you intend to do. You should only use the signals shown in the *Highway Code* if it would help other road users (including pedestrians).

Always signal in good time and ensure that the signal has been cancelled after the manoeuvre has been completed.

Do not beckon to pedestrians to cross the road.

16 Clearance to obstructions

Allow plenty of room to pass stationary vehicles, obstructions and be prepared to slow down or stop. A door may open, a child may run out or a vehicle may pull out without warning.

17 Response to signs and signals

You should understand and be able to react to all traffic signs and road markings.

You must act correctly at traffic lights, and check that the road is clear before proceeding when the green light shows.

Obey signals given by police officers, traffic wardens and school crossing patrols.

Look out for signals given by other road users, including people in charge of animals, and be ready to act accordingly.

18 Use of speed

You should make safe, reasonable progress along the road bearing in mind the road, traffic and weather conditions and the road signs and speed limits.

Make sure that you can stop safely, well within the distance you can see to be clear.

Do not speed. Remember that as a new driver, your licence will be revoked if you accrue six or more penalty points during the first two years, and you have to retake and pass both theory and practical tests.

19 Following distance

Always keep a safe distance between yourself and other vehicles.

Remember, on wet or slippery roads it takes much longer to stop.

When you stop in traffic queues leave sufficient room to pull out if the vehicle in front has problems.

20 Maintain progress

In order to pass your test you must show that you can drive at a realistic speed appropriate to the road and traffic conditions.

You should approach all hazards at a safe, controlled speed, without being over cautious or interfering with the progress of other traffic.

Always be ready to move away from junctions as soon as it is safe and correct to do so.

Driving excessively slowly can create dangers for yourself and other drivers.

21 Junctions (including roundabouts)

You should be able to judge the correct speed of approach so that you can enter a junction safely and stop if necessary.

Position your vehicle correctly.

Use the correct lane.

If you are turning right, keep as near to the centre of the road as is safe.

Avoid cutting the corner when turning right.

If turning left, keep over to the left and do not swing out.

Watch out for cyclists and motorcyclists coming up on your left and pedestrians who are crossing.

You must take effective observation before moving into a junction and make sure it is safe before proceeding.

22 Judgement

Only overtake when it is safe to do so.

Allow enough room when you are overtaking another vehicle.

Cyclists and motorcyclists need at least as much space as other vehicles. They can wobble or swerve suddenly.

Do not cut in too quickly after overtaking.

Take care when the width of the road is restricted or when the road narrows.

If there is an obstruction on your side or not enough room for two vehicles to pass safely, be prepared to wait and let the approaching vehicles through.

When you turn right across the path of an approaching vehicle, make sure you can do so safely. Other vehicles should not have to stop, slow down or swerve to allow you to complete your turn.

23 Positioning

You should position the vehicle sensibly, normally well to the left.

Keep clear of parked vehicles and position correctly for the direction that you intend to take.

Where lanes are marked, keep to the middle of the lane and avoid straddling lane markings.

Do not change lanes unnecessarily.

24 Pedestrian crossings

You should be able to recognize the different types of pedestrian crossings and show courtesy and consideration towards pedestrians.

At all crossings you should slow down and stop if there is anyone on the crossing.

At zebra crossings you should slow down and be prepared to stop if there is anyone waiting to cross.

Give way to any pedestrian on a pelican crossing when the amber lights are flashing.

You should give way to cyclists as well as pedestrians on a toucan crossing and act correctly at puffin crossings.

25 Position/normal stops

Choose a safe, legal and convenient place to stop, close to the edge of the road, where you will not obstruct the road and create a hazard.

You should know how and where to stop without causing danger to other road users.

26 Awareness/planning

You must be aware of other road users at all times.

You should always think and plan ahead so that you can

– judge what other road users are going to do
– predict how their actions will affect you, and
– react in good time.

Take particular care to consider the actions of the more vulnerable groups of road users such as pedestrians, cyclists, motorcyclists and horse riders.

Anticipate road and traffic conditions, and act in good time, rather than reacting to them at the last moment.

27 Ancillary controls

You should understand the function of all the controls and switches, especially those that have a bearing on road safety. These include

– indicators
– lights
– windscreen wipers
– demisters
– heaters.

You should be able to find these controls and operate them correctly when necessary, without looking down.

Boxes 28 and 29 on the marking sheet are normally used by the examiner for any faults relating to eco-driving and for the fleet training test.

As a professional driving instructor you should be completely familiar with the DL25 and the above detailed explanations.

Fault categories

Faults committed during driving tests are assessed under the following categories:

- *Dangerous fault:* recorded when a fault is assessed as having caused actual danger during the test. A single fault in this category will result in failure.
- *Serious fault:* recorded when a fault is assessed as potentially dangerous. A habitual driving fault can also be assessed as serious when it indicates a serious weakness in a candidate's driving. A single serious fault is an automatic failure.
- *Driving fault:* a less serious fault, which is assessed as such because of the circumstances at that particular time. Driving faults only amount to a failure when there is an accumulation of 15 or more.

There is an obvious need for a degree of standardization between the consistency of assessments made in training and those used for the driving test. It is essential therefore that you become familiar with this grading system.

There are, of course, other types of errors that you will be dealing with during a pupil's training. These include marginal errors that could develop into more serious faults or that could lead to bad habits being formed, and they are dealt with in more detail in Chapter 8, Driver Training.

DRIVING TEST ERRORS

Driving fault

The pupil is approaching a junction to turn right into a fairly wide side road. Visibility into the road is good and, after ensuring it is safe to turn and the side road is free of traffic movement, the learner turns into the side road, cutting the corner very slightly. No potential danger was caused to other road users because the pupil had checked the situation before turning. On a driving test this would be recorded as a driving fault. It would not result in failure.

Serious fault

The pupil is approaching the same right turn. This time visibility into the side road is severely restricted by parked vehicles, making it impossible for the pupil to see whether or not there is traffic approaching the end of the new road. The pupil blatantly cuts the corner into this unknown situation. No actual danger occurred because no other road user appeared from the side road. This, however, was purely good luck and not an assessed judgement. The incident involved potential danger and the learner would fail the test.

Dangerous fault

In exactly the same circumstances as the example above, the learner cuts the corner. This time, another vehicle appears approaching the end of the side road. The other driver has to brake to avoid a collision. This incident involved actual danger and, of course, the learner would fail the test.

Driving, serious or dangerous?

It is not necessary for you to be able to grade errors exactly to DSA Driving Test criteria. While some degree of standardization is desirable, it is not absolutely essential to get it right all the time, and you need not worry unduly over this matter. In any event, the difference between serious and dangerous is purely academic, because in both instances the result is the same – failure.

The difference between a driving fault and a serious fault in this situation, however, could mean the difference between pass and fail. Using again the above examples, for comparison, we can define the errors in a different way. The essential difference between the two incidents is that the driver committing the driving fault in the first example was able to see that the new road was clear. In the second example the fault was a serious fault because the driver was unable to see if the new road was clear, but was prepared to take a risk or was completely unaware of any risk.

The fault really is not a difference between two people cutting a corner with one of them getting away with it. One of them was able to see and might well have acted differently had the visibility been restricted; the other proved to be totally unaware of the danger caused by the parked vehicles. It is only possible to assess the actions of a driver in the light of the prevailing situation.

Summary of 'L' driver errors

According to the DSA driving skills book, *The Official Guide to Learning to Drive*, some of the most common causes for driving test failure are:

- **Eyesight test**: unable to read a vehicle number plate at 20.5 metres (67 ft) or 20 metres (66 ft) for the new-style plate.
- **Highway Code**: knowledge of the Highway Code (and application of it during the drive) weak or wrong.
- **Precautions before starting engine**: handbrake not applied, neutral not selected, when starting or restarting the engine.
- **Make proper use of**:
  - **accelerator**: erratic, fierce or jerky use; poor coordination with clutch;
  - **clutch**: not depressed far enough, causing noisy changing or stalling; poor coordination with accelerator;
  - **footbrake**: not used when needed; used late, harshly or erratically;
  - **gears**: incorrect selection; coasting; not in neutral when needed; harsh control of the gear lever; looking at lever; reluctant to change; incorrect use of selector on automatic;
  - **handbrake**: not applied when required; not released when moving; used before stopping;
  - **steering** (position of hands on wheel): one hand off; both hands off; hands on spokes, rim or centre; hands crossed unnecessarily; elbow on window ledge;
  - **steering** (oversteer): erratic control of steering; wandering on wheel; late correction; over- or understeering; jerky or fiddling movements.
- **Moving off – angle, hill, level, straight**: not done smoothly; not safe; not controlled; causing inconvenience or danger to others; not using mirrors; not looking round or not acting sensibly on what is seen; not signalling when needed; incorrect gear; lack of coordination of controls.
- **Emergency stop**: slow reactions; like a normal stop; footbrake/clutch used in a manner likely to cause a skid; handbrake used before stopping; both hands off the wheel.
- **Reverse, left/right**: rushed; stalling; poor coordination of accelerator and clutch; incorrect course; mounting kerb; steering wrong way; too wide or

close (not realized); not looking around before/during reverse; not acting on what is seen.

- **Turning in road**: rushed; stalling; poor coordination of accelerator and clutch; not using handbrake; incorrect steering; mounting or bouncing off kerb; uncontrolled footbrake or accelerator; more moves than needed; lack of observation before or during manoeuvre; danger or inconvenience to others; looking but not acting sensibly on what is seen.
- **Reverse park**: rushed; poor coordination of controls; incorrect course; too wide or too close to parked car; lack of effective observations before/during exercise; poor response to other road users; not using handbrake; not finishing exercise correctly.
- **Effective use of mirrors**: not looking in good time; not acting on what is seen; omitted or used too late; used as or after movement is commenced; not used effectively before signalling, changing direction, slowing or stopping; omitting final look when necessary.
- **Give signals correctly**: signals omitted; given wrongly, or given late; too short to be of value; not cancelled after use; not repeated when needed; arm signal not given when needed.
- **Prompt action on signals**: failing to comply with signals or signs – stop, keep left, no entry, traffic lights, police signals, school crossing wardens, signals given by other road users.
- **Use of speed**: not exercising proper care in use of speed; too fast for conditions or speed limits; too close to vehicle in front in view of speed, weather, road conditions.
- **Making progress**: not making normal progress; too low speed for conditions; crawling in low gear; no speed build-up between gears; speed not maintained; undue hesitation at junctions; over-cautious to the point of being a nuisance.
- **Crossroads and junctions**: incorrect regulation of speed on approach; late appreciation of, or reaction to, junctions or crossroads; not taking effective observation before emerging at a crossroad or junction; not being sure it is safe to emerge before doing so; incorrect assessment of speed and distance of other vehicles, including cyclists; incorrect positioning for right turns, at or on approach; position taken late, too far from centre, wrong position out of narrow road, or from one-way street, wandering, wrong position at end of right turn; incorrect positioning for left turns, at or on approach; too far from near kerb; swinging out before turning; striking or running over kerb; swinging out after turn; cutting right turns when entering or leaving.
- **Overtaking/meeting/crossing other traffic**: overtaking unsafely; wrong time or place; causing danger or inconvenience to others; too close or cutting in afterwards; inadequate clearance for oncoming traffic, causing vehicles to swerve or brake; turning right across oncoming traffic unsafely.
- **Normal position**: unnecessarily far out from kerb.

- **Adequate clearance**: passing too close to cyclists, pedestrians or stationary vehicles.
- **Pedestrian crossings**: approaching too fast; not stopping when necessary, or preparing to stop if pedestrian waiting; overtaking on approach; not signalling (by arm if necessary) when needed; giving dangerous signals to pedestrians.
- **Normal stops**: stopping unsafely or in inconvenient place; not parallel to kerb; too close to other vehicles or hazards, compounding hazards.
- **Awareness and anticipation**: lack of awareness or anticipation of others' actions. (This is marked when the result of bad planning or lack of foresight involves the test candidate in a situation resulting in late, hurried or muddled decisions.)
- **Use of ancillary controls**: not using equipment that is necessary for the conditions.

At the end of the test

Driving Test Report – DL25 (DL9A in N. Ireland)

During the test the examiner uses this form to record any driving errors. Other information regarding the conduct of the test is also itemized. At the end of the test a copy of the marking sheet is given to the candidate. The examiner may also discuss the reasons for failure with the candidate and the instructor. The form lists the main subjects outlined in *The Official Guide to Learning to Drive*. It should be used as a guide for both you and your pupil. For more detail see pages 337 to 342.

When your pupil passes

The examiner will record all driving faults on form DL25, and a duplicate is handed to the candidate. The examiner will discuss any relevant points and the instructor will be invited to listen to this explanation.

A Certificate of Competence to Drive (D10) will also be issued. This allows the candidate to drive unaccompanied on any type of road, without 'L' plates. You should advise your pupils to apply for a full licence as soon as possible, and in any case within two years, otherwise the D10 will become invalid.

The examiner will hand the pupil a copy of the DSA magazine *Drive On*, which contains useful information and advice for new drivers; and a leaflet describing the Pass Plus scheme. This is your opportunity to encourage him or her to take further training in those areas of driving not already covered within your syllabus. See page 24 for information on the scheme. Details of the Pass Plus syllabus are given in Chapter 8, page 291.

If your pupil fails

As well as giving the pupil a copy of the Driving Test Report form, the examiner will give a verbal report on the reasons for failure. You may sit in and listen to this explanation if you wish – it may help you advise the pupil on any further training requirements. The reverse of the form gives an explanation of the markings, and an outline of the appeals procedure.

Application for a retest can be made immediately, but the test must not be taken within 10 working days. Book the pupil a lesson as soon as possible so that your analysis and correction of weaknesses is more valid. This also allows the current standard of driving to be maintained and improved where required.

After the test

Whether the pupil has passed or failed, it is usually appropriate and advisable for you to drive the car away from the test centre as soon as practicable.

There are several reasons for this:

- You can vacate the parking space for candidates who are preparing for the next test time.
- The pupil will be feeling very elated if he or she has passed and will not be able to concentrate properly on his or her driving.
- The pupil will be disappointed, angry or upset if he or she has failed – none of which is conducive to driving.
- The test centre is not the ideal time for carrying out a post-mortem.

Finally, as soon as possible after the test make sure that your pupil signs up for their first session of Pass Plus training.

CAR AND TRAILER TEST

From time to time you may need to train a pupil in a car towing a trailer. This is because the current regulations allow a new driver to tow a trailer where the nett weight of the car exceeds the gross weight of the trailer, and if the total weight of the outfit is under 3,500 kg. For heavier trailers, or where the trailer weighs more than the car (a horsebox, for example), an additional test will be needed for category B+E.

To take this test, the pupil must

- already hold a full category B licence;
- be over 21;
- be accompanied by a person who has held (and still holds) a full licence for B+E for at least three years.

The vehicle must carry 'L' plates (or 'D' plates in Wales if you prefer).

Minimum test vehicles

The vehicle to be used for the test must conform to the minimum test vehicle requirements. For vehicles first registered before 1 October 2003 the vehicle must be capable of 100 kph (62 mph) and the trailer must be at least 1 tonne maximum authorized mass. For a vehicle first registered after 1 Oct 2003, there is an additional rule: the trailer must be 'a closed box trailer – slightly less wide than the towing vehicle, but rear view must be by external mirrors only'.

Test centre

Vehicle and trailer tests are conducted at LGV/PCV testing stations, where there are special facilities for maneouvring and for braking exercises.

Safety questions

At the start of the test the examiner will ask five questions on vehicle safety. As with the car test, these questions are based on the 'show me'/'tell me' principle.

The subjects covered include:

- tyres and wheels;
- brakes;
- steering;
- engine oil and fluid levels;
- lights and reflectors;
- direction indicators;
- audible warning devices;
- loading;
- trailer body condition.

Sample questions include:

- '*Tell me* the main safety factors in loading this vehicle.'
  The trainee's explanation should include 'even distribution throughout the length of the vehicle', 'securely stowed, within the size and weight limits' and 'secured so that there is no danger of the load moving or falling off when cornering or braking'.
- '*Show me* how you would check for air leaks on this vehicle.'
  The pupil would need to show the examiner the location of the air tanks and how to check the gauges for a drop in pressure, and would need to walk round the vehicle to listen for obvious leaks.

Test syllabus

Reversing

This exercise is carried out at the test centre, using an area that is set according to the size of the vehicle and trailer combined. The candidate has to reverse to the right and then to the left between cones, finishing in a simulated loading bay. The maneouvre must be done:

- under control and in reasonable time;
- with good observation;
- with reasonable accuracy;
- inside a clearly defined boundary.

The extreme rear of the trailer should finish within a yellow painted box area at the end of the marked bay.

Braking exercise

The braking exercise takes place on the special manoeuvring area rather than on the public roads. The examiner travels in the vehicle during the exercise. The candidate is asked to achieve about 20 mph in a distance of about 200 feet, and then stop the vehicle on reaching a set of markers. The vehicle should be stopped:

- as quickly as possible;
- under full control;
- as safely as possible;
- in a straight line.

The candidate should avoid:

- driving too slowly;
- braking too soon;
- taking too long to stop.

On the road

The test is about one hour long. Because the braking and reversing exercises are carried out at the test centre, the candidate is not required to do any other manoeuvres, such as turning in the road, reversing round a corner, or emergency stop. There is, however, a requirement to move off:

- at an angle;
- on an uphill gradient;
- on a downhill gradient.

The route includes dual carriageways, one-way systems, and where possible, motorways.

Uncoupling and recoupling

At the end of the test the candidate is expected to park the outfit and uncouple the trailer. The towing vehicle is then parked safely alongside the trailer before recoupling the trailer. Some of the key points:

- Jockey wheel lowered correctly.
- Electric lines disconnected and stowed safely.
- Stabilizing equipment removed.
- Safety chain or coupling removed.
- Coupling removed and trailer moved clear of the towing hook.
- Check that the coupling is secure by using an appropriate method.
- Wheels, legs, etc are raised.
- Operation of the lights and indicators.

The pupil should be able to uncouple and recouple the vehicle and trailer:

- confidently and without any unnecessary delay.

EXTENDED DRIVING TEST

If a driver is convicted of an offence of dangerous driving the court will impose an Extended Driving Test as part of the disqualification process. Similarly, courts have discretion to order an Extended Test for other offences that involve obligatory disqualification.

The Extended Test is much longer than the ordinary test, lasting about 70 minutes, and is much more demanding. During the test a wide variety of different road and traffic conditions are covered, including dual carriageways. As the candidate will hold a provisional licence, motorways are not included. Because of the extra duration of the test a higher fee applies.

The test includes all the exercises that are part of the normal 'L' test, but with particular emphasis on whether the candidate is able to concentrate for the duration of the test and whether his or her attitude to other road users is satisfactory.

DSA SERVICE STANDARDS

Full information about complaints is given in the DSA's Service Standards leaflet, available from the Head Office in Nottingham. The contract for driving tests is between candidates and the DSA. If you have a pupil who has a complaint to make about any of the following, he or she must write to or telephone the appropriate DSA section:

- test cancellations;
- compensation;

- lost applications;
- delays in providing tests or results;
- Theory Test results;
- the conduct of a Practical Test.

The DSA will forward the complaint to the appropriate area customer service unit. The complaint must be set out clearly, including any redress the client is seeking.

You should note that if a pupil has a complaint about the conduct of a Practical Driving Test, the result of the test cannot be overturned. However, if it is felt that the test was not conducted according to the relevant regulations, the pupil should contact a magistrates' court, or sheriff's court if he or she lives in Scotland, which can order a retest.

If satisfaction is not achieved after this procedure has been followed, clients should be advised to write to the Chief Executive at the DSA in Nottingham. If satisfaction is still not achieved clients should be advised to write to their MP asking for their complaint to be investigated by an independent complaints adviser (ICA). In the rare event of these problems arising, leaflets about the ICA and the Parliamentary Ombudsman are available from DSA Head Office in Nottingham.

11

Business Skills and Customer Care

After qualifying as an ADI, the only continuing check on your ability is the periodic Check Test conducted by the DSA. This looks only at your ability to deliver a specific lesson to a specific pupil on the specified date. In other words, it's only a 'snapshot' of your overall instructional ability. At the present time the DSA are not involved in checking on your skills relating to customer care or to your ability to run a business legally or efficiently. In fact, when members of the public occasionally query the business conduct of a particular instructor or organization the DSA response is that they are only concerned with the level of instruction given. This leads to a situation where most instructors think that the ADI Check Test is the only thing they must concern themselves with.

This situation should change over the next few years as a result of several projects that are currently under way. In particular, one programme is looking at all areas of instructor refresher training, and most of the main trade organizations such as the Motor Schools Association are actively preparing themselves to offer the appropriate courses as soon as the requirements are known.

To be an effective all-round instructor – especially if you are working on your own account or with some franchises – you need to develop any of your skills that will enhance your business and keep you fully up to date in all areas, not just instructional skills. Equally important in the current era of consumer rights, customer care skills are becoming ever more important. Business skills – including legal issues, cash flow, insurance responsibilities and public liabilities – are necessary in running a business today.

A lot of work is currently being undertaken to review the needs of instructors in the area of continuing professional development (CPD), including various projects commissioned by the DSA and the Department for Transport (DfT). The results of these projects should be known and implemented by about 2007, but there are already a few indicators that have emerged. One of the main points is that there is currently no real incentive for ADIs to develop their skills and, in fact, only a very small percentage undertake any form of qualification or training other than the basic DSA qualification. The general trend in most other industries and professions is for CPD to be much more widely undertaken (and is an expectation for most people). For example, in the road transport industry there is a European directive that will require all lorry drivers to take a minimum amount of refresher training every few years. This training will include an element of business knowledge and customer care skills. There is clearly a need for more training and development for instructors but, as always, it is uncertain how any CPD courses or initiatives will be funded, because it is extremely unlikely that the majority of instructors will take training or extra qualifications unless they are obliged to or are motivated in some way. Nevertheless it can be shown that CPD is now even more important in a world that is very competitive.

Any properly prepared programme of CPD for driving instruction should include an element of business and customer care skills as well as the personal and instructional skills that are covered in more detail in *Practical Teaching Skills for Driving Instructors*. These subjects include:

- personal:
  - assertive skills
  - affective skills
  - problem-solving skills
  - decision-making skills
  - feedback;
- own driving skills;
- instructor training;
- role-play skills.

As a qualified ADI you are likely to be working either as a completely independent instructor or as a franchisee. Either way, you are in effect running your own business as a self-employed trader. In these circumstances there is a need for you to be fully conversant with many of the requirements of running a small business. Just how much you need to know will, of course, depend on the working relationship between yourself and your franchiser where applicable. In running a small business – particularly in a service industry where there is direct one-to-one contact with your customers – you should also be aware of the need for customer care qualities, standards and responsibilities.

Any programme of CPD should therefore include as many of these areas of knowledge as are appropriate to your particular circumstances. This is likely to be done on a voluntary basis, as the DSA seem to concentrate solely on instructional matters in their Check Tests and in monitoring the standards of ADIs generally.

BUSINESS SKILLS

These should include the skills discussed in the following sections.

Management and planning

Running a business from home can offer several financial advantages. If you use one of the rooms as an office you are able to claim for the expenses such as rent, heat and light. This is in addition to the normal running costs such as telephone, computer, stationery, office staff and so on. However, remember that there will be a certain amount of administrative work: you will need to keep appropriate records to satisfy not only your franchiser, but also the tax and National Insurance authorities.

Take into account that you will not necessarily be able to work all year – you will need to make allowances for time off for illness and for holidays.

Make sure that you understand and make provision for life and health insurance, your pension, savings and any sudden or unexpected downturn in business.

Check whether you would require planning permission to operate from your home address. Find out whether there are any restrictive covenants or lease restrictions that might apply.

Administration

You will need to keep proper records of all your business transactions, especially for income tax purposes and where VAT is involved.

Whether you need to employ an accountant, either to set up a system for you or to deal with your end-of-year affairs, will depend on the type and size of business you run.

If you employ someone part time to deal with these matters (your spouse or partner, for example), you can claim those expenses against tax, but you will also need to make the necessary payments for tax and National Insurance.

Bookkeeping and accounts

To keep accurate records of your business (particularly for tax purposes) you would normally be required to keep details of all income and expenditure including purchase invoices and cash payments. There are plenty of relatively simple systems available either in manual or in computer form. As a minimum, most businesses will need bookkeeping records for purchases, sales and cash payments.

From your records you need to know:

- how many lessons were completed in any particular period;
- what your running costs are for each lesson;
- what profit you have made;
- what monies are owed to your business customers;
- how much the business owes;
- what your cash flow is likely to be;
- what the business's bank balance is at any time.

Any bookkeeping records, including invoices and payments, you use should be retained for five years after the 31 January following the year of assessment.

Insurance – vehicle, premises, personal and public liabilities

Insurance is a necessary expenditure giving cover against a variety of mishaps. For example, you can, for a price, insure yourself or your business for almost any risk including professional indemnity. The main one to consider, of course, is the vehicle you use for training. If this were out of action for any length of time because of an accident it could be disastrous to your income. Shop around to obtain the best deal, but do not necessarily go for the cheapest option – make sure that you get the cover you need.

Other insurance should cover you as a provider of income, by taking out life, critical illness and accident cover. You might also feel that you need cover against loss of income – for example, if your car were to be out of action for a long period of time owing to a breakdown you would need to recover the loss of income. Most of these types of cover can be arranged under a composite business policy that is tailored to your needs. This would normally cover other elements such as public and professional liability.

You should consider whether private health insurance would be appropriate to your needs. If you required hospital treatment or a prolonged period away from work, would it be more efficient to your business if you could decide when it would be more convenient to take the time off? This can often be a worthwhile alternative to the NHS waiting periods, although you will need to balance the advantages against the potential cost of private medical insurance, which can vary greatly from one provider to another, and depending on individual circumstances.

If your home-based office is important to the business, check that your house insurance covers the business use and the contents.

Tax affairs

Taxation can depend on whether you operate as a sole trader, in a partnership or as a limited company.

Self-assessment for income tax purposes requires the taxpayer to retain his or her business records to support the information given on the tax return. The tax return should be submitted before 30 September if you want the tax office to calculate the tax, or by 30 January if you calculate your own tax.

For details of self-assessment for the self-employed, visit www.hmrc.gov.uk or telephone 0845 900 0444 for advice.

Pension planning

Recent surveys have shown that millions of people do not make sufficient provision for their pension requirements and that a significant number make no provision at all. This is a situation that is likely to be even more important in the future, as there are signs that the state pension system will have to change drastically to cope with future demands. One of the changes might involve an increase in the pension age.

Right from the start you should make adequate provision for your pension by charging the right rate for your services to allow for an appropriate regular payment into a pension scheme. Take appropriate independent advice from a registered broker or adviser, as there are many suitable schemes about – especially as a result of the new rules that were due to come into force in 2006. Remember that a large proportion of the payments you make can be offset against tax.

For information and details about state pensions or for a prediction of your pension at retirement age, contact the Pension Service on 0845 3013 011 or at www.thepensionservice.gov.uk, quoting your National Insurance reference number.

VAT

If your annual turnover is more than £60,000 (for 2006/07) you will need to register for VAT. Even though you will then need to charge VAT for all your services, there are some benefits, as you are allowed to claim back the VAT on many of your expenses.

For details about VAT, go to www.hmrc.gov.uk or contact the advice line on 0845 010 9000.

Finance

When you start up a new business it is usually necessary to have sufficient funds available to cover the cost of purchasing vehicles and other equipment. There will also be a need to have access to sufficient funds to support yourself (and your family, if applicable) for a period of time until you generate a regular income. Of course, if you decide to take out a franchise some, but not all, of these expenses will be covered by way of weekly or monthly payments, rather than as capital expenditure.

Financing assets

Manufacturers and retailers usually offer finance packages and will often encourage you to make use of them. Many of these schemes are worthwhile – particularly if there is a genuine special low-cost offer available. However, it is important to shop around for loan arrangements from other sources. It may, for example, be more cost-effective to borrow the money from your bank, a building society or a specialist finance firm. In this way you may be able to tailor the repayments to suit your particular circumstances.

A popular way of financing is to use contract hire, where you do not necessarily own the vehicle, but you do know exactly what your repayment costs will be over a fixed period.

Another fairly common method of paying is by a 'finance lease'. This involves making a payment at the end of the term based on the anticipated value of the car. This method reduces the initial payment and the monthly repayment costs and also provides the opportunity to purchase the car for a predetermined cost at the end of the leasing period.

Hire purchase and lease purchase are other viable alternatives, with some similarities. With both methods you do not legally own the vehicle until you have finished paying all the required instalments.

National Insurance

As a self-employed person you need to pay National Insurance at the flat weekly rate and also a Class 4 contribution based on the level of your profits. If you employ any staff, you will need to pay the employer contribution for them.

Banking

You don't necessarily need a business bank account as well as your normal personal account, but it is usually quite useful as a means of completely separating all your business income and expenditure. If you decide to use a personal account, make sure that you keep details of all business transactions quite separately.

When opening a new business account, shop around to find the most appropriate bank. Many banks and building societies offer reduced charges or even free banking for the first one or two years of a new business.

Health and safety matters

The Health and Safety Act is mainly aimed at preventing accidents and providing a safe working environment for employees. However, the regulations apply equally to the self-employed, who have a responsibility for their own safety.

This should not be too much of an issue, but remember that you have an obligation to your customers and yourself in terms of safety and creating a safe working environment.

If you have any concerns, or need further information, you could check with the Health and Safety Executive on their help line, 08701 545500, or e-mail them at hseinformationservices@natbrit.com to find out which regulations might apply to your particular situation.

Full details of the requirements can be found at www.hse.gov.uk.

CUSTOMER CARE

Customers (and, more importantly, potential customers) now have a great deal of freedom of choice between suppliers – particularly in the service industry. Furthermore, their expectations of efficient service are greater than previously. Your instruction skills may be top-grade, but if you let your customers down in any way your business and your reputation will suffer.

Customer loyalty is an important factor in a one-to-one service industry such as driving instruction. Recommendation is probably by far the most effective marketing tool and is much less costly than any advertising or promotion.

As well as offering good-quality instruction, think of other areas of your business – personal appearance, punctuality and timekeeping during lessons. Avoid 'short-changing' the pupil; give a little extra rather than a little less time.

Customers' expectations include:

- *Efficiency.* Be on time for all lesson appointments. A wait of two to three minutes can seem a long time to a waiting pupil – five minutes is unacceptable.
- *Honesty.* Carry out your business and instruction honestly and professionally, but tactfully.
- *Politeness.* Maintain the instructor–pupil relationship in a friendly, but not over-familiar, manner.
- *Respect.* The pupil can rightly expect to be treated as an individual person, and does not want to be patronized or treated dismissively.
- *Dress code.* You are not necessarily expected to wear formal clothing or a traditional business suit, but at least you should be neat, clean and tidy – whatever style of dress you choose.

Dealing with enquiries

Make sure that your telephone is answered promptly and efficiently. If you use an answer machine, try to follow up enquiries promptly. Research has shown that customers tend to expect their call to be answered within four rings of the phone. It has been shown that many people will give up after six or eight rings.

Whoever answers your phone is the first point of contact for the prospective customer. Make sure that the enquiry is dealt with effectively, with clear, concise and accurate information.

Follow-up procedures

Every enquiry, however vague or imprecise, should be treated seriously and with respect. Have a system in place whereby the enquiry details can be logged for future reference, so that you can follow up the enquiry at a later date and as a memory jogger for any further contact.

Promotions and marketing

Promoting your business is essential. Potential customers need to be made aware of what your business is offering. Marketing is normally vitally important to the home-based business because of the lack of passing trade. However, as a driving instructor, your car is probably your office as well as the training vehicle. Make sure that it is clean and well presented, with clear, sensible advertising material displayed. The name and telephone number of your business must be prominent. Make sure that the service you are offering is what your potential customers would expect.

Selling your services

The most important way of selling your services is by personal recommendation from satisfied customers. A satisfied customer can be a very useful marketing tool.

Make sure that any claims you make – regarding pass rates, for example – can be substantiated. To do this you must keep accurate customer records and not rely solely on verbal claims.

You should be able to organize a system of feedback from customers. This could be done by way of a fairly uncomplicated question form to give out to customers during their course of lessons or send out to them at the end.

Promotional literature

Business cards and leaflets should set out the details of your business in clear terms. Remember that leaflets are easily discarded, so consider whether to include some form of discount to new customers on presenting the leaflet.

Any advertising that you do should be completely honest, accurate and straightforward. You should avoid any inaccurate or misleading claims relating to your qualifications or pass rates.

Customer records

At any one time you could have a large number of pupils under instruction who will all be at different stages in their learning. Even those who have reached the same stage will not have covered identical aspects of driving in exactly the same order. Your students will be of a wide range of abilities and aptitudes. All of them will have individual likes, dislikes and preferences. For teaching purposes alone, this information is vitally important in helping you to create a suitable and effective learning environment for each individual pupil.

From a business point of view you need to have a system in place that will enable you to have an up-to-date picture of the status of each pupil. Without some form of record keeping, it will be impossible for you to carry all of the necessary information in your head from week to week. Apart from the obvious information such as name and address, your records could usefully contain some of the following details:

- driving licence: driver number, categories covered, expiry date;
- eyesight: spectacles, contact lenses?
- Theory Test: application, date and time, result;
- lesson payments;
- tuition record: topics covered;
- assessment and progress report: skills and procedures;
- route record: intermediate/advanced routes (keeping a record will help to avoid unnecessary repetition);
- Practical Test: application, fees, date and time, result;
- Pass Plus sessions.

As well as using a 'driver's record' for each customer, it is also worthwhile having a system to record the details of each customer. This may be done manually or on a computer and may include details of payments made and lessons taken. This kind of system will be helpful in building up a profile of your customer base.

If you take money in advance for lessons, it is important that you keep an accurate record in case of queries. Similarly, if you take money for a test application, make sure that the pupil is aware of the circumstances regarding a refund.

Handling complaints

Complaints from customers can be dealt with in a positive manner. The important issue is to try to ensure that any minor problems are tackled before they become major problems.

Your complaints procedure should be clear, stating that in the first instance clients should approach you with their grievance. If you cannot come to an amicable agreement, clients should be advised to refer to the DSA to consider and advise on the matter. In some circumstances the Registrar of ADIs is prepared to offer advice in an attempt to resolve disputes between instructor and pupil.

The industry has a voluntary code of practice (see below) that deals with this subject. You – or your franchiser – should have an effective procedure in place for dealing with complaints. Dealing with complaints properly and fairly can help to maintain good customer relations. The important thing, though, is to try to deal with minor queries before they turn into complaints.

CODE OF PRACTICE

The DSA and the main ADI consultative organizations have produced a code of practice that places emphasis on professional standards and business ethics. Once you have qualified, you will be expected to operate within this framework. Some of the main criteria are detailed in the following sections.

Personal conduct

You should:

- behave in a professional manner towards clients;
- treat your clients with respect and consideration;
- be polite, punctual and presentable;
- avoid physical contact with clients, except in emergencies or in the normal course of greeting;
- give value for money;
- not discuss with other people any matters that a pupil has disclosed;
- avoid acting in any way that contravenes legislation on discrimination.

Your training vehicle should be:

- properly maintained;
- safe and roadworthy;
- legal for giving instruction;
- clean, both internally and externally.

Business dealings

You should:

- Safeguard and account for any monies paid in advance for driving lessons, test fees or any other purpose. These details should be available to clients on request.
- Provide clients, on or before their first lesson, with a written copy of your terms of business. This should include:
  - the legal identity of your school, together with a full address and telephone number at which you or your representative can be contacted;
  - the price and duration of lessons;
  - the price and conditions for using the school car for driving tests;
  - the terms under which cancellation by either party may take place; and
  - a complaints procedure.
- Make sure clients are entitled to drive your vehicle, have a valid driving licence and can read a number plate from the prescribed distance. Ensure also that when presenting them for driving tests they have all the necessary documentation and your car is roadworthy.
- Forecast clients' readiness, and advise them when to apply for their theory and practical tests, taking into account local waiting times. Do not cancel or rearrange tests without clients' agreement. If you decide to withhold the use of your vehicle for a test, clients should be given sufficient notice to avoid their loss of the test fee.
- If the pupil is having an intensive course of lessons, make sure that he or she is aware of the potential loss of fees if the test is not taken or if the course is not completed.

- The whole of the lesson time should be devoted to the pupil's instruction, not to your own personal business.
- At all times do your best to teach clients correct driving skills according to the DSA's recommended syllabus.

Advertising

Your advertising should be honest. Any claims you make should be capable of verification and comply with the codes of practice set down by the Advertising Standards Authority. Any advertising referring to pass rates should not be open to misinterpretation, and the basis on which you calculate the pass rates should be made clear.

After passing all three exams, when you register as an ADI you will be sent a leaflet containing full details of the code of practice. If you are already qualified, copies are available from the DSA in Nottingham. (For contact details see page 390.)

This chapter is, of course, only a brief summary of the requirements of running a small, home-based business. For more information you should refer to some of the many books that are available from bookshops or libraries, including:

- *Running a Home-based Business* by Diane Baker, published as a *Sunday Times* Business Enterprise Guide – ISBN 0-7494-3665-4;
- *A Guide to Working for Yourself* by Godfrey Golzen and Jonathan Reuvid, published by Kogan Page – ISBN 0-7494-3751-0.

Courses are also available from local colleges and by distance learning. Check with your trade association, because several of them – for instance, the Motor Schools Association – offer occasional seminars at which many of these topics are covered.

12

Driving Large Vehicles

Passing the ordinary 'L' test gives full licence entitlement for category B, that is goods vehicles up to 3.5 tonnes gross weight and for passenger vehicles with up to eight passenger seats. If your first full licence was issued before January 1997 you will have additional entitlement for category C1 and D1 vehicles. These categories cover goods vehicles up to 7.5 tonnes and passenger vehicles (not used for hire or reward) with up to 17 passenger seats.

This chapter covers licences, tests and instructor qualifications for large vehicles in general terms, but for detailed information you need to refer to the official DSA and DVLA publications. These include:

- *The Official DSA Guide to Driving Goods Vehicles.*
- *The Official Theory Test for Drivers of Large Vehicles.*
- Leaflet D100, *What you need to know about driving licences.*

Other books that you might find helpful include *The LGV Learner Driver's Guide* by John Miller and *The Professional LGV Driver's Handbook* by David Lowe. For details of these books see page 392.

Some large vehicles are exempt from the requirement for the driver to hold a separate LGV driving licence. Full details of the exemptions can be found on the DVLA website at www.dvla.gov.uk and in the D100 leaflet.

LGV DRIVING LICENCES

To apply for a provisional LGV driving licence you must first hold a full UK car licence. The provisional licence will be for rigid vehicles only, as you must pass a test on this type of vehicle before moving on to vehicles with a trailer (including articulated vehicles and drawbar outfits). This system of 'staged testing' means that in order to eventually drive an articulated vehicle or large drawbar outfit, you must progress through the following sequence:

- Provisional driving licence for rigid goods vehicles.
- LGV Theory and Hazard Perception Test.

- LGV Rigid Vehicle Practical Test.
- Full rigid vehicle licence (with provisional trailer entitlement).
- Artic or Draw Bar LGV Practical Test.

Full details of all licence requirements and the exemptions are in the DVLA booklet, *What you need to know about driving licences* (D100), or on its website at www.dvla.gov.uk.

YOUNG LGV DRIVER SCHEME

The normal minimum age for driving vehicles with a gross weight of more than 7.5 tonnes is 21 years. However, under the Young LGV Driver Scheme it is possible to drive larger vehicles at an earlier age. This scheme has been brought about as a result of cooperation within the road transport industry. The various bodies involved include:

- Department of Transport;
- Road Haulage and Distribution Training Council (RHDTC);
- Road Haulage Association;
- Freight Transport Association;
- several trade unions.

Under the scheme, trainees between the ages of 18 and 21 receive quality driver training and an opportunity to obtain a National Vocational Qualification (NVQ). This enables the driver to gain experience and licences for the various categories of vehicles from B through C1 and C to C+E.

Table 12.1   Driving licence categories

Type of vehicle	Category	Min. age
Goods vehicle with a maximum authorized mass between 3.5 tonnes and 7.5 tonnes	C1	18
Goods vehicle and trailer As above, with trailer more than 750 kg – total weight not more than 12,000 kg	C1 + E	18 or 21
Large goods vehicle with a maximum authorized mass of more than 7.5 tonnes	C	21
LGV with draw bar trailer Rigid vehicle with trailer of more than 750 kg	C + E (restricted to drawbar trailers)	21
Articulated vehicles	C + E	21

Note: Whether or not you have C1 entitlement on your licence it is permissible to progress straight from category B to C to C + E, subject to the minimum age requirements being met. However, an 18-year-old would need to take the category C1 Theory and Practical Tests before moving on to category C at 21.

The Young LGV Driver Scheme is managed by Skills for Logistics on behalf of the Department for Transport. Under the scheme the young driver follows a structured training programme leading to a Level 2 NVQ in 'Driving Goods Vehicles'.

Full details of the scheme and information about training providers can be obtained from Skills for Logistics, 14 Warren Yard, Warren Farm Office Village, Milton Keynes MK12 5NW (tel: 0870 242 7314; fax: 0870 242 7315; e-mail: info@skillsforlogistics.org; website: www.skillsforlogistics.org). Information about training providers can be found at www.careersinlogistics.co.uk.

HEALTH AND EYESIGHT

To obtain a licence for LGVs you need to undergo a stringent medical examination by a doctor who must complete the medical certificate form D4. You have to pay for the medical privately, but the cost is normally allowed against tax as a business expense. If you are unsure about any aspect of health or eyesight, or your eligibility for a licence for health reasons, you should consult your doctor or discuss the details with the Drivers' Medical group at the DVLA. It can be contacted on 0870 240 0009.

The eyesight standard for driving large vehicles is much more demanding than that of the 'L' driver test where the requirement is simply to be able to read a car number plate at the appropriate distance. To qualify for a licence for large vehicles you must have visual acuity of at least 6/9 in the better eye and at least 6/12 in the weaker eye. If corrective lenses are worn, the uncorrected acuity must be no less than 3/60 in each eye.

The health standards are also much higher for drivers of large vehicles. This is mainly because the responsibilities of handling a large vehicle are much greater, and because accidents involving LGVs are often more serious than those involving cars. A medical report is required with each application for a licence and with each renewal. The law does not allow for a new PCV or LGV licence to be issued to anyone who has had an epileptic attack since the age of five or who is being treated by insulin for diabetes.

Some of the other conditions that might make it unsafe to drive larger vehicles (and which might cause the DVLA to refuse a licence) include disorders of the heart, epilepsy, alcohol and drug dependency, psychiatric illnesses and eyesight defects. A full list of the relevant medical conditions is available from the DVLA.

APPLYING FOR A LICENCE

Application forms (D2) are normally available from main post offices or from commercial LGV driving schools. The form and other documents should be sent to the DVLA at Swansea SA99 1AD. Before applying for provisional entitlement for LGVs you must already hold a full car licence. Your application must be accompanied by the full car licence (or a provisional licence together with a pass certificate) and a completed medical report form (D4). There is no longer a fee for vocational licences, including renewals.

A first provisional LGV licence is valid for category C (rigid) vehicles only. A full category C licence is needed before you can apply for a provisional licence for artics or trailers. The Theory Test must be passed before taking a Practical Rigid Vehicle Test, but this is not necessary for upgrading from rigid to artic vehicles.

The licence application is normally processed by the DVLA within about 10 days, and you have to wait for the licence to arrive before you can drive the larger vehicle. Licence entitlement is normally valid until the driver's 45th birthday. For drivers over 45, the licence lasts for five years. From the age of 65 the licence has to be renewed annually. A medical report is required with each application or renewal.

When driving an LGV, the learner must:

- hold provisional licence entitlement for that category of vehicle;
- be supervised by a driver who has held a full licence for that type of vehicle for at least three years;
- display 'L' plates (or 'D' plates in Wales, if preferred) on the front and back of the vehicle.

LGV THEORY TEST

The Theory Test is in two parts: a multiple-choice paper of 35 questions followed by a hazard perception test. Both parts of the test are taken on the same occasion and must be passed before applying for the Practical Test.

The current Theory Test fee (March 2006) is £21. A Theory Test pass certificate is valid for two years to allow the learner to take and pass the Practical Test in that time.

Syllabus

- *Vehicle weights and dimensions:* vehicle size; stowage and loading; vehicle markings; speed limiters.
- *Drivers' hours and rest periods:* driving limits; keeping records; tachograph rules; tiredness; vehicle security.
- *Braking systems:* types of brakes; maintenance and inspection; connection and proper use of brakes; tailgating; freezing conditions; anti-lock brakes.
- *The driver:* consideration; courtesy; priority; vehicle safety equipment; tiredness; drugs and alcohol.
- *The road:* anticipation; hazard awareness; attention; speed and distance; reaction time; risk factors.
- *Accident handling:* reducing risk; injuries; casualties.
- *Vehicle condition:* wheels and tyres; principles of construction and function of large vehicles; vehicle coupling mechanisms; breakdowns.

- *Leaving the vehicle:* the driver's cab; your own safety and that of others.
- *Vehicle loading:* loading; safety; types of load.
- *Restricted view:* mirrors; signals; parking; moving off; blind spots; observation at junctions.
- *Documents:* for national and international carriage; when receiving, carrying and delivering goods.
- *Environmental issues:* vehicle noise; wind resistance; fuel consumption; refuelling.
- *Other road users:* vulnerable road users; other vehicles.
- *Traffic signs:* road signs; speed limits; regulations.

The procedures for the multiple-choice part of the exam are much the same as for the 'L' driver test (see page 322). You are allowed 40 minutes in which to complete the 35 questions. To pass you must achieve 30 or more correct answers. Most of the questions require one correct answer from four alternatives, but with a few questions having two or three correct answers from five alternatives.

To prepare thoroughly for the test, the DSA recommend that you should study the *Highway Code, Know your Traffic Signs, The Official Theory Test for Drivers of Large Vehicles* and *The Official DSA Guide to Driving Goods Vehicles.* All of the questions and answers are included, together with an explanation for each one. The books also give a complete, detailed breakdown of the test syllabus, as well as a list of all theory test centres.

The Theory Test must be taken if you are applying for a category C or C1 licence, but is not required when upgrading from C1 to C, or from C to C+E.

Sample questions

1. Under EC rules, when may you interrupt the daily rest period?

(Mark one answer)

When part of it is to be taken on board a ferry or train.
When loading or unloading a vehicle.
When there is a gap of not more than one hour between rest periods.
When your journey involves night driving.

2. You are driving a lorry with a wide load. The width of the load is between 3.5 metres (11 ft 6 in) and 4.3 metres (14 ft 2 in). Which three of the following apply?

(Mark three answers)

Side markers must be shown.
The police must be notified.
An attendant must be carried.
Reduced speed limits apply.
Department of Transport approval must be obtained.

3. **An LGV is found to be overloaded. Who is liable to be prosecuted for the offence?**

(Mark one answer)

The person who loaded the vehicle.
Both the driver and the operator.
The operator only.
The driver only.

4. **What could prevent air pressure building up in the air brake system in cold, frosty weather?**

(Mark one answer)

Moisture in the air may form bubbles in the brake fluid.
The air will contract, reducing the pressure.
Moisture drawn in with the air may freeze and cause a blockage.
The dampness may cause valves to rust.

5. **How far can a load overhang at the rear before you must use triangular projection markers?**

(Mark one answer)

1 metre (3 ft 6 in).
1.5 metres (5 ft).
2 metres (6 ft 8 in).
2.9 metres (9 ft 6 in).

6. **You are uncoupling a trailer. Before disconnecting any of the air lines, you MUST .....**

(Mark one answer)

Drain the air tanks.
Apply the trailer parking brake.
Lower the landing gear.
Disconnect the electrical line.

7. **You have been driving non-stop since 5 am. It is now 9.30 am. Under EC rules you must have a break of at least:**

(Mark one answer)

15 minutes.
30 minutes.
45 minutes.
60 minutes.

8. **Exhaust brakes give greatest efficiency when used:**

(Mark one answer)

At high engine speed in low gear.
At low engine speed in high gear.
On stop–start town work.
On high speed motorway runs.

Hazard Perception Test

The second part of the Theory Test is the 'hazard perception' test, and is taken immediately after the multiple-choice test. As with the 'L' driver test (page 324), this consists of a series of video film clips showing potential driving hazards on screen. The test requirement is to 'spot' these hazards by clicking on a computer mouse as soon as the potential hazard is recognized. You are shown 14 film clips, with one hazard on 13 clips and two hazards on the other one. Each hazard is given a maximum of five points – the earlier you spot the hazard, the more points you achieve. Out of a possible 75 points, you need to obtain 50 to pass.

If you fail this part of the test, but pass the multiple-choice part, you will still need to take both parts again on a future occasion.

To prepare for the hazard perception test, the DSA recommends that you train with a professionally qualified instructor using a properly structured course. This training should be supplemented by studying the relevant DSA books and the DSA video or DVD *RoadSense*, which is the official guide to the hazard perception test for all drivers.

Once you have passed both parts of the test you can apply for the Practical Test.

LGV PRACTICAL TEST

Application for a test can be made by post, fax, phone or online. Forms are normally available from the DSA or most commercial LGV driving schools. If you are having training with a recognized school it will normally make the arrangements for your test by using the 'trainer booking' system.

To book online, go to www.driving-tests.co.uk. You will need details of your licence, your theory pass certificate and payment by credit or debit card.

If you apply by post you will need to send a cheque or postal order. Applications by phone or fax can be made using a credit or debit card. In either case, your driving licence details are required unless the application is made under the trainer booking system. With this system the test is allocated to the training organization, with the candidate's details given at a later date. The current fee for a weekday test (April 2006) is £89. For evening and weekend tests the fee is £107.

LGV driving tests are conducted by a team of experienced examiners who are specially trained for the specific requirements of larger vehicles. A list of test centres is given on the application form. The candidate has to provide a suitable vehicle that complies with the following requirements:

- The vehicle must be unladen and of the correct category for which the licence is required.
- It must display 'L' plates (or 'D' plates in Wales if you prefer) on the front and rear.

- It must have sufficient fuel for the test, which lasts up to 1½ hours.
- It must be in good roadworthy condition with all stop lamps and direction indicators working properly.
- Proper seating and a seat belt for the examiner must be provided.
- The vehicle must not be operating on trade licence plates.
- It must not exceed 60 ft in length.
- Nearside and offside mirrors for use by the examiner.

MINIMUM TEST VEHICLES

Vehicles used for LGV driving tests must be capable of 80 kph (50 mph) and must conform to the requirements listed in Table 12.2.

Practical Test format

The DSA book *The Official DSA Guide to Driving Goods Vehicles* is available from most bookshops and training organizations. It explains the contents of the LGV test and how to prepare for it. You should read it in conjunction with *The Official Guide to Learning to Drive*, which gives advice on correct vehicle control and road procedures for candidates on both car and lorry tests.

In order to pass the LGV test you must:

- demonstrate to the examiner that you can handle the vehicle safely and competently in all types of road and traffic conditions;
- show courtesy and consideration for other road users, no matter what the situation;
- show that you have complete control of the vehicle throughout the test, whatever the weather and road conditions.

The test is in several parts:

1. A series of safety questions based on 'show me' or 'tell me'.
2. A test of the driver's ability to control the vehicle in a confined space. This part of the test is conducted at the test centre on a special area of about 300 ft × 60 ft, and includes the reversing and braking exercises.
3. A drive over a route covering various road and traffic conditions. During this part of the test (which lasts about one hour), the candidate has to carry out several special exercises, including a gear change exercise as well as uphill and downhill starts.
4. For drivers of articulated vehicles and drawbars, a practical exercise in coupling and uncoupling the trailer is included.

Table 12.2 Minimum vehicle requirements for LGV Practical Tests

Vehicles first registered before 1 October 2003:

Category C1	4 tonnes maximum authorized mass (MAM)
Category C1 + E (drawbar)	As above, with a trailer of at least 2 tonnes MAM and a combined length of at least 8 metres
Category C1 + E (artic)	MAM of at least 6 tonnes and a combined length of at least 8 metres
Category C	A rigid goods vehicle with a MAM of at least 10 tonnes and a length of at least 7 metres but not more than 12 metres
Category C + E (artic)	Artic with a MAM of at least 18 tonnes and at least 12 metres length
Category C + E (drawbar)	A category C vehicle, with a trailer at least 4 metres in length and at least 4 tonnes weight. Combined weight of at least 18 tonnes, combined length of at least 12 metres

Note: the above standards apply to vehicles first used before 1 October 2003 and will apply until 1 July 2007.

Vehicles first registered after 1 October 2003:
All test vehicles must be capable of 80 kmh (50 mph).

Category	MAM	Length	Width	Cargo compartment/trailer
C1	4 tonnes	5 m		Closed box cargo compartment at least as wide and high as cab
C1+E	4 tonnes + 2 tonne trailer	8 m		Closed box trailer – slightly less wide than towing vehicle, but rear view must be by external mirrors only
C	12 tonnes	8 m	2.4 m	Closed box cargo compartment
C+E drawbar (Cat C towing vehicle)	20 tonnes	1.4 m (trailer at least 7.5 m from coupling eye to extreme rear)	2.4 m	Closed box trailer – at least as high and wide as cab
C+E artic	20 tonnes	14 m	2.4 m	Closed box – at least as high and as wide as cab

Notes:
1 All vehicles must be fitted with ABS and tachograph.
2 Category C and C+E vehicles must have at least eight forward gears, taking account of splitter boxes and range changes.

1   Safety questions

At the start of the practical test, candidates are asked several questions on vehicle safety. The questions are normally of the 'show me'/'tell me' type. This part of the test includes questions on:

- engine oil levels;
- engine coolant levels;
- windscreen wipers and washers;
- tyres, wheels and mudguards;
- brake lights, indicators and reflectors;
- headlamps, side and tail lights;
- windscreen and windows;
- vehicle suspension and power-assisted steering;
- loading mechanisms and safety factors;
- air pressure and leaks;
- cab locking mechanism;
- tachographs and discs;
- instrument checks;
- audible warning devices;
- vehicle body condition.

Typical questions

Show me how you would check that the wheel nuts on this vehicle are secure.

Tell me how you would check the condition of the suspension (or windscreen, wipers, reflectors) on this vehicle.

Show me how the cab locking mechanism is secured on this vehicle.

Tell me how you would operate the tail lift mechanism on this vehicle.

Show me how you would replace the tachometer disc on this vehicle.

Tell me how you would check that the power-assisted steering is working.

2   Manoeuvring exercises

Reversing

The candidate is expected to drive in reverse along a course marked out by cones, involving the use of right and left steering lock, and finishing in a bay 1½ times the width of the vehicle. The object of the exercise is to complete the manoeuvre smoothly, without touching any of the cones, without going over the boundary lines, and to stop with the extreme rear of the vehicle within a 3 ft marked area and close to a simulated loading platform. Throughout the exercise the driver should maintain all-round observations and complete control of the vehicle.

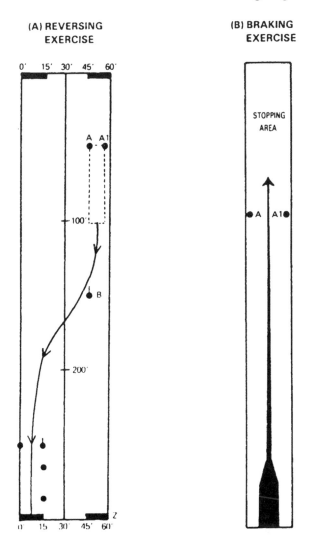

Figure 12.1 Manoeuvring exercises

During this exercise the examiner will be outside the vehicle to check on the accuracy of the manoeuvre and for the driver's observations and vehicle control.

Braking

The vehicle is driven forward over a distance of about 200 ft to a speed of about 20 mph. After passing the marker cones, the brakes are applied, stopping the vehicle as quickly as possible, with safety, under full control.

For this part of the test the examiner travels in the cab to check on the driver's control of the vehicle.

3   On the road

During the 'on-road' section of the test, the candidate is asked to carry out various exercises together with normal driving over a route of approximately 25 miles. The set exercises include an uphill and downhill start and a gear change exercise. In order to show that all gears can be used when necessary, the driver is required to demonstrate progressive upward and downward gear changes. During this exercise it is not necessary to use any auxiliary transmission systems.

Depending on the size of the vehicle used for the test, some degree of tolerance in positioning at junctions is permitted. However, care must be exercised so as not to endanger or inconvenience other road users.

The test route may include a section of motorway driving.

For full details of the requirements of the test, you should take professional tuition and refer to the DSA book *The Official DSA Guide to Driving Goods Vehicles.*

4   Coupling/uncoupling

For tests on category C1+E and C+E (artics and drawbars) there is now a requirement to demonstrate uncoupling and recoupling of the trailer or semi-trailer. The candidate is asked to uncouple the trailer and then park the vehicle alongside. The towing vehicle is then realigned with the trailer before recoupling.

During the exercise the candidate is assessed on:

- control of the vehicle;
- accuracy of the maneouvre;
- effective observations.

LGV Practical Test syllabus

The test covers the following main topics:

- *Vehicle controls:* accelerator, clutch, footbrake, handbrake, steering.
- *Precautions before starting.*
- *Moving off safely and under control.*
- *Use of mirrors:* well before signalling, changing direction or speed.
- *Use of signals:* when necessary, correctly and properly timed.
- *Reversing exercise:* under control and with effective observations.
- *Controlled stop:* promptly and under control.
- *Gear change exercise.*
- *Uphill and downhill starts.*
- *Clearance to obstructions.*
- *Response to signs and signals:* traffic signs, road markings, traffic lights, traffic controllers, other road users.
- *Use of speed.*

- *Maintaining a safe following distance.*
- *Maintain progress:* use of appropriate speed; without undue hesitation.
- *Junctions:* speed on approach; observations; right and left turns; avoidance of cutting corners.
- *Judgement:* overtaking, meeting, crossing the path of other vehicles.
- *Road positioning:* in normal driving; lane discipline.
- *Pedestrian crossings.*
- *Safe position for normal stops.*
- *Awareness and planning.*
- *Ancillary controls.*
- *Uncoupling and recoupling.*

After the test

At the end of the test the successful candidate is given a pass certificate. This entitles the applicant to exchange the provisional licence for full licence entitlement for the relevant category of vehicle. There is no fee for vocational licences.

An unsuccessful candidate is issued with a statement of failure on which the examiner will have marked the points that require particular attention. As with the car test, any serious or dangerous fault or more than 15 driving faults will result in a test fail.

INSTRUCTOR QUALIFICATIONS

As a qualified car instructor, and if you have held a licence for large vehicles for some time, you may be considering moving on to training on LGVs. The job of the LGV instructor can be demanding, as you will be in charge of a much bigger and heavier vehicle, with probably two trainee drivers to teach. It can, however, be very rewarding, as you are preparing your drivers for a professional qualification.

In order to accompany a learner LGV driver, the supervising driver must be at least 21 and have held a full driving licence for that type of vehicle for at least three years. This is the minimum legal requirement. However, most LGV instructors hold other voluntary qualifications, such as the ADI certificate, RTITB approval, the Voluntary Register of LGV Instructors or a training qualification from the armed forces.

VOLUNTARY REGISTER OF LGV INSTRUCTORS

This scheme, which is likely to become compulsory within the next few years, was developed by the DSA in conjunction with various trade bodies, with the aim of improving the standard of training for lorry drivers. It is very similar to the ADI Register in its administration and testing procedures. As with the ADI, there are three examinations – a theory test, a practical test of driving ability and an instructional ability test. An information pack containing the application forms, the syllabus and the complete question and answer bank is available from the DSA at a cost of £6.99 (March 2006).

The register is open to anyone who has held the appropriate licence entitlement for a period of three years and who has not been disqualified from driving at any time in the preceding four years. To qualify for the register, you have to take and pass all three parts of the examination within one year. You are allowed only three attempts at each of the practical tests.

You must take and pass the Theory Test before applying for the practical parts (driving and instructional ability). However, with the practical tests you can decide whether to take them both on the same day or on separate occasions. There are advantages and disadvantages in each case – for instance, if you opt for consecutive tests and fail the driving ability part, you may have to forfeit the instructional ability test. On the other hand, if you take them separately, there may be some delay in booking the third part of the exam.

The Theory Test (Part 1)

The Theory Test is in two parts – multiple-choice and hazard perception – and can be taken at any one of about 150 centres around the country. The current fee (March 2006) is £58.75.

Multiple-choice questions

In this test there are 100 questions with a choice of three or more alternative answers to each. You are allowed 90 minutes to complete the test. The syllabus for the examination covers:

- principles of road safety generally, and their application in particular circumstances;
- techniques of driving an LGV correctly, courteously and safely, including control of the vehicle, road procedure, recognizing hazards and taking proper action, dealing properly with pedestrians and other road users, the use of safety equipment;
- theory and practice of learning, teaching and assessment;
- tuition required to be able to instruct a pupil driving an LGV, including the items set out above, the correction of pupil's errors, the manner of the instructor and pupil;
- the *Highway Code*;
- the DSA publication *The Official DSA Guide to Driving Goods Vehicles*;
- interpretation of the reasons for failure to pass the driving test given in the form DLV 25, the 'Statement of Failure' to pass the driving test.

The questions are grouped into 10 subjects and into four 'bands'. In order to pass you must obtain a minimum of 80 per cent in each of the bands, as well as an overall mark of 85 per cent.

Band 1   Road procedure
                Driving technique
Band 2   Instructional techniques
Band 3   Mechanics
                Vehicle condition
                Drivers' hours and rest periods
                Loading, unloading and load security
Band 4   Driving test
                Environmental issues
                Accident handling

The DSA recommended reading list for this exam includes *The Driving Instructor's Handbook* and *Practical Teaching Skills for Driving Instructors.*

Sample questions

1. **You must drive your vehicle at lower speed limits when its load is wider than:**

   (Mark one answer)

   2.7 metres (9 ft).
   4.0 metres (13 ft).
   4.3 metres (14 ft 2 in).

2. **When part loading a vehicle with an empty ISO container, you should position the container:**

   (Mark one answer)

   Close to the fifth wheel.
   Over the front axle.
   Close to the trailer edge.
   Over the rear axles.

3. **Your tractor unit has three air lines. You are connecting to a trailer with two air lines. What colour is the line you should leave unconnected?**

   (Mark one answer)

   Red.
   Yellow.
   Blue.

4. **What shape are hazardous cargo labels?**

   (Mark one answer)

   Diamond.
   Triangle.
   Circle.
   Oval.

5. **The process of perception can be described as ...**

(Mark one answer)

Shrewdness and foresight.
The interpretation of necessary information.
The selective focusing on a given hazard.

6. **As a pupil's knowledge and driving competence increases the level of instructor involvement is likely to ...**

(Mark one answer)

Remain the same.
Increase.
Decrease.

The complete question bank is available from the DSA.

Hazard perception test

This part of the exam tests your hazard perception skills by using video film clips as in the 'L' and LGV Theory Tests (pages 322 and 366). You are allowed about 25 minutes for this part, during which you are shown 14 film clips, with 15 scoring hazards. The pass mark for the test is 57 out of a possible 75.

Before leaving the test centre you will be notified of the result for both parts of the test, and will be given information about how to apply for the practical driving ability test.

The Practical Driving Test (Part 2)

The driving test can be taken at about 34 LGV centres around the country. It lasts about an hour and a half over a route that is similar to, but more demanding than, the usual LGV test. The test is of an advanced nature and a very high standard of driving is required.

You must provide a suitable vehicle for the test. Depending on which qualification you need it can be a Category C1, C1+E, C or C+E vehicle. It must, of course, meet the minimum test vehicle requirements that are outlined on page 370 and must have right-hand steering and a suitable forward facing seat for a passenger. 'L' plates should not be displayed.

The syllabus for this part of the examination covers:

- special 'off road' exercises, including braking, reversing and (where applicable) uncoupling/recoupling;
- a wide variety of road and traffic conditions, including dual carriageways, one-way systems and, where possible, motorways;
- gear change exercise, which is normally carried out during the on-road section;
- uphill and downhill starts as well as moving off normally and at an angle;

- meet, cross and overtake other traffic;
- keep a safe separation distance;
- negotiate various types of roundabout;
- exercise correct lane discipline;
- display courtesy and consideration to other road users, especially pedestrians, riders on horseback, cyclists and motorcyclists;
- apply correct procedures at all types of road junctions and hazards, including pedestrian crossings, level crossings, traffic signals;
- effective use of mirrors and signals;
- alertness and anticipation;
- speed limits;
- vehicle sympathy.

You will pass if you commit six or fewer driving faults, and no serious or dangerous faults are recorded. At the end of the test the examiner will give you the result.

Test of Instructional Ability (Part 3)

This part of the test is an assessment of your ability to give instruction and to pass on your knowledge to a 'pupil'. The test can be taken at certain selected test centres and usually lasts about one hour. As in the driving ability test, you must provide a suitable vehicle that conforms to all the previously listed requirements. 'L' plates (or 'D' plates in Wales if you prefer) should be displayed on the front and rear of the vehicle.

The examiner must be covered by insurance for the time he or she is driving the vehicle. The insurance should not name any particular examiner, but should cover any DSA examiner.

During the test the examiner adopts the role of a learner lorry driver and will simulate faults that are appropriate to the particular role selected. This is done by using a selection from the following nine preset tests:

PST 1   *Safety precautions/controls:*
Accelerator, clutch, footbrake, handbrake, steering, gears
Move off and stop:
On level, uphill, downhill, angled
Mirrors, observation, control

PST 2   *Signs, signals and road markings:*
Road signs, markings, traffic lights, controllers, other road users
Recognition, appropriate action
Braking exercise:
Safely, full control, promptly, distance

PST 3   *General driving:*
Faults – identification, analysis, remedial
Gear change exercise:
Control, observations, signals

PST 4   *Use of mirrors:*
Moving off, signalling, changing direction or lanes, turning, overtaking, increasing speed, slowing, leaving vehicle, parked vehicles
Uncouple/recouple:
Safe place, brakes, landing gear, taps, air lines, coupling mechanism, number plates

PST 5   *Judgement of speed:*
Road, traffic, weather, vehicle speed limits, hazards
Road positioning:
Keep left, parked vehicles, weaving, lanes, one-way, road markings

PST 6   *Junctions (turning into and emerging):*
Position, speed, observations, priorities
Roundabouts and crossroads:
Mirrors, signal, manoeuvre (MSM)
Position, speed, look (PSL)
Gears, observations, lanes, position through, exit

PST 7   *Approaching or turning at crossroads, roundabouts or junctions:*
MSM, PSL, gears, observations

PST 8   *Meet approaching traffic:*
Mirrors, signal, speed, gears, position, observation
Overtaking/anticipating the actions of other road users:
View, speed, limits, bends, junctions, gradients
Mirrors, signal

PST 9   *Remedial lesson after test failure:*
DLV25, assess, faults

During the test you will be assessed specifically on the following:

- Fault assessment, analysis and remedial action.
- Level of instruction.
- Planning the lesson.
- Controlling the lesson.
- Communication.

- Question and answer techniques.
- Feedback and encouragement.
- Attitude and approach to the pupil.
- The method, clarity, adequacy and correctness of the instruction given.

As with the driving ability test, you will be given the result straight away. The cost of each part of the examination (March 2006) is £96.35. Registration is for four years for a fee of £58.75.

Further details about the examination and registration can be obtained at www.driving-tests.co.uk or www.dsa.gov.uk or by phoning the DSA on 0115 901 2625.

COMPULSORY TRAINING OF LGV DRIVERS

The European Union (EU) has recently introduced a new directive that requires all category C and D licence holders (ie drivers of large goods vehicles and passenger carrying vehicles) to undertake a programme of retraining at regular intervals. The directive will come into force in 2009 for lorry drivers.

The draft EU directive contains proposals for compulsory initial training and periodic refresher training for LGV drivers. On successful completion of the training and test, the driver will be eligible for a 'Certificate of Professional Competence' (CPC).

The proposals include:

- a recognized training syllabus;
- a minimum number of hours of intensive training – either 140 or 280 hours depending on the type of vehicle;
- periodic refresher training of 35 hours every five years;
- training to be carried out only at recognized and approved centres.

One of the advantages of the new CPC is that it allows for drivers to train on large vehicles earlier than the present rules allow.

Appendix I

Useful Addresses

Driving Standards Agency (DSA)
56 Talbot Street
Nottingham NG1 5GU
Tel: 0115 901 2500
www.dsa.gov.uk
For full details of DSA departments, see page 390.

Driving and Vehicle Licensing Agency (DVLA)
Longview Road
Swansea SA6 7JL
Tel: 01792 782 341
Drivers' enquiries: tel: 0870 240 0009; e-mail: drivers.dvla@gtnet.gov.uk
Vehicle enquiries: tel: 0870 240 0010; e-mail: vehicles.dvla@gtnet.gov.uk

ADI consultative organizations

AA Driving School
Customer Service Centre
26–32 Park Row
Fanum House
Bristol BS1 5LJ
Tel: 0800 587 0086
www.theaa.com

Approved Driving Instructors National Joint Council (ADINJC)
47 Sweetmans Road
Shaftesbury
Dorset SP7 8EH
Tel: 01747 855091
www.adinjc.com

British School of Motoring Limited
RAC House
1 Forest Road
Feltham
Middlesex TW13 7RR
Tel: 08705 276 276
www.bsm.co.uk

Driving Instructors Association (DIA)
Safety House
Beddington Farm Road
Croydon
Surrey CR1 4XZ
Tel: 020 8665 5151
Fax: 020 8665 5565
e-mail: driving@driving.org
www.driving.org

Driving Instructors Scottish Council (DISC)
5 North Lodge Avenue
Motherwell
Lanarkshire ML1 2RP
Tel: 01698 268711
www.d-i-s-c.org.uk

Motor Schools Association GB Ltd
101 Wellington Road North
Stockport
Cheshire SK4 2LP
Tel: 0161 429 9669
Fax: 0161 429 9779
e-mail: mail@msagb.co.uk
www.msagb.co.uk

Training Aids and Services

Desk Top Driving Ltd
Unit 6
Gaugemaster Way
Ford
Arundel
West Sussex BN18 0RX
Tel: 01903 882299
Fax: 01903 885599
www.desktopdriving.co.uk

Driving School Aids
East View
Broadgate Lane
Horsforth
West Yorks LS18 4AG
Tel: 0113 258 0688

Driving School News
PO Box 469
Barming
Maidstone
Kent ME16 9PU
Tel: 01622 728898

Driving School Supplies
2–4 Tame Road
Witton
Birmingham B6 7DS
Tel: 0121 328 6226
www.d-ss.co.uk

F I N D (NVQ Assessment Centre)
121 Marshalswick Lane
St Albans
Herts AL1 4UX
Tel/fax: 01727 858068

He-Man Dual Controls Ltd
Cable Street
Southampton SO14 5AR
Tel: 023 8022 6952
www.he-mandualcontrols.co.uk

Porter Dual Controls
Boar's Head Business Park
Brent Way
Brentford
Middlesex TW8 8ES
Tel: 020 8568 2345

RCM Marketing Ltd
20 Newtown Business Park
Albion Close
Poole
Dorset BH12 3LL
Tel: 01202 737999
www.rcmmarketing.co.uk

Royal Society for the Prevention of Accidents (RoSPA)
Edgbaston Park
353 Bristol Road
Birmingham B5 7ST
Tel: 0121 248 2000
www.rospa.co.uk

SmartDriving
Ballinultha
Boyle
Co. Roscommon
Ireland
www.smartdriving.co.uk

The Stationery Office
51 Nine Elms Lane
London SW8 5DR
www.tso.co.uk

Wholesale Book Supplies
Glan Y Wern
Park Road
Barmouth
Gwynedd LL42 1PH
Tel: 0800 195 2208
www.wholesalebooks.co.uk

Disabled drivers' assessment centres

Queen Elizabeth's Foundation Mobility Centre
Damson Way
Fountain Drive
Carshalton
Surrey SM5 4NR
Tel: 020 8770 1151
Fax: 020 8770 1211
e-mail: info@mobility-qe.org
www.qefd.org/mobilitycentre

Cornwall Mobility Centre
Tehidy House
Royal Cornwall Hospital
Truro
Cornwall TR1 3LJ
Tel: 01872 254920
Fax: 01872 254921
e-mail: mobility@rcht.swest.nhs.uk
www.cornwall-homepage.co.uk/homepages/mobile/index/html

DART Driving Assessment and Advice Centre
Cobtree Ward
Preston Hall Hospital
London Road
Aylesford
Kent ME20 7NJ
Tel: 01622 795719
Fax: 01622 795720
e-mail: janicestannard@nhs.net

Derby Regional Mobility Centre
Kingsway Hospital
Kingsway
Derby DE22 3LZ
Tel: 01332 371929
Fax: 01332 382377
e-mail: info@derbyregionalmobilitycentre.co.uk
www.derbyregionalmobilitycentre.co.uk

Hertfordshire Action on Disability Mobility Centre
The Woodside Centre
The Common
Welwyn Garden City
Herts AL7 4DD
Tel: 01707 324581
Fax: 01707 371297
e-mail: driving@hadnet.co.uk
www.hadnet.org.uk

Kilverstone Mobility Assessment Centre
2 Napier Place
Thetford
Norfolk IP24 3RL
Tel: 01842 753029
Fax: 01842 755950
e-mail: kmacmobil@aol.com
www.ridgenage.co.uk/mobility

Mobility Advice and Vehicle Information Service (MAVIS)
'O' Wing, Macadam Avenue
Old Wokingham Road
Crowthorne
Berks RG45 6XD
Tel: 01344 661000
Fax: 01344 661066
e-mail: mavis@dft.gsi.gov.uk
www.mobility-unit.dft.gov.uk/mavis.htm

Mobility Centre
Regional Neurological Rehabilitation Centre
Hunters Road
Newcastle upon Tyne NE2 4NR
Tel: 0191 219 5694
Fax: 0191 219 5693
www.nap.nhs.uk/snrs/index.html

Mobility Service of the Disabled Living Centre
The Vassall Centre
Gill Avenue
Fishponds
Bristol BS16 2QQ
Tel: 0117 965 9353
Fax: 0117 965 3652
e-mail: mobserv@dicbristol.org

Northern Ireland Mobility Centre
Disability Action
Portside Business Park
189 Airport Road
Belfast BT3 9ED
Tel: 028 9029 7880
Fax: 028 9029 7881
Text: 028 9029 7882
e-mail: mobilitycentre@disabilityaction.org

North Wales Mobility and Driving Assessment Service
The North Wales Resources Centre
Glan Clwyd Hospital
Bodelwyddan
Denbighshire LL18 5UJ
Tel: 01745 584858
Fax: 01745 582762
e-mail: info@drivemobility.org

Regional Driving Assessment Centre
West Heath Hospital
Rednal Road
Birmingham B38 8HR
Tel: 0121 627 8228
Fax: 0121 627 8629

Scottish Driving Assessment Service
Astley Ainslie Hospital
133 Grange Loan
Edinburgh EH9 2HL
Tel.: 0131 537 9192
Fax: 0131 537 9193

South Wales Mobility and Driving Assessment Service
Rookwood Hospital
Fairwater Road
Llandaff
Cardiff CF5 2YN
Tel: 029 2055 5130
Fax: 029 2055 5130

William Merritt Disabled Living Centre and Mobility Centre
St Mary's Hospital
Green Hill Road
Armley
Leeds LS12 3QE
Tel: 0113 305 5288
Fax: 0113 231 9291
e-mail: wmmobilityservices@cwcom.net

Wrightington Mobility Centre
Wrightington Hospital
Hall Lane
Appley Bridge
Wigan
Lancs WN6 9EP
Tel: 01257 256409
Fax: 01257 256409
e-mail: mobility.centre@alwpct.nhs.uk

Motoring organizations

Automobile Association
Fanum House
Basingstoke
Hampshire RG21 2EA
Tel: 0800 085 2721
www.theaa.com

Royal Automobile Club
RAC House
1 Forest Road
Feltham
Middlesex TW13 7RR
Tel: 020 8917 2500
www.rac.co.uk

Appendix II

Driving Standards Agency – Contacts

Headquarters:
Stanley House
56 Talbot Street
Nottingham NG1 5GU
www.dsa.gov.uk

Customer service enquiries:
Tel: 0115 901 2500
Fax: 0115 901 2510
e-mail: customer.services@dsa.gsi.gov.uk

ADI (Approved Driving Instructor) enquiries:
Tel: 0115 901 2595
Fax: 0115 901 2820
e-mail: adireg@dsa.gsi.gov.uk

CBT (Compulsory Basic Training) enquiries:
Tel: 0115 901 2595
Fax: 0115 901 2600
e-mail: cbt@das.gsi.gov.uk

To contact a particular department at the DSA by phone, dial 0115 901, followed by:

ADIs	2618
Central operations	2557
Commercial branch	5901
'Despatch'	5874
Pass Plus	2633
PDIs	2629
Policy	5918

Press office   5874
Technical standards   2537
Theory Test unit   5935

Training centre (Cardington):
Tel: 01234 744000

Publications (Cardington):
Tel: 01234 744054

Customer service enquiries and complaints:

London and South-east
Tel: 020 7468 4712
Fax: 020 7468 4550
e-mail: londoncsu@dsa.gsi.gov.uk

Midlands and Eastern
Tel: 0121 697 6762
Fax: 0121 697 6750
e-mail: birminghamcsu@dsa.gsi.gov.uk

Wales and Western
Tel: 029 2058 1218
Fax: 029 2058 1050
e-mail: cardiffcsu@dsa.gsi.gov.uk

Scotland
Tel: 0131 529 8645
Fax: 0131 529 8589
e-mail: scotlandcsu@dsa.gsi.gov.uk

Northern
Tel: 0191 201 8161
Fax: 0191 201 8010
e-mail: northerncsu@dsa.gsi.gov.uk

Appendix III

Reference Books

Your Road to Becoming an Approved Driving Instructor (ADI 14), Driving Standards Agency (DSA) (£5.00)

The Official DSA Guide to Driving – the essential skills, DSA/The Stationery Office (£12.99, ISBN 0 11 552641 2)

The Official Guide to Learning to Drive, DSA/The Stationery Office (£7.99, ISBN 0 11 552608 0)

The Official Theory Test for Car Drivers and the Highway Code, DSA/The Stationery Office (£11.99, ISBN 0 11 552 660 9)

Know Your Traffic Signs, DSA/The Stationery Office (£3.00, ISBN 0 11 551612 3)

The Highway Code, DSA/The Stationery Office (£1.49, ISBN 0 11 552449 5)

The Official DSA Guide to Driving Goods Vehicles, DSA/The Stationery Office (£14.99, ISBN 0 11 552656 0)

The Official Theory Test for Drivers of Large Vehicles, DSA/The Stationery Office (£14.99, ISBN 0 11 552406 1)

Practical Teaching Skills for Driving Instructors, 5th edn, by John Miller, Margaret Stacey and Tony Scriven, published by Kogan Page (£17.99, ISBN 0 7494 4499 1)

The LGV Learner Driver's Guide, by John Miller, published by Kogan Page (£14.99, ISBN 0 7494 3790 1)

Haynes Glovebox Guide: Your car (£9.99, ISBN 1 85960 792 6)

Learn to Drive in 10 Easy Stages, by Margaret Stacey, published by Kogan Page (£8.99, ISBN 0 7494 3019 2)

Instructional Techniques and Practice, by L Walklin, published by Stanley Thornes (£14.65, ISBN 0 7487 1631 9)

The Professional LGV Driver's Guide, by David Lowe, published by Kogan Page (£22.95, ISBN 0 7494 3822 3)

Appendix IV

The Official Register of Driving Instructor Training (ORDIT) – Terms and Conditions of Membership

AIMS AND OBJECTIVES

The aim of the ORDIT scheme is to maintain, produce and promote the current Register (and work towards a compulsory Register) of driving instructor training organisations and driving instructor trainers that can be relied upon by the public, the driver training industry and the Driving Standards Agency to provide good quality training by qualified trainers, from premises that are ORDIT inspected and meet satisfactory standards and from organisations that have agreed to abide by the terms and conditions of the scheme.

The main objectives of the ORDIT scheme are to ensure that:

- Satisfactory standards of training are available for members of the public wishing to qualify as Approved Driving Instructors (ADIs);
- Satisfactory standards of training are available for ADIs who wish to receive further training or retraining;
- All trainers delivering training under the scheme have been tested by the DSA and accepted as being suitable for entry onto the Register;
- Any person seeking training with an organisation or individual whose details are entered in the Register should be protected from unfair business practices and inferior training;
- Those organisations, premises and trainers that are successfully ORDIT inspected will be promoted through the ORDIT list contained within the DSA's Starter Pack for potential ADIs (ADI 14);
- The DSA and the ADI consultative organisations will only promote those organisations, premises and individual trainers entered on the Register;
- Only those organisations, premises and trainers entered onto the Register are entitled to display ORDIT certificates/badges to help the public recognise them;

- Any course offered by ORDIT Members shall be genuinely adequate for the purpose of enabling a trainee to pass the ADI qualifying examination.

CODE OF PRACTICE

Those on the Register must:

- Clearly inform all prospective Trainees in writing of the services provided, with particular reference to the Trainer's qualification, costs, venue, duration and content in relation to the ADI examination structure.
- Inform prospective Trainees of the Organisation's terms of business and complaints procedure.
- Take all reasonable care, skill and diligence in providing training in all relevant aspects of traffic and driver education needed to pass the ADI qualifying examinations, taking into account individual training needs and safety.
- Not disclose to a third party any information given by a Trainee during training or training progress or driving and instructional ability except where under obligation in Law or with the DSA as part of an ORDIT inspection or with a third party who is paying for a Trainee's training but subject to the Trainee's knowledge.
- Ensure all vehicles used in training are maintained in a safe and satisfactory condition, properly insured, taxed and where appropriate certified as roadworthy.
- Apply an honest, moral and professional approach in all business practice and avoid improper language, suggestion or physical contact with Trainees as well as maintaining proper standards of personal hygiene and dress.
- Comply with all current legislation particularly in respect of business premises and practice, staff, vehicles and public liability.

ADVERTISING AND PROMOTIONAL CODE OF PRACTICE

- All advertising shall fully comply with the best practice, as defined by current Codes of Practice issued by the Advertising Standards Authority (ASA), in the spirit as well as the letter.
- All advertising shall be legal, decent, honest, truthful and prepared with a sense of responsibility to both trainees and competitors as well as respecting the principles of fair-trading and competition.
- Any claim made in advertising shall be able to be substantiated objectively by documentary evidence, which shall be made available for inspection upon request.
- The full terms of any guarantee shall be given in writing before any training course agreement is signed.

- Members of the Register convicted of any trading standards or fair trading offence, or having an adjudication made against them by the Advertising Standards Authority, shall have their continued membership of ORDIT reviewed by the ADI Registrar, who shall have the power to remove that person or Organisation from the Register.
- The ADI Registrar shall retain the right to demand timely changes to the advertising of any Organisation or Trainer following ASA OFT or Trading Standards rulings with the ultimate sanction of exclusion from the Register.
- The ADI Registrar shall retain the right to demand timely changes to the advertising of any Organisation or Trainer in the case of it not being covered by any regulatory body.
- The ADI Registrar reserves the right, but not the duty, to make a complaint about a member's advertising (in whatever form) to the appropriate regulatory body if in his opinion such material does not satisfy the above criteria. As an alternative to such a complaint being raised the member may elect to immediately remove the offending material and thus potentially avoid such action being taken.

BUSINESS CODE OF PRACTICE

An organisation shall:

- Provide a full copy of their training course contract or agreement and any other associated terms and conditions and give an opportunity for any prospective Trainee to study them away from the Premises and seek independent advice, if so desired, before they are required to sign any document or make any payment.
- Have a refund policy in circumstances where a Trainee cannot continue with the course at the time or at any reasonable time in the future on serious medical grounds confirmed in writing by a doctor that prevents them from being able to drive or instruct and such refund shall be limited to the savings that an Organisation would make by not having to deliver the remainder of the training course in accordance with the Guidance on refunds provided by the Office of Fair Trading.
- Have a refund policy in the event of the Trainee failing three attempts at Part Two of the ADI examination providing that each exam was taken in good faith by the Trainee and provided any free remedial training offered by the Organisation prior to the failed attempts is taken and such refund shall be limited to the savings that an Organisation would make by not having to deliver the remainder of the training course in accordance with the Guidance on refunds provided by the Office of Fair Trading.
- Have a refund policy in the event of the Trainee being refused their application for registration by the DSA provided the Trainee had not deliberately withheld or falsely stated any relevant information as part of their application

to attend the course and provided it was not as the result of any event or incident following commencement of the training course and such refund shall be limited to the savings that an Organisation would make by not having to deliver the remainder of the training course in accordance with the Guidance on refunds provided by the Office of Fair Trading.

- The refund policy must provide for an automatic and prompt refund to the Trainee for any ADI examination, trainee licence or registration fees paid to the Organisation whether identified separately or inclusive in the overall training course fee. The Trainee's entitlement to this money, at any time upon their written request, should be clearly stated in the course contract or agreement. If the fees are paid on behalf of the Trainee by the Organisation it will be deemed that these fees have been collected as part of the fee for the training and subject to the terms of this clause.

Index

NB: page numbers in *italic* indicate figures or tables

Index of Advertisers